INTERNAL COLO

INTERNAL COLONIZATION

RUSSIA'S IMPERIAL EXPERIENCE

ALEXANDER ETKIND

polity

First published in 2011 by Polity Press

Polity Press
65 Bridge Street
Cambridge CB2 1UR, UK

Polity Press
350 Main Street
Malden, MA 02148, USA

ISBN-13: 978-0-7456-5129-3
ISBN-13: 978-0-7456-5130-9(pb)

A catalogue record for this book is available from the British Library.

Typeset in 10.5 on 12 pt Sabon
by Toppan Best-set Premedia Limited
Printed and bound in Great Britain by the MPG Books Group

For further information on Polity, visit our website: www.politybooks.com

CONTENTS

Acknowledgments		vi
List of Illustrations		viii
Introduction		1
Part I The Non-Traditional Orient		
1	Less than One and Double	13
2	Worldliness	27
Part II Writing from Scratch		
3	Chasing Rurik	45
4	To Colonize Oneself	61
5	Barrels of Fur	72
Part III Empire of the Tsars		
6	Occult Instability	93
7	Disciplinary Gears	123
8	Internal Affairs	150
Part IV Shaved Man's Burden		
9	Philosophy Under Russian Rule	173
10	Sects and Revolution	194
11	Re-Enchanting the Darkness	214
12	Sacrificial Plotlines	231
Conclusion		249
References		257
Index		283

ACKNOWLEDGMENTS

In writing this book, I have built up a number of debts that cannot be returned. My parents, art historians Mark Etkind and Julia Kagan, defined my interests in unaccountable ways. My stepfather, philosopher Moisei Kagan, and my uncle, literary scholar Efim Etkind, gave examples of brilliance and courage. Every page of this book keeps the breath, temper, and care of Elizabeth Roosevelt Moore, my muse, opponent, and editor. Our sons, Mark and Moses, have inspired and distracted me in the proportion that has been, and will always be, quite right.

Igor Smirnov, Nancy Condee, Svetlana Boym, and Mark Lipovetsky gave this work early and invaluable encouragement. Oleg Kharkhordin, Irina Prokhorova, Irene Masing-Delic, and Alastair Renfrew edited the first versions of some of these ideas; their long-standing support is much appreciated. Conversations with Gyan Prakash helped me receive some wisdom from the mainstream of postcolonial studies. Eli Zaretsky and John Thompson were instrumental in making me write it all down. An exciting conference, *Russia's Internal Colonization*, which Dirk Uffelmann and I organized at the University of Passau – an adventure from which we, along with Ilia Kukulin, have still not returned – resuscitated my interest in the subject. Simon Franklin, Emma Widdis, Rory Finnin, Jana Howlett, Caroline Humphrey, and Harald Wydra have been wonderful colleagues throughout these years.

I presented parts of this book at the brown-bag seminar of the Slavonic Department of Cambridge University, a "Found in Translation" conference at the Van Leer Institute in Jerusalem, a Eurasian conference at Hangyang University in Seoul, and also at lively seminars at Durham, Södertörn, and Stanford. The questions and comments of colleagues in these and other places found their way into this book. Several scholars read parts of this manuscript and commented generously. They are, in chronological order, Willard Sunderland, Maria Maiofis, Simon Franklin, William Todd, Mark Bassin, Dirk Uffelmann, Marina Mogilner, Eric Naiman, David Moon, Rubén Gallo, Michael Minden, Peter Holquist, Jana Howlett, Valeria Sobol, Jane Burbank, and Tony La Vopa. Sarah Lambert, Sarah Dancy, and two anonymous reviewers of Polity Press were very helpful.

Parts of Chapters 6, 7, and 12 were published in the Russian journals, *Novoe literaturnoe obozrenie* and *Ab Imperio*. Part of Chapter 10 was published as "Whirling With the Other: Russian Populism and Religious Sects," *Russian Review* 62 (October 2003), pp. 565–88. Part of Chapter 8 was published as "Internalizing Colonialism: Intellectual Endeavors and Internal Affairs in Mid-nineteenth Century Russia," in Peter J. S. Dunkan (ed.), *Convergence and Divergence: Russia and Eastern Europe into the Twenty-First Century* (London: SSEES, 2007), pp. 103–20. Part of Chapter 5 was published as "Barrels of Fur: Natural Resources and the State in the Long History of Russia," *Journal of Eurasian Studies* 2/2 (2011). Part of Chapter 12 was published as "The Shaved Man's Burden: The Russian Novel as a Romance of Internal Colonization," in Alastair Renfrew and Galin Tihanov (eds), *Critical Theory in Russia and the West* (London: Routledge, 2010), pp. 124–51.

LIST OF ILLUSTRATIONS

Figure 1: Joseph Swain, "Save me from my friends!", 1878. 33

Figure 2: Charles Malik and Eleanor Roosevelt working on the Declaration of Human Rights, 1948. 40

Figure 3: Viktor Vasnetsov, *Rurik's Arrival at Ladoga*, 1909. 46

Figure 4: Sergei Uvarov, portrait by Orest Kiprensky (1815). 54

Figure 5: Aleksei Olenin, Demeter–Ceres, a Greek-Roman Goddess 1812. 57

Figure 6: Vasilii Surikov, *Ermak's conquest of Siberia*, 1895. 80

Figure 7: Coat of Arms of the Stroganovs, 1753. 85

Figure 8: The coat of arms of Abram Gannibal (*c.* 1742). 96

Figure 9: Karl Briullov, *A Portrait of an Officer with his Servant* (1830s). 117

Figure 10: Johann Reinhold Forster. The map of German colonies on the Volga,1768. 130

Figure 11: A cavalry training ring in Selishche, near Novgorod, built in 1818–25. 137

Figure 12: The Perovsky descendants of Aleksei Razumovsky (1748–1822). 153

Figure 13: Karl Briullov, Vasilii Perovsky on the capital of a column, 1824. 154

Figure 14: Pushkin and Dal presented on an icon as St Kozma and St Damyan. 163

Figure 15: Andrei Bolotov's self-portrait, c. 1790. 183

Figure 16: Afanasii Shchapov, 1872. 195

Figure 17: Lenin and Bonch-Bruevich, October 16, 1918. 209

Figure 18: Ilia Repin. Portrait of Nikolai Leskov, 1888. 225

Introduction

In 1927 in Moscow, Walter Benjamin noted that Russia had no use for the romantic concept of the east. "Everything in the world is here on our own soil," his Russian friends told him. "For us there is no 'exoticism'," they stated; exoticism is nothing but "the counterrevolutionary ideology of a colonial nation." But having killed the idea of the east, these intellectuals and filmmakers brought it back to life again, and on a huge scale. For their new films "the most interesting subject" was Russian peasants, a group that these intellectuals believed were deeply different from themselves: "The mode of mental reception of the peasant is basically different from that of the urban masses." When these peasants watched films, they seemed to be incapable of following "*two simultaneous narrative strands* of the kind seen countless times in film. They can follow only a single series of images that must unfold chronologically." Benjamin's friends maintained that since peasants did not understand genres and themes "drawn from bourgeois life," they needed an entirely new art, and creating this art constituted "one of the most grandiose mass-psychological experiments in the gigantic laboratory that Russia ha[d] become." Despite Benjamin's sympathies towards both the new film and the new Russia, his conclusion was wary: "The filmic colonization of Russia has misfired," he wrote (1999: 13–14).

Studying imperial Russia, scholars have produced two stories. One concerns a great country that competes successfully, though unevenly, with other European powers, produces brilliant literature, and stages unprecedented social experiments. The other story is one of economic backwardness, unbridled violence, misery, illiteracy, despair, and collapse. I subscribe to both of these at once. In contrast to the Russian peasants whom Benjamin's friends exoticized in line with an age-long tradition, scholars cannot afford one-track thinking. But scholarship is not a dual carriageway, either. We need to find a way to coordinate the different stories that we believe in. My solution is a kind of Eisensteinian *montage* interwoven with an overarching principle, which in this book is internal colonization. I propose this concept as a metaphor or mechanism that makes the Russian Empire comparable to other colonial empires of the past. So, in this book, the two Russian stories combine into one: the story of internal colonization, in which the state colonized its people.

In 1904, the charismatic historian Vasilii Kliuchevsky wrote that Russian history is "the history of a country that colonizes itself. The space of this colonization widened along with the territory of the state" (1956: 1/31).[1] Coextensive with the state, self-colonization was not directed away from the state borders but expanded along with the movement of these borders, filling the internal space in waves of various intensities. At that moment, this formula of Russia's self-colonization had already had a long history in Russian thought, which I describe in Chapter 4. Enriched by twentieth-century colonial and postcolonial experiences, we can draw further conclusions from this classical formula. Russia has been both the subject *and* the object of colonization and its corollaries, such as orientalism. The state was engaged in the colonization of foreign territories and it was also concerned with colonizing the heartlands. Peoples of the Empire, including the Russians, developed anti-imperial, nationalist ideas in response. These directions of Russia's colonization, internal and external, sometimes competed and sometimes were indistinguishable. Dialectic in standstill, as Benjamin put it, but also an explosive mix that invites oxymoronic concepts such as internal colonization.

Exploring the historical experience of the Russian Empire before the revolutionary collapse of 1917, this book illuminates its relevance for postcolonial theory. However, I turn the focus onto Russia's internal problems, which have not previously been discussed in postcolonial terms. Since the 1990s, scholarly interest in the causes and results of the Russian revolution has paled in comparison to the explosion of research on the Russian Orient, orientalism, and Empire.[2]

[1] Here and elsewhere, the translation is mine unless stated otherwise. I refer to multi-volume editions by volume/page, e.g. 1/31.

[2] This literature is too large to be surveyed here. On the Russian east, I benefited in particular from the now classical Brower and Lazzerini 1997; Barrett 1999; Bassin 1999; Geraci 2001. On orientalism in Russia, see Layton 1994; Sahni 1997; Khalid et al. 2000; Sopelnikov 2000; Thompson 2000; Collier et al. 2003; Ram 2003; Tolz 2005; Schimmelpenninck 2010. On the Russian Empire in comparative perspective, see Burbank and Ransel 1998; Lieven 2003; Gerasimov et al. 2004, 2009; Burbank and Cooper 2010.

Historians have learned to avoid the Soviet-style, teleological approach to the revolution and the terror that followed, which explains the preceding events as "the preparation" for the subsequent ones. However, historians – and all of us – need explanations for why the Russian revolution and the Stalinist terror occurred on the territory of the Russian Empire. Such explanations cannot be sought exclusively in the preceding era, but they, or at least a part of them, also cannot be disconnected from the historical past. I do not aim to explain the revolution, but I do believe that a better grasp of imperial Russia can help us toward a clearer understanding of the Soviet century. I am also trying to bridge the gap between history and literature, a gap that few like but many maintain. Some time ago, Nancy Condee formulated the idea that while area studies is an interdisciplinary forum, cultural studies "incorporate[s] interdisciplinarity into the project itself" (1995: 298). This book is a project in cultural studies.

Incorporating different disciplines, voices, and periods is a risky task for a cultural historian. I take courage in the idea that high literature and culture in Russia played significant roles in the political process. As I will demonstrate in several examples, "transformationist culture" was an important aspect of internal colonization. Due to a paradoxical mechanism that Michel Foucault helps to elucidate in his "repressive hypothesis" (Foucault 1998; see also Rothberg 2009), oppression made culture politically relevant and power culturally productive. For an empire such as Russia's, its culture was both an instrument of rule and a weapon of revolution. Culture was also a screen on which the endangered society saw itself – a unique organ of self-awareness, critical feedback, warning, and mourning.

***

In Russia, social revolutions resulted in magnificent and tragic transformations. However, the continuities of this country's geography and history have also been remarkable. Russia emerged on the international arena at the same time as the Portuguese and Spanish Empires; it grew in competition with great terrestrial empires, such as the Austrian and Ottoman in the west, the Chinese and North American in the east; it matured in competition with the modern maritime empires, the British and French; and it outlived most of them. An interesting measure, the sum total of square kilometers that an empire controlled each year over the centuries, shows that the Russian Empire was the largest in space *and* the most durable in time of all historical empires, covering 65 million square kilometer-years for Muskovy/Russia/Soviet Union versus 45 million for the British Empire and 30 million for the Roman Empire (Taagepera 1988). At about the time when the Russian Empire was established, the average radius of a European state was about 160 kilometers; given the speed of communication, a viable state could not dominate more than a 400-kilometer radius (Tilly 1990: 47). The distance between St. Petersburg (established in 1703) and Petropavlovsk (1740) is about 9,500 kilometers. The Empire was enormous and its problems grew with its size. But throughout the imperial period, tsars and their advisors referred to the vastness of Russia's space as the main reason for its imperial empowerment, centralization, and further expansion.

Larger than the Soviet Union and much larger than the current Russian Federation, the Empire of the tsars stretched from Poland and Finland to Alaska, Central Asia, and Manchuria. Russian soldiers took Berlin in 1760 and Paris in 1814. After the victory over Napoleon, Russian diplomats created the Holy Alliance, the first modern attempt to integrate Europe. The Empire was constantly engaged in colonial wars over disputed domains in Europe and Asia; it oversaw the impressive advance into the Pacific; it evoked and suppressed a mutiny in the Urals, several revolts in Poland, and a permanent rebellion in the Caucasus. With the sale of Alaska in 1867, the Empire began to shrink; this tendency would continue in the twentieth century. But the Petersburg rulers dreamed about Constantinople and expansion into the Balkans and the Near East, an ambition that fueled military efforts up to World War I. The series of Russian revolutions changed both the map of Europe and the structure of the Russian state. Starting as a furious outburst of anti-imperial sentiments, the revolutions of 1917 led to new enslavement. After World War II, the growth of the Muscovite state continued when other western empires disintegrated. Even when the USSR collapsed, the loss of territory was smaller than what the western empires experienced with their decolonization. With surprise, the twenty-first century is watching the imperial resurgence of post-Soviet Russia.

The enormity of the space gives the easiest explanation for a "traditional and instinctive Russian sense of insecurity," as it was described by George Kennan in his famous Long Telegram (1946) that ignited the Cold War. Importantly, Kennan added that this "neurotic view" afflicted Russian rulers rather than Russian people. In light of the eventful time that has passed since Kennan sent his telegram off, his point can be sharpened. Throughout the larger part of Russian history, a neurotic fear, which is mixed with desire, focused not only on the enemies beyond the borders but also on the space inside them. This internal space happened to be populated, somewhat unfortunately for the rulers, by the subject peoples, Russians and non-Russians.

Led by Edward Said (1978, 1993), postcolonial scholars have emphasized the significance of oceans that separated the imperial centers from their distant colonies. In some of these writings, overseas imperialism feels different – more adventurous, consequential, and repressive – in a word, more imperialist than terrestrial imperialism. However, before railways and the telegraph, terrestrial space was less passable than the high seas. In times of peace, it was faster and cheaper to transport cargo from Archangel to London by sea than from Archangel to Moscow by land. In times of war, shipments of troops and supplies proved to travel much faster from Gibraltar to Sebastopol than from Moscow to the Crimea. In the mid-eighteenth century, the German scholar, Gerhard Friedrich Müller, led a Russian expedition to Siberia; the distance that Müller traveled there was about equal to the circumference of the Earth. In the early nineteenth century, it was four times more expensive to supply the Russian bases in Alaska by transporting food across Siberia than to carry it by sea around the world (Istoriia 1997: 239–7). It took two years for Russians to transport fur across Siberia to the Chinese border; American ships did the job in five months (Foust 1969: 321). Technically and psychologically, India was closer to London than many areas of the Russian Empire were to St. Petersburg. And there were no subjects living on the high seas, no strange, poor people who had to be defeated, tamed, settled and resettled, taxed, and conscripted. Two theoretically opposing but, in practice, curving and merging vectors of external and internal colonization competed for limited resources, human, intellectual, and financial. The oceans connected, while land divided.

Created by its rulers in their effort to make Russia a viable and competitive power, this Empire was a cosmopolitan project. Much like contemporary scholars, Russian Emperors compared Russia with other European empires. Almost until their end, the tsars focused on the troublemaking areas on Russia's periphery and construed the core Russian population as a God-given, though limited and unreliable, resource. Having colonized its multiple territories, Russia applied typically colonial regimes of indirect rule – coercive, communal, and exoticizing – to its population. Rich in coercion and poor in capital, the Empire had to master and protect its enormous lands, which were taken for various purposes that had been largely forgotten. In Lev Tolstoy's story, "How much land does a man need?," a peasant goes from "overpopulated" Central Russia to a colonized steppe in Bashkiria, where friendly nomads offer him as much land as he can encircle in a day. He walks and runs from sunrise to sunset and dies of exhaustion when he completes the circle. He is buried on the spot: this, enough for a grave, is how much land man needs, says Tolstoy. But he himself bought one estate after another, subsidizing his agricultural experiments with the royalties from his novels.

Human grammar distinguishes between subject and object, while human history does not necessarily do so. Self-imposed tasks – self-discipline, internal control, colonization of one's own kind – are inherently paradoxical. Languages, including scholarly ones, get into trouble when they confront these self-referential constructions. In the twenty-first century, scholars of globalization meet the same logical difficulties as the scholars of Russian imperial history met in the nineteenth century. Of course, I hope that the world of the future will be no more similar to imperial Russia than it will be to British India. But the experience and experiments of the Russian Empire can still teach us some lessons.

***

So, what is internal colonization – a metaphor or a mechanism? Many philosophical books argue that this is an incorrect distinction, but I do not think so. As much as I can, I am relying on the precise words of historical subjects in which they formulated their concerns. One scholar of contemporary empires states that since the concept of empire has been applied indiscriminately, the way to learn what an empire is, is to look at those who apply this word to themselves (Beissinger 2006). In a similar move, I survey the changing use of the words "colonization" and "self-colonization" in Russian historiography. Although in Russia the historical actors employed this terminology infrequently, the historical authors used it profusely, and they started to do it much earlier and with more sense than I had expected when I started this research. As a metaphor that reveals a mechanism, internal colonization is an old, well-tested tool of knowledge.

Two components always comprise colonization: culture and politics. Pure violence manifests itself in genocide, not colonization. Cultural influence leads to education, not colonization. Whenever we talk about the colonization processes, we see cultural hegemony and political domination working together in some kind of coalition, correlation, or confrontation. Jürgen Habermas speaks about internal colonization as a framework for various cognitive and even constitutional developments in modern societies. Social imperatives "make their way into the lifeworld from the outside – like colonial masters coming into a tribal society – and force a process of assimilation upon it" (1987: 2/355). Habermas's analogy is between colonialism overseas and a monolingual European society, which assimilates modernity as if it had been introduced by colonial masters, but which actually imposes it on itself. Even in this broad usage, the concept of internal colonization presumes an aggressive confrontation of alien forces. Habermas clearly describes a cultural conflict, though this conflict is not based on ethnic or language difference.

According to classical definitions, colonization (and its ideological system, colonialism) refers to the processes of domination in which settlers migrate from the colonizing group to the colonized land, while imperialism is a form of domination that does not require resettlement (N.R. 1895; Hobson 1902; Horvath 1972). Theoretically, definitions of colonization do not specify whether any particular migration evolved within the national borders or outside them, or whether such borders even existed at the time. In practice, however, and also in intuition, colonization has usually meant travel abroad. Against this backdrop, the concept of internal colonization connotes the culture-specific domination inside the national borders, actual or imagined. In the late nineteenth and early twentieth centuries, several important scholars used this concept. Prussian and German politicians launched an ambitious program of internal colonization in Eastern Europe, which was fed by all kinds of knowledge, faked and real. Russian imperial historians used the concept of "self-colonization," producing a powerful discourse that has been largely forgotten. The ideas of one of these historians, the brilliant but maverick Afanasii Shchapov (1830–76), expose themselves intermittently in my book.

Following the Russian revolution and decolonization of the Third World, the concept of internal colonization took a long break. In 1951, Hannah Arendt (1970) introduced the concept of the colonial boomerang, the process in which imperial powers bring their practices of coercion from their colonies back home. A few years later, Aimé Césaire (1955) formulated a similar concept, the reverse shock of imperialism, which he saw in the Holocaust. After 1968, social scientists reinvented the concept of internal colonization with the aim of applying postcolonial language to the internal problems of metropolitan countries. The American sociologist Robert Blauner (1969) looked at aspects of the domestic situation of African Americans, such as ghetto life and urban riots, as processes of internal colonization. In his lectures of 1975–6, the French philosopher Michel Foucault used the same concept in the broader sense of bringing colonial models of power back to the west (2003: 103). The British sociologist Michael Hechter (1975) used the concept of internal colonialism in his book about the core and periphery of the British Isles, with a particular focus on Welsh politics. Revising the classical concept, Hechter neutralized the geographical distance between the colonizer and the colonized, formerly the definitive feature of British-style colonialism. However, in his case studies, he still needed the ethnic difference between the mother country and the colony (say, between the English and the Welsh) to make his concept work. After Hechter, the next step was to deconstruct ethnic difference, revealing the internal colonialism inside the mosaic ethnic field that is structured by cultural reifications of power. In this meaning, concepts of internal colonization/colonialism were used by the historian Eugen Weber (1976), the sociologist Alvin W. Gouldner (1977), the anthropologist James C. Scott (1998), the literary scholar Mark Netzloff (2003), and a group of medievalists (Fernández-Armesto and Muldoon 2008). In her book on mid-twentieth-century French culture, the historian Kristin Ross observed how France turned to "a form of interior colonialism" when "rational administrative techniques developed in the colonies were brought home" (1996: 7). Several critics reviewed the idea of internal colonization, usually with mixed feelings (Hind 1984; Love 1989; Liu 2000; Calvert 2001). Some prominent historians have mentioned the colonial nature of Russia's internal rule but have never elaborated on this thesis (Braudel 1967: 62; Rogger 1993; Ferro 1997: 49; Lieven 2003: 257; Snyder 2010: 20, 391). Postcolonial studies all but ignore the Russian aspect of their larger story. In studies of Russian literature and history, however, the concept of internal colonization has been discussed by several authors (Groys 1993; Etkind 1998, 2002, 2007; Kagarlitsky 2003; Viola 2009; Condee 2009).

Developing this worldly concept, I wish to combine it with more traditional, text-oriented concerns of cultural history. This is a triple task – historical, cultural, and political. As a Russian specialist, I cannot agree more with Ann Laura Stoler who specializes in Southeast Asia: "[T]he omission of colonialisms (internal or otherwise) from national histories is political through and through" (2009: 34). However, I demonstrate that this omission has never been complete in classic Russian historiography. It is necessary to understand the political reasons for both the presence and the omission of internal colonization in the national and imperial historiography. Chapter 5, probably the most controversial in this book, historicizes twenty-first-century Russia in a deep, *longue durée* way by moving from cultural history to political economy. I have no intention of finding an invariable condition that spans through centuries, but I do strive to understand the recurrent interplays between the contingent factors of geography, ecology, and politics that shaped Russia's experience. As has happened in other spheres of postcolonial studies, my focus in this book shifts from describing historical events and social practices of the imperial past to engaging with cultural texts that depicted this past before me, the texts that define our very ability to imagine this past along with its events and practices. This shift structures this book thematically and chronologically.

Chapters 1 and 2 expose the Cold War context of Edward Said's concept of "Orientalism" and complement Said by following some of his heroes through their Russian adventures. In Chapter 3, I dig into the debates on the origins of the Russian monarchy, as they articulated the nature of Russia's internal colonization. Chapter 4 traces the robust self-colonization paradigm in the mainstream historiography of Russia, as it developed in the nineteenth century. Chapter 5 discusses the fuel of Russia's pre-modern boom, the fur trade, which established the enormous territory that later underwent troubles, schisms, and recolonizations. Chapters 6 and 7 explore the peculiar institutions of this colonization, such as estate and commune. Constructing an analogy between the classical problems of race and the Russian construction of estate, I invite the reader to St. Petersburg to follow its transformation from a colonial outpost into the wonder of the Enlightenment. Chapter 8 examines the fierce intellectual activities of a ruling institution of imperial Russia, the Ministry of Internal Affairs. The last part of this book consists of case studies in the cultural history of the Empire. Chapter 9 examines an unexpected figure, Immanuel Kant, during his period as a Russian subject. I take issue with the recent criticism of Kant as ignorant or insensitive toward colonial oppression. On the contrary, my perspective presents him as an early (post)colonial thinker. In Chapter 10, I look at the Russian religious movements and explore their revolutionary connections, mythical and real. Exoticizing the people and construing their "underground life," the late nineteenth-century missionaries, historians, and ethnographers ascribed to them the most unbelievable features; as a result, populists and socialists counted on these popular sects in the self-imposed task of the revolution, which was no less incredible. Chapter 11 compares the anti-imperial narratives of two major authors that were, in their different ways, both fascinated with imperial Russia and sharply critical toward it, Joseph Conrad and Nikolai Leskov. Using three classical texts, Chapter 12 explores the Russian novel as a sacrificial mechanism that re-enacts the changing relations between classes and genders within the Empire. This chapter combines Mikhail Bakhtin's and René Girard's theoretical perspectives on the novel with the historical context of internal colonization. Throughout this book, I place some great names, Russian and western – Pushkin and Dostoevsky, Kant and Conrad – in unusual contexts; I also introduce a number of figures that may be less known to the reader. Ever concerned about territory, colonization is about people. Proponents, victims, and heretics of colonizations internal or external, the protagonists of this book constitute a multicolored, paradoxical crowd.

Part I

The Non-Traditional Orient

— 1 —

Less than One and Double

On March 25, 1842, in St. Petersburg, one official lost his nose. This noseless person, Kovalev, had just returned from the Caucasus, the embattled southern border of the Russian Empire. In the imperial capital, he was seeking a promotion that would put him in charge of a nice, bribable province of central Russia. But Kovalev's nose betrayed him. His face was flat. Without his nose, he could not visit his women. He even missed a job interview, so strong was the shame of being noseless. Finally, his nose was captured on its way to Riga, the western border of the Empire. "Russia is a wonderful country," wrote Nikolai Gogol who composed this story. "One has only to mention an official" and all his peers, administrators "from Riga to Kamchatka," unanimously believe that "you are talking about them" (Gogol 1984: 3/42). From the Caucasus to St. Petersburg and from Riga to Kamchatka: it's a long trip for a nose.

Career of Improvement

Gogol's "The Nose" is a beautiful example of what Homi Bhabha calls the "colonial doubling," which summarizes the processes of loss, splitting, and reconfiguration that are essential for the colonial situation. We can lose a part in many interesting ways, from castration, or decolonization, or even from shaving, or some combination of these. Presenting a faceless colonial administrator, Gogol analyzes his nose as an imperial fetish, a "metonymy of presence" where presence is unreachable and its signs, unrecognizable. Indeed, for Kovalev, there was no presence without his nose. Without the part, everything that the whole required – office, power, women – became unreachable. When in its proper place, the nose is just a little part of Kovalev's wholeness, a metonymy of his impeccable functioning as the corporeal and imperial subject. Lost, the nose turns into the all-embracing symbol for Kovalev's unaccomplished dreams and aspirations, the summary metaphor for all those goods, bodies, and statuses – vice-governorship, fortunate bride, social pleasures – which are unreachable for the noseless. The part is made into a fetish only after it has been lost. The Hegelian relations of master and slave are analogous to Gogolian relations of the whole and the part. As long as the part is the slave of the whole, the order is safe; but the rebellion of the part has more dramatic effects than the rebellion of the slave, because it questions the deepest, the most naturalized perceptions of the social order. Colonial differences cross-penetrate all social bodies, including the body of Kovalev. Together, Kovalev and his separatist nose make a wonderful illustration for the enigmatic, Gogolian formula that Bhabha repeats without explaining: "less than one and double" (Bhabha 1994: 130, 166).

An imperial author with an exemplary biography, Gogol was born in Ukraine and moved to St. Petersburg where he failed first as an official and then as a historian, succeeded as a writer, and failed again as a political thinker. He belongs to the list of great colonial authors, along with James Joyce and Joseph Conrad. The plot of *Dead Souls* was an imperial project; with his Napoleonic look, the protagonist Chichikov plans to resettle the purchased peasants to a recently colonized land near Kherson in the southern steppe and to mortgage them to the state. The fact that the peasants were dead makes their transportation easier. Kherson was the land of the notorious Potemkin villages, but the internal provinces that Chichikov visited on his way were no more trustworthy. *Dead Souls* should be read as the saga of Russia's colonization, a text on a par with the British *Robinson Crusoe* or the American *Moby Dick*. When Gogol's *Inspector-General* went on stage in 1836, hostile critics targeted precisely this colonial aspect of Gogol's inspiration. These horrible events could never have happened in central Russia, only in Ukraine or Belorussia; or even worse, continued a critic, they could have happened "only on the Sandwich Islands that captain Cook visited" (Bulgarin 1836). With and without their lost noses and dead souls, Gogol's characters were precise images "of a post-Enlightenment man tethered to . . . his dark reflection, the shadow of colonized man, that splits his presence . . . repeats his action at a distance" (Bhabha 1994: 62). The colonial nature of Gogol's inspiration has been emphasized by a more recent wave of scholarship, which was itself inspired by the post-Soviet transformation of Ukraine (Shkandrij 2001; Bojanowska 2007). Understandably, postcolonial scholars have focused on Gogol's Ukrainian roots and stories. The colonial nature of his works on Russia and the Russians, such as "The Nose" and *Dead Souls*, have eluded them, because such an understanding requires the concept of internal colonization. I believe that postcolonial criticism clarifies Gogol, but the opposite is also true: Gogol helps us to understand Bhabha.

In 1835, when Gogol was teaching Universal History at St. Petersburg Imperial University and Kovalev was starting his service in the Caucasus, Lord Macaulay delivered his *Minute on Indian Education*. Working for the Viceroy of India, Macaulay argued that only teaching English to the Indian elite would create the "interpreters between us and the millions whom we govern." He referred to Russia as the positive model:

> Within the last hundred and twenty years, a nation which has previously been in a state as barbarous as that in which our ancestors were before the crusades, has gradually emerged from the ignorance. . . . I speak of Russia. There is now in that country a large educated class, abounding with persons fit to serve the state in the highest functions. . . . There is reason to hope that this vast empire, which in the time of our grandfathers was probably behind the Punjab, may, in the time of our grandchildren, be pressing close on France and Britain in the career of improvement. (Macaulay 1862: 109–10)

For Macaulay, the west and the east were but steps on the worldwide ladder of history. Where England was in the tenth century, Russia was in the eighteenth and Punjab in the nineteenth. In this vision, the higher stages smoothly replaced the lower ones in the mother country. In the large space of empire, these different stages of progress all coexisted; moreover, they became known to the politician mainly because of their coexistence in the imperial domain rather than because of their obscure traces in the national archive. In India and Russia, higher races, castes, and estates cohabited with lower ones. The imperial task was to make order out of this chaos, which meant creating categories, managing hierarchies, regulating distances. After Peter the Great, "the languages of Western Europe civilized Russia. I cannot doubt that they will do for the Hindu what they have done for the Tartar," said Macaulay.

A few years later, the leading Russian critic, Vissarion Belinsky, wrote that, without Peter the Great, Russia "would probably still have accepted European civilization but it would have done so in the same way in which India adopted the English one" (1954: 5/142). In other words, Belinsky saw Russia's westernization as a response to the anxiety of being colonized by the west, though of course this anxiety was also a European influence, one of those languages that Russia, like India, imported from the west. As a matter of fact, India was a colony and Russia was an empire, which made Macaulay's comparison a little forced; what is interesting is that he did not notice it. For Belinsky and his readers, Russia's sovereignty – its difference from India – was the crucial fact. The imperial gradient between the higher and lower groups was immense in the British and Russian Empires; in the former the difference was mainly between the mother country and the colony, while in the latter the difference was mainly between groups within the mother country. Although straight in the national domain, the line of progress curved and folded within its imperial possessions. Later, Marxist theorists struggled with the same issue. Lev Trotsky called it "combined and uneven development" (1922, 1959). In his vision, advanced and backward societies coexisted in Russia simultaneously and "traumatically"; their contradictions would "inevitably" result in a revolution (Knei-Paz 1978: 95).

During the High Imperial Period, which lasted from Russia's victory in the Napoleonic War (1814) to its defeat in the Crimean War (1856), the Russian educated class spoke and wrote French as well as Russian. German was a heritage language for many, and English was for the *crème de la crème*. The famous works of Russian literature depicted this polyglossia and were often inspired by French examples (Meyer 2009). In Aleksandr Pushkin's novel in verse, *Evgenii Onegin* (1832), Tatiana's letter of love was written in French. Typical for ladies of high society, Tatiana's Russian was worse than her French, explained Pushkin. French was the language of women and family life; Russian was the language of men, of the military service and the household economy where work was carried out by serfs and soldiers. In Lev Tolstoy's *War and Peace* (1869), where the action takes place during the Napoleonic War, the officers and officials who were fighting with the French speak French with their wives and daughters, Russian to their subordinates, and mix the languages when talking to their peers. Unlike Pushkin, who in his novel "translated" Tatiana's letter into Russian verse, Tolstoy wrote these long dialogues in French and published them with no translation, expecting his readers to understand them. But his public was changing rapidly and within a few years he had to translate these French sections into Russian for the next edition of his masterpiece.

After reading Alexis de Tocqueville's *Democracy in America*, a former officer of the Imperial Guard, Petr Chaadaev, asked in 1836: Does Russia also have a destiny? His answer was devastating: "We live in our houses as if we are stationed there; in our families we have the outlook of foreigners; in our cities we are similar to nomads, we are worse than nomads." At exactly the time when the Empire was as rich and large as never before, the imperial elite felt as if they were invaders stationed in their own cities, homes, and lives. "Our remembrances do not go deeper than yesterday; we are foreign to ourselves. . . . Our experiences disappear as we are moving ahead. This is a natural consequence of a culture that is entirely borrowed and imitated" (Chaadaev 1914: 110). Illustrating his thesis, Chaadaev compared the Russians to the Native Americans. He asserted that there were "people of outstanding depth" among the Native Americans, but the Russians had no sages who could be compared to these natives (Chaadaev 1914: 116; Etkind 2001b: 24). These feelings of the foreignness in the native land, the stoppage of time, and the imitative character of culture were subjective components of reversed, internal orientalism (Condee 2009: 27).

Chaadaev wrote his epistle in French, but when it was published in Russian translation, it caused a scandal. Denouncing Chaadaev, one official with Siberian experience wrote that he "denies everything to us, puts us lower than the American savages" (Vigel 1998: 78). Awakened by Chaadaev, a group of intellectuals turned his cultural criticism into the call for nationalist reawakening. Having adopted an unfortunate name, the Slavophiles, they reinvented the global language of anti-imperial protest that was rooted in the French Enlightenment, the American Revolution, Edmund Burke's criticism of British policies in India, the experience of the Napoleonic wars, and, last but not least, the Polish rebellions against the Russian Empire.

In 1836, Gogol described St. Petersburg as "something similar to a European colony in America: there are as few people of the native ethnicity here [St. Petersburg] and as many foreigners who have not yet been amalgamated into the solid mass" (1984: 6/162). Like many Russian intellectuals of his time, Gogol was very interested in America and even dreamed about emigration to the US. Comparing the imperial capital to America sounded good to this outsider. In a remarkable twist, the conservative Russians of the 1840s employed the language of colonial discontent for their criticism against their own culture. A former officer of the Imperial Guard, Aleksei Khomiakov, wrote in 1845 that in Russia, the Enlightenment took "a colonial character."

In 1847, he characterized the educated society in Russia as "a colony of eclectic Europeans, thrown into a country of savages." He also stated that the enlightened Russia "fashioned itself in an aggressive way, like a European colony anywhere in the world, conceiving the conquest with best intentions but without means to realize them and . . . without a superiority of spirit that could give some kind of justification for the conquest." He characterized this "colonial relationship" as "the struggle" between "the entirely unjustified repulsion" on the part of the elite toward the people and "the well-justified suspicion" on the part of the people towards the elite. On this base, Khomiakov diagnosed in the Russian society "fundamental doubling," "imitativeness," "false half-knowledge," "a lifeless orphanhood," and "cerebral deadliness." Like his favorite writer, Gogol, he loved the metaphor of doubling/splitting (*razdvoenie*) and used it profusely. Doubling was induced by the Petrine reforms but increased after that. Doubling was an unavoidable result of too abrupt, too rapid social change. Doubling separated the life of the people and the life of the higher estates. "Where the society is doubled – a deadly formalism reigns the day" (Khomiakov 1988: 100, 43, 152, 96, 139). Much earlier, Khomiakov (1832) wrote a tragedy about the legendary Ermak, a Cossack who conquered Siberia for the Russian crown. Far from glorifying Ermak, it shows a repenting criminal, cursed by his father, convicted by the Tsar, and betrayed by the fellow Cossacks. A Shaman offers him the crown of Siberia, but he prefers suicide. If it were a story about Montezuma, it would have been perceived as an early and strong anti-imperial statement; *Ermak* has never been successful on stage, with either the critics or the historians. Khomiakov spent many years writing a multi-volume saga of peoples' migrations and resettlements, starting from the antiquity. An Anglophone and Anglophile, he speculated about the colonized Celts, Indians, and Hottentots. Colonial practices were in his mind, whether he was writing about Russia or the world. One of the most gifted people of his time – an amateur engineer, artist, historian, and theologian – Khomiakov was piously Orthodox, like other Slavophiles, but in his own creative way (Engelstein 2009). Through the years, he corresponded with a cleric from Oxford about a unification of Orthodox and Anglican churches; he even believed that the same could happen with the Calvinists (Khomiakov 1871: 105).

While the British administration was introducing English in Indian schools, Macaulay's Russian counterpart, the Minister of the Enlightenment Sergei Uvarov, decided that the Europeanization of Russia had gone too far. Reporting in 1843 about the first decade of his ministerial job, he saw his success in "healing the new generation of its blind, thoughtless predisposition towards the foreign and the superficial" (Uvarov 1864). Remarkably, Uvarov drafted his projects for the new "national" education in French but then switched to Russian (Zorin 1997). A dilettante orientalist but a professional administrator, Uvarov was responding to a wave of popular sentiment that was universal for post-Napoleonic Europe.

A long time has passed since Macaulay and Uvarov planned to re-educate their spacious domains. As in India, nationalism in Russia took two competing forms, rebellious and anti-imperial on the one hand, official and pre-emptive on the other. If Peter I was a model for Macaulay, Lev Tolstoy was an influence on Mahatma Gandhi. Russia was a great European power alongside those of Britain or France, *and* a territory that received its civilization from the west, like Africa or India. This is why Macaulay compared the Russian Empire not to the British Empire but to its colony, India. It was to the Russians themselves and not to the Poles or the Aleuts, that the Empire was teaching French with the success that Macaulay wanted to emulate and Uvarov to unwind. This success did not last long, but it was important for all aspects of imperial culture and politics. It divided the intellectuals into those who mourned the lost originality of native ways and those who welcomed the bursting creativity of cultural hybridization, a divide well known to the scholars of colonial cultures. "Learning is nothing but imitation," proclaimed a leading academic historian, Sergei Soloviev, whose son, Vladimir, became the most original Russian philosopher (1856: 501). Through the High Imperial Period, the understanding of Russia as an imperial *and* a colonial country was shared even by those who did not have much else in common. A late and revisionist follower of the Slavophiles, Fyodor Dostoevsky wrote in 1860 that no country is less understood than Russia; even the moon is better explored, wrote Dostoevsky, who was in the know: he had just been released from a Siberian prison camp. In his vision, the people of Russia were sphinx-like – mysterious and omniscient; he called on his public to approach the people with an Oedipal feeling of awe (1993: 12–13). The philosopher and governmental official, Konstantin Kavelin, used the same colonial rhetoric in 1866, justifying the slow pace of the reforms that he helped to write into the law: "Imagine a colonist who starts a household in the wilderness.... Whatever he did his success would not be able to stand comparison with the life standard of a town.... We are the very same colonists" (Kavelin 1989: 182).

Slavic Wilderness

The fierce, transnational polemics that raged between Marxists at the turn of the twentieth century alerted them to the relation between imperialism and national economies. The polemics had a critical stance; many believed that Marx did not understand this relationship. The Russian economist Petr Struve emphasized the "third persons," neither capitalists nor workers, who complicated the class war. Living pre-capitalist lives, these "third persons" consumed the "surplus product" of the economy and provided capitalism with labor and growth (Struve 1894). Responding to this argument, the German socialist Rosa Luxemburg stated that foreign markets play this role far better than Struve's internal "third persons." According to Luxemburg's *Accumulation of Capital* (2003), capitalism would always need fresh markets and, therefore, is inescapably connected to imperialism. Thus, a struggle against capital is also a struggle against the empire. In memorable words, Hannah Arendt observed that by synthesizing two programs of emancipation, social democratic and anti-imperialist, this Marxist message had made recurrent waves throughout our world: "[E]very New Left movement, when its moment came to change into Old Left – usually when its members reached the age of forty – promptly buried its early enthusiasm for Rosa Luxemburg together with the dreams of youth" (1968: 38).

In response to Luxemburg, Vladimir Lenin, in his early book *The Development of Capitalism in Russia*, suggested that in larger countries such as Russia and the United States, the unevenness of development plays the role of global inequality, so that the colonization of these internal spaces would consume the "surplus product" and give a boost to capitalist development. Internal inequalities would play the same role as external ones. Speaking of the underdeveloped Russian territories on the Volga, in Siberia, and elsewhere, Lenin used the concepts of "internal colonization" and "internal colony" (1967: 3/593–6). Responding to his opponents, "legal Marxists" like Struve, Lenin discussed not only the flows of capital, but also the demographical patterns of peasant migrations into the territories of internal colonization. With no hesitation, Lenin applied this concept, internal colony, to those parts of Russia that were populated by ethnic Russians, such as the steppes of Novorossiysk and the forests of Archangel; territories with mixed and changing population, such as Siberia and the Crimea; and lands with ethnically alien peoples, such as Georgia. In Lenin's account, his own homeland on the Volga was one of these internal colonies. He based his speculations about "the internal colonization" and "the progressive mission of capitalism" on a systematic analogy between the Russian Empire and the US, which he abandoned a few years later (Etkind 2001b).

In the US, W. E. B. DuBois wrote about American underprivileged minorities, social and racial alike, in colonial terms: "[T]here are groups of people who occupy the *quasi-colonial status*: laborers who are settled in the slums of large cities; groups like Negroes . . ." (cited in Gutiérrez 2004). Both Lenin and DuBois imported the concept of internal colonization from the Prussian bureaucratic language, where it meant the state-sponsored program of managing the frontier between Prussia and "the Slavic wilderness" to the east. The German colonization of Polish and Baltic lands started in the Middle Ages and was consistently pursued by Frederick the Great. Prussian and, then, German officials called this policy "the program of inner colonization." Starting in the 1830s, the Prussian government disbursed millions of marks for the purchase of Polish manors, dividing them and leasing them to German farmers. Under Bismarck, this policy was strengthened with restrictions for seasonal workers, the introduction of passport control, and even deportations of Slavs from Prussia (Koehl 1953; Brubaker 1992: 131; Dabag et al. 2004: 46; Nelson 2009). Remarkably, the leading figure of these events, Max Sering, found his inspiration in his trip to the American Midwest; in 1883, he returned to Prussia with a determination to organize a similar frontier along the German borders with the east. In 1912, he visited Russia (Nelson 2010). In 1886, the Royal Prussian Colonization Commission was established and the imperial intellectuals started debating what kind of colonization Germany needed: an African-style "overseas colonization" or a Polish-style "inner colonization." Advising on these efforts, Max Weber published a survey, in which he recommended his own version of internal colonization of the "barbarian East" (Paddock 2010: 77). In this work, Weber collaborated with one of the leaders of the colonization movement, Gustav Schmoller, though their ways parted later on. An historian, Schmoller looked back at the Prussian colonization in the east, *Drang nach Osten*, and emphasized the settlement programs of Frederick the Great, which he also called 'inner colonization' (Schmoller 1886; Zimmerman 2006). This historical retrospective, mythologized to a large extent, was crucial for the political plans of Prussian internal colonizers: it was the historical precedence of the earlier colonization that made these newest efforts "inner" and therefore different from British overseas imperialism. But, as we shall see in Chapter 7, historical examples of German colonization spread very far to the east, as far as the Volga river.

During World War I, the Prussian enthusiasts of internal colonization indulged in "a dream spree of wide proportions," envisioning large-scale colonization of the occupied Polish and Ukrainian lands (Koehl 1953). But soon this policy, which would have outraced Russia using Russia's method of contiguous expansion, became insufficient for the wildest dreamers. The Nazis rejected the idea and practice of internal colonization; their ambition was to create an entirely new space of colonial, ethnically purged Eastern Europe, a project which Hitler compared to the European conquest of America (Blackbourn 2009; Kopp 2011; Baranowski 2011). Rejecting Bismarck's legacy that he associated with internal colonization, Hitler opted for external colonization, not in Africa, however, but in Eurasia: "If land was desired in Europe, it could be obtained by and large only to the extent of Russia." When political dreams outpaced historical precedents, the very distinction between the external and the internal had to be overcome. Describing his thoughts in Munich of 1912, Hitler called the plan of Germany's internal colonization a pacifist and Jewish idea:

> For us Germans the slogan of "inner colonization" is catastrophic. . . . It is no accident that it is always primarily the Jew who tries and succeeds in planting such mortally dangerous modes of thought in our people. . . . Any German internal colonization . . . can never suffice to secure the future of the nation without the acquisition of new soil. (Hitler 1969: 125, 128)

Boomerang Effect

In the 1920s, the Italian Marxist, Antonio Gramsci characterized the relations between different regions of his country, the north and the south, as colonial exploitation. Better than his predecessors, he realized the internal complexity of this intra-ethnic colonization. Its cultural vector, which he called hegemony, diverged from its political vector (domination) and its economic vector (exploitation). All three had to be considered separately, because their directions were different or even the opposite. Regions of southern Italy became northern Italy's "exploited colonies" but, at the same time, the culture of the south strongly influenced that of the north (Gramsci 1957: 28, 48). In fact, it was due to the internal structure of Italian colonialism that

Gramsci was able to separate these elements of power, which correlate and stick to each other in many situations of external, overseas colonization. Revising the Marxist teaching that the economic basis determines the "superstructure," Gramscian concepts of hegemony and domination proved to be seminal for cultural and postcolonial studies. Conceived in Italy, they have been applied in India and elsewhere (Guha 1997).

Speculating about the relations between "power," which in her writing was close to hegemony, and violence, Hannah Arendt described the "boomerang effect" that an imperial government would bring to the mother country from the colonies if the violence against the "subject races" spread to the imperial nation, so that "the last 'subject race' would be the English themselves." Arendt suggested that some British imperial administrators (she referred to Lord Cromer) were aware of the boomerang of violence, and this "much-feared effect" constrained their actions in India or Africa (Arendt 1970: 54). With its aboriginal roots, the boomerang metaphor summarized the old, Kantian nightmare that the European peoples would be ruled as if they were savages who could not rule themselves. Anthropologists have repeatedly stressed the role of European colonies as "the laboratories of modernity," which tested the newest technologies of power (Stoler 1995: 17). When the mother countries implemented selected methods of colonial power at home, they appropriately adjusted their functions. The project of the Panopticon, which was first devised as a factory by the adventurous Brits in a Russian colony in Ukraine and later used as a prison in England and elsewhere, is a good example of this creative process (see Chapter 7).

This boomerang imagery was crucial for Arendt's major contribution, *Origins of Totalitarianism* (1966), which surveyed the Soviet and Nazi regimes under one cover along with a variety of western colonies. Despite the long-standing fascination with Arendt's theoretical ideas, this part of her legacy has been discussed primarily by her earliest as well as her most recent critics (Pietz 1988; Rothberg 2009; Mantena 2010). Still, with one significant exception (Boym 2010), the scholarship on Arendt's *Origins* focuses on its German story and downplays the massive Russian-Soviet part of this study. Indeed, Arendt's focus on the pan-Slavic movement as a step in the development of Russian and European racism was not productive for her project. The pan-Slavic movement was a dead-end; it did not lead to the Russian revolution and Soviet totalitarianism in the way that Arendt described. Arendt's idea of the boomerang effect was brilliant, but in application to Russia it needed mediation by an understanding of Russian imperialism as an internal, and not only external, affair. The long-standing traditions of violence and coercion with which the Russian Empire treated its own peasantry could explain the revolution and totalitarianism as a boomerang coming home to the cities, the capitals, and the state. The revolutionary state absorbed the practices and experiences that the Empire projected onto its subject peoples, including the Russians. Unlike the German boomerang that, according to Arendt, flew back across the high seas from the colonies to the heartlands, the Russian boomerang whirled through the internal machinery of the empire. Totalitarianism, Soviet style, was a logical result of this effect.

Talking about the influx of race imagery from the colonies to Europe during the English and French revolutions, Michel Foucault generalized:

> It should never be forgotten that while colonization . . . transported European models to other continents, it also had a considerable boomerang effect on the mechanisms of power in the West. . . . A whole series of the colonial models was brought back to the West, and the result was that the West could practice something resembling colonization, or an internal colonialism, on itself. (2003: 103)

I believe that this combination of concepts, the boomerang effect that Foucault probably borrowed from Arendt, and the internal colonialism that he improvised here though rarely used elsewhere, is productive for understanding Russia's extraordinary history. This claim finds much support in Russian sources. One hundred years earlier than Foucault, the Russian provincial administrator and satirical writer Nikolai Saltykov-Shchedrin wrote a collection of essays, *Gentlemen from Tashkent*, which analyzed essentially the same processes, the boomerang effect and internal colonialism, in the Russian life of the time. Tashkent, now in Uzbekistan, was taken by Russian troops in 1865 and became the center of a huge colonial domain (Sahadeo 2007). Saltykov-Shchedrin chose this event, the largest success of Russian imperialism, for a demonstration of its destructive effect on the policies and mores in the Russian heartland. Returning from Tashkent, the Caucasus, and other "tamed" places, the imperial officers and officials brought their skills and lust for violence home, to St. Petersburg and the provinces. The gentlemen from Tashkent call themselves "civilizers," wrote Saltykov-Shchedrin; in fact, they are a "moving nightmare" that permeates every corner of life. A typical such gentleman had "civilized" Poland even before his stay in

Tashkent, but it is there that he would receive a critical experience that enabled him to "civilize" Russia. In several funny stories, the gentlemen from Tashkent beat and bribe the gentlemen in Petersburg, assuming it as a part of their civilizing mission. If you find yourself in a town that has a prison and does not have a school, you are in the heart of Tashkent, wrote the satirist. Like Major Kovalev who lost his nose when he returned from the Caucasus, the imperial returnees confront a catastrophe that they purposefully create and deeply misunderstand. Focusing on the return arc of the imperial boomerang, from the colony to the mother country, Saltykov-Shchedrin defined the internal Orient – in his terms, "Tashkent-ness" – as a combination of violence and ignorance that he discerned in the exchange between the Russian center and its colonies (Saltykov-Shchedrin 1936: 10/29–280).

Two great struggles, inconsistent but emancipatory, dominated the end of the twentieth century and continue into the twenty-first century: decolonization of the Third World and de-Sovietization of the Second World. Historically, these two struggles have been intertwined. Intellectually, they have been kept separate. But starting from the age of the Enlightenment, academic history has experienced its own boomerang effect: the knowledge of the colonization and decolonization processes in the east illuminates the understanding of the west.

Recent decades have seen a historiographical revolution that has been mostly focused on the role of the state, coercion, and war in the creation of the modern world (Tilly 1990; Bartlett 1993; Mann 1996). Michael Mann observes that in modern history, settler colonies of democratic countries were more murderous than the colonies of authoritarian empires. Liberal democracies were built on the back of ethnic cleansing, which took the form of institutional coercion in mother countries and of mass murder in the colonies. As long as empires were able to sustain the plural "sociospatial networks of power" in their diverse parts, they could escape massive bloodshed. With the transition to the "organic view of society," empires break into nation-states, a process which is usually accompanied by large-scale violence. New nation-states regulate their complexity by redrawing boundaries, organizing population transfers, and sanctioning ethnic cleansing. For Mann (2005), this is the "dark side of democracy," the modern heart of darkness, to use an older metaphor.

In Russia, organic nationalism started during the Napoleonic Wars and was maturing all the way through the nineteenth and twentieth centuries, with the collapse of the Soviet Union in 1991 marking one of its turning points. The fact that it has never fully matured explains both the weakness of Russian democracy and the relative bloodlessness of recent Russian transformations (Hosking 1997). Despite their defining importance for the modern world, these processes have been under-theorized. In a rare postcolonial response to the post-Soviet transformation, David Chioni Moore describes a situation that he calls "the double silence." Postcolonial experts stay silent about the former Soviet sphere and Sovietologists stay silent about postcolonial ideas. Moore gives two separate explanations to this double effect. For many postcolonial scholars, some of them Marxist-leaning, the socialist world seems a better alternative to global capitalism; they do not wish to extend their critical vision from the latter to the former. Many post-socialist scholars have cultivated their new European identities; they do not wish to compare their experience with Asian or African colleagues (Moore 2001: 115–17). Several commentators have shared Moore's surprise (Condee 2006, 2008; Buchowski 2006; Chari and Verdery 2009). Both sides suffer from the disjunction between the postcolonial and the post-socialist. This disconnect is largely responsible for the much-deplored depoliticization of postcolonial studies and for the methodological parochialism that many Russianists have lamented. The reasons for this disconnect are both political and academic. As Nancy Condee put it: "[T]he intellectual Left's silence about the Second world and the Right's anticommunist preoccupations were interrelated processes, mutually enforcing constraints" (2008: 236). I would add only that in the twenty-first century, the continuation of the Left's silence about the past and the lasting present of the Second World can be explained only by inertia.

I propose in this book to take a step back. Not only is the post-Soviet era postcolonial (though still imperial), the Soviet era was postcolonial too. The Russian Empire was a great colonial system both at its distant frontiers and in its dark heartlands. Employed by Bismarck, Lenin, and Hitler; mentioned by Weber, Foucault, and Habermas; and, with slightly different wording, developed by nineteenth-century Russian historians (see Chapter 4), the concept of internal colonization has a deeper genealogy than is usually assumed. To be sure, extending the postcolonial edifice, which has never been very coherent, to the immense space of the Russian Empire requires not just an "application" of the pre-existing ideas, but their deep refashioning. Doing so might help us to understand not only the Russian imperial experience, but also the unused potentialities of postcolonial theory.

— 2 —

Worldliness

Two very different authors, Hannah Arendt and Edward Said, relied on a rare concept that they used independently of one another. This concept was "worldliness." Writing about humanity in dark times, Arendt revealed how people respond to the collapse of the public sphere by pressing up against each other, mistaking "warmth" for "light," and escaping into the worldlessness, "a form of barbarism" (1968: 13). Also writing about dark times, Said protested against the popular idea that literature has a life of its own, a life that is separate from history, politics, and other worldly matters (see Ashcroft and Ahluwalia 1999: 33; Wood 2003: 3). Worldliness is important for reading Gogol, and no less so for Conrad or Kipling. But there are always many worlds on earth; during the Cold War, there were officially three.

Three Worlds

Writing during the Cold War, Edward Said defined "Orientalism" as the way in which the First World has treated the Third World. In this abstract formulation, he skipped the Second World entirely. In his introduction to *Orientalism* (1978), Said spoke of the Cold War, "an era of extraordinary turbulence in the relations of East and West," as the very first of historical circumstances that made his study possible. Indeed, the idea of three worlds came into being around 1955 and expressed western anxiety about the growing appeal of the USSR among the former colonies – the penetration of the Second World into the Third (Sachs 1976; Pletsch 1981; Moore 2001). In the 1970s, the USSR was relevant enough for Said to write: "No one will have failed to note how the 'East' has always signified danger and threat . . . even as it has meant the traditional Orient as well as Russia" (1978: 26). In this beginning of Said's work, the east embraced two major entities, the traditional Orient and the non-traditional one, which was Russia. The subsequent parts of Said's book exclusively discussed relations between the west and "the traditional Orient." The non-traditional part of the east was left for further consideration.

Speaking of an Orient that stretched from the coasts of the Mediterranean Sea to those of the Indian Ocean to the Southern Pacific, i.e. along the borders of the Russian Empire, Said showed that European policies toward this part of the east were accompanied by a public focus on captured territories and their inhabitants; that knowledge about colonial peoples defined the world of those who ruled them and the ways they were governed; and that the great texts of the western tradition were not "innocent" of imperialism but persistently alluded to the colonial experience. Said attacked traditional orientalism for imagining the east and the west as self-sufficient Platonic essences, which split the imperial mind into a "Manichean delirium."

Subsequent critics have corrected Said's arguments in many respects. Using British examples, David Cannadine (2001) showed that the cultural traffic between the capital and the colonies was actually reciprocal. The British who mimicked Indians and other colonials in food or spirituality comprised the rule rather than the exception. Even more importantly, Brits projected onto their subjects a presumption of affinity rather than difference, so that they could deal with familiar hierarchies rather than with exotic and dangerous disorder. Writing about German colonialism, Russell Berman (1998) showed that the cultural logic of orientalism changed its patterns when it worked in western empires other than the French and the British. In Berman's account, German missionaries and scholars were more attentive to the natives and did not deprive their informants of human agency to the extent that was typical of their British and French colleagues. Orientalism was a specific cultural pattern, variable in different situations. Homi Bhabha (1994) destabilized the Saidian opposition between the imperial masters and the colonial subjects by focusing on paradoxically creative dimensions of colonialism. With his work, cultural hybridization has made for a popular subject of postcolonial studies. While Frantz Fanon and Edward Said focused on "the Manichean opposition" between the colonized and the colonizers, it is the enormous "grey zones" and "middle grounds" that have become the focus of postcolonial scholarship (Cooper and Stoler 1997). Finally, Gyan Prakash has noted the connection between Said's arguments and the tripartite world map that he inherited from the Cold War. "Even as we recognize that three worlds have collapsed into a single differentiated structure, the demand for imminent criticism remains relevant," wrote Prakash (1996: 199).

Among European powers, the Russian Empire was distinguished by its liminal location between west and east; by a composite structure that was created of western and eastern elements; and by its self-reflective culture, which accounted for creative combinations of orientalism, occidentalism, and more. It is difficult to think about this historical phenomenon in terms of Platonic ideas of east and west. For many reasons, these ideas are awkward and difficult to handle. It would be better to imagine east and west as Heraclites' elements, which are free to mix in certain, though not in any, combinations. As elements, the west and the east sometimes need one another, like fire and air; sometimes displace one another, like water and fire; and sometimes – most frequently – coexist in complex, multilayered folds, pockets, and mixtures, like water and earth.

Following Said's footsteps, I will show that some of his protagonists, major British authors, documented their Russian fantasies or memories in a way that was simultaneously orientalist and "non-traditional," i.e. deeply different from what Said saw as the norm of western writings about the "traditional East." I will look at Defoe, Kipling, and Balfour, and leave Conrad for a separate chapter. I do not mean that similar readings can be applied to all or many of the protagonists of Said's *Orientalism*. But these four authors are, without doubt, important. At the end of this chapter, I will explore one source of Said's remarkable omission of Russia from his analysis.

Robinson's Sables

Robinson Crusoe was the starting point for some of Said's crucial arguments. Re-reading Daniel Defoe's groundbreaking representations of the western man in an eastern land, Said explored Crusoe's attitude toward money, travel, and solitude. Like many critics before him, Said ignored the second volume of Defoe's trilogy, *The Farther Adventures of Robinson Crusoe* (1719). These adventures brought Robinson much farther than his proverbial island. Covering thousands of miles, mostly by earth, he traveled to Madagascar, China, Tartary, and Siberia, to return to England by way of Archangel. This geographical experience was very different from what he found on no man's island, and he engaged in social adventures that were totally different from his experience with Friday. In Eurasia, he negotiated with savvy eastern traders, had conflicts with his shipmates, lost Friday, decimated a native village, established a settled colony in Madagascar, failed as a colonial administrator, made a new friend, and became rich. Entering Siberia, he felt relief, but also disappointment:

> As we came nearer to Europe we should find the country better peopled, and the people more civiliz'd; but I found myself mistaken in both, for we had yet the nation of the Tongueses to pass through . . . ; as they were conquered by the Muscovites, and entirely reduc'd, they were not so dangerous, but for rudeness of manners . . . no people in the world ever went beyond them. (Defoe 1925: 310)

Taking into account Robinson's previous adventures, this was no small criticism. The horrible Tunguses particularly impressed Robinson with their furs. "They are all clothed in skins of beasts, and their houses are built of the same." As we shall see shortly, Robinson's business vision did not fail him this time. In contrast, his geography was very shaky.

Much concerned, like other travelers of his time (Wolff 1994), with the boundary between Europe and Asia, he reported that this boundary stretched along the Enisey river, but some pages later transferred it thousands of miles farther west, to the Kama river. In Siberia, Robinson was also interested in comparative issues:

> The *Czar of Muscovy* has taken to have cities . . . where his soldiers keep garrisons something like the stationary soldiers plac'd by the Romans in the remotest countries of their empire, some of which I had read particularly were plac'd in *Britain*. . . . Wherever we came, the garrisons and governor were *Russians*, and professed Christians, yet the inhabitants of the country were mere pagans sacrificing to idols, and . . . the most barbarous, except only that they did not eat human flesh, as our savages in America did. (Defoe 1925: 295)

In a un-Robinsonian way, he reported his findings to "the Muscovite governors" of Siberia, who said that it was none of their business, because if the Czar expected to convert his subjects, "it should be done by sending clergymen among them, not soldiers" (Defoe 1925: 311). They added, with more sincerity than Robinson expected, "that it was not so much the concern of their monarch to make the people

Christians as to make them subjects." He also learned that Siberia was the Russian place of exile, which did not surprise this Brit. When he befriended an exiled Russian prince there, he devised a subversive plan to smuggle him to England. This Russian Friday, however, declined the offer in sublime, Puritan words:

> Here I am free from the temptation of returning to my former miserable greatness; there I am not sure that all the seeds of pride, ambition, avarice, and luxury . . . may revive and take root. . . . Dear sir, let me remain in this blessed confinement, banish'd from the crimes of life, rather than purchase a show of freedom, at the expense of the liberty of my reason. (Defoe 1925: 323)

Dostoevsky's characters might have said the same thing in the same part of Siberia, but their final plea would not have been to preserve "reason." Touched by both the offer and its denial, Robinson and the prince exchanged gifts. The prince gave Robinson "a very fine present of sables, too much indeed for me to accept from a man in his circumstances, and I would have avoided them, but he would not be refus'd." Robinson gave the prince "a small present of tea, and two pieces of China damask, and four little wedges of Japan gold, which . . . were far short of the value of his sables." The prince accepted the tea and one piece of gold, "but would not take any more." The next day, the prince asked Robinson to take his only son to England. The deal was excellent: with his new Friday, Robinson obtained "six or seven horses, loaded with very rich furs, and which in the whole, amounted to a very great value" (Defoe 1925: 325). And so it happened.

Rich in realistic details, this part of *The Farther Adventures* sends a complex moral message. The indiscriminate picture of Siberian idolatry fits the perception of Robinson as an orientalizing Puritan traveler. His condemnation of the Tsar's indifference to his Christian mission reveals Defoe's understanding of the imperial burden. The whole picture justified Robinson's plot of cheating the Russian Tsar by smuggling his exiled subject to England. But it was not only Robinson's desperate longing for human contact, another feature of his pilgrimage, which motivated his unlimited affection toward the prince. Because of the generosity of the prince and the value of the furs, their exchange was unfair, a fact that Robinson felt deeply but did not try to correct. Two times in a row, Robinson financially benefited from this friendship. The exchange of gifts in which the western side gains fabulously and unilaterally was a regular ambition of colonial projects. But in *The Farther Adventures*, Robinson gained not because of his intellectual superiority over the native, but because of his moral inferiority. Evidently, Defoe designed the whole exchange in such a way that the exiled Russian prince appeared not only richer but also wiser and kinder than the traveling British merchant. Able to make a distinction between freedom and liberty in perfect English, this prince was also very enlightened, an admirable quality in comparison to Robinson's limited skills. Thrown among barbaric people, the noble prince of a higher nature represented the embodiment of a particularly Russian kind of colonialism, in which the high and the low points of human existence are pushed to the extreme, beyond the westerners' expectations. This friend was a far cry from the first volume's Friday; maybe because of this, it was the prince's son, not the prince, who took Friday's place in Robinson's retinue.

Judging Robinson solely on the basis of the first volume of his travels, Said performed an erasure that has been typical of modern readings of *Crusoe*, who have presented Crusoe as the model and prototype of Puritan orientalism. As Melissa Free (2006) argues in her illuminating essay, this erasure was uncommon among the early readers of Defoe but became increasingly popular in the twentieth century. In her extraordinary statistics from more than 1,000 editions of *Crusoe* in English, Free demonstrates that in the eighteenth century, these editions usually consisted of just the first two or all three of the volumes, with only 4 percent containing the first volume alone. In the nineteenth century, the separate publications of the first volume increased only slightly. But after World War I, more than 75 percent of the editions of *Crusoe* consisted of the first volume only. The story, which resulted in more commerce than any colonial cargo, was simplified by abridgement. The fur-clad Russian prince was sacrificed in preference to the naked Friday. Robinson in Siberia was not orientalist enough, or rather not in the proper way, to deserve reading.

Kipling's Bear

"Oh, East is East, and West is West, and never the twain shall meet," Rudyard Kipling wrote in 1889. But of course they have met myriad times and Kipling, though often misquoted, knew it well: "But there is neither East nor West. . . . When two strong men stand face to face, tho' they come from the ends of the earth!" (Kipling 1925: 231). By focusing on relations between the First World and the Third, postcolonial studies have too literally followed the initial line of Kipling's

Ballad and missed its deconstructive flow. However, in the Great Game between the British and Russian Empires, which Kipling explored in *Kim*, three rather than two elements fight a sort of militarized dialectics: England, India, and, in the background, vicious Russia. The Game pushed India to the west and Russia to the east, a complex geopolitics that Kipling situated in the continuum that spans and curves around the globe. An Irish boy and British spy in India, Kim works against the Russian penetration there in a spirit that is more reminiscent of the future Cold War rather than of India's struggle.

In a later poem, "Truce of the Bear" (1898), Kipling presented a pathetic beggar who tells the story of his fight with a horrible beast, "the Bear that stands like a Man." The fight, if there was any, took place 50 years earlier than the story, but the beggar keeps repeating it as the central event of his life. He describes the bear as "the

PUNCH, OR THE LONDON CHARIVARI.—NOVEMBER 30, 1878.

"SAVE ME FROM MY FRIENDS!"

"IF AT THIS MOMENT IT HAS BEEN DECIDED TO INVADE THE AMEER'S TERRITORY, WE ARE ACTING IN PURSUANCE OF A POLICY WHICH IN ITS INTENTION HAS BEEN UNIFORMLY *FRIENDLY* TO AFGHANISTAN."—*Times*, Nov. 21.

Figure 1: Joseph Swain, "Save me from my friends!" 1878: The Ameer of Afghanistan between the Russian bear and the British Lion. *Source*: "Punch, or the London Charivari", November 30, 1878

monstrous, pleading thing." However, the bear is not unknown; the opposite is true: "I knew his times and his seasons, as he knew mine. . . . I knew his strength and cunning, as he knew mine." When he met this bear 50 years earlier, the hunter had pity on him and did not shoot. In response, the bear ripped his face away. Now, the former hunter asks for money in exchange for demonstrating his wounds. "Over and over the story, ending as he began: / 'There is no truce with Adam-zad, the Bear that looks like a Man!'" Though Russia is not mentioned in the poem, generations of readers have perceived this bear as the symbol of Russia, and the poem as a call to Britain to make no truce with this rival. In 1919, an author of the *Atlantic Magazine* praised Kipling for his "remarkable rightness." After the revolution in Russia, the wartime alliance seemed to her like a bad idea, a Truce of the Bear. To this author, "the Russians were behaving very much, and very vividly, like 'the bear that looks like a man.'" She testified to the fact that Kipling's Russophobia was unpopular before and during the war: "The intellectuals have been Russianizing themselves, in these last years; and Kipling's laughter at that phenomenon must have been unholy. They could scarcely afford to feel him remarkably right, it would prove them so remarkably wrong" (Gerould 1919).

But Kipling's construction is more subtle. While Matun, the narrator, "Eyeless, noseless, and lipless – toothless, broken of speech," does not look like a Man, Adam-zad, the bear, "Horrible, hairy, human, with paws like hands in prayer," does. This resemblance between the Bear and the Man repeats as the central line of the poem; they are like twins who are engaged in an eternal, open-ended fight. Once again, we need to return to the very start of the poem to realize that the narrator is not white; he is bandaged. "[H]e follows our white men in / Matun, the old blind beggar, bandaged from brow to chin" (Kipling 1925: 271–3). The duel and the truce were struck between the Indian man and the Russian bear. As in *Kim*, the construction is triangular, not linear. Like Gogol's "The Nose," this poem turns into doubles what cannot possibly be similar: the whole and the part, the man and the beast, "less than one and double."

Throughout the age of empires, Britain increasingly saw its adversary in Russia. In the time of Kipling, both empires debated the possibility of a Russian attack on India, which was alternatively perceived as revenge for the defeat in the Crimea and as a threat to British rule in Asia. First used by the Brits in 1840, the term "Great Game" referred to their civilizing mission in Central Asia, but the meaning shifted to the zero-sum game when Russia expanded into the region

(Yapp 1987; Hopkirk 1996). In 1879, a certain A. Dekhnewallah published a pamphlet, *The Great Russian Invasion of India*, which described a future war between the two empires. Advancing through Afghanistan, Russian troops occupy the Punjab and Central provinces. Their attack is well prepared by the numerous spies who provoke mutiny among lower castes. British India is saved by an artillery officer, "a quiet man with large dreamy eyes," who withdraws the troops to Kashmir and organizes cunning attacks on the invaders. Finally, the British send navy expeditions into the Black Sea and the Baltic, forcing the Russians to purchase peace at the expense of giving up Afghanistan and Persia (Dekhnewallah 1879: 43, 66). The war of the future was imagined by analogy with the war of the past, the Crimean campaign.

"The Russian is a delightful person till he tucks his shirt in," stated Kipling in the amazing story, "The Man Who Was" (1889). A British regiment in north India hosts a certain Dirkovitch, "a Russian of the Russians, as he said." A Cossack officer and a journalist writing for a newspaper "with a name that was never twice the same," Dirkovitch is evidently a spy. But the Brits treat him with respect: he has done "rough work in Central Asia" and has seen more "help-yourself fighting than most men of his years." With his bad English, this Cossack tries to refresh the idea of the civilizing mission for the White Hussars:

> He remained distressingly European through it all. . . . He would unburden himself by the hour on the glorious future that awaited the combined arms of England and Russia when . . . the great mission of civilizing Asia should begin. That was unsatisfactory, because Asia is not going to be civilized after the methods of the West. There is too much Asia, and she is too old. You cannot reform a lady of many lovers. (Kipling 1952: 29)

Denying the orientals' ability to rule themselves as Brits do, the narrator, one of the White Hussars, holds no illusions about the Russian's sincerity: Dirkovitch knew the hopelessness of changing Asia "as well as any one else." The White Guards recognize this Russian in a racial way that is meaningful for them; although an Indian officer, their ally, cannot not join them at table and knows it, Dirkovitch is able to spend his evenings with the Brits; moreover, he proves his ability to drink more brandy than any of them. But suddenly, a weird figure appears in the living room: The Man Who Was, a miserable Afghan who speaks English and Russian. He turns out to be a former officer of this very regiment, whom the Russians captured in the Crimea and sent to Siberia; decades later, beaten and pathetic, he has found his way back to his regiment, "like a homing pigeon." He cringes before the Cossack who espouses an unclear threat: "He was just one little – oh, so little – accident, that no one remembered. Now he is *That*. So will you be, brother-soldiers so brave – so will you. But you will never come back." The Man Who Was dies three days later. As Dirkovitch departs, the smartest of his British friends murmurs, "A terrible spree there's sure to be when he comes back again." The theme of coming back is central for the story. British troops in India were expecting the return of the experience of the Crimean War. Having read the story to the end, we inevitably go back to the beginning:

> Let it be clearly understood that the Russian is a delightful person till he tucks his shirt in. As an Oriental he is charming. It is only when he insists upon being treated as the most easterly of Western peoples, instead of the most westerly of Eastern, that he becomes a racial anomaly extremely difficult to handle. The host never knows which side of his nature is going to turn up next. (Kipling 1952: 28)[1]

Kipling's contemporary, George Nathaniel Curzon, visited Russia before his appointment as Vice-Roy of India (1898–1905). In his first book, which happened to be his Russian travelogue, he wrote, "Upon no question there is greater conflict of opinion in England than Russia's alleged designs upon India." Based on his experience of traveling to Russia, he felt this split internally: "Every Englishman enters Russia as a Russophobe and leaves it a Russofile" (Curzon 1889: 11, 20). No doubt an overgeneralization, this early version of a "from Russia with love" story speaks volumes about the British attitude toward Russia. Having entered and left Russia, Curzon was still anxious about the Russian threat: "Russia is as much compelled

[1] Kipling probably took the name Dirkovitch from the amazing story of a Russian agent in Central Asia, Ivan (Yan) Vitkevitch (1808–39), who was well known to the Brits. A Pole from Vilnius whom the Empire exiled to Orenburg for conspiracy when he was 15, Vitkevitch served there as a soldier, translated for Alexander Humboldt, made a brilliant career under the governor, Vasilii Perovsky, and, as a Russian resident in Kabul, outmaneuvered British agents in 1838. Recalled to St. Petersburg, he committed suicide after his meeting with the Minister of Foreign Affairs, Karl Nesselrode (Volodarsky 1984; Khalfin 1990: 168–75).

to go forward as the earth is to go round the sun," he wrote. But on the other hand, the Russian advance in Asia would just be "a conquest of Orientals by Orientals" and therefore acceptable (Curzon 1889: 319, 372). As Foreign Secretary (1919–24), Curzon drew a line between revolutionary Russia and the newly independent Poland, which many decades later materialized as the border of the European Union. For all practical purposes, the Curzon line is still dividing the world into the west and the east.

To the revolution in Russia, Kipling responded with the poem, "Russia to the Pacifists." His unexpected mourning for the Russian Empire reflected his anxiety that the distant tragedy would repeat at home: "So do we bury a Nation dead / And who shall be next to fall?" It turned out to be another version of the boomerang story: "We go to dig a nation's grave as great as England was" (Kipling 1925: 274–5).

Balfour's Declaration

According to Said, orientalism was a form of thought and of action, and the two were cyclically connected. The politics created the knowledge, which, in its own turn, guided the behavior of the colonizers and directed their scholarship. One of Said's initial examples was the ideas and policies of the early twentieth-century British statesman Arthur James Balfour, who in 1917 laid the foundation for the Jewish migration to Palestine. Said declared that Balfour's "argument, when reduced to its simplest form, was clear. . . . There were Westerners, and there were Orientals. The former dominate; the latter must be dominated." The double doctrine of western power and orientalist knowledge was based on the "absolute demarcation between East and West." These two categories, of east and west, were "both the starting and the end points of analysis." Their "polar distinction," "binary opposition," or "radical difference" secured the "streamline and effective" operations that Said ascribes to Balfour's type of orientalism. In Balfour's mind "the Oriental becomes more Oriental, the Westerner more Western"; Said calls it "to polarize the distinction." To Balfour, "'Orientals' for all practical purposes were a Platonic essence" (Said 1978: 36–45).

A Platonic essence cannot change, expand, or polarize. It cannot merge with other essences. Finally, it cannot be aware of itself. No doubt, Balfour deserved much of this criticism. In 1917, he told his colleagues in the Cabinet that since "East is East and West is West," they should not use the idea of self-governance when they are talking about places like India. Even in the west, said Balfour, parliamentary institutions had rarely been a great success, "except among the English-speaking people." Curzon found this statement, which could have come straight from an ironical Kipling story, "very reactionary" (Gilmour 1994: 485). Responding to the events that were triggered by the revolution in Russia, Balfour projected his orientalism not only onto Indians and Arabs, but onto Jews as well, especially Russian Jews. When Balfour met the aspiring Zionist leader Chaim Weizmann in 1906, he asked this Belarusian Jew whether his people would go to Uganda rather than to Palestine. Weizmann responded with a question: "Mr Balfour, supposing I was to offer you Paris instead of London, would you take it?" Balfour said, "But Dr Weizmann, we have London." "That is true," Weizmann said, "but we had Jerusalem when London was a marsh." Instead of questioning this concept of "we," Balfour asked, "Are there many Jews who think like you?" To this Weizmann said, "I believe I speak the mind of millions of Jews whom you will never see and who cannot speak for themselves" (Weizmann 1949: 144).

Meeting in Manchester, the statesman and the immigrant discussed oriental places such as Uganda, Palestine, and the Pale. Born in the village of Motol, near Pinsk, in what is now Belarus, Weizmann seemed exotic to Balfour. Of course, Balfour knew how to talk to orientals and his questions were exacting; but Weizmann also knew his game. He conversed with Balfour not just as a member of a foreign tribe, but as a representative of a people who were unknown and unseen, a people who could not speak for themselves. A decade later, as Foreign Secretary, Balfour passed Weizmann his famous Declaration that conveyed British "sympathy" for Zionist aspirations and established "a national home" for the Jews in Palestine. It was not the state, though. Often criticized and rarely understood, Balfour was pursuing the policy by analogy: the Russian Pale of settlement was not a state, either. The stateless Jews from the old, by then destroyed, Pale of the Russian Empire were moving to the newly drawn Pale of the British Empire. The Balfour Declaration was signed on November 2, 1917, five days before the Bolshevik Revolution in Russia. It had a double purpose, to create a British protectorate for Jews in Palestine and to discharge the explosive situation in Russia, where the Bolsheviks, many of them Jews, were contemplating a separate peace with the Germans.

It so happened that Weizmann became a dear friend of Balfour, a distant analogue of Robinson's Russian prince. Balfour's practices and theories were essentialist, but they changed over the decades. His "orientals" included Weizmann from Pinsk and the Mufti of Jerusalem, both of whom were important for British politics in Palestine. British policies toward the east, including Eastern Europe, also changed dramatically. Dividing the vastly different orientals and mediating between them in the name of the Empire, Balfour's east was not really a world of Platonic essences. It was, rather, a Wittgensteinian constellation of images, people, and places that had little in common but their perceived distance from Trinity College, Cambridge, where Balfour received his Law degree.

If for Kipling, Russia was a mythical enemy that had always threatened but never penetrated his India, Joseph Conrad was still living after this event actually happened to his Poland. Russian colonization was the site of the catastrophe, accomplished or anticipated – the crime of partition, the truce of the bear. I find it amazing that Edward Said's first book, *Joseph Conrad and the Fiction of Autobiography* (1966) all but ignored Conrad's tortured relation to the Russian Empire, which was central both to his fiction *and* to his autobiography(see Chapter 11). An enthralled critic of Balfour and Curzon, Kipling and Conrad, Said took no notice of their obsessions with Russia. By doing so, he reduced their multipolar worldliness to the one-dimensional concept of traditional orientalism.

An Uncle's Lesson

There was no Second World in Said's universe. One of the reasons becomes clear from his memoirs, which present an unexpectedly lonely, apolitical portrait of his youth. Protected from real life by the wealth of his father and the warmth of his mother, Edward was awakened by the Egyptian revolution of 1952. As a result of the coup, Edward's father lost a large part of his business, and his mother became an ardent supporter of the militant and increasingly pro-Soviet leader of the revolution, Gamal Abdel Nasser. Edward, then aged 17, became involved in the family debates, the Cold War in miniature. His sympathies were with his Nasserite mother, though he sometimes disagreed with her "socialist pan-Arabism" (Said 1999: 264). The opposite pole, however, was embodied not by his father who was busy restoring his business, but by a relative, Charles Malik, the husband of an aunt.

A philosopher who studied with Heidegger and a statesman who wrote the Declaration of Human Rights together with Eleanor

Figure 2: Charles Malik and Eleanor Roosevelt working on the Declaration of Human Rights, 1948. Edward Said could have been among these children.
Source: http://www.chahadatouna.com/2006/2006-12/Dr.%20Charles%20Malik/Dr%20Charles%20Malik%20Bio.htm

Roosevelt, Malik was an outstanding figure. The Lebanese Ambassador to the US, he also served as the country's Foreign Minister and later, at the end of the 1950s, as President of the United Nations General Assembly. "Polarizing" and "charismatic," as Said depicted him, but also cosmopolitan and visionary, Malik was a true Cold War warrior. Among many subjects of his speeches and pamphlets, the most salient subject was anti-communism.

The young Edward Said was initially attracted to his famous relative, but later found him "troubling." Ascribing to the Soviet Union "the missionary fervor and the imperialist vision," Malik warned the free world of the threat of enslavement. However, when in 1960 he shared a podium with the father of the hydrogen bomb, Edward Teller, Malik chose to espouse his dream of the peaceful disintegration of communism from within. He saw "infinite possibilities, short of war," to help this happen (Teller and Malik 1960). He hated "neutralism" and eagerly operated with the concepts of west and east.

Devoting pages to the philosophical analysis of their relations, he saw two forces, Soviet Communism and Islam, occupying two "intermediary" and "inauthentic" positions between east and west. A Lebanese Christian, Malik distrusted them both, but his passions were focused on the Soviets. "Communism is almost infinitely resourceful in poisoning any normal relationship between East and West," wrote Malik (1953) during the Egyptian revolution. Around this time, Said learned from Malik "about the clash of civilizations, the war between West and East, communism and freedom, Christianity and all the other, lesser religions." Said's distrust is clear in these words, but the intensity and longevity of his struggle against Malik's influence needed another passage: "I see it as the great negative intellectual lesson of my life." For the last three decades, wrote Said in 1999, he was still living through Malik's "lesson," analyzing it "over and over and over with regret, mystification, and bottomless disappointment" (Said 1999: 264–5).

For many Third World intellectuals, the Soviet Union was an inspiration and a model; for some, it was also a source of support. The most notable thinkers of the radical Left took part in the emancipation efforts that were led, and sometimes manipulated, by the Soviet Union. The fate of the American John Reed, a participant of the Bolshevik Revolution who died in 1920 in Moscow after taking part in the Congress of the Peoples of the East in Baku, illustrates this early twentieth-century convergence between communism and anti-imperialism. The lives and works of Rosa Luxemburg, Antonio Gramsci, and Jean-Paul Sartre give further, intellectually more significant, examples. But as the Soviet Union shaped itself into a major imperialist power that competed with other global powers, the free-minded Marxist-leaning intellectuals found themselves deprived of their mental tools. There is a disturbing split between the ways in which many twentieth-century thinkers understood two major developments of the period, decolonization and the collapse of the imperialist order on the one hand, and the Cold War and the collapse of the socialist order, on the other.

Said's oeuvre features the same partial worldliness, which omits the Second World as a nuisance. If, for those who believed in "modernization theory," the Second World did not seem much different from the Third World because both were just steps in the modernization process that led to the First World, then postcolonial critics performed the opposite operation. In their minds, the Second World was not much different from the First World because they both failed to support the Third World. This indifference calcified after fellow-travelers of the Soviet regime watched its collapse, with their hopes betrayed and their respect having turned to contempt. However, Said was never a Soviet fellow-traveler. His memories of his early debates with his mother, the supporter of Nasser, could signal his lifelong disavowal of the pro-Soviet ideas that were popular in his circle. He was trying to find his own, creative way, one that would ignore Nasser and Malik alike. But then not only the Nasserian regime but the Soviet Union also collapsed. Were Malik still alive in 1991, he could have celebrated the triumph of his prediction about the non-violent demise of the socialist system from within. Said had nothing to say about this and subsequent events in the Second World; to comment on them would have amounted to agreeing with his uncle.

However, in one of his last books, Said experimented with a closer look at Eastern Europe. In *Freud and the Non-European* (2003), Said appreciated Freud's reading of Moses, the founder of Judaism, as a non-Jewish Egyptian. Said was right to emphasize Freud's interest in the Orient, but Freud was equally involved in the "non-traditional" east. A subtler analysis would have shown that in Freud's circle, German and Austrian Jews viewed the Jewish refugees from Eastern Europe with stereotypes that were similar to Said's portrait of orientalism. Freud's clientele in Vienna was largely composed of East European Jews (Etkind 1997). As with his Moses, Freud did not trade in stereotypes.

Said's wonderful book on Freud ends in the most unexpected way, with a tribute to Isaac Deutscher, "a non-Jewish Jew," a Polish Trotskyite who became a British critic of both Stalinism and Zionism. Freud chose Moses, Said chose Deutscher: two non-Zionist Jews, non-Western Europeans, betrayed revolutionaries, adopted founders. It was an extraordinary choice that showed Said's late, mature interest in the Second World.

Part II

Writing from Scratch

— 3 —

Chasing Rurik

Ascribed to a twelfth-century monk, Nestor, the *Primary Chronicle* narrates a moment from the ninth century, when some northern tribes failed to settle their disputes and invited a Varangian, named Rurik, to bring order to their "plentiful land." Rurik's name was given to the first Russian dynasty, the Rurukides, which preceded the Romanovs and ruled for twice as long. "The Origin is a silent zero point, locked within itself," writes Edward Said; an Origin, or rather a myth of origin, "*centrally* dominates what derives from it" (Said 1985: 318, 372). But in modern Russian, "to start from Rurik" means to engage in boring and irrelevant talk, to refer to origins instead of confronting problems. Already in 1841, the critic Vissarion Belinsky complained that the debates about Rurik were "bringing boredom and sadness to the thinking public" (1954: 5/94). In this chapter, I will re-visit the debate on Rurik in the context of Michel Foucault's course on French historiography (2003), a remarkable and controversial model.

Inviting Leviathan

In 1818, having read what was the newest version of the Rurik story, General Mikhail Orlov, a hero of the war with Napoleon and a future rebel and exile, wrote to a friend:

> I am reading Karamzin. His first volume is not to my liking. . . . Why no passion for the Fatherland? Why does he want to be an impassionate cosmopolite rather than a citizen? . . . Why does he say that Rurik was a foreigner? That Varangians were not Slavs? What does he find

praiseworthy in the call to the foreigner to take the seat of Novgorod? (Cited in Maiofis 2008: 344)

Like the building of the Russian Empire, the writing of its history was an international project, frequently contested by the emerging Russian nationalism. Nationalisms embodied themselves in history books as well as in novels and newspapers. Part of "print capitalism" but perceived as truth rather than fiction, history books shaped the body of the nation despite the permanent revisions of them and contradictions among them (Anderson 1991; Hroch 1985). Generations of Russians read about Rurik while Russia was fighting with its enemies. In times of peace, they pursued historical studies because of their patriotic desire to learn more about their country. In their classes or textbooks, there was no place to start but with Rurik the Varangian. Who was he, who were they? The ethnicity of Rurik was discussed fervently, while other aspects of his story were largely ignored.

Figure 3: Viktor Vasnetsov, *Rurik's Arrival at Ladoga*, 1909. Three brothers, Rurik, Truvor, and Sineus (which in Russian means the blue moustaches) are receiving "gifts" of fur from a Slavic tribe.
Source: http://www.vasnecov.ru/

The first Russian author to publish the *Primary Chronicle* was Vasilii Tatishchev (1686–1750), a lay historian and high official of the emerging empire, a fascinating and unreliable author (Tolochko 2005). Peter the Great asked him to map his imperial domains, but Tatishchev slipped from geography to history. He created mines in the Urals and suppressed the Old-Believers there, "tamed" the Kalmyks on the Volga and the Kyrgyzes in the southern steppes, and governed the crucial province of Astrakhan, the gateway to the east. Digging in archives was like digging in mines, and writing history was like forging metal; both industries were instrumental for the Empire. Almost 200 years later, Pavel Miliukov, an academic historian who helped to dethrone the second dynasty and set himself up as Foreign Minister during World War I, admitted that this eighteenth-century way of doing history was closer to him than the positivist tradition that lay in between (Miliukov 2006: 35).

Tatishchev's life and work were parallel to those of his French contemporary, a royal historian Henri de Boulainvilliers, who received a focused attention from both Arendt (1970) and Foucault (2003). Like Boulainvilliers, Tatishchev lived in a time of wars and served his monarch in many ways, including history writing. Three major wars between Sweden and Russia punctuated his lifetime, one a failure and two ending in Russian victories. During the truce, Tatishchev went for two years to Sweden, where he explored the mining industry and carried out intelligence work. Tatishchev's rule in the Urals, where he had to enserf the local peasants to make them work in his factories, was notoriously violent. Like Boulainvilliers, who is credited with the scholarly elaboration of the right of conquest, Tatishchev liked the idea that the Russian state was founded by conquest. However, the idea that the conquerors were the ancestors of Russia's current enemy made him uncomfortable: "The arrival of Rurik with his Varangians humiliated the kinship and language of Slavs" (Tatishchev 1994: 1/344). Some consolation was found in the idea that the incoming Vikings were all male and therefore, their descendants were "quickly" Slavonized. It might be true with the Rurikides but the Romanovs invariably married into the Baltic peoples, undoing the previous Russification. After much doubt, Tatishchev concluded that the Vikings came to northern Russia from Finland rather than Sweden. Since parts of Finland had been annexed by the Russian Empire in 1721 and again in 1743, locating Rurik's point of departure in Finland domesticated him into a Russian subject. In response, Tatishchev's nemesis, the German historian August Schlözer who worked in St. Petersburg and Göttingen, said plainly but a little maliciously that the Varangians were Swedes (1809: 2/430).

For Russian readers of the *Primary Chronicle*, it was no easier to accept the idea that Rurik was a Swede than for the readers of the Bible to agree that Moses was an Egyptian. During the early years of the Imperial Academy of Sciences, an unusual debate on this issue animated its halls (Rogger 1960; Obolensky 1982). Starting with the Russian polymath Mikhail Lomonosov, Russian scholars derived the Varangians from the Prussians, Lithuanians, Baltic Slavs, and even the Judaic Khazars. Catherine the Great wrote a play in the style of Shakespeare, "A Historical Scene from the Life of Rurik," and also the monumental *Notes on Russian History*, which showed Rurik as a Finnish Prince, a son of the King of Finland, though no such royalty existed, as Catherine well knew (Ekaterina II 1990: 145; 2008: 44). The Slavic elders summon Rurik after he has returned from a successful expedition to France: those who created France and those who created Russia were of one kin, states Catherine. But she also imagines a Slav rebel who does not recognize Rurik as the ruler (Wachtel 1994: 26).

In the early nineteenth century, Nikolai Karamzin found a semantic solution to the question of the Varangians in calling them Normans. An early source identified visitors to Constantinople, who came from "Rus," as the Normans (Vasil'ev 1946; Franklin and Shepard 1996). More importantly, by equating the Varangians with the Normans, Karamzin equated Russians with other Europeans who had also been dominated by the Normans in the past. A competing school of thought called itself "anti-Normanist." Schlözer wrote, early and prophetically:

> I do not know of another example among the educated nations in which the science of national history would have such a strange pace. Everywhere it has been moving ahead . . . but here [in Russia] it has been returning to the very start, and more than once. (Schlözer 1809: 2/391)

Tatishchev and the Amazons

But the story of Rurik is gentle, even "idyllic" (Kliuchevsky 1956: 1/140). It does read as if the Vikings and the Slavic-Finnish tribes struck some kind of voluntary agreement. One part said to another, come and reign over us. The other part surely asked, is your land rich enough? But Rurik is a foreigner, someone in the crowd must have said. Retelling the story for the first time, Tatishchev had to believe that, first, in order to establish civil peace, a tribe needs a sovereign, and second, that it does not really matter where this sovereign comes from: from within the tribe or from the outside. While the former idea was espoused by Thomas Hobbes and in the eighteenth century had become the mainstream philosophical wisdom, the latter was unusual.

For Tatishchev as much as for us (or even more so), the *Primary Chronicle*'s story of the Varangians reads like a paraphrase from Hobbes's *Leviathtan*: "There was no law among them, but . . . they began to war one against another," until they said to themselves, "Let us seek a prince who may rule over us" (Laurentian Text 1953: 61). In Tatishchev's time, Hobbes's ideas reached Russia through the work of Samuel von Pufendorf (1632–94), a prominent German philosopher who worked most of his life for Russia's enemy, Sweden. But the nature of his teachings made them fit for import. Writing after the peace of Westphalia, Pufendorf made state security central among political values, the common measure for the ruler and the ruled. Only that sovereign who promises and delivers protection to his subjects can be legitimate. Only those subjects who are loyal to the sovereign are worthy of protection.

In Russia as in German lands in the late eighteenth century, debates on Pufendorf provided shelter for discussions of Hobbes (Kempe 2007). This is how Pufendorf rendered the central idea of *Leviathan*:

> Whilst I voluntarily subject myself to the prince, I promise obedience and engage his protection; on the other hand, the prince who receives me as a subject, promiseth his protection, and engageth my obedience. . . . They who create a sovereign, therefore, at the same time promise whatever the nature of subjection requires. . . . And what can we call this but the entering into covenant? (Pufendorf 2002: 595)

This is a version of Hobbes's argument that the sovereign's violence is justified because, in its absence, the unruly subjects would foment even greater violence. In Pufendorf, this idea acquires an active, dramatized form. Subjects "create a sovereign" by exchanging "promises" and negotiating these promises *in vivo*. This exchange is precisely what the *Primary Chronicle* attributes to the Slavs and the Varangians. As in Pufendorf, the Slavs promise obedience to the Varangians, who reciprocate by promising them protection. The conquerors' need to convert their conquest into contract is well recognized in postcolonial studies. A historian of India, Ranajit Guha, explains:

> The conquistador must . . . move forward from the *Augenblick* of his flashing sword to history, from instantaneous violence to law. . . . And the moment he does so he ceases to be conqueror and sets himself up as ruler, although the habits of thought and speech may still continue to designate him by the terms of his erstwhile project. (Guha 1998: 86)

In a theoretical chapter of his *Russian History*, Tatishchev referred to Machiavelli, Hobbes, Locke, Wolff, and Pufendorf. He admired Christian Wolff more than the others, but only Pufendorf was available in Russian translation and Tatishchev relied on him. Peter the Great personally commissioned this translation, which was published in Russian in 1724. Adjusting Hobbes's system to the post-Westphalian world, Pufendorf purged it of any reference to the divinity or other ideas that Catholics and Protestants would understand differently (Hunter 2001). To end the war of religions meant to develop a system of peace that made religions irrelevant. Now, the Orthodox could also accept it.

Tatishchev began his own political philosophy not with Hobbes's "war of all against all," which is a collective experience, but with the idea of a solitary man. By himself, man is helpless; he cannot obtain "pleasure, peace, or profit." Therefore, he creates civil unions "naturally." The first exemplary union is marriage. It is based on a free choice but after the parts sign a contract, they cannot break it and each part can force the other to follow the contract. The same is true of the state, said Tatishchev. In the family, men "naturally" dominate women and children; this is also the foundation of a monarchy, because "the monarch is the father and his subjects are children" (1994: 1/359).

In Tatishchev, a patriarchal philosophy coexisted with a fantastic history. He claimed that the Slavs originated from the Amazons, the female warriors whom Herodotus connected to the Scythians. Tatishchev argued that in ancient times, the Amazons came from Africa to the banks of the Volga and there became the Slavic tribes. He attributed this discovery to Feofan Prokopovich, archbishop of Novgorod and one of the closest associates of Peter I, and gave a specific date, 1724, when Feofan supposedly presented this idea to Peter I. These amazing Amazons, the great-grandmothers of Russians, played a peculiar role in Tatishchev's historical imagination. In line with his idea of marriage as the paradigm for contract relations, he assumed the contract between the Vikings and the Slavs was a marriage in which the Vikings played the masculine role and the Slavs the feminine role. That is why the Russians, having originated from the Amazons and the Vikings, were good warriors. Later, Catherine the Great created a cult of Amazons that included an "Amazon" outfit, an "Amazon" way of riding horseback and an "Amazon" regiment of female warriors, the wives of local gentry who greeted Catherine in the Crimea (Zorin 2001; Proskurina 2006). Catherine even told Diderot that in St. Petersburg she was missing "the first Russians," the Varangians (Diderot 1992: 123).

An elaborate speculation on the Amazons and the marriage model of the state helped Tatishchev to reconcile Rurik with Hobbes and Pufendorf. Famously, Hobbes distinguished between two types of Commonwealth, by Institution and by Acquisition. The former comes from a voluntary agreement among the insiders, the latter is imposed by force of war onto the outsiders. Both are based on fear, and the rights of sovereignty are the same in both. The terror of an occupation by foreigners helped Hobbes to explain the horrifying methods of the sovereign power. At the same time, this equation allowed him to neutralize the legacy of the Norman Conquest, which was still significant in the England of his time. "Leviathan's invisible adversary is the Conquest," wrote Foucault (2003: 98). Tatishchev knew the logic of *Leviathan* well enough to feel a similar pacifying intention in the *Chronicle*. The voluntary invitation of a foreign sovereign would combine both types of Commonwealth. The agreement is voluntary but the contractor is foreign. This combination neutralized the racial model of the Russian state as the domination of the Viking Rurikides over the enslaved Slavs. There were two ways to develop this logic. One, which was probed by later historians, was to reduce the difference between the counterparts (Varangians, Slavs, and Finns) and present the situation as a multiethnic commonwealth that was electing its sovereign in consensus. Tatishchev chose the opposite and more complex solution, exaggerating the distance between the Vikings and the Slavs by way of his gender metaphors and the marriage model.

Schlözer was skeptical about this peaceful picture. Asking himself and the reader what the Russian north looked like in the year 800, he relied on the colonial experience that his contemporaries obtained overseas. It was "a little bit like Siberia, California, Madagascar," said Schlözer; "the Enlightenment that the Normans brought to the Russian desert was not better than what the Cossacks brought to the Kamchadals some 120 years ago" (Schlözer 1809: 1/419–20; 2/180; Miliukov 2006: 142). From reports by Georg Wilhelm Steller, who explored Kamchatka in 1740, Schlözer knew that the Russian conquest was one of the bloodiest in colonial history. In just 40 years the population of the vast land had shrunk to one-fifteenth of what it was before the Russians arrived. Foreign to Russian nationalist sentiment, Schlözer applied the idea of colonization to the very origins of Russian history. Russia was an exotic, deserted land that was colonized by the Vikings.

Remembered in Russia mainly as Normanists, Schlözer and his one-time patron, Gerhard Friedrich Müller, were also the founders of the discipline that has become known as ethnology. The new ethnological discourse came out of the clash between the universalist ideas of the Enlightenment and the actual diversity of peoples of the Russian Empire, which resonated with the diversity and desolation of German lands after the peace of Westphalia (Vermeulen 2006, 2008). Later, two Prussians, Kant and Herder, ignored the Russian-based contributions of Müller and Schlözer. Though Herder's philosophical writings defined the future of anthropology, in Russia an influential trend in history, classical studies, and education drew its roots from "the great Schlözer." Preparing his ill-fated academic career as a professor of history, in 1832 Gogol wrote a fascinating essay, "Schlözer, Müller, and Herder," which portrayed these three as "the great architects of universal history." Attributing to Schlözer the gift of throwing lightning bolts, Gogol preferred him to the other two, and to Kant as well:

> Schlözer was the first to feel history as one great whole. . . . His writing was like the lightning that illuminates objects almost at once. . . . He destroyed his enemies with one word of thunder. . . . Schlözer's genius had to be in opposition. . . . Him, rather than Kant, it is fair to call all-destructive. (Gogol 1984: 6/88–9)

After the end of Seven Years War (see Chapter 9), Schlözer returned to Germany. He developed "universal history" and social statistics in Göttingen; he was also a prolific journalist, one of the creators of the pan-German public sphere. He wrote *Nestor* before any comparable edition of a German chronicle was produced; for his analysis of the Russian chronicles, he appropriated the Protestant methods of critical reading of the New Testament (Butterfield 1955: 56). He also wrote a study of the north, from Iceland to Kamchatka. Following Pufendorf, he was one of the first to distinguish between the state and the people. He originated the term ethnography and, starting in 1772, exchanged hostile reviews with Herder, who disliked the word (Stagl 1995).

Within *Nestor* and on a broader scale of lifelong scholarship, Schlözer made pioneering use of the epistemological boomerang, an interpretative method that applies colonial knowledge to the understanding of metropolitan societies.

Uvarov and the Black Athena

In 1812, Sergei Uvarov, a career official as well as a self-trained classicist, applied the concept of colonization to the emergence of ancient Greece:

> It is probable that, of all the European countries, Greece was the first peopled by Asiatic colonies. . . . We know that Greece, peopled by Asian colonists, was subjugated in turn by races of men different among themselves, but of one common origin. These new colonies brought with them the elements of their religious worship. . . . The Egyptian and Phoenician colonies imported into Greece, with their religious modes of faith, their languages and their traditions. (Uvarov 1817: 73–4)

Uvarov had studied in Göttingen with Schlözer in 1801–3. The idea that ancient Greece produced myriads of Mediterranean colonies had been well established in classicist scholarship. However, Uvarov made a deeper and more radical claim, that ancient Greece was itself the result of colonization. Two oriental peoples, Egyptians and Phoenicians, invaded Greek lands in several waves and mixed with the local population, which Uvarov identified with the Pelasgians. He also learned from Schlözer, who was the first to describe the Semitic language family, that Egyptians and Phoenicians were "of one common origin." To name these processes, Uvarov used the term "colonization" extensively and with no sign of hesitation or novelty. He saw the analogy between the colonial situation that he described as the emergence of Greece, and the colonial situation that Schlözer described as the emergence of Russia; recent studies also indicate this analogy between Hellenistic and Russian colonization (Malkin 2004). Under Uvarov's influence, Schlözer's historiography became mainstream reading in the empire. In 1804, Alexander I ennobled Schlözer and gave him a coat of arms with Nestor, the legendary author of the *Primary Chronicle*, in the center (Kliuchevsky 1956: 8/448).

Figure 4: Sergei Uvarov between an Oriental tablecloth and a Classical column. Portrait by Orest Kiprensky (1815), in the Tretyakov Gallery, Moscow.
Source: Wikimedia Commons

Later, Uvarov published a proposal for the setting up of an Academy of Asian Studies in St. Petersburg (Whittaker 1984; Maiofis 2008). "It is to Asia that we owe the foundations of the great edifice of human civilization," wrote Uvarov (1810); studying and enlightening continental Asia is Russia's task, its civilizing mission. The German linguist Julius Klaproth, who had just returned from a trip to Mongolia and the Caucasus, helped Uvarov in this venture (Benes 2004). In 1932, the Soviet scholar and former Orthodox priest, Sergei Durylin, interpreted Uvarov's project as if he had just read Foucault: "With Napoleon or against Napoleon, with England or against England, Russia had to know its own and the neighboring East in order to reign over it: this is the idea of the Asian Academy" (Durylin 1932:

191). Forging an illustrious career, Uvarov became President of the Imperial Academy of Sciences (1818), an organizer of St. Petersburg Imperial University (1819), and Minister of the People's Enlightenment (1833–49). Seeing his role as the promotion of the ancient languages and classical education, he described Greece using the historical concepts that he had acquired in Russia and understood Russia in terms that he had learned from classical scholarship. Colonized and colonizing, both countries had much to share.

Uvarov's ideas matured in the international Romantic circles that – as Edward Said (1978: 98) told us with irony – were fascinated with "nations, races, minds, and peoples as things one could talk about passionately – in the ever-narrowing perspective of populism first adumbrated by Herder." In 1813, when Russian troops were fighting all over Europe, Uvarov composed a plan for perpetual peace. Referring to Hobbes, the abbé de Saint-Pierre, Rousseau, and Kant, whose projects of perpetual peace he knew but deemed outdated, Uvarov singled out one new idea that could provide a purpose for the postwar world. The idea was the colonization of the east, a sublime project that would keep the victors in business well after the war. Nations perform their noblest deeds after long and bloody conflicts, declared Uvarov. The war with Napoleon was large and its outcome, peace, would be proportional. Uvarov's Eurocentric project amounted to a project of colonization so large that it would be proper to call it, globalization. "The world is still spacious. . . . One half of the earth consists of deserts, of wild lands and . . . of barbarian societies. Powerful states will create a new world," wrote Uvarov (cited in Maiofis 2008: 78).

An alliance between two empires, the Russian and the British, was crucial for this project of global imperialism. But Great Britain suspected Alexander I of plans to create a world empire, declined to take part in the Holy Alliance of 1815, and prevented Russia from taking Greece from the Ottomans. Uvarov's idea of perpetual peace and his historical analogy between Russia and Greece became dated. In his correspondence with the highest authority among his contemporaries, Goethe, Uvarov reformulated the role of Russia as "the new Egypt" rather than Greece – not the "center" of the modern world but rather the "bridge" between its two separate halves, the east and the west. Like a bridge, Egyptians brought Asian culture to Greece and Europe; Russia should play the same role between Europe and Asia (Durylin 1932: 202). Three worlds were clearly on Uvarov's map, – the First World, Europe; the Third World, Asia; and the Second World, Russia. The new Egypt, Russia, would bring civilization to Asia in the same way as historical Egypt had brought it to Greece.

Beginning in 1987, the Sinologist Martin Bernal published several volumes of a controversial work that argued essentially the same thesis that had been proposed by Uvarov in 1812. Bernal's historical argument stated that the land of Greece had indeed been colonized by the Egyptians and Phoenicians and that the mixing of these peoples with the Pelasgians gave birth to ancient Greek civilization. This late twentieth-century study employed the same terminology of colonization that Uvarov had used much earlier. In the light of Bernal's historiographical argument, his proximity to Uvarov is not that surprising. Until about 1800, European classicists shared the belief in the eastern roots of Greece, asserts Bernal. Then, some scholars realized that this genealogy made Greeks the descendants of the Egyptians and the Phoenicians, i.e. the Africans and the Semites. Because of the growing racism of the pan-European intellectual elite, a new era started that Bernal described as the rise of India and the fall of Egypt. Denying the idea of the black and Semitic Athena, historians and linguists invented the Indo-Europeans.

Bernal attributed this early nineteenth-century revisionism to Göttingen's circle of the anti-Semitic Semitologist Johann David Michaelis, who proposed the colonization of the sugar islands in the Caribbean by the deported European Jews (Hess 2000). While Michaelis's student and Uvarov's teacher, Schlözer, was the first to describe the Semitic language family, Uvarov's one-time assistant, Klaproth, was instrumental in the construction of the Indo-German language family (Benes 2004). Schlegel and the Parisian orientalists soon took up the fateful contrast between the Semites and Aryans. Connected to all of them but unable or uneager to choose between their positions, Uvarov synthesized them in his book on the mysteries of Eleusis. Supplementing the idea of the Semitic colonization of Greece, Uvarov identified some inscriptions that were connected with the mysterious Eleusis as sacral Sanskrit words, such as the famous Om. One illustration in the book, which was created by Uvarov's friend Aleksei Olenin, then Russia's Secretary of State, showed the Greek goddess, Ceres/Demeter sitting on a pedestal that featured the images of Indian and Egyptian gods and holding a parchment bearing mystical words in Greek. It was a wonderfully inclusive image; as a historian, Uvarov was more tolerant than he was as a bureaucrat. He chose the epigraph to this book from Virgil (Eclog. III): "Non nostrum inter vos tantas componere lites" – "Tis not for us to end such great disputes."

Figure 5: Demeter-Ceres, a Greek-Roman Goddess, sits on a stone which exhibits on one side the Indian gods, Brahma, Vishnu, and Siva, and, on the other, the Egyptian Goddess Isis. The inscriptions say "Demeter" and "Homer."
Source: From Sergei Uvarov's *Essay on Eleusinian Mysteries* (Uvaro 1817); drawing by Aleksei Olenin

Origin is Destiny

Being a colony means having a sovereign abroad. But both Russia and ancient Greece were different; at different stages of their history they were both colonized and colonizing. The potential of this system of similarities and differences was realized while Uvarov combined his duties as Minister of the Enlightenment and President of the Imperial Academy of Sciences. Working in Uvarov's spirit of enlightened, even utilitarian, monarchism, the writer Nikolai Karamzin supported the Hobbesian idea that the unruly Slavs created an autocratic regime to tame themselves. Internal conflicts and long-term misery revealed for the Slavs "the danger and the harm of the rule of the people"; as a result, they acquired a "unanimous belief in the value of Autocracy." But taking the next step, Karamzin contrasted the origins of Russia with other processes of state-building: "Everywhere else Autocracy was introduced by the sword of the strong or the cunning of the ambitious. . . . In Russia, Autocracy was founded with the general consensus of the citizenry: this is what our *Chronicle* says" (1989: 1/93). In Western Europe, the Normans occupied France or England, but in the east, the Normans were invited to Slavic lands. Mikhail Pogodin, a professor of the Moscow Imperial University whose father was a serf, developed this contrast just a bit further. For him, the story of Rurik amounted to the "providential and fateful text," a parable that resolves "the mystery of Russian history" (Pogodin 1859: 2; Maiorova 2010):

> The history of any state is nothing but the development of its foundational event. . . . The beginning of the state is the most important part of . . . its history and it defines its fate for ever and ever. It is in the beginning that we need to find the difference of Russian history from any other, Western and Eastern histories. (Pogodin 1846: 2)

Origin and History are clearly different and the former overdetermines the latter.[1] For Pogodin, the invitation to Rurik, "to come and rule over us," was not a one-time event, as the *Chronicles* described it, but an ever-continuing romance. "In the West, everything started with the occupation; with us, everything originates from the free call, the undisputed takeover, and the loving deal." This is why the Russian sovereign has always been "a peaceful guest, a desired protector," while in the west the sovereign has been "a hated invader, an arch-enemy" (Pogodin 1859: 187, 218). The Origin found its place as the eternal center of the Empire.

Adjusting Rurik's story and creating a theory of Origin, Pogodin centralized his own domain, Russian history, around the concept of colonization by consent. His idea of the "loving deal" responded to the colonial doctrine of his boss Uvarov. In 1818, when Pogodin was a student, Uvarov formulated the idea that remained central for his Enlightenment and orientalist initiatives:

[1] In Russia, Petr Chaadaev was the first to elaborate this philosophy of foundational events, that the origin of a people determines its destiny. After finding similar thoughts in Alexis de Tocqueville's *Democracy in America*, Chaadaev wrote to a friend, seriously or not, that Tocqueville had stolen this idea from him (Ermichev and Zlatopol'skaia 1989: 388; for details, see Etkind 2001b: 22).

> Hegemony cannot be established or kept only by the sword. . . . Conquest with no respect for humanity, without the new and better laws, without correcting the condition of the defeated, is a futile and bloody dream. Gaining victories by the enlightenment, taming minds by the humble spirit of religion, by the spread of arts and sciences, by education and the prosperity of the defeated – this is the only method of conquest that could be stabilized for eternity. (Maiofis 2008: 281)

If this project did not sound realistic, Rurik's example could make it digestible. After all the blood spilled in their internal and external endeavors, the statesmen of the post-Napoleonic Restoration wished to reign over the hearts and minds of their subjects. Increasingly conservative, Uvarov coined the triple slogan of "Autocracy, Orthodoxy, Nationality," which the Romanovs preached and practiced until 1917 (Riasanovsky 1959; Zorin 1997). But Uvarov was also attentive toward religious minorities, such as the Jews, expressing his hope early in 1836 for "the moral and intellectual rapprochement of the Jews and Christian society" (Stanislawski 1983: 68). Sergei Soloviev, who became a professor of history under Uvarov, quipped that his boss worshiped Orthodoxy though he did not believe in Christ, preached Autocracy though he was a "liberal," and called for Nationality though he had read "not a single Russian book" (Soloviev 1983: 268). The latter was definitely an exaggeration.

Under Uvarov, Russian historians became increasingly professional. They felt an obligation to write and teach Russian history in a worldly, comparative context that displaced bizarre and unique events, such as the story of Rurik, to the margins of scholarship. This perspective did not prevent their histories from evolving into imperial narratives of the steady, irresistible growth of Russian power. But first, they had to deal with Rurik, who opened their courses. The founding father of modern Russian history, Sergei Soloviev, closed the circle by connecting Rurik with Peter the Great and situating Rurik's arrival at the site of St. Petersburg: "The location of the great waterway that connects Europe and Asia determined the foundation of St. Petersburg: here in the ninth century the first half of Russian history started, here in the eighteenth century its second half began" (1988: 1/60). But his great student, Vasilii Kliuchevsky, retold the story of the Varangians with noticeable irritation:

> What is this but not a stereotypical formula of the law-abiding power that rises out of a contract, a theory very old, but always re-emerging . . . ? The tale of the Call to the Princes, as it is told in the *Primary*

> *Chronicle*, is not a popular legend. It is a schematic parable of the origins of the state, which is adjusted to the comprehension level of schoolchildren. (Kliuchevsky 1956: 1/144)

With the irony that he sometimes smuggled into his writings, Kliuchevsky attributed the contract theory of political power to the Orthodox monks of the twelfth century. He knew that this was an anachronistic hypothesis. Was it Nestor who adjusted his stories for the schoolchildren? The famous historian questioned this part of the *Primary Chronicle*, but confined his doubts to the notes (Kliuchevsky 1983: 113; Kireeva 1996: 424). Indeed, the idea that the story of the Varangians appeared in the *Primary Chronicle* in the milieu of Tatishchev and under the influence of Pufendorf and Hobbes would have made perfect historical sense. However, several versions of the *Chronicle* had recorded this story much earlier. A symbol of larger historiographical and ideological problems, Rurik embodies the controversies of autonomy, freedom, and modernity that re-emerge with every new turn of Russian and global history. Tired of chasing Rurik in the archive and unable to erase him, Russian historians ventured a set of creative concepts, the epistemological Rurikides, which developed their own reproductive energy.

— 4 —

To Colonize Oneself

The Romantic and then the Soviet poets sang of the warmth and beauty of the Russian land. But historians of Russia expressed deep insecurity about the Russian environment, both natural and social. Russian nature was not the mother for Russians, but the stepmother, said Sergei Soloviev (1988: 7/8–9). During the crisis of the seventeenth century, Muscovites felt alien in their own state, "as if they were accidental and temporary dwellers in someone else's house," wrote Vasilii Kliuchevsky (1956: 3/52). Surprisingly, this historian also applied the same oxymoronic trope, homesickness at home, to a man of the eighteenth century, Peter I: he was "a guest in his own home" (1956: 4/31). Strikingly, the same author also applied the same trope to a typical early-nineteenth-century noble who, "strolling with Voltaire's book somewhere in his own village," felt himself "an alien among his own kind" (1956: 5/183). In his wonderful essay on Pushkin's *Onegin*, Kliuchevsky applied the same characteristic to its fictional character: "[Onegin] was foreign to the society in which he moved" (1990: 9/87). An important trope of the High Imperial Period, this persistent image was sometimes based on historical evidence and sometimes not; what is clear is that the historians preferred to see their favorite protagonists in this light.

"Why did God make me a stranger and an outcast in mine own house?" wrote the renowned African American intellectual, W. E. B. DuBois in 1903 (Washington et al. 1965: 214). Postcolonial theorists have also speculated about this experience of being "strangers to ourselves" (Kristeva 1991). "The 'unhomely' is a paradigmatic colonial and postcolonial condition," states Bhabha (1994: 13). In the nineteenth century, the pioneers of Russian historiography found their own formulas for the same intuition.

Soloviev and the Frontier

Having visited Russia in 1843, August von Haxthausen wrote that this country was involved not in a colonial expansion but, rather, in an "internal colonization," which was "the most important subject of the whole internal politics and economy of this Empire" (1856: 2/76). Unlike the other Russian discoveries of this Prussian official, this one failed to attract public attention. However, mid-nineteenth-century agricultural experts eagerly used the concept of colonization (*kolonizatsiia*) when they discussed and regulated migrations of Russian peasants to the peripheral regions of the Empire, mainly to southern Russia, Siberia and, later, Central Asia. One of many such debates took place in 1861 at the Russian Geographical Society. The journalist Nikolai Leskov, who managed some of these internal resettlements (see Chapter 11), responded to the speech of the geographer Mikhail Veniukov, who had traversed Asia and a little later presided over the agricultural reform in eastern Poland. Leskov stated that, in practice, many organized migrations were directed toward "the central areas of our Empire" rather than its distant possessions, and this was a major difference between Russian and British modes of colonization (Leskov 1988: 60).

The mid- and late nineteenth century was the moment of imperial expansion on a large scale (Arendt 1970). Taking its part in the conquest of America, the Great Game in Asia, and even the scramble for Africa, the Russian Empire was no less concerned about its vast hinterland. Having appropriated imperialist language, it needed to adjust the overseas concept of colonization to its terrestrial, provincial realms. The Moscow historian, Sergei Soloviev, made the conceptual breakthrough. Drawing his academic genealogy directly from Schlözer, he was engaged in a fierce polemics with Khomiakov and his Slavophile followers, whom he deemed "an anti-historical school" (see Chapter 1). He appropriated Khomiakov's critical notion of Russia as a colony, but gave it an interpretation that was deeper both historically and logically. Applying the discourse of colonization to pre-Petrine Russia, Soloviev rejected the very difference between the colonizers and the colonized: "Russia was a vast, virgin country, which was waiting to be populated, waiting for its history to begin: therefore ancient Russian history is the history of a country that colonizes itself" (1988: 2/631).

Soloviev formulated this astonishing dictum in his survey of Russia's ancient history. If there is no point in differentiating between the subject and the object of Russia's colonization, then let us avoid doing so. Soloviev gave a dynamic depiction of the concerns of a self-colonized country:

> To populate as soon as possible, to call people from everywhere to come to empty places, to tempt them with various benefits; to leave a place for newer, better lands, for the most profitable conditions, for an edge that is quiet and peaceful; on the other hand, to cling to the people, to bring them back, to force others not to accept them – these are the important concerns of a country that colonizes itself. (1988: 2/631)

For a colonial mind, there is no greater distance in the world than that between the metropolitan land and its colony. How can a country colonize itself? Soloviev knew the problem and emphasized it:

> This country [Russia] was not a colony that was separated from the metropolitan land by oceans: the heart of the state's life was situated in this very country. . . . While the needs and functions of the state were increasing, the country did not lose her self-colonizing character. (1988: 2/631)

In Russian, the reflexive form that Soloviev used, "to colonize itself," is as unusual as it is in English. In the original even more than in the translation, this formula sounds dynamic, even forceful, and paradoxical. But Soloviev and his disciples were consistent in the use of this verbal form. Going into detail in his multiple volumes, Soloviev explained that the direction of Russia's self-colonization was coherent, from the south-west to the north-east, from the banks of the Danube to the banks of the Dnieper. Going north, the ancient Russian tribes went to Novgorod and to the coast of the White Sea. Going east, they colonized the upper Volga and the neighborhood of Moscow. There they established the Russian state, but the direction of colonization remained the same, to the east and all the way to Siberia. Importantly, Soloviev did not apply the idea of "Russia colonizing itself" to the history that he perceived as modern. In his later volumes that described the "new" Russian history as opposed to the "ancient," he did not use the term "colonization."

In a pioneering essay, Mark Bassin (1993) compared Soloviev's idea of Russia's "colonization of itself" with Frederick J. Turner's concept of the American "frontier." There are many resemblances and differences between these two concepts, both of them crucial to the histories of Russia and America. Like the American frontier, the external line of Russia's colonization was uncertain, diffuse, and constantly moving. As in America, this line was centrally important for the development of Russian imperial culture. Persecuted religious minorities were equally important in the American and Russian frontiers (Turner 1920; Etkind 1998; Breyfogle 2005). However, there are also significant differences between Turner's and Soloviev's concepts.

Turner explored the modern developments on the frontier, while Soloviev restricted his use of the concept of Russia's self-colonization to its "ancient," i.e. early medieval, history. This difference is not as serious as it sounds because there is nothing in the concept of colonization that prevents using it for the modern Russian period; indeed, as we will see shortly, Kliuchevsky made this move, but Soloviev did not. While Turner focused on the characteristic culture of the western frontier and explored the mechanisms of its impact on the eastern states, Soloviev did not produce a comparable portrait of the external line of colonization. However, historians have produced remarkable studies of various parts of the Russian frontier.[1] The pioneers of the frontline – the hunter, the trader, and the sectarian - were similar, but the second and third lines of colonization were vastly different. In America, as Turner saw it, lands behind the frontier were cultivated in a regular "four-stages order" by ranchers, farmers, and industrialists. The frontier was pushing the cultivated space to the west. In Russia throughout centuries, the movement of the colonization line to the east left huge lands behind it as virginal as they had been. Later, these empty spaces had to be colonized again, and then again. America's frontier and Russia's colonization had different topologies, the former relatively continuous, the latter leaving in its wake holes, pockets, and folds.

Mapping these internal lands was tough; exploring the peoples who populated them was no easier (Widdis 2004; Tolz 2005). Although in various segments of the immense frontline of Russia's external colonization, "middle grounds" were created that hybridized the colonized and the colonizers, these synthetic cultures were local, variegated, and dispersed over huge stretches of time and space. It is all but impossible to describe them all in one ethno-sociological portrait, as Turner did in his work on the American frontier. Developing centrifugally, these local formations were crucial to the economic development of Russian centers, from Novgorod to Moscow to St.

[1] To me, the most illuminating have been Lantzeff and Pierce 1973; Barrett 1999; Khodarkovsky 2002; Sunderland 2004; Breyfogle 2005; Dolbilov 2010.

Petersburg. With gunpowder, alcohol, and germs on their side, the Russians exterminated, absorbed, or displaced many of their neighbors. But these processes took centuries. Multiple waves of adventure, violence, labor, and breeding rolled between Russia's centers and the moving frontline of colonization. Culturally thin, Russia's frontier was geographically broad. However much it changed with time, it always covered huge areas of space. Within these areas, there was no regular transition from hunting to herding or from planting to industrial development. Sometimes trapping remained the only profitable business for centuries; huge cities were sometimes built on land that had never been ploughed. Even Russian capitals were established on territories that were foreign to their founders. Indeed, the lands of Novgorod and Kiev were as foreign to the Varangians who ruled there as the land of St. Petersburg was for the Muscovites. From the borders to the capitals, the space of internal colonization extended throughout Russia.

Shchapov and Zoological Economy

A significant influence on the further development of the self-colonization idea was the historian Afanasii Shchapov, who wrote most of his works not when he was a university professor, but when he was either a state official or a political exile. He was the first who actually thought of Russian colonization not as a vigorous adventure but as a bloody, genuinely political process. It had its victims as well as victors, and the task of a historian was to see both. Teaching history at Kazan Imperial University in the late 1850s, Shchapov sorted out an ecclesiastical archive of the Solovetsky monastery in the far north, which was evacuated to land-locked Kazan as Russia was preparing for the Crimean War (the monastery, thousands of miles from the Crimea, was nonetheless bombed by the British navy in 1854). It was in this remote archive that the leading historian of the next generation, Vasilii Kliuchevsky, wrote his first monograph about "the monastery colonization" of northern Russia; his first critical review was also on Shchapov, of whom he had a "very high opinion" (Nechkina 1974: 434). But by then Shchapov was no longer in Kazan. In 1861, he was accused of fomenting unrest, was arrested, brought to Petersburg, pardoned by the Tsar, and, in a sensational move, was appointed to the Ministry of Internal Affairs. Later, exiled to his native Siberia, he still published his revisionist articles in the mainstream Russian journals.

Agreeing with Soloviev that the history of Russia was the history of colonization, Shchapov described the process as a "millennium of colonization and cultivation of woods and swamps, the fight with Finnish, Mongol, and Turkish tribes" (1906: 2/182). An ethnic Creole – son of a Russian deacon and a Siberian Buriat – Shchapov emphasized racial mixing more than any other Russian historian. He was also the true pioneer of ecological history. Two methods of colonization were primary: "fur colonization," with hunters harvesting and depleting the habitats of fur animals and moving further and further across Siberia all the way to Alaska; and "fishing colonization," which supplied Russian centers with fresh- or salt-water fish and caviar. In this attempt at ecological history, Shchapov made an important step forward from Soloviev.

From Rurik the Varangian to Ivan the Terrible, Russia's wealth was measured in fur. Coining the concept of "zoological economy," Shchapov understood fur as the clue to Russia's colonization (1906: 2/280–93, 309–37). Beaver led the Russians to the place where they founded Novgorod; grey squirrel secured them the wealth of Moscow; sable led them to the place that became mapped as Siberia; sea otter brought them to Alaska and California. Throughout the Middle Ages and what elsewhere was known as the Renaissance, man-made migrations of small, wild, furry animals defined the expansion of Russia. Winter roads, trade stations, and militarized storehouses for fur spanned across Eurasia, playing roles that were not dissimilar from the Great Silk Route in medieval Asia. Ecologically, colonization also meant deforestation. "Agricultural colonization" followed "fur colonization" and gradually replaced it. It was not a sword but an axe that moved Russia's colonization, said Shchapov, with the plough following the axe. But the bow and the trap preceded them all. For Shchapov, colonization was an easy and positive concept, which he used on almost every page of his wordy and warm writings. It meant the multi-edged process of exploring, populating, cultivating, and depleting new lands. Russia's colonization had to be understood as parallel histories of peoples moved, animals exterminated, and plants cultivated. It was an unprecedented vision, multidimensional, environmental, and human.

Kliuchevsky and Modernity

Decades later, Kliuchevsky repeated the motto of his teacher, Soloviev, and revised it in one significant respect, which I attribute to the influence of Shchapov: "The history of Russia is the history of a country that colonizes itself. . . . [T]his centuries-long movement has continued until the current moment" (Kliuchevsky 1956: 1/31). If for Soloviev, Russia's self-colonization started in ancient times and stopped in the Middle Ages, Kliuchevsky extended this concept well into the modern age. When he revised his work in 1907, he added a long passage about the early twentieth-century state-sponsored migrations to Siberia, Central Asia, and the Pacific Coast, in which he saw the newest manifestations of the "centuries-long movement of Russia's colonization." It was the only significant change that Kliuchevsky made in his multi-volume *Course of Russian History* for its new edition. Covering Russia's long history from ancient to modern times, he wished to apply the concept of colonization to his era as well.

Talking about the ancient Russians, Soloviev gave a description of the Russian national character that was widely quoted:

> Because of [the Russians'] high mobility, their shapelessness, their habit of leaving after the first difficulty, they developed a semi-settledness, a lack of commitment to a place, a weakened moral focus, and lack of calculation; Russians developed the habit of looking for easy work, of living in limbo, from one day to another. (Soloviev 1988: 2/631; see also Bassin 1993: 500; Sunderland 2004: 171)

Kliuchevsky argued that this set of characteristics was a consequence of self-colonization. He generalized that this "particular relation of the people to the country," the relation of colonization, "worked in Russia over centuries and is working now." In this, Kliuchevsky saw "the main condition" that defined the development of "changing forms of community" in Russian history. Repeating and varying Soloviev's formula, that Russia is "a country that colonizes itself," Kliuchevsky wished to emphasize and extend this process even more than his teacher. Thus, this most influential of Russian historians stated that "the colonization of the country is the single most important fact of Russia's history" and that, from the Middle Ages to the modern era, the standard periods of Russian history are nothing more than "the major moments of colonization" (Kliuchevsky 1956: 1/31–2).

Self-applicable judgments have an unusual logic. If X does Y to Z, as in the statement "Britain colonizes India," that implies that X and Z were there before Y occurred. But this straightforward logic wouldn't work for the colonization of Russia because, according to Soloviev and Kliuchevsky, Russia has constituted itself through the process of colonization. There was no X that preceded Y and no Z that was different from X. It all has evolved together. Therefore, in "Russia colonizes itself," X does Y to X. As Kliuchevsky said, the area of colonization expanded along with the territory of the state. Since the colonized areas did not retain their special status but were absorbed by the Russian state, there is no reason to distinguish between Russia's colonies and its metropolitan center. With the territorial growth of the state, Russia colonized the newly appropriated territories, but it also (though probably in different forms) colonized itself at its imperial core, which has recurrently undergone this process of colonization.

"The history of Russia is the history of a country that colonizes itself." There is an awkward repetition in this formula but there is also a feeling that it could not be worded differently. Structurally, the formula combined the most trivial, even banal repetition in the first half and the paradoxical, deconstructive second half. By saying, "The history of Russia is the history of a country," Soloviev and Kliuchevsky alerted the reader to the fact that, this time, they were talking about Russia as the country and not as the people, the state, or the empire. In Russian, as in English, "country" stands somewhere between the geographical "land" and the political "nation," which is exactly what is needed. They could not say what they wanted to say without this rhetorical repetition, because an alternative formula such as "The history of Russia consisted of self-colonization" would assume that Russia existed before this self-colonization, while the very idea was to describe the process in which Russia was created by a process that it also performed. Polished by so many hands, the formula could not be rendered in any other way. This is why it was repeated.

Self-Colonization School

Kliuchevsky's followers distinguished between various modes of Russia's colonization, such as "free colonization" that was led by private men, mostly runaway serfs and deserted soldiers or Cossacks; "military colonization," which happened as a result of regular campaigns; and "monastery colonization," which was centered around major Orthodox sanctuaries that owned thousands of serfs, carried trade, and built outposts. For them, the trails of Russia's eastward colonization were blazed by fur hunters, beatified by monks, fortified by soldiers, and cultivated by settlers. Their purpose was a systematic, balanced overview of these events that would show the civilizing mission of Russia in the vast, wild expanse of Eurasia. Loyal to the cause of Russian nationalism, Kliuchevsky's school tended to ignore the huge amounts of violence that these colonizing activities entailed. Although it was violence that made necessary all the fences, walls, and towers of the outposts, monasteries, and towns that these historians described in detail, sensitivity to this violence and compassion for its victims came mainly with the next generation of historians, who would experience the Russian revolution, take part in it, and often find themselves either under arrest or in emigration.

A student of Kliuchevsky's, Pavel Miliukov, elaborated on this colonization theme with a new emphasis. As a young professor, Miliukov was dismissed from Moscow University for political activism, was imprisoned, released, and mixed history with politics for decades. In his multi-volume course of Russian history, he realized better than his predecessors how much violence the process of colonization required, and mapped large ethnicities who were either absorbed or exterminated by Russians on their path of colonization. In a special article of the Russian Encyclopedia, Miliukov wrote, "Russia's colonization by the Russian people has continued throughout the whole duration of Russian history and has constituted one of its most characteristic features" (1895: 740).

In the early 1930s, Matvei Liubavsky, a prominent disciple of Kliuchevsky who served as the Rector of Moscow Imperial University until 1917, presented a systematic exploration of the favorite idea of his teacher. Liubavsky (1996) repeated that "Russian history is the history of a country that colonized ceaselessly": instead of the reflective mode that was used by his predecessors, he used a simpler construction – "colonized ceaselessly" rather than "colonized itself." This shift is subtle but significant. It matched a further statement by Liubavsky, that he wrote his treatise as an exploration of "the predominantly external colonization that created the territory of the Russian state." Bringing his long narrative to the late nineteenth century, Liubavsky included a chapter on the colonization of the Baltic lands, which embraces the area of St. Petersburg. Ironically, his book about external colonization ended with a chapter on the colonization of the territory of the imperial capital. But he did write his history of Russia as a history of external colonization – how Russia colonized the others rather than colonized itself – and his awareness of this fact shows that he understood better than his predecessors the political meaning of the concept. His book remained unpublished because he wrote it after he was arrested, interrogated, and exiled to Bashkiria, one of those colonized regions about which he wrote.

In the late imperial period, Russian historiography was dominated by the self-colonization school. From history textbooks, its ideas found their way into encyclopedias. Russian historians wrote detailed accounts of Russia's takeover of the Crimea, Finland, Ukraine, Poland, and other lands. However, they did not describe these areas as Russian colonies. (In this respect, a remarkable exception among Russian authors was Nikolai Iadrintsev, whose book *Siberia as a Colony* (2003; first published in 1882), was a great example of an anti-imperial history.) Instead of talking about the Russian Empire colonizing the Caucasus or Poland, Soloviev and Kliuchevsky argued that "Russia colonized itself." However, they held a critical stance toward the peculiar character of this particular empire. "As the territory of the Russian state was expanding and the external power of the people growing, the internal freedom of the people was decreasing," wrote Kliuchevsky (1956: 3/8). He used the concept of self-colonization as a shortcut for this "inverse proportion" between the imperial space and internal freedom, a usage that modern philosophers such as Habermas would probably approve. Kliuchevsky's disciples, who saw the worldwide processes of decolonization, reproduced his definition with minor variations. By merging subject and object, this formula provided them with an inverted, maybe even perverted, language that they reserved for talking about Russia and did not use when talking about other parts of the world (Etkind 2002).

The discourse of self-colonization was a specific, though long-term and surprisingly robust, moment in Russian historiography. Living in the age of colonial empires and working for a country that competed with these empires, leading Russian historians found the language of colonization appropriate and necessary for their work. However, they transformed the western idea of colonization in quite a radical way. First, in Russia, the process of colonization was construed as self-referential and internal, rather than as object-directed and external. Second, in Russia, we often find approval of the processes of colonization, which is different from the British and French historiographical traditions and from the strongly ideological, postcolonial approach to colonization. Whereas twentieth-century historians generally denounced imperialism, their nineteenth-century predecessors did not always use "colonial" words in a critical way. Even Shchapov, a pariah and exile, admired the heroism of those who accomplished the colonization of a large country. The most critical among historians of Russian self-colonization, Miliukov, became a hawkish politician as Minister of Foreign Affairs. His objective in World War I was to take Constantinople for Russia.

Soviet historians largely abandoned the discourse of self-colonization: it did not fit the class approach and the idea of the socialist commonwealth. In late nineteenth-century Russia, colonization was still perceived as progress; in the Soviet Union, it was reactionary and Russia's history was supposed to have little to do with it. A student of Kliuchevsky, who became his Soviet biographer, counted the concept of Russia's colonization among his weaker ideas (Nechkina 1974: 427). However, the colonization paradigm continued in the work of a largely forgotten group of political geographers, led by Veniamin Semenov-Tian-Shansky (1915; Polian 2001). For a while, the Soviet activities in the Arctic continued under the name of colonization, which engaged some historians of the Kliuchevsky school (*Ocherki* 1922; Holquist 2010a). Ironically, the colonial terminology vanished from official discourse in the early 1930s, when the Soviet government implemented the most massive and brutal methods of colonization, by the forced labor of the gulag prisoners.

To conclude, the historians of the self-colonization school were not anti-imperialist thinkers; they were not particularly critical toward Russian imperial appropriations. Their historiographical tradition was secular, liberal, and nationalist. Like some Russian rulers before them, these historians were engaged in "cross-imperial knowledge acquisition" (Stoler 2009: 39), which connected the Russian Empire to other empires of the world via relations of selective and sometimes reciprocal mimesis. The notebooks of the all-time leader of this tradition, Kliuchevsky, surprise the reader with the political despair that is hidden in his famous course of lectures: "In the Europe of kings, Russia was a decisive force; in the Europe of nations, Russia is but a thick log that is caught in an eddy" (2001: 406). Three generations of nineteenth- and early twentieth-century Russian historians, whose teachings and textbooks constitute the core of Russian historiography, disagreed about many features of the Russian past but there was one formula that they kept repeating one after the other: "Russia colonized itself."

— 5 —

Barrels of Fur

Historians write from the past to the present, but think from the present to the past. Twenty-first-century Russia's successes and problems are plentiful; along with some others, I believe that the dependency on oil and gas exports is an important source of many of them (see, e.g., Ross 2001; Friedman 2006; Goldman 2008). But I intend to show that a resource dependency far predates post-Soviet Russia and the Soviet Union.

Protego Ergo Obligo

Suppose that some valuable resource, say a rare metal, is available at a single spot on earth. The labor theory of value does not work there; the price of the metal is not dependent upon the labor that is needed for mining this metal. Since the whole population depends on the redistribution of income that comes from a single spot, this state has no reason to develop the governance mechanisms that enable fair taxation, competition, and rule of law. The security costs are serious because the state that owns this spot would likely have many enemies. The transportation costs are also substantial, because this spot is likely to be far from the traditional centers of population, which developed according to an entirely different logic. Growth in the resource-bound state requires relatively little labor or knowledge. Instead, it develops a security apparatus that protects the source of wealth and its transportation routes, and a bureaucracy that redistributes the wealth and demands respect.

Political philosophers have always known that those who provide security tend to grasp property. "The *protego ergo obligo* is the *cogito ergo sum* of the state," wrote Carl Schmitt (1976, 56; see also Bates 2001). In our hypothetical case it means that the group that trades the resource is the same group that protects the state. Besides the classical monopoly over the legitimate use of violence, as it was defined by Max Weber, such a state develops a monopoly over the legitimate trade of its resource: a double monopoly that could be best compared to a Mobius strip, with one side managing the resource, and another side managing security, and both sides smoothly merging with each other (Etkind 2009).

Let us also imagine that the state controls a territory that is larger than the spot with the valuable resource, and there are many people living everywhere in the land. This situation creates a rigid, caste-like structure. Two classes of citizens emerge: the small elite of producers who extract, protect, and trade the resource, and others whose existence depends on the redistribution of the rent that this trade provides. The state is fully dependent on the trading group; moreover, these indispensable people *are* the state. But this state does not necessarily ignore the people; it provides them with security and other goods, indeed all that can be done after the state satisfies its own needs. Human capital does not determine the wealth of this nation. On the contrary, the resource-bound state provides charity to the people.

In a neighboring land, which I call labor-bound, the work of citizens creates the wealth of a nation. There is no other source of wealth there than the competitive work of its citizens. Value is created by labor; this old axiom still works in this economy. The state taxes this labor and has no other income. The health and education of the citizens are not only in their best interest but also in the interests of the state, because the better they work, the more taxes they pay. But then, these happy citizens find out that the growth of their economy depends on a resource they do not have. As they buy more and more of this resource, its price grows, production diminishes with depletion, and labor becomes relatively cheaper than the resource. From now on, both trading states become resource-bound. Nothing on earth could change this common dependency unless the labor-bound society focuses a part of its creative labor on substituting the deficient resource with something that it has in abundance.

This process has not occurred with oil, but many centuries ago it did happen with another valuable resource.

A Divine Marvel

In a lively tale dated 1096, the *Primary Chronicle* describes the first resource curse in Russian history:

> We have encountered a divine marvel. . . . There are mountains, which slope down to the arm of the sea, and their height reaches to the heavens. . . . Within these mountains are heard great cries and the sound of voices and [some people] are struggling to cut their way out of this mountain. . . . Their language is unintelligible. They point at iron objects and make gestures as if to ask for them. If given a knife or an axe, they supply furs in return. (Laurentian Text 1953: 184)

These people, the Iugra, were unclean, continues the *Chronicle*, and with God's help Alexander the Great locked them inside this mountain in the northern Urals. They will be released when the world comes to its end; until then, they will be trading fur for iron. They are imagined as a trading machine, speechless and subhuman. They do not speak because their trade does not require language. Nothing but fur justifies the humans from Novgorod to be there, among the Iugra.

Apart from the reference to Alexander, the tale is not far from the truth. In their quest for fur, the Russians colonized a huge, exotic, and inhospitable space, called "the land of darkness" with early Arabic travelers (Slezkine 1994; Martin 2004). Combining barter with coercion, the Russians locked the peoples of the Arctic north into a trading system that led to the extermination of animals and humans. The people of Novgorod thought that these operations would continue until the end of the world as they knew it; indeed, their termination would signal the end of Novgorod. It was a straightforward case of colonization that was recognized as such by major historians, Russian and western alike. Continued by the Muscovite state, which expanded the fur trade much further to the east, this colonization led to a huge accumulation of wealth and a proportional desolation of the natives, both processes being of outstanding scale in colonial history.

The Russians arrived in small numbers and did not hunt the animals. They needed locals to do the highly skilled jobs of hunting animals and dressing furs. The natives had the skills but were not much interested in fur, which they used mainly for their own warmth. Only force or commerce could turn these fishermen or reindeer herders into full-time hunters. The state established the fur trade in several steps. First, the military teams confiscated the furs that were already stored there. Second, the invaders imposed a tribute that obliged each native man to deliver a certain number of pelts annually. Third, the servitors established customs in towns and on the roads that collected the tithe in fur, usually a tenth of every transaction. Corruption was high and uncontrollable; bribes and other illegal fees ate up a big part of the state income (Bushkovitch 1980: 117). Novgorod and, later, Moscow had to send more servitors to these vast lands, though the number of Russian men was never high. The tale of the divine marvel was prophetic: the native tribes were locked into the fur trade. As long as they provided fur, it was in the interest of the servitors to maintain their conditions rather than to christen and educate them. If baptized into the Orthodox church, natives would stop paying the tribute in fur and start paying tax in rubles. This was undesirable; later, even Christian communities had to pay tribute instead of tax if they were perceived as non-Orthodox (Znamenski 2007). Since in many cases, the partners did not share a language and were scared of one another, they developed a method of "silent trade" that was surprisingly similar to the Iugra trade of 1096:

> For many years, [the Chukchi] would have no dealings with [the Russians] except at the end of a spear. They would hang a bundle of furs . . . upon a sharp polished blade of a long Chukchi lance, and if a Russian trader chose to take it off and suspend in its place a fair equivalent in the shape of tobacco, well and good, if not, there is no trade. (Kennan 1870: 286)

In Siberia, as well as in North America, the fur business was different from most "cross-cultural trades" because it involved a meeting between the organized Europeans and the natives, who had been isolated for centuries. Hunting and trapping was intrinsically violent, did not entail the long-term cycles that were characteristic for agriculture, and had no need of the participation of women (Curtin 1984: 219). Trade was also violent; even when the Russians used barter, it was barely distinguishable from robbery. They exchanged furs for iron and other products of their superior civilization, such as alcohol, tobacco, beads, knives, and, later, traps and rifles. The Soviet scholars politely called this method "the non-equivalent exchange" that was characteristic for the "initial accumulation of the capital."

In their quest for fur, Russian traders explored the vast lands that stretch far to the north and east from the metropolitan centers, Novgorod and Moscow, all the way to the White Sea, across the Ural Mountains, and into Siberia. Firearms were the key to this success, even though they often worked merely as fireworks. But violence was not easy to convert into power. Technical terms that were foreign to both sides, usually of Arabic or Turkish origin, were meant to mask the rude force. Concepts and practices traveled across the land, from the Caucasus to Alaska. *Yasak* referred to the special regime of taxation, a tribute in fur. Judging by later evidence from the eighteenth and nineteenth centuries, another typical method of extracting fur from the natives was kidnapping, which was known as "taking *amanats*." Capturing the native women and children and holding them in captivity, Russians demonstrated them to their men in exchange for furs. If the children survived to maturity, these *amanats* would speak Russian; baptized, they could marry Russians and contribute to the creolization of the locals (Liapunova 1987: 59). In 1788, the Russians held as many as 500 children of the Aleuts as *amanats*. Russian emperors, including the enlightened Catherine the Great, authorized this method for "taming the natives" in official documents (Slezkine 1994). First recorded in the late sixteenth century in the southern steppes, "taking *amanats*" was practiced by all sides during the long Caucasian wars of the eighteenth and nineteenth centuries (Khodarkovsky 2002: 57). Broadly used as a method of Russian colonization of Siberia and Alaska, this institutionalized kidnapping was practically unknown in the British, French, or Spanish colonization of the Americas (Grinev n/d).

Hunting the hunters, the invaders met with formidable resistance on the part of some tribes such as the Chukchi, the Kamchadals, the Aleuts, or the Koryaks (Slezkine 1994; Iadrintsev 2003; Bockstoce 2009). When challenged, the Russians responded with increasingly violent methods, starting with public flogging and ending with indiscriminate killing. The Orthodox priest Innokentii Veniaminov, bishop of Alaska and later Metropolitan of Moscow, reported that in 1766 Ivan Soloviev with his seamen exterminated about 3,000 Aleuts, more than a half of the rebellious tribe (Veniaminov 1840: 188–90). Hundreds of the survivors were forced to resettle to another archipelago to hunt sea otters. Reportedly, natives hated Russians so much that they did not accept their superior tools, such as traps, and continued to hunt with bow and arrow, therefore losing the competition to the incomers (Pavlov 1972). Like almost all ventures of the Russian state, the fur trade was multinational. Along with the ethnic Russians, the newcomers included their allies, such as the Cossacks; their exiles, such as the Swedes and the Poles; and their merchants such as the Tartars and the Jews (Glebov 2009).

Gradually, Russian servitors learned to bring the natives "under the exalted hand of the great sovereign" by demonstrating force rather than applying it. In a ceremonial way, cannons and muskets were discharged while the native chiefs took an oath to the sovereign and the tribesmen were lined up as if they were an imperial guard (Lantzeff 1972: 93). While the sovereign understood the fur business as a kind of taxation and the natives understood it as a kind of slavery, the local servitors had to improvise a middle ground on which they could establish a relatively peaceful and profitable trade. Giving "gifts" to the chiefs of the tribes, befriending the shamans, raising or even adopting the "amanats," and arming one tribe against another were ordinary methods of bringing people to tribute. In many respects, the system of Russia's rule in northern Eurasia was comparable with the later British system in India. The rule was indirect, many tribes preserved their autonomy, and the number of colonizers in relation to the colonized territory was miniscule. However, there were many differences. Because of fur, Russian colonization was a very lucrative enterprise. Local tribes in Siberia were exterminated to an extent that would have been unthinkable in India; actually, the population losses were close to North American levels (Curtin 1984: 208). Finally, even with the depletion of the key resource, fur, the Russian Empire kept its hold in Siberia, while the Brits preferred to quit when they found maintaining the colony to be untenable.

In their sub-Arctic colony, the Russians created a four-layer political pyramid that consisted of the distant sovereign, his Russian servitors, the native hunters, and fur animals. Violence spread down from the top to the bottom and profit grew from the bottom to the top. Formulating an entirely different experience, the philosophers Giorgio Agamben and Jacques Derrida wrote about proximity between the sovereign and the beast, both of whom are exempt from the law. In this they are like the criminals, who populated Siberia along with animals. "Beast, criminal, and sovereign have a troubling resemblance: they call on each other and recall each other . . . outside the law" (Derrida 2009: 38). This resemblance of beasts and sovereigns created a thick layer of political mythology, with Behemoths and Leviathans, the wolves of Rome and lions of Venice, and Russian sables and bears. Novgorod and Moscow based their political economy on the direct connection, economic as well as aesthetic, between the fur-clad tsars and the fur-carrying animals, with little or, ideally, no participation from those who were irrelevant to this connection.

The resource-bound economy makes the population largely superfluous. An essential part of this system is land. In its enormous northern and eastern stretches, the geographical space of Russia was largely shaped by the fur trade.

Boom and Depletion

The fur pyramid was fragile. The closer we are to the recorded history, the more we know about the rebellions of the locals, the depletion of the animals, the corruption of the servitors, and the discontent of the sovereign. The fur trade brought many tribes to the edge of extermination; in some cases the population loss went so deep and happened so quickly that it is proper to speak of genocide. In 1882, the Siberian Nikolai Iadrintsev was able to mention about a dozen ethnicities that had been fully exterminated earlier but whose names were still remembered. From the mid-eighteenth to the mid-nineteenth centuries, the Kamchadals lost about 90 percent of its population, the Vogules about 50 percent, etc. (Iadrintsev 2003: 137–9).

Replacing the natives, Russian trappers had better access to markets and courts. With their arrival, fur trade normalized, but it coincided with the depopulation of animals. Only sables provided enough profit to support a Russian trapper; squirrel, otter, and other animals remained the business of the natives. In the early seventeenth century, a good trapper could get as many as 200 sables a year; closer to the end of the century, the numbers were 15–20 sables a year, which made the trade unprofitable (Pavlov 1972: 224). Then, Russian trappers dropped the business, but native hunters stayed in the trade. Objects of desire and vanity, Siberian furs fed conspicuous consumption at the pan-European level for a longer period of time than any other class of colonial goods. Silver from Spanish colonies, spices from Dutch colonies, or tea from British colonies could have generated even more wealth and suffering; but in their symbolic value, furs were difficult to compete with. For just one of Henry IV's outfits, London skinners used 12,000 squirrel and 80 ermine skins, which were extracted from the wild tribes thousands of miles to the east (Veale 1966: 20).

The fur trade became the backbone of the Hanseatic League, which included Novgorod as its eastern member and established a trading colony there. Upon purchase, the Germans bounded the fur into bundles and packed them into barrels. In the spring, the Germans shipped the fur barrels by Russian lakes and rivers to the Neva and the Baltic. In exchange, Russian merchants received weapons, silver, cloth, salt, and sweet wine; beer, herring, and metal products also appeared on the market. The fur trade provided a significant part of hard currency that Russian principalities needed for buying weapons and mercenaries. In the late fourteenth century, about 95 percent of all furs that were imported to London were of Hanseatic origin and most of them came from Novgorod. The numbers were huge. During one year, 1391, London imported 350,960 squirrel skins (Veale 1966: 76). It was the time when the Novgorod teams had already crossed the Urals and collected tribute from the western Siberian tribes of the Khanty, Mansi, and others. It was also the time when the English language made one of its very few appropriations from Russian, the word "sable."

Though Russia was not the only source of furs, this source became increasingly important with the deforestation of Europe. Until the end of the fifteenth century, squirrels were available near Novgorod and beavers were trapped near Moscow (Pavlov 1972: 57, 67). However, London's import of fur started declining in the fifteenth century, which some authors put down to the changing fashions in England; it was also the result of the depletion of the Russian forests. The fall of revenue from the fur trade was a reason for the escalating conflict between Russian centers. The fall of Novgorod in 1478 followed after the decline of both the export volumes and the prices of grey squirrel in Europe. Instead, Europeans discovered sable. The routes to Siberia, the land of sable, went through oriental Kazan, which was taken by the Muscovite troops in 1522 in what was the turning point of Russia's history of colonization.

The burden of the resource-bound state only increased with these events. In 1557, each male inhabitant of Iugra had to give one sable a year to the sovereign of Moscow; in 1609, he was obliged to pay seven sables (Pavlov 1972: 70). In 1581, 800 men led by Ermak defeated the khan of Siberia. Carrying the Viking-style boats between Siberian rivers and rowing upstream, they reached the tribes that they could fight with. Their firearms gave them the advantage. Historians, poets, and artists have imagined these events by analogy. Let me try to do so too:

> We penetrated deeper and deeper into the heart of darkness. It was very quiet there. At night sometimes the roll of drums behind the curtain of trees would run up the river. . . . We were wanderers on prehistoric earth, on an earth that wore the aspect of an unknown planet. We could have fancied ourselves the first of men taking possession of an accursed inheritance. (Conrad 1988: 37)

After two years of fighting, Ermak was killed. Meanwhile, 2,400 sable, 800 black fox, and 2,000 beaver pelts were sent to Moscow

Figure 6: Vasilii Surikov, *Ermak's conquest of Siberia*, 1895 (in the Russian Museum, St. Petersburg). Note the abundance of firearms on one side and furs on the other side of this battle.
Source: Wikimedia Commons

(Fisher 1943: 26). According to an historian of Siberian fur, Oleg Vilkov (1999), more than seven million sables were procured in Siberia in the 70 years between 1621 and 1690. An American historian gives an estimate that is considerably lower.[1] Janet Martin (2004) estimated the average price of sable at the end of the sixteenth century in Moscow to be one ruble per pelt. Using this low estimate, we arrive at a sum of 50,000–100,000 rubles a year – a healthy and long-term revenue that the state was learning to appropriate. While Russian sources estimated the proportion of the fur trade to represent a quarter of the gross income of the Muscovite state, one American historian gives the more believable figure of one-tenth (Fisher 1943: 122) and a Soviet scholar, one-fifth (Pavlov 1972). However, the fur's part in the state treasury was much higher. Another major commodity was salt, but it was traded only on the internal market; the role of grain export was minuscule until late in the eighteenth century. As a matter of comparison, in 2005–10, the share of the oil and gas industry in Russia's gross national income was about 25 percent, and represented 60–75 percent of Russian exports. Though it works

[1]Bushkovitch's estimate is 50,000 sables a year from 1630 to 1660 "at the very least" (1980: 94, 69).

nicely for the export side of the Russian trade, this comparison does not work for its import side. In its late period, the Soviet Union and, now, post-Soviet Russia have been able to exchange their raw commodities for a large proportion of their food, clothing, and other vital goods. This feat was unimaginable in Muscovite Russia. Fur was traded for luxury goods and military equipment, both of which fueled the growing structures of the state and remained unavailable to the general population.

The centuries-long income from the fur trade helped to create a state that some Russian historians, most prominently Pavel Miliukov, called "hypertrophic" or "hyperactive" (Emmons 1999). However, manifestations of this role of the state were different in different periods and regions. In Novgorod, fur merchants created a primitive republic that was able to sign defense contracts with the prince. In Moscow, the merging of trade and protection went much further, with Ivan the Terrible trading fur himself and granting "privileges" to others. Providing a lion's share of the state's disposable income, the fur trade played its role in financing military campaigns, diplomatic activities, and even religious treaties of the state. Upon the arrival of a Russian envoy to the ruler's court in the southern steppes, he would disburse pelts to the ruler and his nobles. In the seventeenth century, a good present would consist of 40 sable furs, one marten coat, and several other coats of lesser value (Khodarkovsky 2002: 66). Internal consumption of the fur was also significant. When silver was scarce, fur played the role of currency. There were periods when officials of the Muscovite state, officers in the army, and doctors in the court received half their salaries in fur (Pavlov 1972: 102). The profitability of colonies has been a subject of much debate, but there is no doubt that Siberia was very profitable. A Siberian scholar compared the effect of the fur trade on Russia's economy with the flood of silver that came to Europe from the New World in the sixteenth century (see Pokshishevskii and krotov 1951: 57).

After the termination of Hansa shipping from Novgorod, the Siberian pelts were delivered through Moscow to Leipzig, their distribution base in Europe, over land. Though the Hansa had other goods to trade over the Baltic, its collapse in the sixteenth century followed the changing routes of the Russian fur trade. In the 1660–70s, the trade in furs sharply fell, which coincided with the start of the inflation that lasted through the Time of Troubles (Kliuchevsky 1959). With the depletion of animals, trappers and hunters were moving to new areas in the east. Looking for squirrel, beaver, sable, martin, ermine, sea otter, and other wonders of the north, the Russians moved farther and farther into the north-eastern corners of Eurasia, all the way to Kamchatka and then to Alaska. In the late seventeenth century, the state monopolized the export trade in all furs and the domestic trade in sables and black foxes (Fisher 1943: 65). These measures did not help; the trade was in decline. Afanasii Shchapov's statistics of the Muscovite "gifts" to foreign powers demonstrated that, through the seventeenth century, the share of sable in these collections was diminishing (1906: 2/330–2). As he formulated it, the depletion of the "zoological wealth" caused the crisis of the Russian state. Shchapov tells how hunters, dressers, tradesmen, and drivers strove to find new ways of subsistence. The ecological disaster turned adventurists into peasants, a long process that took place over generations, some of whom barely survived the transition. It was equally bad for the Russian state, whose infrastructure was dependent on fur. When hare replaced sable in the Kremlin treasury, the Moscow period of Russian history approached its end.

Fed by the fur trade, the state experimented with new commodities and institutions. Hemp, iron, and, finally, wheat replaced fur in Russian exports. *Oprichnina*, serfdom, and, finally, imperial bureaucracy became substitutes for the fur trade network. However, the state remained, or strived to remain, hyperactive. Its institutions flourished when they could develop a political economy that provided the resource-bound income that was largely independent of people's labor. These were periods when, as Kliuchevsky put it, "the state grew swollen and the people sick" (1956: 3/12). There were also periods when it was the state that was sick. Establishing their trade with Archangel in 1555, the British were interested in timber, wax, cordage, and other forest products; fur comprised a minor part of the trade (Bushkovitch 1980: 68). King James estimated the value of the region high enough to consider its outright colonization in 1612–13, when the Polish troops and stateless Cossacks took Moscow (Dunning 1989; Kagarlitsky 2003). Then, the Volga merchant, Kuzma Minin, saved Russia from default and defeat by financing the war effort from the revenue of the salt trade, a harbinger of the mining economy to come. When the troubles were over, the hopes for commerce were projected onto the south-west rather than the north-east. Expansionism replaced the prudence of the Muscovite state in respect to the steppes (Boeck 2007). Even more importantly, the state experimented with new practices of controlling and disciplining the population. Wheat, the commodity of the future, required much more labor than fur, and of a very different quality.

In the mid-eighteenth century, the share of fur in Russia's budget was small, but it still dominated the country's exports to China (Pavlov 1972: 119; Foust 1969: 344). Changes in both production and consumption were involved in this decline. Internationally, the Russian fur now competed with North American fur, which was cheaper because of lower transportation costs and customs fees. Moreover, fur was losing out to wool, which was at the peak of its success in Europe and the Americas. Converting a state monopoly into a royal one, Catherine II moved the fur trade from the Siberian Chancellery to the Personal Cabinet – her private treasury (Slezkine 1994: 67). To a certain extent, the collections of the Hermitage were financed from the revenue that came from Siberian pelts. In this enlightened era, the fur trade was discussed in terms of economic mercantilism, which called for state monopolies in colonial trade. In his comments on the *Instruction* by Catherine II, Denis Diderot wrote that in order to get rich by trade, a state should maintain a monopoly if its source is far away and there is no law in that land. In Russia, that meant Siberia and its fur. Diderot was writing these comments while returning from his visit to St. Petersburg and receiving his salary from Catherine's Personal Cabinet (1992: 135, 159). Even by the end of nineteenth century, the fur tribute comprised more than 10 percent of the Cabinet income (Znamenski 2007: 125).

Sable was gone and squirrel was out of fashion. But then came news from an expedition of Captain James Cook about the sea otter. Cook's sailors traded several pelts on the east coast of Australia for a few glass beads each, and then sold them on to the Chinese in Canton for two thousands pounds. Published in 1784, this story caused new British and French expeditions to Alaska. Catherine the Great commissioned the young, British-trained captain Grigory Mulovsky to head a Russian expedition. George Forster, a participant of Cook's expedition and the author of its best-selling account, agreed to take part in it. But with the start of still another Russo-Swedish war, the expedition was canceled; Mulovsky was killed in action (King 2008). Later voyages found the sea otter in abundance and Chinese customers in waiting. In 1802, Johann von Krusenstern was the first Russian captain to circumnavigate the world, though the reason for his expedition was still the same: fur (Foust 1969: 321). Founded in 1799, the Russian-American Company traded fur for the next half-century, after which quick depletion of the sea otter brought it to a close; the company never made a profit. It was fur alone that attracted the government in St. Petersburg to Alaska and California.

In 1867, the company was liquidated and the imperial domains in North America were sold to the US.

Venus in Furs

Beginning from the seventeenth century, European thinkers formulated "the four stages theory" which stated that the original mode of human economy was hunting and fishing, which gave way to pasturage, which was replaced by agriculture, and, finally, by commerce. This narrative was based mainly on what was happening in the recently colonized America, where the four stages had followed one after the other (Meek 1976). But the Russian fur trade demonstrated a coexistence of distant stages, such as hunting and commerce. Those European thinkers who were closer to Russia, such as Pufendorf, did not agree with the four-stage theory but believed that various modes had in fact coexisted from biblical times. In his version of European history that was translated into Russian in 1718, Pufendorf talked about the Russian Empire as "vastly extensive" though "barren and uninhabited." However, the Emperor's revenue was "very considerable" and "the Trade in Sables which is entirely in his own Hands is a vast Addition thereto" (1764: 2/347–8). Pufendorf knew that although the whole world could, at the beginning, have been like America, at its next stages it had become like Russia, mixed and twisted.

Though the fruits of the Russian north, fur pelts, had been familiar to the Europeans, only in the eighteenth century did the literate world learn about these lands. Then, a mixed group of German academics, Orthodox missionaries, and political exiles found themselves in Siberia and were able to write back to Europe. Exiled to Siberia in 1790, Nikolai Radishchev was the first to explain the takeover of Siberia as colonization and its motive as fur. In his *Concise History of the Acquisition of Siberia*, he wrote that the tsars gave rights to the Siberian pioneers "over the lands that did not belong to Russia" and that they were exempted from taxes in exchange for supplying furs to Moscow (1941: 2/148). Writing in the 1830s, another Siberian historian, Piotr Slovtsov (1886), described in detail how, in their search for beaver and sable, the first Siberian pioneers ignored everything else, including the metals that were discovered later on the same lands. When the merchant family of Stroganovs, the oligarchs of west Siberia who financed Russian tsars, obtained their coat of arms in the eighteenth century, they chose sables as their emblem.

Figure 7: Coat of Arms of the Stroganovse, 1753. Two sables hold the shield picturing another creature. Stroganov's motto said, "Ferras, opes patriac, sibi nomen" ("Will give wealth to the fatherland and name to myself").
Source: Wikimedia Commons

A traveler, who visited Moscow in 1716, reported the local interpretation of the Greek myth of the Argonauts: the Golden Fleece was understood as the Siberian sable and the Argonauts as fur traders (Pogosian 2001: 282). The peak of this fur-clad myth-making was the famous novel by the Austrian writer Leopold Sacher-Masoch, *Venus in Furs* (1870), which featured a Slavic beauty who gave and received pleasure from playing with Russian sables and the knout. But Peter the Great rejected the ancient symbol of Russian power, Monomakh's Cap with its sable trimming, for the imperial crown made of gold and diamonds.

In his *Capital*, Marx compared primitive accumulation with original sin, which European empires committed in their colonies. "In the tender annals of Political Economy, the idyllic reigns from time immemorial" (Marx 1990: 354): the origins of the imperial capitals in the bloody commodities such as silver, fur, or ivory elude memory. On a more scholarly note, it was Afanasii Shchapov who in the mid-nineteenth century understood the crucial role of the fur trade in terms of history, geography, ethnology, and ecology (he did not know the latter word). A Siberian, Shchapov realized the historical meaning of the depletion of the fur trade. He knew about the tragedies that developed at the frontlines of this hunting colonization, where the Cossacks were exterminating the hunting tribes in order to force them to exterminate the fur animals. One such example, which Shchapov used extensively, was the colonization of the Aleut Islands, where Russians forced the locals to hunt sea otter until almost all of them, otters and humans, had perished (1906: 2/291). Victims were illiterate, the perpetrators complicit, and historians mute about these early catastrophes. In this situation Shchapov developed his anachronistic method, imagining the past by analogy with the present.

Immensely influential among Russian radicals (see Chapter 11), Shchapov's ideas can be traced far into the twentieth century. During his Siberian exile in 1900–2, the young Lev Trotsky worked for the Siberian merchant Yakov Chernykh, who bartered fur with the local tribe of the Tungusy in exchange for vodka and cloth. Illiterate, Chernykh had a revenue of millions and many thousands of people in his employ, and he operated on land that spanned from the Lena to the Volga. This Chernykh was the "indisputable dictator" of the whole district, wrote Trotsky (1922), who knew the meaning of the word "dictator."

Trotsky made this view public while debating Russian history with the leading Marxist historian, Mikhail Pokrovsky, in 1922. They both agreed that Russia featured an "uneven development," a phrase that Trotsky made famous. But Pokrovsky attacked Trotsky for producing too static a picture of this unevenness. What created these extreme differences? He cited the final chapters of Marx's *Capital*, which narrated how, after the Middle Ages, "the colonial system" played the "preponderant role" in Europe and how the "strange God" of colonialism "perched himself on the altar, cheek by jowl with the old Gods of Europe" (Marx 1990: 374). A student of Kliuchevsky, Pokrovsky easily applied these colonial idioms to the rewriting of Russian history (1920, 2001). Trotsky's work for a Siberian fur oligarch gave Pokrovsky just another example: Chernykh was a new version of the Stroganovs, wrote the historian. As a result, Pokrovsky revealed a belief that he ironically called one of his "heresies" – namely, that Russia had developed "according to the colonial type." Trotsky misunderstood this primary cause for Russia's "combined and uneven development." Pokrovsky asked Trotsky:

> Is the concept of the colonial system applicable only to the countries with hot climates and colored populations, or could one imagine it also in the Siberian forest or in the Northern Russian marshes? Does it require ostriches and rhinoceroses, or are foxes, sables, and martins enough for the colonial system? (Pokrovsky 1922)

On the other side of the ocean, an American scholar, Frank A. Golder, gave a boost to the scholarly studies of Russian colonial trade. Born in Odessa, Golder started his career with teaching English in Alaska in 1899. Alaska was still a land where the natives preferred Russian to English; Golder even had to give his Fourth of July speech in Russian. After this experience, he studied Russian history at Harvard and in 1921 took part in the American Relief Administration (ARA), trying to help the victims of famine on the Volga. He wrote a magisterial book on the Russian expansion in the Pacific (1914). Fed by his personal experience, his interest was in demythologizing the fur trade and traders, who were still perceived as like the Argonauts:

> The Siberians of the 17th and 18th centuries were part of the movement in which they were caught . . . yet we are expected to fall on our knees and bow to heroes. As a matter of fact they were, at best, very ordinary men and some of them were vicious and depraved. . . . In every seaport town and in every frontier community one will find [similar] men. (Quoted from Lantzeff and Pierce 1973: 224)

Two Californian historians, Harold Fisher (who was Golder's associate in the ARA) and George V. Lantzeff, continued Golder's work (Dubie 1989; Emmons and Patenaude 1992). Writing in the 1950s, Lantzeff (in his introduction to Lantzeff and Pierce 1973) stated that "no search for any single commodity has ever resulted in the acquisition of as huge an area as the one acquired by Russia in this quest." One could add that no other quest for any single commodity has been so well forgotten in the history of human suffering. We know a thing or two about Cortez or Kurtz; but looking at the splendid portraits of British kings, nobody thinks about those little peoples in the Arctic who exchanged these furs for "protection."

Space Through Time

Catherine the Great justified monarchical rule in Russia by its unusually large territory. But how was this territory acquired in the first place? She asserted that the Russian Empire appropriated a big part of the world, "from the Irtysh River to the Kuril Islands," because of the Russians' "proclivity for adventure" (Ekaterina II 1869: 256). Catherine misrepresented a crude economic reality: this land was taken in the quest for fur. However, the Russian Empire retained its hold on the colonized land even after the fur was depleted. With the one big exception of Alaska, the areas of the fur trade were all held under Russian sovereignty even after this trade was discontinued and the lands had no mercantile value. In the nineteenth century, these lands were used mainly as penal colonies. Even Soviet military-industrial sites did not change this large picture. A huge expanse of northern Eurasia, of a size much larger than Europe, remains underdeveloped and underpopulated (Hill and Gaddy 2003).

In the twentieth and twenty-first centuries, these lands of the fur trade have played a new and precious role, which feels uncannily similar to the old one. The same geographical areas that fed the fur trade of medieval Novgorod and Moscow have provided the Soviet Union and post-Soviet Russia with their means for existence. The oil and gas fields of western Siberia have been found in those very spaces that the greedy sons of Novgorod colonized for the fur trade with the Iugra, Hanty, Mansi, and others. Like then, with the exhaustion of older sites, the drillers are moving eastwards, to the coasts and islands of the Pacific. The main consumers of Russian gas and oil are also located in many of those same places, from Hamburg to London, which consumed Russian fur. The large pipelines of Gazprom run along the terrestrial route, from Moscow through Poland to Leipzig and further to the west, which was used for the export of fur. The future North Stream, the underwater pipeline that will provide northern and Western Europe with gas from western Siberia, runs almost precisely along the routes of the ancient Hanseatic trade.

Geographically, this resemblance is accidental. Aesthetically, fur and oil could not be more different. Ecologically, there is no correlation either: people drill for oil and gas in forests as well as in deserts, but fur animals are to be found only in forests. But politically, there is much in common between an economy that relies on the export of fur and an economy that relies on the export of gas. Both economies are victims of the resource curse, the one-sided development of a highly profitable extraction industry that leaves the rest of the economy uncompetitive and undeveloped. In the *longue durée* of Russian history, taxing the trade in these commodities has become the source of income for the state; organizing their extraction, its preoccupation; securing the lines of transportation that stretch across Eurasia, its responsibility. The extraction takes highly specialized skills that have little to do with the occupations of other parts of the population. Very few people take part in business, with the result that the state does not care about the population and the population does not care about the state. A caste-like society emerges in these conditions. The security apparatus becomes identical to the state.

This is the political economy of what Arendt called "the mass man's superfluousness," a situation that she believed to be foundational for totalitarian rule (1966: 311). More recently, institutional economics has described two modes of relations between resources, the state, and the subjects (North et al. 2009). In the "natural state," a dominant group limits access to valuable resources, creates rents out of these resources, and rules over the population by applying suppression and bribery. A different social order is "the open access state," which controls internal violence by providing equal opportunities to its citizens. In such a society, there is no legal or metaphysical difference between the elite and the populus. Historically, the lack of natural resources leads to the development of human capital and the creation of the open-access system, while the abundance of such resources keeps a state in its resource-bound condition. However, there are many exceptions from this rule of thumb. Norway and Canada remain balanced economies despite the abundance of oil. Holland overcame its mid-twentieth-century "Dutch disease." In Russia, Trotsky's "unevenness of development" meant that while some regions in some periods were entirely dependent on raw commodities such as fur, other regions developed crafts, processing industries, and labor shortages. Politically, resource-dependence can be dealt with. Historically, it can come and go.

There have been two resource-bound periods of Russian history: the era of fur and the era of gas. Historically discontinuous, these two periods feature uncanny similarities – structural and geographic, essential and accidental. Processing these commodities is unusually messy. The state's dependence on them makes the population superfluous. Extracting, storing, and delivering these resources makes security more important than liberty. Reliance on these resources destroys the environment, natural and cultural. And as fur was centuries ago, so oil too is counted in barrels.

We know how the first period ended. The depletion of the key resource, fur, drove the state into a major crisis. It forced a radical change in Muscovite mores, which included the election of a new dynasty by vote, the import of the European Enlightenment, and the institution of the formal empire. The state redirected its colonization activities from the fur-rich eastern forests to the grain-rich southern steppes, and later to the silk-rich Transcaucasia and cotton-rich Central Asia. However, nothing in this later history would be comparable in profitability, duration, and scale of expansion to the fur trade. Consumers also changed, though it is amusing to notice how long it took the west to kick its fur habit.

Part III

Empire of the Tsars

— 6 —

Occult Instability

In 1849, an organizer of settlements in New Zealand blamed British colonial administrators for being "deeply convinced of the inferiority or nothingness of the other classes." To strengthen the argument, he said that these people had already been "more privileged than any class in any European country at present, excepting Russia perhaps" (Wakefield 1849: 59). In New Zealand and other British colonies, the distance between the privileged and the underprivileged was structured by race, defined primarily as the color of the skin. Visible race marked the total sum of differences between human groups and had a particular kind of metrics. It squeezed the variety of humanity into a few categories, white, black, and everything in between (Gates 1985). But in a society of internal colonization that had annexed, absorbed, and exterminated its others, almost everyone was of one and the same color. To play the function of race, this society created estates, a legal category that was also similar in function to caste. Like race, estate defined people's roles and regulated their relations. Like caste, it was inherited and for many practical purposes, unchangeable. Like race and caste, estate clashed with capitalism and the early attempts at democratic politics. Race was supposedly biological and estate was supposedly legal, but both constructs belonged to culture. The cultural construction of race naturalized power; the cultural construction of estate legalized it. The larger the distances these constructions created, the less stable they were. Low estates, races, or castes were particularly unsteady. It was, as the Caribbean psychiatrist and philosopher Frantz Fanon wrote about the colonial situation, "the zone of occult instability where the people dwell" (1967: 183).

Terra Nullius

British colonists applied English law to any territory that they found lawless; they called this foundational principle of imperialism *terra nullius*. A land was construed as empty even though it was inhabited. This claim terminated all existing customs, property rights, and lines of inheritance in the land. In practice, this principle was followed a long time before it was codified by the British (Gosden 2004). For the eighteenth-century physiocrats, *terra nullius* justified imperial domination by claiming the duty to cultivate the land: those who did not do it in the way that was considered proper were not recognized by law (Nelson 2009; Boucher 2010). The principle of *terra nullius* was metaphorically connected to the biblical idea of creation *ex nihilo* and to Locke's idea of *tabula rasa*, creating a comfortable unity of imperial politics, theology, and epistemology (Arneil 1996; Bauman 2009).

Terra nullius probably was an intuitive strategy of Peter I, but this idea is more evident in the writings of those imperial intellectuals who glorified his rule throughout the nineteenth century. Peter presented himself as the creator not only of the Russian Empire, but of the land, of the people, and even of himself. He did change many laws and institutions, but he wished to exaggerate their novelty even more; he played a foreign conqueror, suggests Richard Wortman (1995: 1/44). One hundred years after Peter's death, the imperial Minister of Finances, Egor Kankrin, said that Peter had changed the Russians so much that they had better stop calling themselves Russians and start calling themselves Petrovians, and their land Petrovia (Riasanovsky 1985: 109). The literary critic Vissarion Belinsky developed the analogy between Russian history and the book of Genesis even further: "With his powerful 'Let there be . . . !' Peter dispelled the chaos, separated the light from the darkness, and called the country to its great, global destiny" (Belinsky 1954: 5/117). Belinsky called upon the Russian historians to terminate their debates about Rurik and to focus on Peter, who was "incomparably more important" for the creation of the state (Belinsky 1954: 5/94). Piotr Chaadaev wrote that "in his hand Peter the Great found only a blank sheet of paper"; he "swept away all our old institutions; he dug out an abyss between our past and our present" (Ermichev and Zlatopol'skaia 1989: 205, 225). Completed in 1782, the Bronze Horseman, the monument to Peter in the center of St. Petersburg, showed Peter and his horse jumping to the present over an abyss.

Both Chaadaev and Pushkin were eager to call Peter's period a "revolution" (Riasanovsky 1985: 104; Etkind 2001b: 32). If it was a "revolution," as some historians also believe (Kagarlitsky 2003: 222; Cracraft 2004), it followed the Dutch and English revolutions but preceded those in America, France, and Haiti. Working on his unfinished novel, *Peter the Great's Negro*, Pushkin presented the story of his ancestor, the black African Abram Gannibal, as an exemplary case of reshaping humankind:

> With grief, Peter saw that his subjects resisted the Enlightenment and in the interest of proving the changes that could be wrought on a perfectly foreign breed of man, asked his envoy to send him a talented little Arab. . . . The Emperor was very satisfied with the boy and educated him diligently, always with this goal in mind. (Pushkin 1995: 67)

Having refashioned his valet from a harem boy into an artillery officer, Peter failed with larger tasks, said Pushkin: his subjects "persisted with their beards," and "Asian ignorance reigned over the tsar's court" (1995: 64). This was reversed orientalism in action: while a black African was fully accepted as an individualized, powerful figure, Russian subjects were orientalized in a non-differentiated, anonymous way. Pushkin's ancestor, the black builder of a fort in Siberia and a port in Estonia, was an admirably imperial figure (Barnes 2005). However, for the idea of *terra nullius* he was rather a counter-example. Gannibal did not downplay his black origins but, instead, publicly celebrated them, and Pushkin followed his example. As a Russian noble, Gannibal chose a coat of arms with an elephant in the center. He built a manor house near Pskov in a Southern style that was unknown to the Russian province. Still, "Fortuna vitam meam mutavit optime" was his motto ("Chance changed my life entirely") (Leetz 1980: 117; Teletova 1989).

"Immobility and petrification belong to Asia like the soul belongs to the body," wrote Belinsky, an extreme orientalist, as Said defined the term. Drawing a picture of the pre-Petrine Russia as the land of ignorance and torture, Belinsky saw it "Asian, barbarian, Tartar" (Belinsky 1954: 5/103). He applied *terra nullius* to a period of history rather than a piece of land. In Chaadaev's philosophy of history, "the starting point defines destiny," and this starting point for Russians was either Rurik, or Peter, or both (for more details, see Etkind 2001b: 21–34). In 1836, Chaadaev's essay in the journal *Telescope* caused a scandal. Nicholas I exiled the editor of *Telescope*, the philosopher Nikolai Nadezhdin, and put Chaadaev under house arrest.

Figure 8: The coat of arms of Abram Gannibal (*c.* 1742).
Source: Grigiorii Fridman, Gipotezy i legendy o proiskhozhdenii Abrama Gannibala, *Zametki po evreiskoj istorii*, 2/63, 2006

A military doctor, Ivan Iastrebtsov, was sent to visit him daily to check his state of mind. He became one of Chaadaev's disciples. Under the pressure, all three men articulated a new idea. Russia's freedom from historical legacies was not a liability but an advantage. Precisely because of their innocence, Russia and the Russians were ideal objects for imperial transformation. Iastrebtsov wrote with a reference to his patient and friend Chaadaev: "Russia is free of prejudice. . . . It is as if the past does not exist for Russia. . . . Its people are white paper, write on them" (1833: 197). From his exile, Nadezhdin formulated emphatically and almost comically:

> We are children, and our childhood makes our happiness. . . . With our simple, virgin nature, unspoiled by any prejudice, one can do what is needed without labor and without violence. It is possible to shape us

> into perfection as if we are a pure, soft wax. Oh, what an unimaginable advantage before the Europeans we have with our saintly, blissful childhood! (1998: 96)

After Chaadaev's scandal, this idea of Russian civic infantilism became common. The critic Belinsky wrote that the Russian people were "fresh, young, and virgin" (1954: 5/119). The historian Soloviev wrote more specifically that the Russian man in the eighteenth century was "perfectly clean and ready to perceive the new ways – in a word, he was a child" (1856: 500). Changing its metaphors from white paper to pure wax and from barbarity to infancy to virginity, the idea of *terra nullius* affirmed the transformative energy of the imperial power.

Point of Rule

In one of the first Russian victories of the Northern War (1700–21), Peter I took the delta of the Neva. With a fort there, he restored control over the strategic river route from the Baltic Sea to the great Russian lakes and Novgorod. In 1712, Peter transferred a part of his administration, military and civil, to St. Petersburg (many offices remained in Moscow for another 50 years). By the right of conquest, the land was his. But the right of conquest functioned in the colonies; in eighteenth-century Europe, international treaties transferred land from one state to another. According to these treaties, Swedish rule over this territory was confirmed in 1617 and remained valid until 1721. "In Russia, the center is at the periphery," wrote Kliuchevsky (2001). Even more, the imperial capital was established on foreign land. Peter "needed a land entirely new, without tradition, where the Russians would find themselves in an entirely new space and could not help but change their mores and habits," explained Belinsky (1954: 5/145).

The new land was called Ingria. Under Russian rule, it kept its name and identity for a number of years. Peter even created the Duchy of Ingria there, but the land was treated as *terra nullius*, with no legacy or identity apart from the idea that it should be Russian. Sparsely populated by dispersed Finnish people, Ingria was not very appealing. The low land, the barely passable harbor, and regular flooding precluded urban development. But Peter loved his place on the Neva. It was deceptively similar to Amsterdam, where the young tsar spent his apprenticeship. The memory of the Hansa was still alive on these banks. In order to shape Russia as if it was an empty land, Peter needed an external point of leverage from whence to push the project.

The historian Nikolai Karamzin in 1811 mocked Peter's project as "turning Russia into Holland" (1991: 36). Having spent four months with the East India Company in Amsterdam, Peter was aware of Dutch colonial practices, mercantilist theories, and Calvinist energy. A mercenary from Geneva, Franz Lefort, a major influence on Peter who accompanied him on the European tour, had introduced him to his adventurous Calvinism even before their trip to Holland in 1697. Late seventeenth-century Holland was the commercial leader of Europe and the cradle of the radical Enlightenment. No less importantly, Holland was the center of the world's largest empire, whose sources of wealth spread as far away from Amsterdam as Russia's did from St. Petersburg.

There were (and are) no two countries more different in Europe than Russia and Holland. However, Russia was not alone in choosing to follow this model. Prussia was also reshaping itself after Holland, with huge success. Historical sociologists generalize that, for changes of this scale, the alliance between an enthusiastic sovereign and a popular religious awakening was always crucial (Gorski 2003). Frederick William of Prussia counted on Pietism, but Peter ostracized the Russian religious activism in which he saw just another expression of barbarity. His reform of Russian Orthodoxy submitted the church to the state and left no place for popular enthusiasm.

Historians have variously described Petrine policies as "reforms," "modernization," or "revolution." Arguably, they were a decisive move in Russia's internal colonization, with a Calvinist touch. This colonization was mainly about the population rather than about the territory. While the resource-bound Muscovite economy largely left the people to themselves, the emerging Empire was dependent upon its population. Peter's subjects "are his only mines of gold and silver," wrote a foreign observer (Hughes 1998: 135). Starting with Peter, taxation, draft, disciplinary innovations, and grassroot resistance marked the history of the Empire. To transform a tribute-based domain into a bureaucratic, tax-collecting, law-abiding state was a task that Peter started and nobody completed (Raeff 1983). His economic ideas are mostly understood as an authoritarian version of Dutch and British mercantilism. For these competing empires, mercantilism was a strategy of maximizing the income of the mother countries by monopolizing their dealings with their daughter colonies. From his apprenticeship in old and new imperial centers,

Königsberg, Amsterdam, and London, Peter learned the rules of this game. But he also knew what some historians still find it hard to comprehend: that in Russia, the mother and the daughter were the same and the Emperor was their master. Practiced though never theorized by Peter, this incestuous idea revised the calculus of mercantilism. Having its colonies inside itself, Peter's Empire did not bother about tariffs, piracy, and trade surplus, the concerns of the mercantilist Europe. Most importantly, the Empire did not bother about the incomes in the mother country. Having imposed a poll tax and other duties on the Russian population, Peter's financiers could ignore the imperial shareholders, because, apart from the crown, there were none. They extracted smart colonial profits without being concerned with the greedy rentiers of the metropolitan lands. It was a good deal for the Empire.

As built by Peter and his heirs, the new Russian capital embodied the universalist imaginary of ancient Rome. The results were magnificent and disruptive. They erased not only the vague memory of the native semi-Christian, semi-shamanistic tribes of Ingria, but also the traditional culture of Russia. There was no resemblance between the imperial St. Petersburg and the medieval Moscow or Novgorod. Struggling to over-compensate for its self-perceived backwardness, the Empire amassed huge collections of European art, purchased Europe's best architects and sculptors, and trained Russian artists in European academies (Cracraft 1997). Russian museums document a full break between the imperial culture and the pre-Petrine past. Leaving the rooms of "icons" and entering the wing of "Russian art," one feels the same rupture as when moving from a section of native art into the imperial section in any colonial museum in America, Australia, or India. Beginning in the eighteenth century, the imperial arts became increasingly similar all over the world, with the result that there is more resemblance between the imperial art of India and the imperial art of Russia than there is between either of them and their own folk arts.

Founded by a great warrior, St. Petersburg was first and foremost a military capital. Peter and Paul Fortress was its focal point and many of its spectacular squares, parks, and edifices were the living and training quarters of the Imperial Guard. The Guard was the supreme master of the city and the Empire. It started and ended wars, ran balls and duels, enthroned and dethroned emperors and empresses, and glorified or killed romantic poets. Officers of the Guard were partially European and largely bilingual; soldiers were overwhelmingly Russian. Until 1762, the gentry was obliged to serve. Peter III abolished this regime, but a career in the Guard and, later in life, in a provincial administration remained the typical path for a gentleman. Disseminating the ways and manners of the imperial capital throughout the provinces, these careers helped to colonize the Empire.

A diplomat from Hanover wrote in 1714 that the new capital was still "a heap of villages linked together, like some plantation in the West Indies" (Hughes 1998: 215). Forcing the court and government to move to St. Petersburg meant that this time not only the peasants but also the gentry were subject to a mass resettlement. Reportedly, families lost about two-thirds of their capital in the move (Rogger 1960: 12). The new capital emulated Amsterdam not only in its islands and channels, but also by being very far from the vital sources of the imperial economy. Grain, timber, and even stone for the new city were delivered from the heartlands. The gentry had to abandon the old way of living off their estates; accustomed to getting their supplies for free, they had to buy them for prices that were five times higher than in the central provinces.

Unlike older European metropolises, St. Petersburg was never enclosed within walls. Divided into two parts, the official center and residential suburbs, it sprawled in all directions from the center. Like the Empire itself, the periphery had no limits and the central part of the city developed more slowly than the suburbs. The enormous central squares and construction sites of the future palaces stretched along the spacious river, creating a gigantic void in the center which was analogous to the larger geography of this Empire. Throughout the High Imperial Period, the center of St. Petersburg was still a work in progress, which was completed only after this period ended, with the ensemble of the Palace Square finished in 1843 and St Isaac's Cathedral in 1858.

The abundant columns, the painted brick, and the regularity of streets and squares followed Palladian examples. Everywhere on the four continents of the colonized world, one could find similar porticos, heroic sculptures, coats of arms, Greek columns, lions, eagles, balconies, fountains, meadows. Against the flat, cold terrain, the painted, multicolored façades look irreconcilably alien: a beautiful embodiment of the occult instability of a colonial situation. As in Washington DC, all was big and sublime in St. Petersburg. One feels a resemblance between these two capitals that were both built on no-man's land, a territory that was cut out from the existing polities so that it could rule over them from an outstanding point, specifically designed as the site of power. A central part of Washington, the empty mall that divides and connects the city, is similar to the line of St.

Petersburg squares and parks along the Neva. Rooted in the same European tradition, both capitals promoted their self-images as aspiring masters of the world. They also had similar insecurities, one being too far to the north, another too far to the south, both distant from the economic and demographic centers of their lands, and both ridiculously available to their common enemy, the British Navy.

St. Petersburg's consumption outweighed any trade advantage that it could provide as a seaport. Peter's idea was to launch an export of grain from the city to Germanic lands; but since the construction of St. Petersburg led to the increase of grain prices in Moscow, the authorities regularly stopped the export of grain altogether. Exporting goods from the existing Russian ports in Riga and Archangel was more efficient than from St. Petersburg, and the government restricted operations in these older ports (Jones 2001).

As St. Petersburg was developing its current shape, with large apartment buildings facing its straight, flat streets, another feature of the city became apparent. Colder than Berlin or almost anywhere in the urban world, Petersburg winters required serious amounts of firewood. Food was a problem in Ingria, but at least firewood was readily available in the country. In the well-ordered plan of the city there was no place to store it but in the internal courtyards – large, passable spaces of relative wilderness. Classical façades and low gates hid the chaos of life from the eye of power. Courtyards contained the real economy of storage, stables, workshops, outhouses, sewage systems, and huge piles of firewood. Three centuries after Peter, many of these spaces are still awaiting cultivation. On several levels, the development of the capital reproduced the script of internal colonization.

A Big Shave

Catherine II famously observed to Diderot that he should be happy to write on paper – monarchs write on skins. Writing on the bodies, faces, and minds of its subjects, the Russian Empire needed a substitute for race, which proved to be even more problematic than race itself. Physical, visible, and, preferably, unwashable signs of distinction had to be found or made between the newly created estates. If estate could be written on skin, this racialized status would work for police officials, road patrols, and plantation managers. "Culture can also function like nature," writes Étienne Balibar; culture can selectively mark individuals and groups and lock them into immutable, intangible categories of discrimination and privilege that work as races (Balibar 1999: 22).

Peter the Great produced a great experiment on the subject. Immediately after his return from a grand European trip, he demanded that the gentry's beards be shaved. As the Austrian envoy wrote on that day of August 26, 1698, "the razor plied promiscuously among the beards of those present" (quoted in Hughes 2004: 22). Peter began with his immediate entourage, then sent police barbers into the streets, and then introduced national legislation that included a beard tax. The history of beards is a rich subject (Reynolds 1949; Peterkin 2001) but nothing similar in scope to Peter's shaving reform has ever been recorded. Dress code was also changed, with the additional advantage that it embraced both genders. During the following decades, several decrees on shaving became more discriminate. The purpose was not to shave all Russian males, but to differentiate between them (Hughes 2004: 31). The gentry had to be clean-shaven; the clergy and peasantry remained bearded; townspeople existed in a gray zone with the rules constantly changing.

The big shave of 1698 preceded the other founding acts of internal colonization, such as "The Manifesto on the Summoning of Foreigners into Russia" (1702), the foundation of the new capital on the occupied land (1703), and the birth of the Russian Empire (1721). In a very Petrine way, abrupt and foundational, shaving established a class structure where there was not one. Before Peter, Russia did not have estates (Freeze 1986) though it had myriad self-conscious groups – ethnic, religious, professional, genealogical, and others. Though some of the previously accepted laws had codified social differences, estates – large non-ethnic social groups that were recognized and differentially treated by the government – were created by Peter's decrees on beards.

While estate was a substitute for race, the beard was a substitute for skin color. In *A Sportsman's Sketches*, Ivan Turgenev presents a serf called Khor who was prosperous enough to buy freedom from his master, but who chose not to do so. The narrator insists, "It's always better to be free." To this Khor objects that even after buying his freedom he would keep his beard, even though he knows that he would be considered inferior because of it. The narrator's solution is easy again: "Then shave your beard." But Khor chooses to stay with his serfdom, his beard, and his money (Turgenev 1963: 4/12).

In Europe during this period, beards also connoted Romanticism and something like a return to nature. The early Russian nationalists, the so-called Slavophiles, had grown beards, but in 1849 the government ordered them to shave these off, as being "unsuitable for the nobility" (Tsimbaev 1986: 13). Garibaldi's rebels were all bearded; in 1853, the Austrian Emperor ordered his civil servants to shave off their beards. With the advent of populism in Russia in the 1870s, facial hair sprouted again: the higher estate emulated the lower one. As Russia approached its twentieth-century turmoil, the beards of artists and bureaucrats, favorites of the imperial court and leaders of popular sects, became longer and longer. Following western fashion and characteristically exceeding it, the length of the Russian beard, black and white, found expression in the symmetrical figures of Rasputin, the folk prophet who became a favorite of the Imperial court, and Tolstoy, the aristocratic writer who became a folk prophet.

In the estate society, inequality was legal. Estates were defined by their rights and duties, which were different for each of them. There was a separate system of law for each estate and only those who belonged to one and the same estate were equal before law. These different systems of law were codified with diligence, much more so than was customary in nations with racial inequality. It was precisely because estates were invisible that their codification needed more effort. The matrix of four estates was simple: gentry, clergy, townspeople, and peasantry. The gentry could own people and land and had to serve the state, usually in the military. The clergy could not own people or land and had to serve God. With the right to marry, Russian priests had many children. Their sons did not serve in the army, but they could receive education and make careers in the ranks of bureaucracy. Neither of these estates paid taxes. The third estate, the townsfolk or merchants, could own property but not people, and had to pay taxes. The peasantry could not own land or property, had to serve their masters, and also paid taxes. Along with their houses, horses, tools, allotments, and families, peasants were owned either by their masters or by the state. But individually or collectively, peasants had some "use rights" with respect to their belongings, rights that before 1861 could exist in practice but not in law. Differing legal codes punished peasants with corporal punishments and the gentry with a penitentiary system. The gentry and townsfolk had some ability to travel, but the peasantry were usually bonded to the land, the master, and the commune. In the army, peasants served as soldiers, gentlemen as officers, and clergymen were exempt from service. Only sons of the gentry and clergy could enter universities. The law and custom conditioned estate differences in food, clothing, healthcare, education, living conditions, marital behavior, and everything else that mattered.

Since many people did not fit into any of the estates, new categories had to be invented, chaotic and porous (Freeze 1986; Wirtschafter 1997; Confino 2008). People of different estates defined themselves by their relations to one another. Like races and castes, estates were produced by merging native traditions and imperial categories. Like races and castes, estates also survived reforms and revolution. In 1917, estate law was abolished, but Soviet practice soon re-established it in the form of "social origin," which reversely discriminated against those who originated from the gentry and clergy (Fitzpatrick 1993). Even in post-Soviet Russia, sociologists suspect there has been a re-emergence of the old system of estates under new names (Kordonsky 2008).

Race and Estate

"Estate" is a poor translation of the Russian word *soslovie*; a literal translation would be "a coordinate." Indeed, the estates provided the system of coordinates in which the Russian Empire structured Russian society. Dividing society into several layers, the Empire codified divisions and strengthened boundaries between social classes in a way that helped to avoid political conflicts, but that hampered economic and cultural development. The sociologist Michael Mann asserts that organic states, which aimed at national homogeneity, were often more dangerous than stratified states; when organic states colonized distant lands or identified an internal enemy, they were prone to commit genocide (Mann 2005). Large religious, ethnic, and service groups – Cossacks, Jews, Poles, Tartars – received their own lists of rights and duties which worked as if they were estates. Small ethnicities were categorized and treated in a summary way: "mountaineers," "nomads," and "little peoples of the North." From the start, the polity was pluralistic and fragmented, which enabled it to absorb more elements and create new coordinates. In the colonial frontiers, with their cycles of rebellion and oppression, and in the internal provinces, with their routine of corporal punishments, the level of violence was high. But when the revolution abolished the estate system, violence only increased.

Like the system of castes in India, the system of estates was created by the modernizing efforts of the imperial state, which appropriated local traditions and changed them for its own purposes (Dirks 2001). The idea that the condition of the bearded Russian peasants was similar to that of a colonized race was formulated immediately when the critics of the Enlightenment discovered colonialism. Abbé Raynal wrote in the *History of Two Indies* about Russia:

> Civil slavery is the condition of every subject in the empire, who is not noble: they are all at the disposal of their barbarous masters, as cattle are in other countries. Amongst these slaves, none are so ill used as those who till the ground. . . . Political slavery is the lot of the whole nation, since the foreigners have established arbitrary power [there]. (1777: 246)

Modern Russian literature started when Raynal's volume was smuggled into St. Petersburg. The customs officer who did it was Nikolai Radishchev, the author of *Journey from St. Petersburg to Moscow* (1790). When interrogated, Radishchev said that he modeled his *Journey* after Raynal and Herder. He wrote:

> Just imagine, – my friend told me long ago, – that the coffee in your mug and the sugar that you put there, deprived a human being, who is like you, of his peace. . . . My hand started trembling and I spilled my coffee. . . . And how about you, dwellers of St. Petersburg? (Radishchev 1992: 75)

For this and similar passages, Radishchev was exiled to Siberia. In the mid-nineteenth century, the radical-minded Alexander Herzen blamed the world for forgetting about the Russian serfs while banning the slave trade. Writing in English, he explained this discrepancy by unfolding serfdom's "extravagant and unparalleled history, that . . . almost def[ies] belief" (1957: 7, 10). A literary critic, Vissarion Belinsky, wrote about serfs as "white negroes"; Herzen wrote about them as "nègres gelés" (frozen negroes) (1956: 302). Belinsky described "the horrifying state of the country where people trade people, having no sly justification even of the sort that American slave-owners have when they say that the negro is not a human being" (1954: 10/213). Mocking the idea that American slavery was better than Russian serfdom because it was justified by belief, Belinsky saw their difference. Nobody in Russia, definitely not the state, claimed that serfs were neither human nor Christian. They attended churches and their pastoral care was a recognized duty of the clergy. For the gentry, Christians who owned Christians, this arrangement caused problems. It was also a problem for the clergy, who did not have serfs of their own, but gave Christian sermons to congregations that mixed the masters with their serfs.

The orientalization of serfs was part of the cognitive machinery of serfdom: treating humans like property, one needed to construct a difference between them and oneself. This oceanic gap between gentry and peasantry is well known, but the distance between gentry and clergy is no less illuminating (Manchester 2008). In the 1830s, a highly successful philosophy professor from Moscow Imperial University, Nikolai Nadezhdin, offered his hand in marriage to the daughter of a noble whom he taught privately. The love was mutual and the reason for her family's rejection was his origins in the clergy. The marriage never happened. In the 1880s, the young historian Pavel Miliukov, of impoverished gentry, happily married the daughter of a highly positioned Moscow clergyman. They had to keep their wedding secret; Miliukov's mother rejected her daughter-in-law; Miliukov (1990: 1/152) wrote about their experience of being newly wed as "a social dead-end." For a lady or a gentlemen, it was much easier to marry a foreigner than to marry a person from a lower estate. The introspective, free-minded Miliukov felt the impact of the estate boundary even in his academic affairs. He could not learn from his professor, Vasilii Kliuchevsky, who was from the clergy, because Kliuchevsky "understood the meaning of Russian history from the inside," and he did not. With a bit of irony, Miliukov explained that "the clergy retained a better connection with the old tradition" while the gentry had lost it (Miliukov 1990: 1/115). Indeed, having come from a dominated estate, Kliuchevsky made the development of estates and their struggles against each other a central theme of Russian history. Like Kliuchevsky, many Russian historians were sons of the clergy and owned nothing; the major Russian critics were also from the clergy rather than from the gentry. In contrast, the major nineteenth-century Russian writers and poets were gentlemen and owned estates, often more than one, and serfs. It was as if, in Russia, the distinction between fiction and non-fiction was also based on the estate origin.

Emancipation of the Russian serfs in 1861 happened almost simultaneously but in a more peaceful way than the abolition of slavery in the United States. There were many more serfs in Russia than there were slaves in America; in Russia, emancipation re-engineered the life and work of many millions (Kolchin 1987). Since serfs were property, the state-sponsored program of withdrawing this property from its legal owners was perceived as illiberal, even revolutionary. The gentry were left with little in way of a role in post-emancipation Russia. Around 1857, the government discussed and rejected a project to provide them with the functions of the rural police – to turn the former owners into the sheriffs of their former serfs (Saltykov-Shchedrin 1936: 5/73); later, the reformers built a mechanism of local governance that was led by the elected gentry. With emancipation, the state compensated the owners and the former serfs had to pay their redemption fees back to the state. Almost everyone – peasants, nobles, state officials, and public intellectuals – was unhappy about the details of emancipation, but they did serve to prevent or defer major outbursts of violence. In 1913, an underground activist, Vladimir Lenin, wrote a short essay, "Russians and Negroes," which argued that though the emancipation of Russian serfs and American slaves had taken place almost simultaneously, the procedures and results were different. Slaves received their freedom as the result of a violent war, serfs as the result of a peaceful reform. Precisely because of this difference, observed Lenin, "there are more traces of slavery kept among the Russians than among the negroes" (Lenin 1967: 22/346). Thus, in 1913, Lenin believed that the reforms of 1861 in Russia had deferred an American-style civil war, not prevented it. Great violence was necessary after which the races, or estates, would truly mix together. Lenin did what he could to realize this prophesy: he succeeded with the first part but failed with the second.

A Trip to the Countryside

Since the establishment of the Empire, Russian and foreign explorers had traveled into its lands with the thrill of discovery. Mostly organized by Germans on Russian service, the eighteenth-century expeditions went to Siberia, to the Caucasus, to the southern steppes, and also into the heartlands (Moon 2010). The enlightened voyagers of this period appreciated their travels to the central, and also exotic, parts of the Empire. Having led a huge expedition to Kamchatka in the 1730s, Gerhard Friedrich Müller died while exploring the countryside around Moscow (Black 1986; Müller 1996). Responding to Abbé Raynal's *History of Two Indies*, Radishchev wrote his *Journey from St. Petersburg to Moscow*. In the nineteenth century, a trip through European Russia was included in the nobleman's Grand Tour along with visits to Paris and Rome (Kozlov 2003). Nineteenth-century literature depicts many of these travels to a strange land that was populated by compatriots, including the officials who suspected every visitor of being an inspector-general. Responding to Byron's *Childe Harold Plilgrimage*, in which the protagonist travels to the exotic Mediterranean, Pushkin wrote "Onegin's Journey," in which the eponymous character travels through Russian provinces, from Novgorod to Astrakhan and then to Odessa (see Hokanson 2010: 126). Pushkin's drafts demonstrate how in this journey Onegin traded his pan-European dandyism for an improvised nationalism, a development that became emblematic for the mid-nineteenth century. Grand Duke Konstantin, arguably the most liberal member of the dynasty, urged the government to focus on Russia's central parts, which "all share one faith and nationhood." He advised disposing of those edges that were impossible to protect and cultivate, and "keeping only those which it is possible to keep" (Istoriia 1997: 3/386; Dameshek and Remnev 2007). Under Konstantin's pressure, the Navy Ministry and the Russian Geographical Society organized systematic travels into the depths of Russia. Together, political liberalism and cultural nationalism turned their focus towards the heartlands.

On June 21, 1826, the Russian diplomat and playwright Alexander Griboedov entertained himself with a day trip from St. Petersburg to Pargolovo, a village near the capital, now a suburb. Having had posts in the colonial administration of the Caucasus and the military mission to Persia, Griboedov had recently been brought back to St. Petersburg. He spent six months under arrest for being involved in the recent rebellion of the troops in the capital, but the inquest resulted in an acquittal and Griboedov was preparing to head back to Tiflis (now Tbilisi). But then his comedy, *Woe from Wit*, was forbidden from being presented on the stage. In the midst of this turmoil, the local festivities in Pargolovo proved memorable:

> Beneath us, on the banks of a quiet stream, along the wooded alleys, we spotted groups of girls; we chased them, wandering for an hour or two; suddenly we heard the ringing sounds of singing and dancing, female and male voices. . . . Songs of motherland! Where have you come from the sacred banks of the Dnieper and the Volga? – We returned: that hill was already full of fair-haired peasant girls, with ribbons and necklace, and also a boy choir; I liked two boys, with courageous features and free movements, more than others.

After chasing the local girls for an hour or two, the group of gentlemen joined the local festivities. At this idyllic moment, Griboedov's findings in Pargolovo turn from the banal to the astonishing:

> Leaning on a tree, I turned my eyes from the loud-voiced singers to the damaged class of the half-Europeans to whom I also belong. It was all wild for them, all that we saw and heard: these sounds were incomprehensible to them, these outfits seemed strange. What black magic has

> made us alien among ourselves! The Finns and the Tunguses are more easily admitted to our community, grow higher than us, become models for us, but our own people, the folk of our own blood, are separated from us, and for ever! If by any chance a foreigner got here, one who would not have known the Russian history of the century, he would conclude from the sharp difference of mores that our masters and our peasants originate from two different tribes, which have not had enough time to mix their mores and customs. (Griboedov 1999b: 276)

With his fresh colonial experience, Griboedov grasped the meaning of the event better than others. Common Russians in Pargolovo seemed "strange," "incomprehensible," even "wild" to the dwellers of St. Petersburg. Griboedov described a trip to the nearest suburb as if he was a romantic traveler visiting a distant land, enjoying the girls and songs of noble savages but misunderstanding their meaning, toying with an idea of mixing with them, and admitting to his sorrow that it was impossible. In the Caucasus, Griboedov would have been in these situations often, though his future marriage to a Georgian princess demonstrated that there, in a truly exotic land, the cultural gap was less noticeable. But Pargolovo was different from Tbilisi: there was no exoticism in the village, only a gap. The civilized Finns were close to Pargolovo and the wild Tunguses were far away in Siberia, but they had a better chance of being absorbed into the imperial elite than Russian peasants, said Griboedov. The contrast between geographical proximity and cultural distance could not have been stronger. Space did not matter; this was an empire in which social distances were greater than geographic ones, which themselves were huge. This empire's heart of darkness throbbed in places like Pargolovo.

There were no natives there. Originally a Swedish land with a Finnish population, the suburb was inhabited by settlers whom the Empire brought there to service and feed the capital. Griboedov guessed that these particular peasants came from "the sacred banks of the Dnieper and Volga." His friend, who accompanied him to Pargolovo, specified that these peasants had been resettled from the "internal provinces" about 50 years earlier (Bulgarin 1830: 155). Both reported a touristic, ethnographic interest in these peasants, their looks and their songs. Meaningfully, Griboedov filled his parable with erotic hints, which were typical for many narratives of the contact zone (Pratt 1992).

In Griboedov's formula, the Russian gentry failed to become good Europeans because they were foreign to their own people. A trained historian, Griboedov knew that it was exactly the perceived foreignness that defined the mechanism of imperial power in Russia. Apart from illicit moments, the elite did not mix its blood and customs with the commoners because self-segregation was the condition of self-preservation (Wortman 1995: 5). There is a powerful feeling of discontent in Griboedov's narrative. Rather than naturalizing differences, Griboedov felt unsettled by them. The inability of his friends, the Russian gentlemen, to understand a peasant festivity, or to take part in it, made these gentlemen a "damaged class of half-Europeans." Griboedov seemed to believe that a truly European elite would have been better connected to the folk in their heartland. But he probably remembered how, a few decades earlier, his French peers observed the same gap among their people. The nobles, wrote abbot Sieyès (2003), was "an isolated people," "a stranger to the nation" in the land where "third estate was everything."

Traveling between Tbilisi and St. Petersburg, Griboedov (1999a) devised a grand-scale project that would, if accomplished, have reshaped the Empire. In 1828, he applied to the government with a plan for the Transcaucasian Russian Company, which would be modeled after the British East Indian Company. His plan would resettle many thousands of peasants from central Russia to the Caucasus, creating massive colonies there: dozens of new Pargolovos. As the best model for the Russian colonization of the Caucuses, Griboedov presented the British colonization of North America. It was an unfortunate example; American colonies had emancipated themselves a few decades earlier and the Russian government closely followed these events, which renewed its anxieties about the fate of Siberia and the Caucasus. For this reason or another, Griboedov's project was rejected. He was appointed ambassador to Persia, where he was murdered by a Muslim mob in Tehran in 1829, less than a year after his marriage to the Georgian princess.

Black Magic

Older than Griboedov, Arthur Young wrote from the other end of Europe: "What a melancholy reflection is it to think that more than nine-tenths of the species should be the slaves of the despotic tyrants!" (Young 1772: 20). The promenade to Pargolovo connoted the same melancholic reflection, but there was more to it. In colonial situations, racial difference defined statutory difference; Griboedov knew how it worked in the Caucasus. Now in the countryside near St.

Petersburg, he discovered the same correlation between race and power, but the causality was reversed. Status inequality changed the perceived racial characteristics of people so much that they seemed to belong to two different tribes. Griboedov's experience was close to a colonial construction of race as the instrumental divide that cuts across humanity to benefit its minority. If Griboedov was right in his perception, a Russian village, an army platoon, and even a noble manor were all places of intercultural miscommunication, "contact zones" (Pratt 1992) that hosted myriad routine dramas typical for a colonial order. In a similar trope, Kastor Lebedev, a respected lawyer and member of the Russian Senate, wrote in 1854 about his routine trip to a village near Orel:

> Peasants are not far from domestic animals. This old man, unwashed, unkempt, barefoot; this half-naked woman; these dirty, disheveled boys lying in the mud and straw, all them are not human figures! It seems as if they all are beyond the boundary of the State, all are illegitimate children of Russia, all are defeated by a conqueror who does not belong to their tribe; as if all our memos, boards, and committees, all these cases in the courts are not about them, not for them. (Lebedev 1888: 354)

The law was not for the peasants and they were not for the law; they lived, worked, and traded outside the law. Unless a serf fled his master or was killed by his master, the state did not interfere in the life of the manor. The serf's life was bare: though they could be punished, they could not be sacrificed (Agamben 1998). Griboedov described the oceanic difference between the masters and the serfs by saying that they seemed to belong to two different, unmixed races. He clearly referred to the invasion of the Varangians, and the idea that the gentry were their descendants.

On January 28, 1974, Michel Foucault gave a lecture in the Collège de France:

> One must say . . . that two races exist whenever one writes the history of two groups which do not . . . have the same language or, in many cases, the same religion. . . . Two races exist when there are two groups which, although they coexist, have not become mixed. (2003: 76)

Like Griboedov, Foucault detached the concept of race from colonial discourse and applied it to the relationships between groups inside Europe. Exploring the war-like nature of politics in a time of peace, Foucault suggested that the struggle between races was at the origin and the center not only of colonial, but also of metropolitan politics. Two groups form "a single polity only as a result of wars, invasions, victories, and defeats" (2003: 76). In other words, races merge only as a consequence of great violence. Examining how the English and French revolutions reactivated the ancient memory of wars between the races of Romans, Celts, Saxons, and Normans, Foucault generalized about the internal colonialism that the pre-revolutionary Europe imposed on itself (2003: 103). When English or Scottish kings claimed their divine right to govern, they had to present themselves as heirs of William the Conqueror. It was not that the theory of divine right was connected to the theory of Norman succession; these two theories were the same. Those who questioned their power, like the radical sectarians of the English revolution, protested against the kings' "Norman yoke" and referred to the people's "Saxon right." Foucault detected similar constructions in medieval France. He could also have mentioned the Russian myth of Rurik or the revolutionary idea that the Romanovs were a "German dynasty."

While Marxian social historians interpreted these racial ideas as a disguised form of class war, Foucault neutralized the very difference between class and race. He presented two mythological languages, one of race and another of class, as mutually convertible. Sometimes the former, sometimes the latter was closer to the actual experience of historical agents. But theorists and ideologists always had their preferences. In a broad stroke, Foucault presented Hobbes's and Marx's political philosophies as attempts to pacify the race war. Like Marx, but in a different way, Hobbes proposed a scheme of things – the state of nature, covenant, sovereignty – that made races irrelevant. "In a word, what Hobbes wants to eliminate is the Conquest" (Foucault 2003: 110).

There is much that is exciting and much that is exaggerated in Foucault's narrative of the European race wars (Stoler 1995). Unlike his many other ideas, this peculiar emphasis on European races has not been integrated in the main body of the contemporary humanities; the leading American theorists of race, enthusiastic followers of Foucault in some other respects, have declined to assess the contrast or similarities between their "race" and Foucault's. Rather than pointing at weaknesses in Foucault's arguments, I wish to transfer the focus closer to my subject. There was an important moment in Russian historiography that closely followed the script that Foucault portrayed in his course, the struggle between race and class in the interpretation of history. In the mid-nineteenth century, two historians from Kazan, Stepan Eshevsky and his student Afanasii Shchapov, produced an important body of racial history. Soon, their work was overshadowed by two historians from Moscow, Sergei Soloviev and his student Vasilii Kliuchevsky, who devised the Russian version of social history as the history of estates.

An old Tartar capital, Kazan was taken by Russian troops in 1552, which was a huge step in Russia's empire-building. Throughout almost all of the nineteenth century, the university there was the easternmost one in the Empire. It was the site of unusual achievements in scholarship, such as Nikolai Lobachevsky's "imaginary geometry," which was built on the assumption that parallel lines converge. Eshevsky's history was also counterintuitive but was more closely linked to the local, Russian and Tartar, realities. An expert in ancient and early medieval Europe, Eshevsky taught courses such as "The Center of the Roman World and its Provinces" and "Races in Russian History," which presented unusually rich and balanced narratives of colonization, resistance, and transcultural exchange. The guiding idea of his courses was the unconquered spirit of the colonized peoples, which enriched the imperial culture and survived it. He observed a similar dialectics in his contemporary Russia and even in America. In 1864, he began his course on race at Moscow University with an extended reference to the American Civil War: "However great the significance of race is for the political life of the United States, it is even more important for scholarly history" (Eshevsky 1870: 22). He believed that it was an achievement of science to be able to look at humanity not just as "an indifferent mass, everywhere and always the same," but as divided into races, which had physical and spiritual manifestations. For him, races were recognizable and stable, but he also emphasized their internal complexity and ability to merge, mix, and change. Pursuing a synthesis between history, linguistics, and ethnography, Eshevsky responded critically to the field of physical anthropology, the nineteenth-century science of races. He distinguished between two concepts, creolization and hybridization. The difference is that animal hybrids cannot reproduce, but mixing human races gives prolific results. He surveyed and rejected the racist idea that the fate of creoles was degeneration; on the contrary, he described the mulatto and other mixes as more viable and productive than pure races. While his famous French contemporary, Arthur de Gobineau, claimed that "the fall of civilization is due to a degeneration of race and the decay of race is due to a mixture of blood" (cited in Arendt 1966: 172), Eshevsky celebrated the racial mixing that he saw as the source of progress, in Russia as well as in America. Races are analogous to breeds rather than species, humanity is one whole, and historical change is not a process of racial displacement and substitution but a process of racial mixing and absorption. This course on race, taught at Moscow Imperial University in 1864, was remarkably anti-racist even in comparison to the later ideas of the so-called "liberal anthropology" (Mogilner 2008).

Revising concepts of colonial anthropology helped Eshevsky to offer a new view on Russian history. A large part of European Russia was originally populated by the Finnish race, taught Eshevsky. At the start of the recorded history, the Finns lived not only where Novgorod stands, but also where Moscow is located; in the earlier period they lived as far to the south as Kiev. However, they were all substituted by the Slavs.

> What does it mean? History does not know about the deportation of the Finns, or even less so, their systematic extermination by the Russians. . . . The process occurred inconspicuously. There is no memory of the bloody race war in the Russian chronicles or in folk legends. However, only Russians live now in the purely Finnish land that was populated by the purely Finnish tribes; and these are the Russians who believe that they are the purest, the most typical Russians. (Eshevsky 1870: 97)

The Slavs did not have firearms like Cortez or superior organization like the Romans. They could not exterminate the Finns, but they mixed with them and absorbed them. Referring to his own observations in Kazan, where he watched "all the grades of absorption of the Tartars and the Finns by the Russians," Eshevsky claimed that only this peaceful process of intermixing could explain the growth of the Russian people. It had left no historical memory because of its gradual, non-violent character. Remarkably, Eshevsky imagined a process that both Lenin and Foucault denied for purely theoretical or rather, ideological reasons: a non-violent, gradual racial mixing.

Negative Hegemony

One idea proved seminal for Russian letters: that while the fruits are national, the roots are foreign. The source of strength and pride should be sought outside among others, even among very distant others ranging from the Vikings to the Amazons. A classical example is the ode that Gavriil Derzhavin, a poet who also served as the governor of Tambov, the Minister of Justice, etc., wrote to Catherine II in 1782. According to the convention of its genre, the ode depicts

Catherine as the embodiment of virtues and the author as a humble subject climbing the ladder of perfection. "The Kyrgyzes-Kaisaks" (now called Kazakhs), the nomadic tribes of the later Orenburg province, had just been brought under Russian sovereignty, and the ode celebrates this event. However, its rich oriental symbolism is so unusual that this ode became a puzzle for many generations of scholars. It is not that the German-born Empress is presented as the source of the westernizing influence and Derzhavin, who was of Tartar blood, as her oriental subject. On the contrary, the Empress is called "the God-like Tsarina of the horde of the Kyrgyzes-Kaisaks," her Russian courtiers are called "murzas" (the Tartar nobility), and the whole Empire is transposed into the Orient, a fairytale space somewhere between "Baghdad, Smyrna, and Cashmere." While the humbler narrator tames his passions in the process of a personal Enlightenment that had, no doubt, European origins, he identifies his sovereign with her base oriental subjects. This is not a satire or parody; this is an ode, for which success in the court testified to the seriousness of the orientalization process. Reversing the order of domination, this exoticizing vision of sovereignty signaled the early and deep revision of the European legacy of orientalism as it was appropriated by Russian literature.

The Russian romantic novel often depicted love between partners who are racially or socially unequal, presenting the death of one of them as a sacrificial mechanism that reveals the deep dynamics of the underlying historical situation (see Chapter 11). In stories of external colonization, it was love between an imperial officer and a native beauty, as in Pushkin's *The Prisoner of the Caucasus* and Lermontov's "Bela." In both stories, love is fatal to the native woman and both of the male characters, Russian officers, are clearly blamed for causing the deaths of their loving, noble savages. This recurrent plot effectively redeems, I would even say deconstructs, the imperialist slogans that one can find in the very same texts. The apparent contradiction between the structure of the romance and the explicit ideology of prologues and epilogues creates a dynamic that has long interested readers.

Students of Russian literature love Mikhail Lermontov's novel, *The Hero of Our Time* (1840). With its multiple narrators and egocentric protagonist, this novel gives a complex and critical picture of the Russian imperial experience. Like Lermontov, its central character, Pechorin, fights in the Caucasian War. He dies during a diplomatic mission to Persia, like Griboedov. The novel features memorable adventures with Russian and native beauties, an inevitable duel, and a portrait of a rank-and-file imperial officer, Maksim Maksimovich, a counter-balance to the brilliant, unstable Pechorin. Having served in the Caucasus for about 25 years, Maksim Maksimovich launches the novel by cracking a typically colonial puzzle. The Ossettians drive two Russian carriages through the mountains. One carriage is light and six bulls cannot move it; another is heavy but four bulls pull it easily. The light carriage belongs to a novice in the Caucasus, the heavy one to Maksim Maksimovich. The Ossettians and even their bulls employ the "weapons of the weak," deception and sabotage, to deceive the Russians and to get more money for the service. "Horrible beasts are these Asians," says Maksim Maksimovich (Lermontov 1958: 4/10). Apart from this generalization, he manifests a detailed knowledge of the locals. He smokes a pipe of the Kabarda people, wears a hat of the Cherkess people, and strongly prefers the Chechens to the Ossettians. A storyteller, he is the first source of our knowledge about the enigmatic Pechorin, whom he leads through the incomprehensible Asia.

In a short essay of 1841, "The Caucasian," which is the best companion to *The Hero of Our Time*, Lermontov presented an anthropological analysis of people like Maksim Maksimovich, the backbone of the empire, the officers of an imperial army that was stationed in a rebellious colony. In this essay, the Caucasian is a typical Russian officer who, said Lermontov, knew and loved his enemy, the untamed tribes of the Caucasus. "A half-Russian, half-Asian creature," with every year of service the officer had become more and more orientalized. He had first learned about the Caucasus from Pushkin, but since then he collected much information about the customs and leaders of various tribes. He knew their genealogies. He preferred their weapons, horses, and women to the Russian ones. He admired the mountaineers' manners of riding, fighting, and living. He started learning their languages, more than once. Discussing the Caucasian tribes in comparative detail had become his and his peers' favorite preoccupation. "The true Caucasian deserves much surprise and respect," wrote Lermontov. A primary agent of imperialist rule, the Russian officer in the Caucasus turned into a lay anthropologist who felt the temptation to "go native" and had not much reason to resist (Lermontov 1958: 4/159; see also Layton 1994; Barrett 1999).

Lermontov was highly critical of these feelings. He distanced himself in equal measure from the destructive snobbery of Pechorin and the naive orientalism of Maksim Maksimovich. Throughout the long nineteenth century, the growing body of Russian literature and thought experienced the temptation to go native. Abandoning the

Figure 9: Karl Briullov, *A Portrait of an Officer with his Servant* (1830s). Note the oriental ambiance and the physical resemblance between the two.
Source: http://gallerix.ru/album/Brullov/pic/glrx-863742065

privileges of the higher estate and merging with the common Russian folk was often depicted as the mission of the educated class. Maksim Maksimovich exemplified a similar affection for non-Russians. Historically, this longing for non-Russian peoples preceded the mid-nineteenth-century prose about the Russian folk and the actual Going-to-the-People movement (Hokanson 1994).

In about 1820, a Baltic German in the Russian Navy, Captain Ferdinand Vrangel, visited Yakutsk on his way to Russian America. He found there a major fair that traded fur for grain, tobacco, and vodka. All the Russians in town were busy with the fur trade. All the craftsmen, hunters, and horse-drivers were Yakuts. Most of them had been christened; they even painted the icons in the town's five churches. However, they also retained their shamanistic customs, wrote Vrangel.

Many were of mixed ethnic origin. Wealthy Russian families used Yakut nurses to help raise their children and they spoke Yakut. In any case, the Russians and the Yakut all looked the same because of the fur clothing that helped them survive the climate. Their diet was also similar; grain was too expensive and flour was made of dry fish. The overall picture presented an unusually rich cultural hybridization, in which the assimilation worked in both directions and the urbane society spoke Yakut instead of French:

> At the higher level of the local society the Yakut language played the dominant role, similar to French in our capitals. I was extremely surprised by this situation at a glorious dinner party in the house of the richest fur trader. . . . The society consisted of the chief of the district, the respected priests, the officials and some merchants, but the conversation was so interspersed with Yakut phrases that I could barely take part in it. (Vrangel 1841: 171)

After 1821, "Creole" became an official term in Siberia. Pure or mixed ethnically, many Russians there were bilingual and bicultural. Built on long-term processes of ethnic- and gender-specific displacement, the results were culturally productive on the Russian, imperial side. Himself a Creole, Afanasii Shchapov documented these processes in a series of essays that he wrote in political exile in the 1860s (1906: 2/365–481). He argued that Russia evolved as the result of the millennium-long Slavic colonization of lands that belonged to Finnish, Tartar, Yakut, and many peoples (Shchapov counted 111 altogether). This colonization was the substance of Russian history; "all our truth and our guilt" are connected to this process. Referring to the examples of the outright extermination of the Pacific tribes, which were known because they had happened recently, he implied that the earlier Slavic invasions in Europe were no less bloody, but that their memories had been forgotten. Shchapov was more realistic than his teacher, Eshevsky, in his understanding of the violence and oblivion that was characteristic of this colonization process. Giving many examples, Shchapov emphasized an entirely unknown aspect of Russian colonization. In two huge areas that he knew well, in the Tartar lands near Kazan and in Western Siberia, Russians effectively assimilated the natives by christening some of them, passing their crafts to the natives, and involving them in markets. But the opposite process also took place: the Russians acquired the skills, customs, dress, language, and even the physical appearance of the local communities.

Though this reversed assimilation was not rare in the history of the empires, the Yakuts could be an exception. A people with a traditional culture of hospitality and relative immunity to European diseases, they benefited from the fur trade more than others. Further east and north from Yakutsk, several warlike tribes rejected contact with the Russians and became targets of ethnic extermination. However, Willard Sunderland (1996) gives multiple examples of the "nativization" of Russians in various areas of Siberia. Whether it was civil peace in Yakutsk or an imperialist war in the Caucasus, Russian influences on the natives met with the natives' influences on the Russians. As Lermontov demonstrates with a persuasiveness unavailable to the historian, even while waging a bloody war, the people of the dominating power admired and imitated the mores of the oppressed.

Domination without hegemony, a concept that the Indian scholar Guha (1997) used to summarize British rule, created an unbalanced situation that featured distrust, resistance, and the frequent discharge of violence. The situations of reverse assimilation in Yakutia and the Caucasus were different. In both these colonial situations, one peaceful, the other violent, domination and hegemony developed in opposing directions. With cultural hegemony not just absent but evolving as a negative entity, the officers of the Empire were going native with an unexpected agility. As Edyta Bojanowska (2007: 107) notes, in his sketch of "universal history," Gogol depicted the Roman Empire in a way that was similar to what he, a colonial himself, perceived to be the situation in the Russian Empire: "The Romans adopted everything from the conquered peoples; first they adopted their vices, then their enlightenment. Everything mixed again. Everyone became a Roman and there was no genuine Roman, not a single one!" (Gogol 1984: 6/39). The way to describe these situations is to posit a negative hegemony and reversed orientalism as corollaries of internal colonization. A negative hegemony could coexist with a relatively non-violent domination, as in Yakutia, but its combination with the massive violence in the Caucasus was doomed. From Gogol to Conrad and from Pushkin to professional Russian orientalists (Berezin 1858; Morrison 2008: 288), intellectuals on both sides of the colonial divide perceived this situation as abnormal, unviable, and reversed in comparison to western imperialism. It also gave ground for hope that as an imperial nation, Russians possess a uniquely cosmopolitan, universal comprehension. Though readers of Russian literature associate this idea with the Pushkin speech by Dostoevsky (1880) and its poetic elaboration by Aleksandr Blok (1918), these ideas were developed throughout the High Imperial Period. Writing, in the 1840s, a cultural history of migrations in world history, the polymath, Aleksei Khomiakov, was first to describe this reversed situation as the advantage of the Russian way of colonization:

> There is no American in the United States . . . who speaks the language of the red-skinned. . . . In his colonies, a fat, phlegmatic Hollander looks at the natives as a tribe that God created for service and slavery, as cattle and not as human. . . . The Russian looks at the dwellers of the enormous Northern land as his brothers. The Siberians often use the language of their neighbors, the Yakuts and the Buriats. A dashing Cossack marries a Chechen, a peasant marries a Tartar or Mordovian, and Russia finds its joy and glory in the great-grandson of the Negro whom the American proselytes of equality would have refused to consider a citizen. (Khomiakov 1871: 1/107)

Fireworks

Domination can be effective with or without shared language, beliefs, and schooling; but hegemony presupposes a common culture. Throughout two centuries, the Empire experimented with various combinations of these factors. Gunpowder was a major factor that made it possible for the Empire to acquire and control its enormous space. The early drivers of Russian industrialization, canons and rifles figured in every confrontation between the Empire and its subjects from the Time of Troubles. It was only because of two unique features of firearms, their killing power and the ease of controlling their proliferation, that the state could monopolize violence on its territory. The sail created Britain's Empire, the canon created Russia's.

But of course the gun was important for all modern empires. In Russia, gunpowder, the universal substance of domination, also provided a means of hegemony over the hearts and minds of the imperial subjects. In rare moments of unity, salutes and fireworks provided an official language that integrated the sophisticated and the illiterate, those who understood the changing assortment of languages of the Empire and those who did not. In its ability to emulate the acts of God, fireworks affirmed and allowed the Empire to speak with its subjects in a language of light, movement, and explosion that was uniquely free of culture.

Starting with Peter I and through a large part of the High Imperial Period, fireworks demonstrated the might and beauty of the Empire. The actual fireworks were over-saturated with allegorical meanings;

they impressed everyone, but only the culturally literate deciphered their subtle messages. Emblems and verses literally shone, whirled, and exploded in the heavens, emulating the acts of God via the rituals of the Empire. Peter saw the connection between fireworks and firearms: those subjects who were used to the fun of fireworks would withstand the fire of cannons, he asserted. To celebrate the victory over the Swedes in 1710, a flaming Russian eagle launched a rocket into a burning Swedish lion. The scale was truly modern: in 1732 on the Neva, 30,000 torches could be ignited in two minutes (Sarieva 2000: 89). Creating fireworks in St. Petersburg was one of the main functions of the Imperial Academy of Sciences, a way in which it proved its utility to the state. These regular events were among the few festivities in imperial Russia which involved both the masses and the elite, the first means of mass communications. Fireworks represented battles, landscapes, maps, and other images of colonial conquest – Turkish forts, Swedish ships, and once in 1748, even a Siberian pine tree (Werrett 2010). The coronation of Catherine the Great included a firework with "an allegorical figure of Russia" accompanied by a 101-gun salute (Wortman 1995: 1/118). In 1789, there appeared a do-it-yourself instruction for those gentlemen who wished to impress their families and serfs with fireworks on their estates (Sarieva 2000). In 1857, Nikolai Ignatiev was traveling through Central Asia with a group of Cossacks. Attacked by hundreds of Turkomans, he dispersed them with fireworks. Allegedly, they were so impressed by "the Devil's fire" that they "craved forgiveness" (Stead 1888: 272). Andrei Bolotov, a Russian officer who studied philosophy in Königsberg, subtly interpreted the function of fireworks as "blinding the common people with [their] very splendor" (1986: 448).

Man-made images of paradise, fireworks illustrated the most difficult tenet of imperial philosophy, the power to transform nature and sublimate culture by the sheer will of the sovereign. For those few who understood the Russian technology of manufacturing gunpowder from manure, ashes, and filth, the process of sublimation seemed even more impressive. There was a universalist energy in these performances that could, if but for a moment, integrate the free and the bound, the rich and the poor, in one awesome climax. No other experience was as inter-estate, cross-ethnic and therefore multicultural as were fireworks. Firearms were means of domination; fireworks were means of hegemony.

But as the enterprising subjects of the empire eroded the state monopolies on both firearms and fireworks, the High Imperial Period was coming to its end. "Gunpowder in Russia is no more precious than sand," quipped a Danish envoy to the court of Peter I (Juel 1899: 257), and there was a predictive power in his observation. The same black powder that was employed for defeating enemies and celebrating victories was also used for assassinating emperors and overthrowing the Empire.

— 7 —

Disciplinary Gears

Serfdom has become an increasingly unpopular subject in post-Soviet historiography; the contrast between the non-existent Serfdom Studies in Russia and the booming Slavery and African American Studies in the USA could not be stronger. In what remains the best study of serfdom, the American historian Stephen Hoch researched the archive of a large estate near Tambov, a black-soil region of European Russia and a proverbial territory of the Russian interior. In the early nineteenth century, the peasants' productivity and diet on this estate were equal to or better than what was common in Germany or France. The difference lay in their motivation, property rights, and principles of management. Since neither the land nor a major share of the product belonged to the peasants, they worked under the threat of corporal punishment, which was used routinely. In Hoch's data, in about 1826, 79 percent of males were flogged at least once, and 24 percent twice a year. For more serious misdemeanors, peasants were also shaved on one side of the head (Hoch 1989: 162).

Founded in 1636, Tambov was a fortress that protected the Muscovite state from the nomadic tribes that had populated this land before the Russians invaded it. Tambov was thus a contemporary of Williamsburg (1632), an early center of plantations in Virginia, and of Cape Town in South Africa (1652). Near Tambov, however, the security situation made stable agriculture impossible for 100 years after its foundation, and a plantation-type economy unfeasible for another 100 after this. Centrally located, the estate that Hoch studied was still far from the markets; it took a week to deliver grain to the river hub, and to transport it to Moscow took months. Forced resettlements of serfs populated this land, and immigration continued into the nineteenth century. Even then, the demographic growth on this estate did not compensate for the draft of recruits and the flights of the serfs (Hoch 1989: 5). Though the estate was relatively rich, it could not sustain the imperial demands. It is counterintuitive to consider Tambov as a colony, but anywhere else in the world a land that was populated by forced settlers at a time of high imperialism and, in addition, cultivated under the permanent threat of the lash would be so designated. It so happens that scholars of the Russian peasantry have rarely addressed its particularity from a colonial perspective, though some remarkable exceptions exist (Rogger 1993; Frank 1999).

Serfs and Colons

Serfdom became law in Russia after the turmoil of the Time of Troubles (1598–1613). A little earlier than the Thirty Years War in Europe (1618–48), this Russian crisis also included a confessional conflict, a civil war with foreign intervention, celebrated cases of fake identities, and the general breakdown of the state (Dunning 2001). As part of the European crisis of the seventeenth century, the situation in Russia was provoked by the collapse of the resource-bound economy (see Chapter 5). With no fur or silver for mercenaries, land remained the only currency available to Moscow. But making any profit on land was problematic. The three-field agricultural system, which was the condition for productivity in central Russia, demanded long cycles (Confino 1963). But bonding people to the land involved a high level of violence. With the arrival of firearms, the servitors obtained a decisive advantage over the peasants; armed with muskets or rifles, a small number of soldiers could control a crowd of peasants carrying axes and knifes (Hellie 1971; Pettengill 1979). Eventually, the new regime was codified as a serfdom and became a major feature of the Russian state. The import of firearms made a larger contribution to the establishment of serfdom than any economic consideration. But violence was difficult to translate into power; complex institutions were needed for this task.

While in Western Europe, serfs became farmers and free toilers, in Poland and Russia, free men became serfs. Some historians explain this "second serfdom" as a result of the growing export demand, with Eastern Europe becoming the supplier of cereals and livestock to the west (Bideleux and Jeffries 2007: 162). But in contrast to Baltic lands, in Russia there were few opportunities for a landowner to export his crops. Until the Black Sea ports became available in the mid-eighteenth century, Russia's largest agricultural export was the hemp and flax that the Brits were buying in Archangel. However, serfdom developed not in Archangel but in those land-locked provinces of Russia that had the worst export opportunities. Racially white, religiously Orthodox, ethnically Russian, centrally located peasants suffered from serfdom more than anybody else. Kliuchevsky showed that the closer a province was to Moscow, the higher was the percentage of serfs there. He interpreted this distribution in security terms: "the fortress of serfdom" (Kliuchevsky 1913). There were few privately owned serfs in northern Russia and Siberia; no serfdom among Kalmycks, Kazakhs, Jews, or peoples of the north; few serfs among Tartars; only some serfs among the Russian Old-Believers and sectarians; and millions of serfs among the Orthodox Slavs (Kappeler 2001: 30). However one defines the core of this Empire, the closer one got to it, the more serfs there were. Despite the intellectual challenge that this situation presented, there was no racial or religious theory that explained or justified such selectivity. Neither the church, nor the state, nor the intelligentsia formulated anything equivalent to the American planters' belief that African Americans were fit for slavery and Native Americans were not (Nash 2000). But the practice of enserfment was consistent with the idea that Orthodox Russians were fit for enserfment and other peoples were not. Much later, the emancipation of serfs also fitted in with this idea. The great reforms of the mid-nineteenth century were first tested on the periphery of the Empire, in those Baltic and Polish lands where Russian and non-Russian peasants were serfs, and then applied to its core. In the long history of serfdom, the peasants of the internal provinces were enslaved earlier and emancipated later than the peasants of the imperial periphery, and in much higher proportions.

In his comparative study, Orlando Patterson characterizes Russian serfdom as "highly extrusive," with the serf imagined as "an internal exile," who had been deprived of the protection of law and all claims of community. The Orthodox Church encouraged the enserfment of the Orthodox by the Orthodox but did not provide a justification for their inequality: "Russia was the only Christian state whose church did not help to define the slave as a converted infidel." Instead of defining serfs as the foreign enemy within their land, the Russian serf-owner "chose exactly the opposite way in defining himself as the foreigner of noble ancestry" (Patterson 1982: 43–4). Whether Rurikide or Petrovian, the typical serf-owner kept hundreds or thousands of his serfs in a state of social death. From 1649 to 1861, masters could legally sell, buy, and mortgage serfs, though in most cases they could not do this to individual serfs, only to whole families.

Masters could force their peasants to work, but they could not legally kill them. Serfs could not sign contracts, could not testify in courts, and could not denounce their masters.

"Ruling the countryside like local satraps or colonial administrators" (Frank 1999: 8), landed nobles had to feed themselves with the help of their serfs. If they failed to do so, the state subsidized them, as it would do with the administrators. The nobles benefited in two ways, socially and economically. While the social benefits – conspicuous consumption, lifestyle preservation, and various privileges of power – were primary, the economic benefits were unreliable and increasingly unsustainable. The non-economic nature of serfdom made it different from slavery in America (Kolchin 1987). There, plantation owners would not keep their slaves from generation to generation if they did not bring a profit. But the standard property of a Russian noble, with many square miles of land and hundreds of peasants, was a not-for-profit institution. Keeping serfs despite losses was the rule rather than the exception. Starting with the early nineteenth century, the empire offered nobles ways of mortgaging their lands, together with the peasants, in state banks. Unpaid mortgages converted into foreign debts and inflation. Serfs subsidized the Empire but the Empire subsidized serfdom. Introduced by Egor (George) Kankrin, the Imperial Minister of Finances (1823–44), this policy was much ridiculed by Marxist historians. In the twenty-first century, when an average European farm receives about a third of its income from the state, Kankrin's policy seems forward-looking. Serfdom did not have an economic rationale; the social interests of the nobility and the disciplinary interests of the Empire dictated its preservation. In 1856, about two-thirds of male serfs (6.6 million "souls") were mortgaged, but foreclosures on the landed gentry could be counted in the dozens (Pintner 1967: 37–42). The government gave loans to the rural gentry on the security of their serfs and refused to credit manufacturers and merchants. During most of its reign, the Empire restricted industrial development in favor of unproductive agriculture. In its core areas, serfdom was a mechanism of social policy and preservation of lifestyle (Moon 1999).

The mechanism of land grants to the state servitors was not different from what went on, during approximately the same period, in many parts of the colonized world, from the American South to New Zealand. To make money on these lands, servitors needed labor. This labor could be found locally or had to come from afar. In either case, the new masters of the land had to employ various regimes of coercion. The choice was narrow, from slavery to serfdom, with hired labor as a distant possibility. Already, Soloviev and Kliuchevsky understood the low density of the population as the cause of serfdom, and contemporary economists agree (Domar 1970; Millward 1982). In the newly colonized lands, labor was brought from afar, as in the British colonies. In central Russia, it was already there, but the peasants had to be guarded so that they would not leave their native land. In its original form, serfdom was an institution of the internal colonization of the Russian heartland.

But external colonization also required peasant labor. Masters could resettle their serfs to new lands or buy serfs and transport them to a new settlement. In the eighteenth and early nineteenth centuries, these forced resettlements of serfs were massive operations; they were also expensive (Sunderland 1993). Since nobody would move, guard, and feed hundreds of families without expecting a profit, these colonial resettlements changed the nature of serfdom. The leading Marxist historian of the 1920s, Mikhail Pokrovsky, acknowledged the development of "plantation serfdom" in Russia only in the early nineteenth century (2001: 10; also Kagarlitsky 2003). It is meaningful that the most important Russian novel about serfdom, Gogol's *Dead Souls*, is a story of the resettlement project.

In his major work of 1885, *The Origins of Serfdom in Russia*, Kliuchevsky argued that early serfdom was not introduced by the state, but grew as a result of multiple deals in which peasants could not pay back rents and other debts to landowners (1956: 7/245). Instead, they accepted lifelong contracts that deprived them of personal freedom. Later, these contracts were codified by the state. As a model for this speculation, Kliuchevsky used the study of the Roman "colonate" by the French classicist, Fustel de Coulanges, whose books were later translated by Kliuchevsky's friends. Coulanges argued that the colonate, an institution of bondage in the late Roman Empire and Byzantium that acted as a gray zone between slavery and free farming, grew from the debts of peasants. When free peasants became "colons," their lords owned them and their descendants; their freedom was restrained (Coulanges 1908). Like the Russian serfs, the Roman colons were used both in the new Roman colonies and in the Italian heartland. Etymologically and historically, these Roman colons rested at the very origins of the idea of colony and colonialism (Morris 1900: 1/6).

The enserfment of Russians by Russians was a mechanism of internal colonization, a regime of population management, *and* an institution of production. Order rather than profit was its utility function; coercion rather than investment was its method; the reproduction of the population and the colonization of land rather than the production of goods was its purpose.

German Colonies

In 1763, after taking the Russian throne by force, Catherine the Great issued the *Manifesto* that invited foreign colonists to settle in Russia and promised substantial benefits to the immigrants, such as free agricultural land, exemption from military service, relocation subsidies, free loans, and tax immunity for 30 years (Bartlett 1979: 3). They were guaranteed freedom of faith. Those newcomers who would like to establish factories (the *Manifesto* called them "capitalists") would be able to purchase serfs. Attached was a long list of available lands, from western Russia to Siberia. The official name for the future immigrants was "colonists." Catherine created a special chancellery to take care of the colonists and commissioned her favorite, a hero of the Seven Years War, Grigorii Orlov, to head this agency. As Orlov explained in his report to the Imperial Senate in 1764, with the accommodation of the large numbers of colonists, "Russia will seem no longer to be as strange and wild as it has seemed until now, and the firm prejudice against it will inconspicuously disappear" (Svod 1818: 5/128). The idea of the civilizing mission was redirected from the margins of the Empire to this empire's exotic interior. Ideologically, internal colonies were also connected to Catherine's vague desire to abolish serfdom, with foreign or native colonists replacing serfs in some sectors of the economy. But this experiment was realized only in a few estates belonging to the royal family (Bartlett 1979: 92).

In the post-Westphalian world, moving Germans around the world was a business. Prussia moved large groups of colonists into the reclaimed territories on the Rhine and settled large numbers of Calvinists from France, a success that Catherine II tried to repeat in Russia. England used German conscripts to suppress the rebellion in America, a plan that Catherine rejected when the Brits offered her a profitable deal. Lured by the riches of Russia, foreign advisers came to help its enlightened Amazonian Empress. A French adventurist and later famous writer, Bernardin de Saint-Pierre, arrived in Russia in 1762 with a plan to establish a "European colony" to the east of the Caspian Sea. This colony would pacify the natives "with the power of example or arms." It would cultivate the desert and open trade with India. Bernardin asked Catherine II for a loan of 150,000 rubles but did not receive this huge sum of money. He became famous for his novel, *Paul and Virginie*, set in the French Mauritius, but before he died in 1814, he was working on a major novel that was set in Siberia. The story was set in 1762, when Bernardin was in Russia, and Catherine's coup d'état is repeatedly referred to as a "revolution" (Cook 1994, 2006). Another adventurous Frenchman, Abbé Raynal, in his *History of Two Indies* explained:

> The best method [for Russia] would be to choose out one of the most fertile provinces of the empire and . . . to invite free men from civilized countries. . . . From thence the seeds of liberty would spread all over the empire. . . . We are not to bid them [Russians] to be free; but we are to lay before their eyes the sweets of liberty. (Raynal 1777: 248)

Later, Raynal visited St. Petersburg and met Catherine, but his *History* was not welcome there. In 1765, Catherine invited a trustworthy German, the pastor Johann Reinhold Forster, to promote the first steps of colonization on the Volga. He came along with his adolescent son, George, mapped the new colonies and took part in the efforts to create a legal code for them (Bartlett 1979: 100). There were rumors in St. Petersburg that Forster wished to create his own colony (Dettelbach 1996: lx). He was never paid for his service, but the publication of his maps with the Royal Society was his first scholarly achievement (Forster 1768). As for his son, George Forster, then aged 11, his first work was a translation of Lomonosov. Both Forsters became famous later, when they took part in James Cook's second expedition.

For the media-savvy Catherine, it seemed perfectly correct to call the organized immigration of Europeans into Russia "colonization," the newly cultivated areas, "colonies," and the new subjects, "colonists." The colonization of what? The Russian Empire. Colonization by whom? European settlers. Under whose authority and in whose interest? The Russian Empire. While many newcomers took money and perished in the open steppe, one particular category of settlers redeemed the project. The successful colonists were the heirs of the radical Reformation and supporters of very special ways of life, some of the strangest people who ever lived in Europe. Persecuted in many countries, these non-violent people found in Russia what they wanted, i.e. virgin land and exemption from military service. Catherine and her favorite, Orlov, found their model in Frederick's colonizing activities on the Rhine (Blackbourn 2007), the success of which Orlov could observe, or at least hear about, while he was fighting with Frederick a few years earlier.

147

At the end of the Sixth Section is represented Ceres, sitting on a stone, which exhibits on one side the Indian Triad, composed of Brahma, Vishnù, and Siva or Mahadeva, as it appears among the ruins of the famous temple in Elephanta, near Bombay, described by Niebuhr. (Voyage en Arabie, *Amst.* 1780, tom. ii. p. 25.) *The other side exhibits the head of Isis, as found on an ancient Egyptian brick, of which Count Caylus has given the figure in his* Recueil d'Antiquités (tom. iv. pl. xv. no. 4).

Figure 10: The first publication of Johann Reinhold Forster, who would later circumnavigate the world with Captain Cook.
Source: *Philosophical Transactions of the Royal Society*, 58 (1768), pp. 214–16

Competing with Frederick for a steady supply of colonists, Catherine made them a better offer; exemption from conscription was particularly important for the radical sectarians. Their organized communities survived the new life much better than the individual adventurists. The largest and the most successful group of colonies was established by the Moravian Brothers. They created booming towns on the Volga and daughter colonies in the south. Active missionaries, they converted thousands of Estonian peasants and played conspicuous roles in the imperial capital. In Russia they became known as Herrnhuters, from the Saxonian village, Herrnhut, where Count von Zinzendorf settled the Moravian refuges in the 1720s. Alexander I particularly favored them, visited Herrnhut, and gave the Brothers highly unusual privileges in the Baltics, which were soon withdrawn. Having had their best moment in the early nineteenth century, the Brothers remained influential for a long period. Aleksandr

Golovnin (2004: 53), the Empire's Minister of Enlightenment (1861–6), wrote in his memoirs: "In my mind there is much from my childhood, from the Quakers, from the Herrnhuters." Lev Tolstoy mentioned the Herrnhuters surprisingly often; he was influenced by their non-violence and by how hard they worked.

Immigrants came by ship to Kronstadt near St. Petersburg – the Ellis Island of Imperial Russia – and swore an oath to the Empress. They were then assigned to vast, practically unknown lands thousands of miles away. Accompanied by army officers, they traveled up the Neva, across the lake of Ladoga and further to Novgorod, repeating the ancient route of Rurik, whose story they might have known. Much later, Gottlieb Beratz (1871–1921), a parish priest on the Volga who was murdered by the Bolsheviks in Saratov, began his history of the German Colonies by mentioning Rurik, "the Norseman of German blood," as proof that Russia always welcomed foreigners (Beratz 1991: 2). From Novgorod, the colonists traveled overland to the Volga and floated downstream. The trip from St. Petersburg to the lower Volga took many months; many had to spend a winter on the way. Catherine's plan was such a success that, in 1766, some German rulers and princes collectively prohibited emigration from Germany. Nevertheless, it continued. After the Russian occupation of the Crimea in 1774, another religious group, the Mennonites, resettled from Prussia to contemporary Ukraine. Around 1818, still another wave of immigrants came from Germany. This time they were Pietists, who wanted to meet the coming end of the world, which they believed would happen where Noah had embarked on his ark, in the Caucasus. Some German colonists cultivated the lands around St. Petersburg, a difficult job in which the English Quakers, specialists in drying marshes, also participated.

Two colonial administrations, in Odessa and Saratov, were created. The new daughter colonies were organized in various places, from the Caucasus to the Altai. The Empire encouraged the communal character of these settlements. Leaving them was hard; a defector would have no property or rights whatsoever. With the consent of the state, members of the community were bonded to it, spiritually and economically. It was an example of success in indirect rule, which created stable and prosperous, albeit illiberal, proto-socialist communities. The Moravian Brothers did not own individual property. Land, cattle, and income belonged to the communities. They lived in dormitories that were segregated along gender lines and had their children raised in separate houses. They used no arms, obeyed their elders in everything including marital choice (which in some communities was entrusted to a lottery), ate meals collectively, entertained themselves by reading the scriptures, and worked the land with amazing efficiency. On the Volga, their towns, gardens, and fields looked like islands of prosperity and high culture. They influenced the Orthodox Russians, Muslim Tartars, and Buddhist Kalmyks who lived around them; some of the Russian sects on the Volga copied the radical beliefs of the Herrnhutters. But discontent among the colonists was also high. Reportedly, about 100 Germans joined the rebels of Pugachev when they massacred the Volga colonies in 1774 (Beratz 1991).

One hundred years later, the population of German colonists in the Russian Empire reached half a million. Exemplary tax-payers, they did not mix with their neighbors but they influenced them. Some of their children grew up bilingual; their contribution to Russian culture was immense and non-appreciated. The Moravian Brothers built Sarepta, which became a part of the city that would turn out to be best known as Stalingrad. Eduard Huber (1814–47), born in a little colony on the Volga, produced the first translation of Goethe's *Faust* into Russian. Working in Sarepta, Isaak Jacob Schmidt translated the New Testament into Kalmyk and Mongolian (Benes 2004). The colonies gave employment to some first-class Russian intellectuals, including Alexander Pushkin, who served in the administration of the southern colonies during his exile in the early 1820s.

The leader of the mid-nineteenth-century radicals, Nikolai Chernyshevsky, grew up in Saratov, the center of the Volga colonies. In his youth, Chernyshevsky befriended Pavel Bakhmetev, a son of the local seignior, and Alexander Klaus, a son of the German organist (Eidelman 1965). Bakhmetev later went to New Zealand to establish a utopian community there. Chernyshevsky was arrested in 1862, wrote his radical novel, *What is to be Done?* in prison, and was exiled to Yakutia. Klaus became head of the Saratov colonial administration. In 1869, he published his own book, which was provocatively called *Our Colonies*. In a move that was no less radical than Chernyshevsky's, Klaus presented his people, the German colonists in Russia, as the model for Russian peasants after Emancipation. Objecting to the liberal idea of individual rights, he contrasted it to the land arrangement of the Mennonites and other "sectarians." When they came to Russia, land was granted to them collectively, not individually. They could leave their colony but could not take with them their share of the collective property. As a result, a few of them left, definitely a lower proportion than that of the peasants who fled their fields after Emancipation. Klaus argued that this collective arrangement should be replicated in the legislation on the Russian peasant commune (Klaus 1869). His book continued the unusual tradition in which nineteenth-century social utopianism converged with the legacy of the sixteenth-century's radical Reformation. His recipe for Russian development was similar to the revolutionary gospel of Chernyshevsky, a trained historian who prophesized a leap from the peasant commune straight to socialism. The unique social arrangement of these internal colonies impressed many Russians, who found there a template for the good life before Marxism and independently of it. It was probably no accident that both Lenin and Trotsky had grown up in the colonized areas, the former among German colonists on the Volga and the latter among Jewish colonists in Ukraine.

The decline of the colonies started in the 1870s, when the imperial administration broke its promise by subjecting them to conscription and introducing Russian in their schools. In response, thousands of sectarians sold their land and left for North America. Ethnographic studies of these immigrants in America reveal that, even decades later, their local co-religionists perceived them as "Russians" (Kloberdanz 1975). About a million German descendants of the "colonists" stayed in Russia and Ukraine. They suffered terribly during the revolution and civil war of 1917–19, famines on the Volga in 1921–2 and 1932–3, and the massive deportations in 1937–8 that were ordered by Stalin's government. At the start of World War II, Alfred Rosenberg claimed all the land in southern Russia that was cultivated by Germans for the German Empire; this land, he said, was larger than all the plowed land of England (Yampolsky 1994: 165). A Baltic German who studied engineering in Moscow and loved to quote Dostoevsky, Rosenberg had educated Hitler in his early Nazi organization, "Reconstruction: Economic and Political Association for the East." He later became Hitler's Minister for the Eastern Territories during World War II (Kellogg 2005). The memory of German colonies provides some historical context to bizarre statements made by Hitler, such as "the Volga must be our Mississippi" (Blackbourn 2009: 152). It so happened that the battle of Stalingrad took place around the prosperous colony of Sarepta, which was created in Russia by the industrious, non-violent Germans.

Panopticon

In his famous rediscovery of the Panopticon, Michel Foucault (2003) did not mention that its first invention took place in Russia. The

British naval engineer Samuel Bentham traveled there in 1780. He was invited by Prince Potemkin to perform a wide variety of duties, from ship-building to brewing beer. In 1785, Potemkin invited Jeremy Bentham as well. The Bentham brothers worked in Krichev, one of Potemkin's estates in the newly conquered Ukrainian lands. Foreigners on the Potemkin estates were exempt from all taxes for five years. The land where Ukrainians, Jews, and Tartars had lived for centuries was being quickly settled by the colonists, most of them Germans and Greeks. Jeremy Bentham served as a secretary, while Samuel received the rank of Russian colonel. British industry was introduced into the Potemkin villages by military force. Samuel, however, was resourceful and flexible. He built an amphibious boat, which could be driven by oars in the water and run on wheels on land. He also built a "vermicular vessel," which could follow the course of Russian rivers. However, the Bentham brothers' major invention in Krichev was the Panopticon. It was a structure that combined the functions of factory and dormitory. The windows of the round-shaped multi-storied building looked inwards toward its courtyard. In the center there was a tower, which was devised in such a way that the workers would believe that they were under surveillance, whether the tower was empty or not, thereby creating the "apparent omnipresence" of power (Bentham 1995). British bricklayers started to build two such structures, in Krichev and further south, in Kherson. In Krichev, Jeremy Bentham wrote his treatise, *Panopticon*, which made him famous. The actual constructions, however, were not completed, because of the outbreak of another Russo-Turkish war and the unexpected sale of Potemkin's estate (Pypin 1869; Christie 1993; Etkind 2001a; Stanziani 2008).

Samuel Bentham was involved in the construction of an even more famous architectural phenomenon, the Potemkin village. Façades erected along the path of the Empress, who was heading south along the Dnieper river in 1787, the decorated villages deceived the eye with their splendor. In their games with truth, power, and vision, both inventions, the Bentham Panopticon and the Potemkin villages, wonderfully complemented each other. In fact, two key strategies of power – visual control and visible fiction – combined in the project of the Panopticon. It was while living on Grigory Potemkin's estate that Jeremy Bentham started to work on his famous theory of fictions. As if summarizing his various interests, the word "panoptikum," defined as a collection of sights and curiosities, entered Russian and German languages. Samuel Bentham traveled twice to Siberia and in 1788, presented Potemkin with a new project, a voyage to America:

he wanted to sail from Siberia, land on the Pacific coast, and reach New York with a detachment of Russian soldiers under his command. Potemkin showed little enthusiasm, so Bentham went instead for a vacation to England (Christie 1993: 253). He did not return, but, in accordance with his advice, a Panopticon was actually built near St. Petersburg, on the banks of the Okhta river in 1807. This time, it was designed as a shipbuilding wharf and school. The six-rayed building was 12 meters high, with a lift in the middle, so that all five floors of the building could be seen from the central tower (Priamursky 1997). On exactly the same spot where this panoptical structure stood, the Russian gas and oil corporation Gazprom was planning to build its headquarters, an enormous, cucumber-like tower that symbolized its power overseeing the land. This controversial project was suspended in 2010.

Conceived in Russia as a factory, the Panopticon was used in England as a prison. Jeremy Bentham left Russia in late 1787. Much later he wrote to Alexander I that two years in Krichev brought him "the richest observations" of his life. While Bentham saw the Napoleonic Code as "mere chaos," he proposed that the tsar adopt a new all-embracing legislation, which would all follow, as if from a central tower, from the principle of the general good (Pypin 1869). Time passed, and the project of the Panopticon caught the eye of Foucault. The Brits invented the Panopticon for a Russian colony and redesigned it for the Russian capital; nearly 200 years later, in Paris, it was redescribed as the prototype for all disciplinary practices.

Military Self-Colonization

After the victorious war with Napoleon, the Empire launched another large-scale colonial experiment. The returning veterans of the army that took Paris settled in newly constructed settlements, where they did the plowing and drilling. These large, scientifically organized plantations were first established near Novgorod, in the very heart of Russia; later, they were created in Ukraine and elsewhere. About a third of the imperial army was settled this way, and there were plans to locate all the infantry in northern Russia and the cavalry in the southern provinces (Pipes 1950). To create the necessary space, the local peasantry were resettled or mixed with the soldiers. The manor houses in these areas were bought for a symbolic price and the owners were forced to move out. In the bureaucratic documents of the time, routinely written in French, the new administrative units were called colonies; in Russian documents, they were called settlements. As happened in nineteenth-century France and its overseas colonies (Stoler 2009: 37), the Russified terms "colonist" and "colony" acquired multiple, interconnected referents. In various discourses, it could apply to an orphanage in Central Russia, a military settlement in Ukraine, a penal camp in Siberia, an outpost in the Caucasus, or a huge domain in Central Asia.

All military colonies were included in one imperial structure that was led by the artillerist Aleksei Arakcheev (1769–1834). Life in these colonies mixed various cultural elements. Bachelors married women who were chosen by their superiors, though one witness wrote that couples were chosen by lottery, exactly as with the Hernhutters (Petrov 1871: 159). Boys were educated in the "Lancasterian schools," which emphasized a system of mutual education, with the more advanced children helping to teach the less advanced. Invented by a British Quaker, Joseph Lancaster (1778–1838), these schools were popular in the English and Spanish colonies. Every colony had a standard plan, with a central square, huge public edifices, and an observation tower. On Arakcheev's estate, he had a particularly tall observation point which one of his better-informed guests compared to the Panopticon (Svin'in 2000: 143). Military colonies were outposts in a land that was foreign to them, and the purpose of their planners was to make these spaces entirely different from Russia. The Minister of Internal Affairs, Viktor Kochubei, wrote to Arakcheev that leaving a colony was like being "thrown from a land of education to a country of barbarism," as if by "some revolution of the globe" (Kartsev 1890: 87). Even now, the enormous ruins of colonial, classicist edifices stick out of the woods and marshes, with a local population insufficient to reuse its abundant brick.

"Foreign colonies" and "military colonies" in Russia were intimately connected. In the 1810s, which was the booming period for both experiments, two brothers, Pavel and Andrei Fadeev, directed the two state chancelleries that ran these colonies. Some German colonists were settled in military colonies as role models. But military colonies evoked much resistance. In a series of cholera riots in the 1830s, soldiers and peasants killed hundreds of officers and doctors; the rebels received corporal punishments, usually by gauntlets that often led to death on the spot. The concept of Arakcheevism became a popular signification for acts of arbitrary, cruel rule; one can find instances of this word even in Lenin's writings, more than 100 years after Arakcheev's death. The promise of financial self-sufficiency was never fulfilled. In 1857, a few years before the emancipation of the

Figure 11: A cavalry training ring with a church, part of the military colony in Selishche, near Novgorod, built in 1818–25.
Source: Wikimedia Commons

serfs, Alexander II disbanded the military colonies. The lands and works were transferred to the same Ministry of State Properties that was also administering the "foreign colonies."

Communes and Gauntlets

In the culminating scene of Aleksandr Pushkin's masterpiece, *Evgenii Onegin*, there is a peasant song, which is performed by young women while collecting berries for their mistress. They were forced, no doubt by the threat of lashes, to sing in a choir so that their mouths would be busy and they would not eat the berries: an "invention of rural wit," said Pushkin (1950: 3/66). In Lev Tolstoy's *Anna Karenina*, the seignior, Levin, finds a resolution to his existential problems in the ecstatic experience of collective, rhythmical scything with a group of peasants who accept him as a peer. It is not an accident that, in both examples, collective manual work was supplemented by an aesthetic activity – coerced singing while picking berries, or choreographed movements while scything. Though functional for specific forms of peasant labor, collective work was unusual. Still, the Empire treated peasants not individually, as they were most often treated in Europe, but in collectives.

When drafted into the army, which in the nineteenth century was all about collective movement, peasants were difficult trainees. Following the Prussian model, the Russian army practiced a highly specialized technique of scapegoating that consolidated the soldiers' collective. The soldier was dragged through the ranks of his colleagues, who beat him, one after another, with wooden rods of a standard length. A soldier who neglected this duty risked becoming the next victim of his community. Punishments were public not because the public watched the performance of an individual perpetrator, but in the deeper sense that these punishments were performed by a community of peers, with each member contributing exactly the same share of the punishment as the others. The death penalty was officially abolished in 1753, but running the gauntlet in the Russian Army often resulted in death. In 1863 the gauntlet was replaced with lashes, which were used as a supplement to the developing penitentiary system. As Foucault (2003) showed, public execution on the scaffold symbolized the power of the king. The gauntlet symbolized the power of the collective or, rather, the unity between the power and the collective.

In civil life, the peasant commune realized a similar function. It was publicly discovered by the Prussian official, August von Haxthausen, who visited Russia in 1843. He traveled into the heartlands with money and a translator provided by the Ministry of State Properties (Morozov 1891; Starr 1968). He went to the Volga to explore the German colonies there and interviewed some of the most radical Russian sectarians. His experience with the regular, Orthodox peasants was limited (Dennison and Carus 2003). But among them, he made the discovery that made him famous, the peasant commune which practiced regular repartitions of land among the peasants. The commune was "a well-organized free republic," wrote Haxthausen. In his Romantic vision, while the Russian elite lived westernized, petty lives that were based on private property and public corruption, the Russian peasant followed an entirely different tradition, hidden and hitherto unknown. Giving a racial interpretation to the concept, Haxthausen believed that the commune had its origin among the ancient Slavs. He found the same institution among the Serbs and believed that the indigenous Slavic population of Prussia also lived in the communes, before Germans arrived and destroyed them.

Widely practiced all over Russia, the commune remained unknown to westerners as well as to westernized Russians. One estate, the peasantry, lived in communes; other estates knew nothing about them, and the life of the gentry was particularly anti-communitarian. Haxthausen wrote that the peasants in the secrecy of their communal ways had already realized the "dreams of some of the modern political sects, particularly the St Simonians and Communists" (Haxthausen 1856: 132). Approaching the revolutionary year 1848, the word "commune" was in fashion; Haxthausen contrasted what he saw as the false French theories of communism to the true, noble Russian practice of the commune. As a conservative Romantic, a graduate of Göttingen, and a friend of the brothers Grimm, Haxthausen found in Russia precisely what he was looking for. No revolution, he said, would ever occur in Russia, because it had already been accomplished in a conspiracy shared by millions. Impressed by Haxthausen, Friedrich Engels started learning Russian, but Marx remained skeptical (Eaton 1980: 108; Shanin 1983). Engels referred to Haxthausen's discovery of the Russian commune in his famous *The Origin of the Family, Private Property, and the State* (1840) and even in the *Communist Manifesto*.

The first Russian review of Haxthausen's book emphasized parallels between his discoveries in Russia and colonial adventures in Africa and America with a healthy bit of irony:

> Our educated people will find a lot to learn from Haxthausen's book. Many of its pages will seem like a perfect trip to the interiors of Africa or even to Eldorado. . . . Yes, dear gentlemen, Eldorado is in Russia. But in order to see it, you have to take away the blindfold that your governors tied around your eyes in your childhood and that, in your maturity, the exceptional reading of western books supports. ([Anonimous] 1847: 10)

Enthusiastically supported by various groups of Russian intellectuals, Haxthausen's discovery of the commune produced an unusual consensus among the public. In 1851, the French historian Jules Michelet compared Haxthausen with Columbus and the newly discovered commune with the New World. Bitterly, Alexander Herzen concurred that Russians had to wait for the German to discover their own treasure, the commune (1956: 301). But as with Columbus, arguments about priority soon emerged. Aleksei Khomiakov claimed that he had discovered the commune on his own estate earlier than Haxthausen. They actually met in May 1843, and this conversation was probably the most important source of Haxthausen's information about the commune (Bogucharsky 1912; Druzhinin 1968). Apart from the petty question of priority, Khomiakov and the Slavophiles concurred that the Russian commune was an ancient, noble institution that embodied the soul of the Russian people.

In the 1840s, the Slavophiles grew beards, read Herder and Hegel, and explored the Orthodox Church. They condemned the foreign influences that they associated with the Petrine Empire, but found it difficult to articulate their own positive ideas. Rich serf- and landowners, they felt that the Empire did not provide them with existential comfort. In their quest for an organic community that would rely on Russianness and Orthodoxy, the Slavophiles struggled with the multi-ethnicity of the Empire. Their theocratic nationalism was adversely affected by the fact of the Russian religious schism, a seventeenth-century religious conflict that made a significant number of the bearded, pious Russians non-Orthodox (see Chapter 10). It was the Schism that made it impossible to imagine a Russian nation based on Orthodoxy. Repeatedly returning to this theme, Khomiakov developed an original strategy, which was different from that of his more fundamentalist friends. It was not so much theocratic but, rather, communitarian and racialized. He was one of the first to identify the colonial nature of Russia's clash with modernity (see Chapter 1). Like his French contemporaries such as Francois Guizot (Foucault 2003: 226), Khomiakov racialized the political problems of his time. The Russian aristocracy, the descendants of Viking warriors, presented themselves as racially different from other estates, the clergy and the peasantry, the descendants of the peaceful Slavs. While the monarchy strove to neutralize this racial discourse, Khomiakov re-enacted it. Perceiving the written law, governmental rationality, and, most of all, property rights as the legacy of the European colonization that started with Rurik, he elaborated the idea of the commune. According to this contrarian idea, the commune was the ancient custom of the Slavs that preceded the Norman conquest of Russia and survived it. This idea came as salvation and became the central tenet of Slavophilism.

Thus, from romantic nationalism the Slavophiles shifted to communitarianism, which valued custom over law, the oral over the written, and the community over the individual. Furthermore, they declared Russia's priority in these anti-modern values. Later, the commune had become equally important to those radicals who believed in socialism but who preached a particularly Russian path to it. Nikolai Chernyshevsky, who would soon go into Siberian exile developed a theory that, because of communal land-holding, Russia would escape capitalism. Since the future socialism would be built on the same principle of collective property as the commune, Russia would be able to reach socialism directly from its current condition, bypassing the hateful capitalism (Chernyshevsky 1856; Bogucharsky 1912; Walicki 1969; Dimou 2009). Nationalist movements in the colonies often affirmed their differences from the west in a similar way, constructing the "west" as materialist and individualistic and their own cultures as spiritual and communitarian (Chatterjee 1993).

Blending socialism with nationalism and combining ethnography, history, economics, and politics, the commune was a truly big idea, the grand narrative of Russian intellectual history. Boris Chicherin, a legal scholar who would become the major proponent of Russian liberalism and an elected mayor of Moscow, attacked Haxthausen in a much-discussed essay, which today would be called revisionist. Chicherin denied that the commune was an "ancient" institution and claimed that it was created in the imperial period. "The commune is a modern institution," wrote Chicherin (1856); it had nothing to do with the ancient Slavs and was created by the state for fiscal purposes. Essentially, Chicherin understood the commune as an incomplete analogue of the German-style municipality and credited Catherine the Great with importing it to Russia. But while the intellectuals were debating the origins of the commune, its actual power in the countryside was only increasing. The commune repartitioned land among its members, collected annual and special taxes, mediated between the peasants and the manor or the state, and chose recruits among the available young men, so that it could get rid of the troublemakers (Mironov 1985; Moon 1999). In the 1840s, the government strengthened the commune's disciplinary power even more, giving it the right to subject its members to corporal punishment or to send them to Siberia. The legislation of 1861 codified the emancipation of serfs from their lords but strengthened their dependence on the commune, which became the primary institution to structure Russian peasantry. Closer to the twentieth century, the commune became the main target of the struggle between the government, which wanted to emancipate the peasants from the commune and bring the land to the market, and the populists, some of them terrorists, who saw in these attempts the betrayal of both Russian and socialist ideas (Bogucharsky 1912; Gleason 1980; Wcislo 1990).

The peasant agricultural commune shared important features with the military institution of the gauntlet. In both cases, the gauntlet and the commune, the Empire delegated the execution of disciplinary practice to the grassroots level. The function of both institutions was to discipline the collective, suppress the private interests of its members, and, finally, reveal, expose, and destroy dissent. But of course, the commune was perceived as having deep national roots, while the gauntlet was regarded as an imported Prussian tradition – even the Russian name for it, *shpitsruteny*, sounds German. Russia's illiberal empire (Engelstein 2009) was based on an alliance between monarchical power at the top and practical communitarianism from below: both prevented the growth of the individual and capitalist development. As Chicherin showed, the commune was founded on the remains of customary law from the mid-eighteenth century, which was about the time that the gauntlet replaced the knout. "Such a communism is very easy to arrange, it is only necessary that there are lords and slaves," wrote Russian liberals (Kavelin and Chicherin 1974: 33).

Nowadays, scholars largely agree that the peasant commune was contemporaneous with the Empire, though the formative role of the state is a different issue (Atkinson 1990; Moon 1999). In the late nineteenth century, agricultural experts noted that in Siberia and other areas of recent colonization, the resettled Russian peasants created land communes spontaneously and without encouragement from officials, sometimes even despite new regulations that insisted on private ownership. Summarizing this evidence, an influential economist and historian of the peasants' resettlements, Aleksandr Kaufman, disagreed with the Russian liberal historiography. He maintained that the commune in the central and southern provinces also developed in a "self-generating way" that was similar to its development in Siberia (Kaufman 1908: 440; Shannon 1990). But he recognized that in the areas with an ancient agricultural population, e.g. in northern Russia, peasants developed individual farming practices with well-established property rights.

Kaufman was close to the conclusion that I formulate in my own language, which is not very different from his. In Russia, the commune was an institution of colonial ownership of land, which the settlers did not own or feel was theirs; it was also an institution for managing the population of settlers who were not attached to their land. In this institution, the peasants' interest in survival met with the state's interest in taxation and discipline. There was also a long-term tendency toward privatizing communal land, which eventually destroyed communes by converting its property to individual ownership. But only in the areas of the most ancient colonization, in the north, did this cycle reach its later phase.

Russia's most peculiar institution, the commune was different from the Soviet collective farm that replaced it. In neither institution did members own the land that they cultivated. However, members of the commune worked land individually or with their families, while members of the *kolkhoz* worked land together, in a collective which was modeled on an assembly line. First attributed to the industrial workers, the Marxist idea of the proletarian collective was then applied to peasants, prisoners, children, and the intelligentsia (Kharkhordin 1999). If there was a communitarian sentiment in the Russian village, through the Soviet period the *kolkhoz* destroyed it. Historically, the Russian commune showed huge variability over periods, areas, and types of property, but its mythology was more uniform. It was all about building a contrast between the higher and lower classes in Russia, a contrast as great as could possibly be imagined. While the higher classes of the Empire developed sophisticated laws of private property and means of self-expression, among the lower classes, so the story goes, life and land did not belong to the individual but to the collective.

The Reversed Gradient

The maritime empires made a clear, sharp distinction between their citizens and the subjects in their colonies. While citizens in the metropolitan areas enjoyed a progressively growing number of political rights, the subjects in the colonies were deprived of them. Throughout the course of the nineteenth century, metropolitan territories were developing into nation-states while preventing their colonies from doing the same. The difference between the political rights of the citizens of the metropolitan states and those of their colonized subjects translated into perceived and, often, real differences in their economic freedoms, educational access, and, finally, their life standards and prosperity. One could call this complex sum of inequalities, which was constitutive for western empires, *the imperial gradient*. Its consequences were simple: the centers of empires enjoyed a better life than their colonies.

In a way that was unusual for "traditional empires" but probably typical for terrestrial ones, the Russian Empire demonstrated a reversed imperial gradient.[1] Only Russians and some other eastern Slavs were subject to serfdom. At the beginning of the nineteenth century, the majority of the nobles in the Empire were non-Russian, though this situation changed later (Kappeler 2001). In about 1861, education and income were higher among Poles, Finns, Ukrainians, Siberian settlers, and, arguably, even among Tartars and Jews, than among the Russians of the central provinces. The Emancipation began with reforms at the periphery of the Empire and from there moved to the heartland. After Emancipation, Russians were still subjected to heavier economic exploitation than non-Russians. In the 1880s, an administrator in the Caucasus reported to the Ministry of Finances that while the local population in the Caucasus was "much richer" than the "hungry dwellers" of the central Russian provinces, the taxes on the former were four times lower than those on the latter (Pravilova 2006: 265–8). At the end of the nineteenth century, the average resident of the 31 provinces with a predominantly Russian population paid twice as much tax as a resident of the 39 provinces with a predominantly non-Russian population (Mironov 1999). Financially and demographically, colonization of the Caucasus and Central Asia throughout the nineteenth century produced losses for the central provinces: their population was decreasing, while taxation was increasing. In Siberia, the natives paid 2–10 times less to the state than the Russian peasants of the same region; in addition, they were exempted from the draft (Znamenski 2007: 117). The life expectancy of Russians was lower than that of the Baltic peoples, the Jews, Ukrainians, Tartars, and the Bashkirs. The internal oppression of the imperial nation was a "remarkable feature of the socioethnic structure" of Russia (Kappeler 2001: 125; Hosking 1997). On the eve of the revolution, "the impoverishment of the center" became a popular topic in political debates. Even the Jews, who were oppressed by the special regime of the Pale, recognized that their condition was better than that of the Russian peasants in the central provinces (Nathans 2002: 71).

[1] Making a similar point, Brian Boeck (2007) explains the unusual privileges of the Russian periphery by detailing the special deals that the Russian Empire cut with the frontier societies in the early eighteenth century. Peter Holquist (2010b: 462) attributes the concept of the privileged peripheries and the underprivileged core of the Empire to Boris Nolde, a politician and historian who served in 1917 as the Deputy Minister of Foreign Affairs under Pavel Miliukov (Nolde 1952).

Indirect Rule

In Russia, colonization often meant collectivization. Subordinating large ethnic communities, the Empire divided them into smaller, collective units of indirect rule that mediated between the sovereign and individual families. On vital issues such as taxation, draft, and even crime, the sovereign dealt not with the individual or his family, but with the community. Created as socio-spatial units, these communities were imagined like cells in a healthy organism, separate but connected. Such a cell could be led by a noble who owned the land and the peasants, or by an administrator who was appointed by the state, or by an elder who was elected by the community. Most of their duties before the sovereign were the same. Much smaller than the Ottoman *millets*, Russian territorial communities were endowed with some rights of self-government and self-taxation. In exchange for tribute, taxes, and recruits, they received non-interference into their religious and cultural life. As scholars of colonialism know well, indirect rule prevented the development of national sentiments and outbursts of violence (Hechter 2001); but it had its limits. The advance of modernity brings the individual subject, and his family, into immediate contact with the state. Intermediary levels, apart from the temporary and voluntary ones, tend to lose their power (Gellner 1998; Slezkine 2004). Individual freedom and mobility provide the economy and culture with the vibrancy that is characteristic of modern societies. Competing with European powers, the Russian Empire could not escape the same process. However, leveling the boundaries between the estates and destroying the particularity of the communes had its dark side (Mann 2005). The advance of modern nationalism, the universal draft, and a uniform educational system increased the chances of ethnic discrimination, forced migration and emigration, pogroms, and other forms of ethnic cleansing.

Having developed within various national traditions, liberal theory presented voluntary associations as the primary institution of civil society. On the contrary, "involuntary association is the most immediate cause of inequality" (Walzer 2004: 2). For the Russian Empire, the idea of free entry and exit was entirely foreign. The subjects did not create their groups and did not choose among them. The enforced, territorial character of their communities meant their members were bonded twice: to the land where they lived and to the group to which they belonged. These groups contained the whole life cycle of their members. Born within these groups, most of them worked and married within them, had children who stayed within these groups, and died as their members. Therefore these groups were strong, their meanings thick, and their boundaries barely passable. While the ruling elite structured itself as a solar network of individuals and institutions with the Emperor at the center, the subjects of the Empire were organized as a cellular structure, like the body or, perhaps, a beehive.

The sovereign gave the land not to individual settlers, but to the entire collective as a whole. This land could not be sold or mortgaged. Individuals and their families did not own the land they used; in the case of the Russian peasantry, the land was repartitioned with every new generation – or even more often. People were settlers on this land, not masters of it. Various obstacles hampered departure from these communities. Until its very end, the Empire did not encourage the development of a market in land, particularly of agricultural land. It did not wish to deal with individual agents, only with nobles, administrators, or elders, who managed hundreds of peasants each. Communes did not communicate amongst themselves; all transactions were vertical, between each commune and the hierarchy leading to the sovereign. For a long period, starting from the mid-eighteenth through the turn of the twentieth century, this beehive system organized the enormous space of the Empire. Throughout the imperial period, this system emerged among peoples with very different traditions. A system of indirect rule, it had to be neutral in terms of culture and ethnicity.

As a codified law, the cellular system of settlers' colonization was first written for the German colonies on the Volga. Moving from one province to another, a group of top imperial administrators introduced this system elsewhere, though the practical results were different. Trying to create a uniform imperial pattern that could be applied to all ethnic cases, they compared their policies across the Empire and exchanged good practices among themselves: "We permit a *mufti* for the Islamic peoples, and so why not a leader among the Jews?" asked Gavriil Derzhavin; in his project of reforming the Jewry, he used the model of the German colonies on the Volga (Klier 1986: 107). Among the Tartars, the Empire applied the same template and created the magistrates in the Muslim environment (Lowe 2000). In western Siberia, Mikhail Speransky divided the Kazakhs into districts, with the elders collecting taxes from the communities on the basis of customary law, "adat" (Martin 2001). One of the most seasoned Russian bureaucrats, Speransky, came to Siberia from St. Petersburg after he helped to codify the innovations into serfdom and drafted the Charter of Military Colonies. The imperial Minister of Finances who oversaw many of these developments, Egor Kankrin, started his career as the inspector of the German colonies near St. Petersburg.

The Pale of Settlement was the Jewish colony of the Empire (Rogger 1993). Though overall restrictions on the migration of Jews were unusual, in many other ways their treatment was not unique; in fact, the policy toward the Jews did not much depart from governmental actions toward other religious minorities. In the 1830s, the Jews of the Pale were treated by law in the same way as the minor Polish nobles, whom the Empire downgraded to a taxable estate. Having colonized the Jewish part of Poland, the Empire found in operation there the ancient Jewish unit of self-governance and tax collection, the *Kahal*. In 1844, the Empire issued a decree that forbade the *Kahal*, forcing the Jewish settlements to conform to the structure of the Russian commune, which was then in the process of codification. In fact, the Empire failed to change the structure of Jewish self-government, but it did undermine its traditional authority (Dubnow 1920: 227; Stanislawski 1983: 48, 124). This story has usually been told as the unsuccessful application of the institutional norms of the Russian commune to the Jewish *Kahal*. However, the reverse was also true: known to Russian administrators since the eighteenth century and much debated in the 1840s, the collectivist structure of the *Kahal* was transposed onto the peasant commune. In fact, indirect rule helped to reduce violence and other expenses of the Empire. The abolition of the *Kahal* reflected the imperial pattern toward the uniform, cellular regulation of all populations, Russian and non-Russian alike. Like serfdom, the Pale was an instrument of imperial domination, with communes and *Kahals* as parallel structures of indirect rule. Imperial administrators explained their resistance to the emancipation of serfs and the desegregation of the Jews in similar terms, referring to their immaturity or backwardness. As Hans Rogger demonstrated, governmental anti-Semitism corresponded to a similar complex of sentiments and prejudices about the Russians. While the imperial "elites shared a genuine and deep-seated fear of the destructive, anarchic power of the Russian mob," imperial administrators agreed on "a pessimistic assessment of their own ability to control popular violence" (Rogger 1993: 1219). Much earlier, Vasilii Kliuchevsky characterized this state of affairs, which he felt was typical for the nineteenth-century Russian gentry, as "complete moral confusion: nothing can be done and nothing needs to be done" (1990: 100). This self-fulfilling pessimism helped the managers of the

Empire to avoid their responsibility: when a peasant rebellion, a Jewish pogrom, or an abuse of their own power occurred, the authorities did little because they felt they could do nothing.

Though the advance of imperial rule was everywhere different, its unwinding was more uniform. Like a boomerang, the Empire's increasingly violent methods of domination spread centripetally from the periphery inwards. Massive migrations, forced or voluntary, accompanied the process. In the spirit of "imperial revisionism" (Mann 2005: 31), the new, organic ideology translated into attempts to make the draft, taxation, and official language universal across the Empire. While the active introduction of indirect rule began with the German colonies, the unwinding of this mechanism began with the Jewish Pale. Forbidding the *Kahal* while preserving the Pale meant introducing direct rule over an enormous ghetto. East European Jews under the Russian yoke responded with two protest movements that defined the twentieth century, Zionism and Communism (Slezkine 2004).

The bet on the Russian land commune was equally fateful. Started as a cultural myth, the commune materialized into a disciplinary mechanism that organized life and work in an enormous space, from the Atlantic to the Pacific. Closer to the end of the nineteenth century, the economic liberals in the imperial government wished to dismantle the commune, to bring land to the market, and to emancipate labor. To replace the commune, they created new, larger and relatively democratic institutions of indirect rule in the countryside, *zemstva*. Further legislation allowed many thousands of peasants to start their own farms. Despite the economic success of these reforms, they met resistance from an unusual source, the armed intelligentsia. Inspired by the intelligentsia's populist beliefs, its terrorist underground tried to force the leap from the commune to communism. This confrontation between the fans and foes of the commune was a major factor leading up to the Russian revolution. Finally, the collectivization of 1928 resuscitated the communal myth in a new and pernicious form.

With the end of the High Imperial Period, Russia approached its age of reforms, but in the final account, things went wrong. Despite the emancipation of serfs and many other changes, the Empire failed to escape its collapse and the waves of violence that followed it. This lesson has been discussed myriad times, but it is still pertinent for the twenty-first century globalization, which confronts some of those very problems that Russia's rulers faced in the nineteenth century. Direct rule over a segregated society – a collection of estates, ghettos, and state-patrolled borders – is not viable. The last Romanovs successfully dismantled the old imperial order that kept different communities under an indirect rule, which prevented violence but was economically inefficient. But in this Empire, the undoing of indirect rule was followed by massive outbursts of violence. Polish rebellions and Caucasian wars marked the first half of the nineteenth century. The massacres of the sectarian villages in the 1870s, the Jewish pogroms of the 1880s, and the populist terror marked its second half. Culminating in the revolutions of 1905 and 1917, these events responded to the innovations in imperial unification, such as equal taxes for different estates, the universal draft, the destruction of the commune, and mandatory primary education. Steps on the ladder of modernity, these innovations had their dark side, which was "the ladder of violence" (Mann 2005). In good conscience, the imperial reformers built the shining ladder of progress, but they misjudged the danger of its dark side, the ladder of violence. Or it was one and the same ladder.

The dismantling of the old order of collective, territorial subjects should have gone hand-in-hand with the cultural neutralization of the state and universal access to education and careers (North et al. 2009). If the Russian imperial experience can teach us anything, the image of the interconnected but antithetical, light and dark vectors of modernity is the lesson. To avoid a Russian-style collapse, the transition from indirect to direct rule should provide an equal chance for prosperity to every individual citizen. The metaphor of progress is not a single, vertical ladder but a free-standing, folding one. The two parts of the ladder of modernity, global unification and universal access must be of equal height or they will collapse.

— 8 —

Internal Affairs

In a recent essay, Willard Sunderland (2010: 120) asks why imperial Russia never created a Ministry of Colonial Affairs. The person who asked this question the first time, August von Haxthausen, stated that Russia had to establish a colonial ministry, "like England, although in a somewhat different sense" (1856: 2/76). But even this proposal was too little too late. An answer to the question of why Russia did not have a colonial ministry is that it did have one, or two.

Intellectuals in Power

The motto on the coat of arms of Count Lev Perovsky, Minister of Internal Affairs of the Russian Empire (1841–52), said, "Being, not Seeming." An illegitimate son of Count Aleksei Razumovsky, Minister of the Enlightenment (1810–16), Perovsky earned his title by service in proximity to Nicolas I. His motto was devised by Vladimir Dal, a military surgeon who authored the magisterial dictionary of the Russian language and was also the head of Perovsky's special chancellery (Melnikov-Pechersky 1873: 310). As it happened, to achieve "being," the minister surrounded himself with writers and scholars, experts in deceitful disciplines of "seeming." In Russian intellectual history, people of the 1840s have usually been represented as highbrow idealists, connoisseurs, and devotees of German romantic philosophy (Berlin 1978). Those in the Ministry of Internal Affairs belonged to a different species. Political foxes rather than romantic hedgehogs, these intellectuals knew a lot about power and eagerly demonstrated their value, as intellectuals, to those in power. Within their lifetime, knowledge gave power over nature. Science created vaccinations, navigation tools, and other successes that everyone could appreciate but only specialists could apprehend. In a similar way, sophisticated, specialized knowledge about the population – as these intellectuals would say, about the People – would provide power that would be beneficial to the People and the Empire. Being was different from hearsay, though only trained professionals could differentiate between them. The apparent phenomena that were accessible to the public were irrelevant to the art of governing. In the 1840s and 1850s, the Ministry of Internal Affairs hired first-rate philosophers, orientalists, and, in particular, many writers.[1] This was a brilliant group of intellectuals. The contemporaneous staffs of the imperial universities in Moscow or Petersburg were negligible in comparison to this group.

The Empire was entering the new age of rational, bureaucratized modernity, when the nobility needed experts and became experts themselves (Weber 1979: 973). Producing millions of documents every month (Lincoln 1982), the Ministry of Internal Affairs controlled enormous areas of general administration, including the nation-wide police force, healthcare, and censorship. It managed most of the communications between the sovereign and the provinces; it appointed provincial governors, sent inspections, drew maps, oversaw roads, and ruled over the religious and ethic minorities. Though it did not have power over the serfs, it defined rules for the seigniors. The habits of aristocratic rule felt obsolete, but replacing them was difficult. Cameralism, a Germanic science of government, introduced the statistics of population, budget accounting, and economic rationality; but its practice was very different from its theories (Wakefield 2009). Though edited by the philosopher Nikolai Nadezhdin, the journal of the ministry was increasingly filled with statistical tables along with detailed maps, technical blueprints, and psychiatric case studies. The famous Schlözer had taught statistics to Perovsky's father, and the ministry tried to introduce some of these scientific devices; but they were not the only methods in vogue there. Under Perovsky and even much later, the majority of high officials in the ministry were generalists (Orlovsky 1981: 111). Even by nineteenth-century criteria, many were still dilettantes: a medical

[1] The philosophers were Nikolai Nadezhdin, Konstantin Kavelin, and Petr Redkin. The Orientalists were Ivan Liprandi, Vasilii Grigoriev, Pavel Savel'ev, and Iakov Khanykov. The writers were Pavel Mel'nikov, Ivan Turgenev, Ivan Aksakov, Vladimir Odoevsky, Vladimir Sollogub, Nikolai Saltykov-Shchedrin, Evgenii Korsh, Nikolai Leskov, and others.

doctor wrote a dictionary, a philosopher practiced ethnography, an intelligence officer invented religious studies, and an orientalist censored the press. There were aspects of the imperial experience and control which found better expression in high literature or collections of folklore than in the emerging statistics. The very scale of the Empire, the enormity of its problems and the miniscule numbers of the ministerial stuff, required a writer, preferably a romantic sentimentalist with his broad vision, quick pen, and heroic propensity for simplification. As one of the employees of the ministry, the satirist Nikolai Saltykov-Shchedrin, wrote in the 1860s, "I am a publicist, a metaphysician, a realist, a moralist, a financier, an economist, and administrator. If needed, I can become even a friend of the people" (Saltykov-Shchedrin 1936: 10/71).

The minister's father was a Ukrainian Cossack, a nephew of the secret husband of Empress Elizabeth. Trained at home, he became Minister of the Enlightenment. Married to the richest heiress in Russia, he fathered 10 children with a daughter of his horse groom, one of them the future Minister of Internal Affairs, Lev Perovsky. The most popular novel of the period, *Ivan Vyzhigin* (1829) by Faddei (Tadeusz) Bulgarin, featured a bastard, the illegitimate offspring of an aristocratic, Ukrainian-based family, who made his way through various trials, including beggary, prostitution, and a clandestine religious sect, to finally reach high imperial posts. A Polish intellectual, Bulgarin shifted his allegiances from being an officer of Napoleon's army to an agent of what today would be called Russia's secret service; he penned hundreds of pages of reports and denunciations for this agency (Reitblatt 1998). In the Empire, the rivalry between various law-enforcement agencies was routine; Bulgarin provided it with a literary dimension.

Though illegitimate, the Perovsky brothers occupied the very top of the imperial pyramid. After his spell as Minister of Internal Affairs, Lev became Minister of Crown Lands and Director of the Imperial Cabinet until his death in 1856. The eldest bother, Nikolai, a member of the mission to China in 1805, was later Governor of the Crimea. Vasilii was General-Governor of Orenburg in the Southern Ural, from where he led a series of colonial endeavors that began with remarkable failures but resulted in the Russian annexation of Central Asia. Close to literature and very close to the dynasty, in 1839 he read to the imperial family the most sacrilegious text of Russian poetry, Lermontov's *Demon*, which would be forbidden for publication for several decades (Gershtein 1964: 69–73). In the 1870s, Lev Tolstoy planned to write a whole novel about this Perovsky.

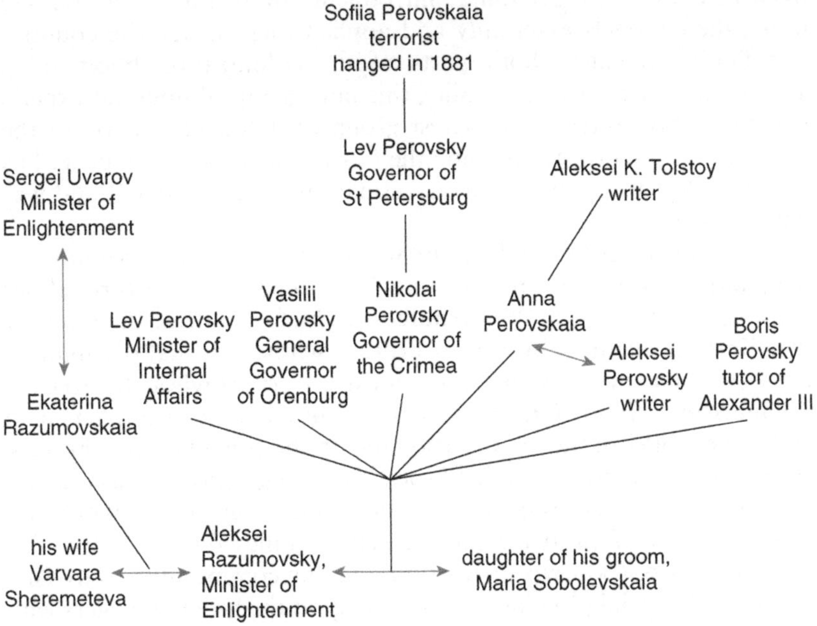

Figure 12: The Perovsky descendants of Aleksei Razumovsky (1748–1822).
Source: A. Etkind

The younger Aleksei became known as the writer Antonii Pogorelsky. A socialite and the author of several novellas, he is remembered mainly for a fairytale, "Black Hen," in which the little protagonist sees a group of ministers even in his night dream. The youngest brother, Boris, was tutor to the future Emperor, Alexander III. Sergei Uvarov, Minister of the Enlightenment and the author of many initiatives of the period, was a brother-in-law of the Perovskys. Through the decades of the rule of Nicolas I, the clan of Perovsky brothers competed with the clan of Pashkov sisters, who were married to the Minister of Justice and the two most powerful leaders of the State Council (Korf 2003: 73).

The Perovsky brothers collaborated on many levels. A friend of Pushkin and other literati, Aleksei connected his brothers to the literary elite; he recruited Vladimir Dal for his service in the colonial administration in Orenburg under Vasilii Perovsky. Later, Dal moved from Orenburg to Petersburg to serve in Lev Perovsky's Ministry of Internal Affairs. Some other officials moved in the opposite direction, from Petersburg to Orenburg. Introducing innovations, the Empire tested their models externally and applied them inside the country; one family managed both parts of the colonization boomerang. Trained in justice and rationality, this new group of imperial experts inevitably gave birth to the latest group of dissidents. A son of the eldest Perovsky brother became the Governor of St. Petersburg. His daughter, Sofia, organized the assassination of Alexander II and was hanged in 1881.

The Ministry of Internal Affairs was in charge of legal, administrative, and agrarian reforms. Starting from the 1830s and throughout the larger part of Perovsky's tenure, the chief of staff of the ministry was Karl von Paul, a Moravian Brother whose unusual disciplinary ideas created conflicts with the provincial governors whom he oversaw (Shumakher 1899: 109). From early 1840, Perovsky implemented collective works in the estates belonging to the royal family. This new regime, which Perovsky called "social plowing," forced peasants not only to pay their taxes collectively, but to do their actual work in a collective way. Typical for the German colonies on the Volga, this method was not known in Russian peasant communities. Perovsky introduced "social plowing" with the help of the hired managers who

Figure 13: Vasilii Perovsky on the capital of a column, 1824. Portrait by Karl Briullov.
Source: Wikimedia Commons

received, in a very capitalist way, a percentage of the output. A little later, the Ministry of State Properties, led by Count Pavel Kiselev, emulated and rivaled Perovsky's model among the state peasants. Kiselev's previous job had been the administration of lands that constituted contemporary Moldavia and Rumania; he also brought his external experience to the internal governance. His ministry sponsored Haxthausen's trip to Russia and, therefore, the discovery of the Russian commune. The idea of the commune flourished among philosophers and lawyers within the Ministry of Internal Affairs, though the agricultural specialists of the ministry knew that communal land usage was an impediment to productivity (Lincoln 1982: 123). The Emancipation of 1861 made the commune the central mechanism of social and financial control in the countryside. Though the actual reforms were penned after Perovsky's term expired, the leading authors made their careers under his auspices. Lev Perovsky was also a very rich landowner who was able to hire a British manager to oversee his estates. In anticipation of the reforms, he was buying up cheap peasants in the impoverished central provinces and resettling them to his land in the south. Unlike the protagonist of *Dead Souls*, Perovsky speculated with living peasants (see Chapter 10).

As minister, Perovsky once ordered a map "of all the corners of the State, with marking by different colors all the various tribes, aliens, and natives" (Liprandi 1870b: 111). Empires have always been obsessed with maps, which often were models for, and not models of, their actual possessions (Brubaker 1992; Suny 2001; Stoler 2009). Perovsky had no interest in standardizing political rights or economic goods across the Empire, but rather welcomed the variety of the imperial colonies, provided that they could be controlled, mapped, and taxed. The imperial space was filled with these imagined communities, colorful and exotic. Groups, not individuals, were the units of imperial rule. The ministry took responsibility for drawing the correct boundaries between these multicolored groups, for comprehending their organic essences, and for harmonizing their relations for the sake of the common good. In these ceaseless efforts, the ministry was concerned even more about confessional communities than about ethnic ones.

Especially Dangerous Sects

In 1843, Ivan Liprandi organized the ministerial "Committee for Schismatics, Castrates, and other Especially Dangerous Sects." With origins in the Spanish gentry, Liprandi founded Russian counter-intelligence during the Napoleonic Wars, pursued lifelong studies on oriental languages and politics, and sought police measures against the Slavophiles whom he believed to be a sect. He was a friend of Pushkin and the protagonist of some of his stories (Grossman 1929; Eidelman 1993); his investigation of a political conspiracy resulted in Dostoevsky being sent to a labor camp in Siberia. A true imperial thinker, Liprandi wrote:

> Fortunately or unfortunately for Europe, the idea of natural boundaries and national unifications has been disseminated among the nations. . . . In itself, the idea is sublime and enduring, as it satisfies the natural inclinations of human nature, but in practice it . . . will drown Europe in crimson flows of blood. At first, Turkey and Austria will become sacrifices of this great but fantastic idea; then it will overturn all of Europe, and finally spread beyond its borders to other parts of the world. (Liprandi 1870a: 234)

Since "different lands of one and the same tribe" are often more hostile to one another than to "an alien race," Liprandi predicted the collapse of German and Italian unification efforts. Russian imperial power had to rest not on tribal pan-Slavic feelings, but on the power of information and coercion. Since "tribes" did not matter, Liprandi saw his task as exploring and exploiting other, less evident units of imperial management. Following this logic, he singled out religious communities as his special subject. Working mainly with police files and missionary reports, he made himself into an early and incomparable expert in the Russian Schism, which he categorized into "sects," some of which manifested a "dangerous" or "very dangerous" character. He evaluated the total number of these sectarian communities at six million people, which was approximately ten times more than what had been estimated earlier. Interestingly, his intuition of the mutual hatred between similar peoples (better known to us as the Freudian "narcissism of small differences") did not apply to the sectarians. On the contrary, he believed that many of these variegated communities were integrated into one "confederative religious republic." This republic within the monarchy had large capitals, its own means of communication, and even a secret language, which the ministerial linguist, Vladimir Dal, was commissioned to put to paper. It was precisely the sectarians' secrecy that justified the efforts of the illustrious intellectuals of the ministry (Liprandi 1870b: 107). A discovery of a colony inside the mother country, this confederation was mapped not geographically but theologically. But it needed policing, and urgently. Among the sects, Liprandi revealed such horrifying vices as "incest, sodomy, the unpunished cohabitation of women with women," and the belief that "movable property belongs to everyone" (immovable property, land, did not belong to peasants anyway). "Is it not a true communism?" asked Liprandi (1870b: 82–5). Equally grave was Liprandi's suspicion that these religious schismatics from the people communicated with the political dissidents from the elite, an inter-estate conspiracy that had been the nightmare of Russian authorities since the famous trial of the publisher Nikolai Novikov in 1792.

Liprandi published this memorandum, "A Brief Survey of Russian Schisms, Heresies, and Sects," in 1870 and dated it 1855, but intellectual circles in St. Petersburg had already read it in 1851 (Annenkov 1989: 510). The memo invented new realities on a giant scale. Huge numbers of people, some of them rich, some noble, and many entirely obscure, were described as a single political community, a republic within the monarchy, which was arranged on an unheard-of, revolutionary base and was fundamentally hostile to the empire. It was possible though, Liprandi believed, to take action, and if not destroy this underground community completely, then at least reduce its danger. Liprandi proposed to chose individual agents among both the sectarian and intellectual communities and, "having established personal relations with them, smartly induce mutual hostility between the communities." He also proposed to start "a focused, secret surveillance of the Schismatics, whose very existence is an important Evil" (Liprandi 1870b: 131).

Liprandi composed this memo while embedding one of his spies in the reading group lead by Mikhail Petrashevsky, a translator for the Ministry of Foreign Affairs whom Liprandi and his colleagues sent to Siberia in 1849 after a mock execution. Fyodor Dostoevsky was also a member of this group. Using his agent, Liprandi was trying to uncover the connection between these western-minded elitists from St. Petersburg and the folkish Schismatics. Simultaneously, he was trying to launch a new and larger affair, a trial of the Moscow Slavophiles, whom in his "Brief Survey" he listed as a sect, "the secular Schismatics." In fact, the Slavophiles did communicate with the Old-Believers; for example, they organized theological debates with them in the Kremlin.

Rumors that the sect of Skoptsy (Castrates) had bribed Liprandi destroyed his reputation, and in 1855 Pavel Melnikov, a provincial official who later became a writer most known for his novels about the Schism, replaced him in his position. Other religious experts in the ministry were Afanasii Shchapov, a former professor of history and a future Siberian exile (see Chapter 9), and the young journalist Nikolai Leskov, another future celebrity (Chapter 11). Leskov recorded the fierce debate between two parties, "the hesitant Melnikovians" and "the resolute Shchapovians," that was taking place in the 1860s. According to the former, every Schismatic was a debaucher, while, according to the latter, every Schismatic was "a little Fourier of a sort" (Stebnitsky 1863: 39). Divergent narratives by the two leading experts on the Schism, the conservative Melnikov and the radical Shchapov, competed for control over governmental policies. In the bureaucratic world of the Ministry of Internal Affairs, these visions complemented one another. Shchapov's idea of the political nature of the Schism only justified police measures against sectarians.

The New Alliance

In Gogol's *Inspector-General*, the central character is an impostor who pretends to be doing what officials of the Ministry of Internal Affairs regularly did: an inspection of a distant province with all its ignorance, chaos, and corruption. Curiously, among the things that this character brags about is his friendship with Pushkin, which makes the provincial officials and their daughters tremble.

In 1843, Ivan Turgenev started his service in the Ministry of Internal Affairs. His boss there was Vladimir Dal, and he worked on another project of agrarian reform. An extended memo, "Some Remarks about the Russian Economy and the Russian Peasant," was one of Turgenev's first written works (1963: 1/459–75). A rich landowner, he resigned in 1845 to publish his great masterpiece, *A Sportsman's Sketches*, in several parts, starting in 1847. Turgenev's *Sketches* had a larger impact on Russia's internal affairs than did dozens of ministerial memos. The mainstream Russian encyclopedia declared with a characteristic mixture of dependency and hubris: "[T]he role of *A Sportsman's Sketches* in the emancipation of serfs was equivalent to the role of Beecher Stowe's *Uncle Tom's Cabin*, with the difference that Turgenev's book is, aesthetically, incomparably higher" (Vengerov 1902: 99). In 1852, Turgenev was arrested for his obituary of Gogol and, after a month in the police station, was exiled to his own comfortable estate. Later, he wrote his novels about Russian life while living in Western Europe.

After his appointment to the ministry in 1848, the young lawyer, Ivan Aksakov, went to Bessarabia (Moldova) to study its remote though powerful community of Old-Believers. There in the steppes, he started writing a poem, *The Wanderer*, with a free, wandering peasant as the protagonist. Upon his return to St. Petersburg the following year, he was arrested in the context of the forthcoming investigation of the Slavophile circle, which his chief in the ministry, Liprandi, proclaimed to be a dangerous sect. Nicolas I personally ordered Aksakov's release (Sukhomlinov 1888). Aksakov was sent to the province of Yaroslavl as an inspector-general, a job that to a recent prisoner probably felt too close to Gogol's play. Known as a center of the Schism, Yaroslavl fascinated Aksakov. Combining both his tasks, of inspector of bureaucracy and researcher of the Schismatics, he wrote to his father that Russia would soon split into two halves: the Orthodox that takes bribes and the Schismatic that gives bribes (Aksakov 1994: 177). In one village on the Volga, Aksakov and his colleagues from the police discovered a sensationally new community, the Beguny (Runners). These people saw it as a sin to spend two nights in one place. They rejected money, property, and family. Understandably, Aksakov gave up his poem, *The Wanderer*, and wrote an extensive report on the "sectarian community" of wanderers. His report became the only source of information about the sect; nobody else could locate them, though many tried (see Chapter 9). Having heard about the poem, Perovsky requested its text and must have been puzzled by the coincidence. Though he found nothing dangerous there, he asked Aksakov to make a choice between creative writing and state service. Aksakov resigned and returned to his estate. He became a leading figure among moderate Russian nationalists, an editor and publisher.

Among these aristocrats, heirs of beautiful manors with hundreds of peasants attached, the boundary between the office and the prison was strangely unstable. Another writer with the blood of a Rurikide, Nikolai Saltykov-Shchedrin, was exiled for his writings in 1848 to the remote though still European province of Viatka. He served there in the governor's office and continued writing, until he was given a position in the Ministry of Internal Affairs in 1855. Traveling for inspections, he collected impressions for an astonishingly broad and equally aggressive satire on many aspects of Russian officialdom. He later became Vice-Governor of Riazan province and the favorite writer of Lenin.

Though most of the classical Russian authors did not serve in offices, many of their male protagonists did. One of the explanations is that the officials and their families constituted a major part of the reading public. Seeking readers' responses, the seigniorial authors imagined scenes in harems, battlefields, madhouses, and other interesting places. But very often, they depicted scenes in the offices. Having turned from Romanticism to Realism, mid-nineteenth-century literature provided narrative models and the stylistic training that were required for paperwork in the imperial offices. The Deputy Minister of Internal Affairs, Aleksei Levshin, who came to the ministry after a long service in the colonial provinces of Orenburg and Odessa, wrote that during the preparation of the Emancipation of 1861, "literature provided a great service to Russia by espousing its variegated views and explications on the question [of serfdom], which had earlier remained a full mystery, a *terra incognita*" (Levshin 1994: 84). The influence went both ways, from the office to fiction and from fiction to the office. History, philology, and the erstwhile Tsarina of the humanities, ethnography, were construed as applied sciences that had their legitimate places in the tool-kit of the rulers. Applying this rhetoric to the practice of governing, the Ministry of Internal Affairs could pursue its agenda despite the virtual absence of social statistics and economic data. Nikolai Nadezhdin, then a professor of philosophy at Moscow University who would later become a top official of the ministry and the founding father of Russian ethnography, said early in 1831 that a new "Holy Alliance" was about to emerge, between the humanities and the practical life of the people. He derived this formula from the ruins of the Holy Alliance between the European powers, created by Russia at the Congress of Vienna in 1815. Nadezhdin's dream of the new Holy Alliance would lead Europe on the basis of uniquely Russian discoveries, made within the applied sciences in their studies of the Russian people (Nadezhdin 2000: 2/736–48). Working in the Ministry of Internal Affairs from 1843, Nadezhdin took part in the production of an outstanding body of scholarship, in which he partially realized his dream of the new Holy Alliance. The Russian Geographical Society, with its vanguard section of ethnography, was created by Nadezhdin, Dal, and other associates of the ministry and was financed from its funds (Lincoln 1982; Knight 1998). Supported by Grand Duke Konstantin, the Minister of the Navy who was also the leader of the 1861 Emancipation reforms, the Russian Geographical Society focused on the investigation of the Russian heartland rather than the global world. The richest collection of Russian fairytales, the ground-breaking study of Russian sects, the best-known dictionary of the Russian language, and the pioneering studies of non-Russian subjects of the Empire were all realized in the ministerial circles. The participants of this movement knew of its colonialist nature as well as of the crucial connection between power and knowledge. As Vladimir Dal wrote in 1842:

> Let's take an example which is close to our purposes. Say you have the task of developing the principles and foundations for processing the language of some Pacific islanders; it is supposed to transform, to re-educate these savages, to give them literacy, upbringing and to adjust their baby-like babble. . . . What would you begin with? Of course, you would start from the very beginning, from the study of their language, as coarse, wild, poor, and unprocessed as it is. Then on this foundation . . . you would build further on. This is what we have to do. (Dal 2002a: 424)

Writing the Dictionary

A close friend of Pushkin, Vladimir Dal nursed this poet in his mortal agony after a duel in 1837. Dal was trained as a Navy officer and military doctor; he was also an engineer, ethnographer, linguist, and popular author. His father was a Danish Lutheran, his mother a French Huguenot. He was born in Lugan, on the territory of contemporary Ukraine, a colony which was shaped in the mid-eighteenth century by refugees from the Balkans. A few decades later, a Scottish engineer found ore and coal there and Dal's father, the German-trained theologian, settled in Lugan to serve in the mining factory. Vladimir learned Russian from his St. Petersburg-born French mother, who spoke five languages. His written Russian was beautiful, but there is little doubt that his foreign origin contributed to his interest in this language. The author of the most famous dictionary of Russian, Dal completed most of this enormous work far from the Russian heartlands; his informants were soldiers, craftsmen, and other folk involved in imperial projects.

Dal started to work on his Russian dictionary during his Navy service in 1819 on the Baltic Sea. Interviewing soldiers, he enriched his collection of Russian words when he served as a military doctor in imperial campaigns in Turkey, Poland, and Central Asia. The major work on the dictionary was done during his service as a civil official in Orenburg, the steppe frontier of the Empire, where he also took part in the military expedition to Khiva (contemporary Uzbekistan) in 1839–40. Though this ill-conceived expedition was a tragic failure, it paved the way for the Russian colonization of Central Asia. Dal completed his dictionary while he served in St. Petersburg as head of the personal chancellery of the Minister of Internal Affairs, Lev Perovsky. His unusually long and rich career as an imperial officer creatively combined the tasks of external and internal colonization. His multiple moves between geographical locations and bureaucratic offices reflected the shifts between what were then "the external" and "the internal" in the Empire.

Wherever Dal's uniformed body fulfilled his imperial duties, his unquiet mind remained in the heartlands of Russian language and folklore. Walking before a dinner near his friends' estate near St. Petersburg, Dal met a cleric who introduced himself as a monk of the Solovetsky monastery. In a brief conversation, Dal recognized his Volga accent and was able to identify the province and even the district of his actual dwelling. A moment later the alleged monk, who was a runaway serf, was groveling at the feet of the linguist (Melnikov-Pechersky 1873: 289). Besides his magisterial dictionary, Dal published multiple volumes of Russian fairytales which he allegedly heard from the common people and wrote down during his travels. "I think in Russian," he wrote. "A human mind belongs to those people whose language this mind uses" (Dal 2002b: 258). But he was pursued by nationalist hostility throughout his entire career. In 1832, he was arrested for his fairytales, in which authorities found political hints that they found unacceptable. Dal's literary friends helped him get out of jail. In 1844, Lev Perovsky commissioned Dal to compose a study of the Skoptsy, the Russian sect that castrated its followers for pious reasons. When Nicholas I learned that the author was a Lutheran, he ordered Perovsky to find an Orthodox author for such a delicate subject (Nadezhdin reworked and signed this essay). Also in 1844, Perovsky ordered a new investigation of the old question: did the Jews of the Empire commit ritual murders? The ministry issued an anti-Semitic pamphlet in two versions, though neither of them was circulated; one pamphlet was signed by Dal.

In the late period of Dal's life, his essays took a distinctively counter-Enlightenment turn. From objecting to the spoiling of the Russian language with foreign words, he switched to an outright denial of the value of literacy for the folk. A radical historian who belonged to the next generation noted that Dal and his circle perceived a "dissonance between the life of the educated class and the life of the common folk. They hoped that this dissonance could be ameliorated by their new cult of the people, but they had no idea how. . . . The writers and ethnographers of this school actually

«А. С. Пушкин и В. И. Даль в виде святых Косьмы и Дамиана».
Икона XIX в.

Figure 14: Pushkin and Dal presented on an icon as St Kozma and St Damyan.
Source: Pravoslavie i ateizm v SSSR. Muzei istorii religii i ateizma. Leningrad: Lenizdat 1981

played the hostile role of spies and detectives in the life of the people" (Pypin 1890: 1/418–19). Dal's dictionary, the huge success of his life, also invited many doubts and criticisms. Some ethnographers accused Dal of inventing entries; others glorified this dictionary as a monument to the richness of Russian language. This debate continued well into the twentieth century, when Vladimir Nabokov admired the dictionary and used it routinely, while Boris Pasternak ridiculed its artificial language. A Swedenborgian and a committed believer in spiritism who organized experiments with rotating tables and ghost apparitions, Dal converted to Orthodoxy before his death.

In 1848, Perovsky asked Dal to destroy his notes because keeping them at this anxiety-ridden time could be dangerous even for these high officials; Dal obeyed and burned hundreds of pages of precious material. The few pages that survive present him in a strangely melancholic light. He was pursued by suspicions and accusations; his only consolations were his domestic life, his irreproachable service, and his humility:

> The generosity of the Minister of Internal Affairs secures my domestic needs. . . . Should I be listening with quiet humbleness to accusations that are insulting to the loyal citizen and subject? Should I give up the best part of my noble name, of my honor? . . . Our feelings and contemplations are hidden; a human being cannot reveal them before his judges. . . . But one finds humility in suffering. Humans are given patience and unshakeable faith in the future. (Dal 2002b: 262)

These unhappy musings sound as if they came from the memories of his Huguenot mother; it is surprising to read them in the notes of a highly successful imperial bureaucrat. If Dal had not destroyed his papers under the pressure of his chief, we might have had many more documents of this genre. Executing disciplinary power over the Empire, this quintessential intellectual wrote and thought under ceaseless suspicion from the outside and under doubt from within. Was he exploring Russians or inventing them? Was he legitimate in doing either of these things? Were he, his power, and his work real or merely spoken of? Adoring the language of the common folk and devoting his lifetime to writing down their words, he denied literacy to these same people. Embodying truly imperial, cosmopolitan skills and talents, he abused them for the sake of a gruesome nationalist message.

In mid-nineteenth-century Russia, sentimentality turned into the grotesque. This affinity was also a part of the imperial experience. It is exciting to reimagine Gogol's story, "The Nose," as happening in the Ministry of Internal Affairs, with Kovalev asking Dal for the position of vice-governor, Dal interviewing Kovalev about his provincial dialect, and both anxiously guarding their disobedient parts.

System of Tenderness

An official of the Ministry of Internal Affairs, a colonial administrator, a professor of oriental languages, and the chief censor of the Empire, Vasilii Grigoriev (1816–81) applied his orientalist knowledge to various tasks of imperial power. Promoting projects of external and internal colonization, he mixed them as he and his bosses saw fit. By training, Grigoriev was a typical nineteenth-century orientalist who graduated from a specialized department at St. Petersburg University, spoke several Asian languages, and wrote on issues ranging from archeology to linguistics to cultural criticism. In 1837 the young Grigoriev applied to the University Council with the syllabus for a new course, "History of the East":

> The spreading and strengthening of Orientalist interests in Russia would give us more autonomy and work as a counter-balance to the Western elements which oppress our national development, and would support this development. . . . The best way to resist the influence of the West is to rely on the studies of the East. (Veselovsky 1887: 33)

Orientalism was Grigoriev's profession, nationalism his preoccupation. Russians needed to study the east because it facilitated a particular way of understanding themselves. As at other moments of his career, Grigoriev's positions seemed more hawkish than those of his superiors, and his program was rejected. From 1844, he served as a civil servant in the Ministry of Internal Affairs. He helped Nadezhdin to edit the journal of the ministry and penned multiple studies on subjects as diverse as the condition of peasants in the central provinces, book-printing in Riga, and the newly discovered Judaic sects. In the Hasidic Jews, he saw "extreme ignorance, horrible illiteracy"; in the "sect of Talmudists," as he called the majority of the Jews, he saw "a major danger for Russia" and "the misery of human kind" (Grigoriev 1846). In 1847, Grigoriev and his friend, Pavel Savel'ev, who was also an orientalist, bought a St. Petersburg journal, *The Finnish Messenger*, which they renamed *The Northern Review*. Among others, this journal published Mikhail Petrashevsky who would soon go to Siberia; curiously, while Liprandi was implanting an agent into his group, Grigoriev was publishing essays and translations that were written by the same group. In this journal, Grigoriev started the propaganda of Haxthausen's views on Russia ([Anonimous] 1847; Seddon 1985: 267). In 1848, Grigoriev traveled into the central provinces with the commission to learn how the nobles and the peasants were responding to the rumors of revolution in Europe. In 1849, he inspected bookstores in Riga, confiscated 2,000 books, and fell sick as a result of the book dust.

Invited by Vasilii Perovsky, in 1851 Grigoriev left the capital for Orenburg, the actual east that had become a part of Russia. Until 1863, he served in the provincial governance of Orenburg and also as chief of the administration of the Kyrgyz frontier. Living the tumultuous life of a colonial administrator, he organized punitive expeditions and took part in military offensives. He mapped borders of the occupied territories and arrested rebels. He wrote laws, established courts, and ran investigations. He performed all these multiple tasks without any legal training or even military experience. However, he never stopped studying the "orientals" and never failed to miss any opportunity to refer to his background in academic orientalism. "As an orientalist, I, for my sins, understand Asia and the Asians, while those who control my actions know nothing about either," he wrote from Orenburg in 1858. "The Kyrgyz steppe is trembling before me. I arrest the sultans and catch the bandits but, extremely unfortunately, I have no power to hang them." Justifying his cruelty, Grigoriev did not hesitate to use his academic erudition. While the Kyrgyz unrest was developing, he wrote in a personal letter: "I invented a fine method . . . a deeply Machiavellian trick, and I did it because I read books and was not an official from the cradle. Long live books!" His method was another series of punitive measures. With much excitement, he positioned himself somewhere between Genghis Khan and Liprandi: "Now, Genghis Khan is nothing for me. I have purchased a beautiful Kyrgyz hat, have grown a beard, and in a glorious robe . . . run 16 investigations at once, *à la* Liprandi" (Veselovsky 1887: 134, 139, 118).

Grigoriev believed in his superiority over his bureaucratic colleagues because of his professional, orientalist knowledge: "What would happen to these gentlemen if something seriously dangerous were actually to occur on our borders?" In response, these colleagues, most of them military officers, saw him as an extremist and put restraints on his activities. When another rebellion began in the steppe, Grigoriev blamed the pliability of his superiors. "This system of tenderness brought the administration of the Kyrgyses to the same end that brought Russia its pliability in relations with Europe." Exoticizing the natives, Grigoriev presented them to the Emperor and the metropolitan public on the basis of racist preconceptions; he proposed sending to the coronation of Alexander II "several fine-looking figures in tall hats with golden embroidery and brocade caftans with galloons" (Veselovsky 1887: 140, 146). In the end, the orientalist became involved in a conflict with the governor-general, Vasilii Perovsky, and applied for retirement. His academic background made this linguist even more hawkish in colonial policies than were his military-trained colleagues. From Orenburg, he also managed to take part in literary debates in the capital. One of his essays, a long and disrespectful obituary of his former classmate, a historian of Europe, Timofei Granovsky, caused a scandal. On top of his gossip about Granovsky, Grigoriev tried to show that Russian scholars should turn their backs on western history and literature; only oriental studies could be useful for Russia and only in this field was Russian scholarship higher than European. "The dirtiest among dirty men," wrote the leading Russian liberal, Boris Chicherin, about Grigoriev (Pirozhkova 1997: 146).

To be sure, Grigoriev's orientalism was non-traditional (Knight 2000; Schimmelpenninck 2010). With his knowledge, Grigoriev worked for the imperial domination over the eastern colonies *and* over the imperial nation itself. Immediately after his return from the Kyrgyz Border Administration, Grigoriev became a professor of oriental languages at St. Petersburg Imperial University. He also took part in several ministerial committees: for Asian trade, for taxation of the Kyrgyzes, for surveillance over university students, and for convict prisons. In 1872, he became a member of the "Jewish Committee" which considered proposals to abolish the Jewish Pale. Grigoriev's opinion was based on his "scholarly" knowledge of the issue. "All evil results from the fact that Jews do not want to work productively." To allow Jews to settle beyond the Pale would be dangerous to all the peoples of Russia, he wrote in another anti-Semitic memo. "Whoever once falls into the hands of the Jews will never be free of them" (Veselovsky 1887: 251).

At the end of 1874, Grigoriev was appointed Head of the Ministry's Main Directorate on Print, i.e., the highest censor in the Empire, a post he fulfilled while remaining a professor at St. Petersburg University. He controlled the opening of new publications and the curtailment of existing ones, the process by which they would pass through censorship, and the system of fines for those who transgressed. He was involved in various high-profile affairs. He authorized the publication of Dostoevsky's controversial *A Writer's Diary* without preliminary censorship, but the sick and disgraced Nikolai Nekrasov, known for his populist stance, had to plead for leniency on behalf of Grigoriev. When an unhappy journalist visited him in his high office to complain about the prohibition of his newspaper and received cynical treatment, this journalist wrote that he felt like a Kyrgyz whom Grigoriev had left to die in the steppes (Gradovsky 1882: 499). Grigoriev interfered in state policy on the Ukrainian language, which he preferred to call a "little-Russian dialect." In a long note, he explained that the ban he had imposed on Ukrainian publications was a response to the danger of separatism: "To allow the creation of an autonomous folk literature in the Ukrainian dialect would be to promote the separation of Ukraine from the rest of Russia" (Veselovsky 1887: 265). Almost at the same time, in 1876, he chaired the International Congress of Orientalists in St. Petersburg and opened it by giving his speech in French.

Grigoriev's career is broader than Said's concept of orientalism; probably the best concept for it is Saltykov-Shchedrin's term "Tashkent-ness" (see Chapter 1), the Russian version of the imperialist boomerang that applied the orientalist habits of rule onto the imperial nation. Moving from the university to the Ministry of Internal Affairs to a provincial administration in the east, and back to the university and to the Ministry of Internal Affairs, Grigoriev had an ambitious career as an imperial administrator whose variegated duties were based on his orientalist expertise. In St. Petersburg and Orenburg, his knowledge and attitudes were in demand by the highest powers, which was why he succeeded in making a grand career. What, indeed, was not the east in Grigoriev's Russia? The Kyrgyzes were definitely oriental and, thus, were subject to orientalist rule. But so too were Jews, and Ukrainians as well. And also convict prisoners on their way to Siberia. And also university students, who were restless and therefore, subject to Grigoriev's expertise. And of course, the writers in Petersburg and Kiev, who were trembling in front of Grigoriev like the Kyrgyzes in the steppe. For Vladimir Dal, internal colonization led to a positive version of orientalism, a stereotyped reasoning that affirmed the moral superiority of the exoticized subjects, Russians and Cossacks. For Vasilii Grigoriev, orientalism worked straightforwardly as discrimination and coercion, which, "extremely unfortunately" for him, stopped short of hanging the natives. But he did hang novels.

Through the High Imperial Period, Russia's internal affairs were intrinsically connected to Russian literature. Top officials of the Ministry of Internal Affairs maintained close relations with well-known writers even after the illustrious Lev Perovsky, the man who wanted "Being, not Seeming," had departed from the ministry. Perovsky's successor, Sergei Lanskoi, married the writer Vladimir Odoevskii's sister. Lanskoi's successor, Petr Valuev (who was a prolific author himself), married the writer Petr Viazemsky's daughter. Some famous characters in Lev Tolstoy's novels, such as Ivan Ilich and Karenin, are described as officials of the Ministry of Internal Affairs. The realist novel became the genre of nationalism everywhere in the western hemisphere (Anderson 1991). The same was true in Russia, but despite the nationalist motifs of many of its classical pieces,

Russian literature played an integrative rather than a divisive role. More than any other aspect of imperial culture, literature accepted the Shaved Man's Burden and carried it nobly. Throughout the enormous space of the Empire, the cult of Pushkin became a belief system for people who shared little or nothing else. In Dostoevsky's *Idiot*, two unusual friends, an impoverished prince and an Old-Believer merchant, spend time reading "all of Pushkin" together. A Russian rebel, Vladimir Lenin, studied Pushkin in the gymnasium, where his teacher of Russian literature was the father of his arch-rival, Alexander Kerensky; Lenin loved Saltykov-Shchedrin and, unexpectedly, Turgenev (Valentinov 1953). A Zionist rebel, Vladimir (Zeev) Jabotinsky, wrote in his memoirs that he knew "all of Pushkin," as well as Shakespeare in the Russian translation, from the age of 14; but he also wrote extensively about the imperial, chauvinist, and anti-Semitic motifs in Pushkin and other Russian classics (Jabotinsky 1989). A Polish rebel, Apollo Korzeniowski, the father of Joseph Conrad, self-consciously modeled his major play on Griboedov's *Woe from Wit*. When Russian populists, Zionists, and Muslim activists met in a tsarist prison, or later in the Soviet gulag, they discussed the great Russian writers up to Tolstoy. In the long run, Russian literature proved to be an extremely successful instrument of cultural hegemony. With its classics, heretics, and critics, it conquered more Russians, non-Russians, and Russian enemies than any other imperial endeavor. Standardizing the language, creating a common pool of meanings, and integrating its multiethnic readership on an enormous scale, this literature was a great asset. The tsars and the censors rarely understood or appreciated it. Thus, the Empire collapsed, but the literature outlived it.

Part IV

Shaved Man's Burden

— 9 —

Philosophy Under Russian Rule

"Grass is needful for the ox, which again is needful for man . . . but then we do not see why it is necessary that men should exist," wrote Kant in *The Critique of Judgment*. However, casting his thoughts to the north and asking the same question about "the Greenlander, the Lapp, the Samoyed, the Yakut, etc.," Kant gave an answer and it was negative: "[I]t is not clear why people should have to live in there at all. . . . It could only have been the greatest unsociability among men which thus scattered them into such inhospitable regions" (Kant 2007a: 155–61).

The postcolonial philosopher Gayatri Chakravorty Spivak states that while Kant's readers understand his philosophy as universal speculation about humanity, he drew a line between the savages and the people of reason: "The subject as such in Kant is geopolitically differentiated" (Spivak 1994: 26). Indeed, "Why should men exist?" is a different question from "Should men live in Tahiti or in Siberia?" In Kant's logic, living in places like Königsberg, being sociable, and making use of their reason, men could realize the purpose of their existence. But in places such as Yakutsk, unsociable men could not understand themselves and, therefore, had no purpose. However, people always travel to places like Yakutsk in search of furs, oil, or diamonds. So the next question would be: in these inhospitable but profitable places, which men should live – natives with no purpose, or whites with it, or both, in some sort of hierarchical order?

Königsberg

In this part of the world, the Middle Ages started fiercely but ended quietly. Founded by a monastic order of Teutonic Crusaders, Königsberg became the center of hostilities between the Germanic,

Baltic, and Slavonic peoples. But then, the Northern Crusade, the fur trade, and, finally, the Hanseatic league were all exhausted. Throughout the eighteenth century, several northern wars ended in Russian triumphs (Frost 2000; Scott 2001). More than anywhere else, Russians combined military conquest of this area with the absorption of local elites. Starting with Peter I, the Romanovs recruited their spouses and successors from the Baltic coast. In the early years of the Russian Academy of Sciences, which opened in 1725, four out of five of its presidents came from the University of Königsberg (Kostiushev and Kretinin 1999).

During the Seven Years War (1756–63), the Russian state annexed eastern Prussia. The war followed fervent pan-European negotiations that historians call, with some justification, a "diplomatic revolution" (Kaplan 1968). When the war started, increasingly bizarre events occurred in Königsberg. In 1757, the Russians came close to its gates but retreated for no apparent reason: the poor health of the Empress, Elizabeth of Russia, was the reason for hesitation, though this was a state secret (Anisimov 1999). While the Prussians celebrated this turn of events, Elizabeth recovered, arrested the top Russian commander, and sent the troops back. Meanwhile, the Prussian king, Frederick the Great, was busy protecting his capital, Berlin. With the Russians near its gates, Königsberg accepted the same deal as Riga had in 1710: the city became a part of the Russian Empire and escaped massacre. Annexing eastern Prussia, the Russian Empire turned it into its province "forever." On 24 January 1758, the officials of the city took an oath to the Russian Empress.

Winston Churchill called the Seven Years War the very first world war. Its imperial context is well established (Anderson 2000; Schumann and Schweizer 2008). Starting with the attack of the young George Washington on a fort in French Canada, the war extended into the Old World. While England and France were fighting over colonies overseas, other powers were struggling for colonies in Eastern Europe. A true product of the Empire, the Russian army featured many Baltic Germans in its leadership. Its infantry was mostly Russian, and its omnipresent light cavalry included the Kalmyks, Bashkirs, and Cossacks, who fought under their native commanders. Frederick the Great explained the power of the Russian assault by "the number of Tartars, Cossacks, and Kalmyks that they have in their armies" (Wolff 1994: 171). Later, Kant considered the "Kalmuckians" as a separate race along with Negroes and (Native) Americans (2007b: 92), a highly unusual racial classification based on his personal experience with the Kalmyks in Königsberg.

The eighteenth-century military revolution was indecisive in Eastern Europe (Frost 2000); although the Russian Army employed the latest artillery inventions, it still relied on light cavalry and ethnic troops. Even the Russians perceived these oriental regiments as exotic and fearsome. The young officer, Andrei Bolotov was shocked to see the "strange," "half-naked," "horse-eating" troops massacring German villages for the sake of the Russian crown (1986: 124). The Kalmyks were allowed to loot the old Prussian arsenals; armed with medieval helmets and sabers, they probably looked ridiculous. Those were the last years of their service to the Russian Empire; in 1771, the Kalmyks left the Russian steppes for China in a mass exodus (Khodarkovsky 1992: 182). The Cossacks were equally unhappy. In 1773, they started a large anti-imperial mutiny in the Urals, which was led by Emelian Pugachev who fought as a Cossack in eastern Prussia. The general who finally defeated and arrested Pugachev also started his career there in Prussia. Bolotov (1986: 125) saw the summary execution of Prussian non-uniformed combatants who were captured shooting the Russians. Two were hanged publicly; eleven had their fingers cut off by Russian soldiers. Later, Bolotov attended Pugachev's execution in Moscow. For him, orientalizing the part helped to rescue the whole, which was the overall feeling of his and his peers' Europeanness:

> Everywhere was devastation, arson, and burglary. . . . The cruelty and barbarism of our Cossacks and Kalmyks was against all the rules of war. . . . Nothing was seen in all these places but fire and smoke and the greatest ferocity and dishonor to the female gender. . . . These actions of our Cossacks and Kalmyks gave us little honor because, having heard of their barbarity, the European nations imagined that all our army was this way. (Bolotov 1986: 123)

The Russian armies and their allies made quick successes against Frederick. Berlin was taken and overrun by Russian and Austrian troops in 1760. Bolotov (1931: 2/34) heard that journalists in Berlin were supposed to run the gauntlet for writing "bold and hurtful things" about Russians, but they received an eleventh-hour reprieve. In any case, Berlin suffered more than Königsberg; Frederick was on the verge of suicide. Nobody doubted that once the Russian crown had annexed eastern Prussia, it would remain a part of the Empire, and locals would have to adjust to the new order.

The brief colonization of Königsberg, with its Teutonic glory and enlightened university, was an outstanding event. But the situation changed spectacularly with the death of Empress Elizabeth in January 1762. Her heir, Peter III, adored Frederick the Great and all things Prussian. In no time, Peter pulled Russia out of the Seven Years War and signed a separate peace with Frederick. The scale of the change in St. Petersburg surprised everyone. Officially, Königsberg became a Prussian city again in August 1762. The Russians were preparing the general withdrawal of troops from Prussia when Peter III was dethroned by a conspiracy that was led by his wife, Catherine. The Russian governor, who was still stationed in the city, issued a declamation about his return to power. The story seemed to take yet another turn, but Catherine the Great decided against a new war and withdrew the troops from Prussia. After the long and victorious war, Russia had made no gains. The bloody series of events turned out to be entirely senseless.

Intrigue and Melodrama

Centuries later, Hitler hoped for a repeat of Frederick's miraculous survival when the Soviet troops encircled Berlin. Historians have ceaselessly debated the causes and results of those mid-eighteenth-century events that shaped Europe. The Cambridge historian, Herbert Butterfield, called this series of diplomatic and military events "intrigue and melodrama"; it was more intense than at any other time in European politics, "the last two decades excepted," he wrote in 1955. Butterfield believed that Russia was the main culprit behind the conspiracy against Frederick the Great, but the philosopher-king did not understand this fact even after the war ended, and nor did historians: "The attention of historians suffered a lapse in regard to those things which related to Russia" (Butterfield 1955: 162, 158). In the later writings of the German historian and theorist, Reinhart Koselleck, a sense of shock still surrounds the Seven Years War. Koselleck compared the events at the start of the war with the German–Soviet pact of 1939, but he characterized the events at its end as "historically matchless." Writing in 1968, he used the whole episode to illustrate the role of chance in history (Koselleck 2004: 118, 124). Later historians agree that the chief players all featured an extraordinary "talent for the unexpected" (Schweizer 1989: 179, 217; Palmer 2005: 150). Unknowable factors such as secret diplomacy, personal chemistry, and rulers' health, played decisive roles in this confrontation of absolutist regimes. For those who observed the war from within Königsberg, it was stripped of any understandable meaning. If historians are still running out of metaphors when confronting these events in Prussia, what could the citizens of Königsberg, who did not know a fraction of what we today know about their war, think about it and about their ability to understand it?

The Russian occupation of Königsberg established a colonial regime that was not unique in Europe but was unusual for German lands. From 1757 to 1762, eastern Prussia was a colony of the Russian Empire, as Livonia had been earlier (since 1710) and eastern Poland would be later (since 1772). Nobody in the land could know what we know now, that the Russian regime in Königsberg would end in less than five years, any more than they could know that it would be re-established centuries later.

One could agree that the Russian occupation of Prussia was not too painful, relatively speaking. The Russian administration there struggled with cultural and political problems that are typical for any colonial regime. Troops were stationed in the city, a Russian governor took over the administration, and Russian currency was introduced. The burgers of Königsberg became Russian subjects. However, Elizabeth promised to respect their traditional rights, including religious liberty. Wartime taxes were reduced, but the draft of recruits, which was tough under Frederick, was replaced by an additional tax. Only one of the many Lutheran churches of the city was converted to Russian Orthodox. Various projects streamed from St. Petersburg, some of them utopian or, rather, dystopian. By special decree, citizens of eastern Prussia were invited to resettle in Russia, though no results were achieved at that time (Bartlett 1979: 20; Kretinin 1996). This project of inward resettlement, in which the victors invited the defeated to settle on their territory rather than the other way around, was unusual in the history of imperial conquests. In his attempt to play a political strategist for the Russian crown, Denis Diderot propagated population transfers and used the Russian–Prussian war as a case in point:

> If the Russians had done the right thing when they were in Berlin, they would have taken away the whole capital – men, women and children, workers, manufacturers, furniture – and left behind only the walls. . . . If this transfer of population had been proposed to me, I would have taken care that it should occur in the most orderly way possible. (Diderot 1992: 112)

Diderot wrote this retrospective advice to Catherine II after his return from Russia in 1774, when the Seven Years War had become history but a civil war between the Empire and the colonized peoples of the Southern steppes, led by Pugachev, was under way. The philosopher did not fail to instruct Catherine about what to do with the Cossacks: "What I say of the Prussians, I say too of the Cossacks." What was good for external colonization was good for internal colonization too. In fact, there was not much difference between the two.

The colonization of Königsberg encountered silent resistance on the part of the natives, who were convinced of their superior culture, complied with Russian rule and rulers, detested them in their quiet way, and responded with a pioneering nationalist movement that had tremendous consequences for European thought. I submit that Russian rule established a "domination without hegemony" (Guha 1997), a typically colonial situation in which the rulers practiced coercion without managing to persuade the natives of their right to do so, or even of their ability to rule. This situation invited deep questions about power, reason, and humanity, some of them for the first time ever. The Russian attempt at colonizing Königsberg became an entry point into modernity, a prototype of the condition that has been re-enacted myriad times later and often, with reference to those who experienced it then, in Königsberg.

Kant

In 1755, Kant defended his dissertation and became a university lecturer. His major work of this period, *Universal Natural History*, began with a dedication to Frederick II, "the mightiest king and master," from his "most humble servant." In the same formula, he promised to serve his king "with the utmost devotion until my dying day." Scholars do not doubt that he was sincere: "Kant's identification with the king's program has long been recognized" (Zammito 2002: 58). But only two years later, Kant had to take an oath to Frederick's mortal enemy, Elizabeth, promising her that he would be "loyal and true to the Illustrious and All-powerful Empress of all the Russias . . . and to her heir"; moreover, if anything were undertaken against them, not only would he "inform the authorities forthwith, but also try to thwart the deed" (Gulyga 1987: 31). In 1758, Kant submitted to Elizabeth his application for a professorship, calling her, oxymoronically, "the most enlightened, the most autocratic Empress" and signing his letter, "in the deepest humiliation," "the most faithful subject and slave" of Her Imperial Greatness. Separated by three years, these ritual constructions promised perpetual service to two mortal enemies. Later, Kant would call such flip-flopping people, "turnspits." It was precisely this lack of autonomy that was the target of the great critical offensive that Kant later undertook.

The professorship was given to one of Kant's rivals. A Soviet scholar of Kant believed that the reason for his failure was the interference of a Russian officer, Andrei Bolotov (Gulyga 1987: 36). Bolotov, a translator who worked for the Russian governor of Königsberg, brought a small group of Russian students to lectures at the University. Having discovered philosophy among the other pleasures of Königsberg, Bolotov preferred Pietism to what he perceived as the spoiling, even criminal, influence of the Enlightenment. For many months, he attended lectures on philosophy given at the university by Kant's rival, Daniel Weymann. On top of the university course, Bolotov took private lessons with Weymann "almost daily." Weymann refused to charge fees for these lessons, but when departing from Königsberg, Bolotov left his teacher of philosophy "a Kalmyk fur coat," a perfectly Russian present (1986: 382).

We know only that Bolotov liked Kant's enemy, but there is no evidence that Bolotov influenced Kant's promotion case, though he probably could have. Together, Bolotov and Weymann read the works of philosopher-theologians such as Christian August Crusius, whom Frederick II declared his enemy and banned from Prussian universities (Zammito 2002: 272). Under Russian occupation, these right-wingers came into vogue again. Bolotov felt that their moralistic, scripturalist philosophy helped him to discipline his mind, to live a moral life, and to resist the seduction of gallant balls and commercial sex that were booming under Russian rule (Bolotov 1986: 347). One can understand that he responded better to this instruction than to those exercises in natural history that were Kant's official interest in the time. When Kant called Weymann "a Cyclops" (1992: lvi) and declined to participate in a public debate with him, he probably knew about Weymann's connections in the Russian administration. The long-standing conflict between Kant and Weymann was re-opened by their publications on optimism, a crucial issue in the occupied city. "Why, I ask in all humility, did it please Thee, Eternal Being, to prefer the inferior to the superior?" asked Kant in an essay written in 1759. In response, he reverted not just to Leibniz but much further back, to the Stoics: "To all creatures, who do not make themselves unworthy of that name, I cry, 'Happy are we – we exist. And God is well pleased with us'" (Kant 1992: 71, 76). This is indeed optimistic, the source of which is not the wisdom of God but a solidarity with all existing creatures, such as animals or slaves. As for Weymann, Kant was right in being optimistic: the owner of the Kalmyk fur coat was expelled from the university 15 years later (Kuehn 2001: 215).

Kant also had important friends among the pro-Russian wing of the Königsberg elite. Every biography of Kant describes Countess Caroline von Keyserlingk, a good friend of Kant's; over several decades, he taught her children, frequented her dinners, and called her his "ideal of a woman." However, their views on Russia, and probably on the Russian occupation, were diametrically opposed. It was 30 years later that their mutual friend recorded a dinner conversation from Keyserlingk's manor, which showed that Russia was still on their minds:

> There was a political discourse in which the officers were very active. Kant, as did I, declared that the Russians were our main enemies. . . . The Countess [was] of a different opinion. . . . "If my husband was still alive, he would certainly have made clear to the king by means of a concrete deduction that his best ally is Russia." . . . I still did not believe that they did not have any interest in Eastern Prussia. . . . The Countess did not change her mind. (Kuehn 2001: 337–8)

Bolotov's memoir leaves no doubt that in 1759–60, von Keyserlingk was a mistress of the Russian governor of Prussia, Baron Nikolai von Korf, and that their liaison was public knowledge in the city (Bolotov 1986: 289). Von Korf was a Baltic-German aristocrat who spoke but did not write in Russian. He was close to the Empress; in Königsberg, he was so important that Bolotov called him Vice-Roy. After his service in Königsberg, von Korf was appointed chief of the St. Petersburg and, later, of all Russian police. Once again, the experience in external colonization was deemed interchangeable with the success in internal policing. A rich and flamboyant bachelor, von Korf used every occasion to throw balls or masquerades to honor the Countess von Keyserlingk. Luminaries attended these dazzling events, including Grigorii Orlov, a hero of the Russian–Prussian war who would soon become a powerful favorite of Catherine the Great. It is tantalizing to imagine a conversation between Kant and Orlov, whom one Englishman described as "colossal in stature but totally unimproved by reading" (Wolff 1994: 234). Kant was then in his "gallant phase," worldly, fashionably dressed, and in demand, if not at balls then at dinner parties. In his writings and lectures from this and slightly later periods, there are signs of his discontent with philosophy and intellectual life, a midlife crisis of a sort (Zammito 2002). Historian Anthony La Vopa discerns "an element of self-caricature, and indeed of self-hatred" in Kant's lectures during the occupation and his writings that followed the withdrawal of Russian troops (La Vopa 2005: 17). Among the explanations for this important though temporary crisis, one comes from the postcolonial tradition. Under a colonial regime, the local intellectuals often registered similar feelings of internal splitting, doubling, and self-hatred. Much of twentieth-century existential thought came out of these situations, in Algeria and elsewhere. Reinstating Kant in occupied Königsberg helps us understand his relation to this tradition.

Apart from his teaching at the university, Kant also taught geography, applied mathematics, and pyrotechnics to the German-speaking Russian officers, people like Orlov or Bolotov (Gulyga 1997: 32). Presumably, he took money for this service. After the Russians left the city, Kant continued to give similar lessons to Prussian officers. Indeed, during those early years Kant was developing a kind of scholarship that he could teach equally well to the Prussians and the Russians. His published research during the years of occupation was very scant. During the almost five years of Russian rule, he published a few essays that all focused on a rather special theme, earthquakes. Geographically, earthquakes were very distant from the experience of Königsberg; metaphorically, these inexplicable, senseless disasters were close to Kant's world. Voltaire, who spent part of the war in Berlin, combined the same crucial themes – the Lisbon earthquake of 1755, the Seven Years War, and theodicy – in *Candide* (1759).

Whether the reason was anxiety or trauma, the fact is that the occupation created a writing block in Kant. Immediately after the abrupt end of the occupation, in 1762–3, Kant's publications burst forth. "It is striking that Kant should have published so much in so short a time, in light of rather spare publications of the preceding six years," wrote John Zammito (2002: 61). It is no less striking that Zammito and other scholars have failed to attribute this dynamic to the most obvious reason, the Russian occupation and its end. Under Russian rule, Kant was a subaltern and he did not speak. To be more precise, he did not speak publicly about anything but earthquakes.

Bolotov

From Isaiah Berlin to John Zammito, research on Kant is of very high quality. However, these scholars invariably fail to detect the formative impact of Russian rule in Königsberg on their hero, and neglect an important primary source: the memoir of Andrei Bolotov, which bore almost singular witness to the events. Many biographers of Kant mention Bolotov, though he has not been translated; they know about Bolotov from the only English-language biography of Kant written by a Russian author (Gulyga 1987). A major Soviet philosopher, Arsenii Gulyga, presented the Russian occupation of Königsberg with a light touch, as an innocent affair with negligible results. Writing about Bolotov, he chose the episodes that showed his power over Kant and not his tortured relations with the Prussians.

Apart from his voluminous writings, which have remained largely unpublished (see Newlin 2001: 4), Bolotov was a typical figure of the Enlightenment: a modest officer, a dilettante naturalist, and a successful administrator who later in his life managed many thousands of the crown peasants near Moscow. His father, also an officer, commanded Russian regiments that were stationed in the occupied Baltic countries. There, Bolotov learned his German, which in Königsberg sounded native. Mediating between Russians and Germans, collecting philosophical books, and drawing aquarelles, Bolotov was eager to become a good European, a feat that few Russian authors presented to their readers. He was in despair when his superior ordered him to return to Russia. Deeply influenced by his tenure in Königsberg, he imposed some of his new skills and ideas on the peasants that he owned or managed. He created Prussian-style ponds and gardens in central Russia and was one of the first to introduce potatoes as an agricultural product there. Writing about his time in Königsberg decades after it ended, he recognized the Germans' advantage over Russians in fashions, haircuts, cuisine, bookstores, schools, and much more. These feelings did not prevent him from being a loyal officer abroad and an ordinary master of his serfs at home. Filling many pages with exalted words about the Prussians, about the Russians he wrote with the impersonal brutality of an aristocrat: "the stupidity and the extreme unreasonableness of our mean folk was all-too-well-known to us" (1986: 604). Experimenting on his peasants, he subjected 1,500 of them to electric treatment, the results of which are unrecorded.

Giving us the perspective of a colonizing power, Bolotov's memoirs differ from the Prussian evidence that reveal the hidden transcripts of the colonized (Scott 1990). A major event of the occupation was a fire panic during a service in the Schlosskirche, which was memorable because it was mysterious; there was panic but there was no fire. Months earlier, the preacher Daniel Heinrich Arnoldt, who was also a professor of theology, gave a sermon there that the Russians perceived as slandering Empress Elizabeth. He quoted from Micah

Figure 15: Andrei Bolotov's self-portrait. The caption reads, "Precise depiction of the room and place where this book was written in 1789–90."
Source: *Zhizn' i prikliucheniia Bolotova, opisannye samim im dlia svoikh potomkov*. vol. 2, Moscow-Leningrad 1931

7:8 about the inner light: "Rejoice not against me, O mine enemy: when I fall, I shall arise; when I sit in darkness, the Lord shall be a light unto me." Bolotov remembered though that this pastor spelled out some "indecencies about our Empress." Arnoldt was arrested and spent six months under investigation; Bolotov remembered that he "suffered very greatly" in jail. In order to avoid Siberia, Arnoldt promised to retract. But when he started the assigned sermon, a group of students yelled "Fire!" and created panic, so that he was spared his apology. We know this from Prussian sources (Kuehn 2001: 113; Kuehn and Klemme, n.d.). Bolotov also described a church panic, with "many" citizens wounded or mutilated and one killed when she jumped out of the Gothic windows. Depicting both events contiguously – the arrest of the "most beloved" pastor because of his sermon and the fire panic in his church – Bolotov saw them as unrelated. He explained the panic as a result of the little heaters that ladies of Königsberg used to bring to the service. In his rendering of the episode, he was much concerned about the gunpowder magazines that were located nearby, a detail that led to panic on the Russian side as well (Bolotov 1931: 1/518). "Seeing like the state" meant objectifying the event so that its physical course was depicted correctly, while its meaning and context were ignored. In contrast, the perspective of the colonized emphasized agency and the hidden intention of those involved.

Despite Bolotov's German, he soon learned that the natives did not accept him as their peer. In the governor's office he worked together with the Prussians and felt alien:

> I could not even think about engaging these Germans in conversation. Not only these colleagues but, in general, all the best dwellers of Königsberg felt some kind of disgust towards all of us Russians. . . . Though I was courteous with them in all possible ways so that I would become somehow closer to them, all my efforts were in vain. They were as polite as I was, and that was all that I got. (Bolotov 1986: 221)

Hurt by this attitude and ever interested in the Germans, Bolotov mused upon their rejection of him more than once. With Kantian clarity, he distinguished between his own stereotype of the Germans and their specific response to the Russian occupants:

> My surprise disappeared when I learned to know the Prussians and the Königsbergians better. I did not ascribe their responses to their unsociability but discerned their general indisposition towards Russians, for whom they expressed respect but, internally, deemed to be their enemies. (Bolotov 1986: 221)

Bolotov spent every Sunday in Prussian cafés and beer gardens, which he loved for their "order, quietness, and decency." Shy and defensive when with his Russian peers, he was never bored in Prussian company. Everything there was "polite," "courteous," and even "timid"; these were all the features of character that Bolotov presented to his readers as his own. He also realized that these cafés and beer gardens, all entirely new to him, worked as the centers of local community life and popular information; some of his observations resemble the idea of the public sphere, which historians articulated, with reference to the same German cafés, some 200 years later.

The Prussians were right to be wary. Desperately wishing to become one of them, Bolotov was forever concerned about Russian interests. He worked hard and, gradually, his cultural skills improved. He was a good spy.

> At first, the Prussian gentlemen shunned and avoided me as a Russian officer, but as soon as I talked to them in German with all tenderness, they treated me as a natural German and became totally tender. They eagerly brought me into their company and entered into various speculations with me, even political conversations sometimes. And as I eagerly allowed them to be deceived and to think that I was a German, and sometimes purposefully encouraged them in this error, so it happened not rarely that I learned much of what one could not find out and learn otherwise, particularly in those matters that concerned the current military events. They were all very well informed in those matters, which greatly surprised me; . . . often I learned things from them two or three weeks before the newspapers wrote about them. (Bolotov 1931: 1/462)

Once, the governor asked Bolotov to arrest a Prussian aristocrat who had been denounced by his servant because of his anti-Russian sentiment. Armed with his knowledge of German and a team of Cossacks, Bolotov accomplished the mission. The count had to go to a trial in St. Petersburg together with his denouncer (Bolotov 1986: 370). At the same time, Bolotov frequented a bookstore in Königsberg, maybe the same one in which Herder started to work a little later. Bolotov loved German books and believed that they improved his character:

> By reading novels, I formed an idea about the customs and mores of various peoples and about everything that they have there, good and bad. . . . I developed an understanding of the life of different classes, from the masters of the earth to the very lowest. . . . I started to look at all events in the world through different, nobler eyes. (1986: 280)

Bolotov believed that personal aggression was a character flaw. He did not like to see it manifested either in himself or in others; his boss, Governor von Korf, was particularly aggressive and Bolotov detested his explosions. After reading novels, Bolotov became more reserved and felt he had mastered himself. Now, he could control his response even when a servant stole his money. With pride, he attributed this civilizing process to his reading of German novels and philosophy: "I tried to observe those very rules that were prescribed in my books and I should say that I succeeded in refashioning myself during that one summer so much that I ceased to look like myself and many were truly surprised about that" (1986: 304).

This refashioning under the influence of the culture that Bolotov was supposed to control is still surprising. It was an essential fact of his life; having acknowledged it during that summer in Prussia, Bolotov did not fail to mention it many decades later back on his Russian estate, when he wrote his memoirs. While exercising political power over the Prussians, he found himself to be deeply dependent on them. Domination was his; hegemony was theirs. Both sides were out of balance.

Camera Obscura and Fireworks

In an occupied Prussian village, Bolotov saw an optical instrument that was essentially a box with a little hole. The light reflected on the internal side of the box and produced a picture, which was upside down. This instrument was also called a perspective box or, more poetically, camera obscura. Bolotov was enchanted:

> I just loved this perspective box and could not stop thinking about it and I would give I do not know what for such a box. . . . Prisms and other optical instruments excited me enormously, but my fascination with the camera obscura was such that I cannot describe it. (1986: 208)

He made a camera obscura for himself; it was portable, so that he could take it with him wherever he went with his regiment. It allowed to him to project "natural pictures" onto the canvas and then to paint them. He used this device for looking at Königsberg. He also could project pictures into the box and show them to his friends, Russian officers, who came in large groups to enjoy the new amusement. These pictures "represented the best street views of Venice and other noblest European cities" (Bolotov 1986: 212). With the help of this magic lantern, Bolotov took his Europe back to Russia. Decades later, when he was writing his memoir at his estate, his camera was still with him, as "a kind of monument for a time bygone." Buying a camera, making another one, improving them, showing them to his friends – these stories mark the happiest pages of Bolotov's memoir.

Neither his promotion nor his wedding nor, to be sure, going home made him as happy. It was his pleasure and his enlightenment, the camera that showed Europe upside down.

Discovered by Johannes Kepler in the early seventeenth century, the camera obscura was a common reference for Enlightenment thinkers. Hume often compared cognition to the dark room, partially and suddenly illuminated; to Locke, the camera obscura seemed to be the best metaphor for the mind (Abrams 1953: 57). The Pietist idea of the inner light, which brings truth into the soul without further mediation, matched the simple design of these obscure cameras. Within them, the Enlightenment became private, even idiosyncratic. At the same time that he was reinventing the camera obscura, Bolotov had to master the Cameralism system of governance. He was commissioned to work as a translator in the office, *Kammer*, that the Russian governor inherited from the Prussian administration and used for collecting taxes and fees from the province. Remarkably, Bolotov used one and the same non-Russian word, *kamera* or *kamora*, for both operations that he learned in Königsberg: the optical device and the administrative system. Although he did not comment on the analogy or contrast between the two cameras, his description of the physical space where he was working suggest it strongly:

> I had to sit alone and entirely solitary in a huge and dark camera, that was illuminated only by two smoky windows, with metal grids, and to sit not near the windows but at a distance from them, – sit like a bird in a cage, and spend the nesting time of spring there. (1931: 1/370)

Like many eighteenth-century Russians, Bolotov was a great fan of fireworks. In 1759, the Russian governor of Königsberg, with the help of his Italian assistant, created an elaborate fireworks performance on the bank of the Pregel River to celebrate the Russian conquest of the city. Bolotov had never seen such a thing. Nor had the Prussians, who came in "countless numbers" and experienced "very great pleasure." Even when observing their Orthodox rituals, Russians in Königsberg fired canons, which "all the dwellers watched with particular pleasure" (Bolotov 1931: 5/48). In 1763, Bolotov was present at the grand fireworks on the Neva in St. Petersburg, when Peter III was celebrating Russia's reconciliation with Prussia. Again, all the banks of the spacious river were crowded, and the fireworks were "blinding" (1986: 299; 1931: 2/149). Long before the era of television, fireworks were the closest analogues to the state-sponsored visual propaganda. Having his camera obscura for private pleasure, the dark *Kammer* for public service, and fireworks for mass communication, Bolotov entered the world of modernity.

Herder

Kant's early student, Johann Gottfried von Herder, was the first to use the term "nationalism" and to explore its peaceful, humanist aspects (Berlin 1996, 2000). A native of a Prussian village that was occupied by the Russians, Herder received unusual help from their surgeon, who operated on his eye and then financed his education in Königsberg. This Russian surgeon wanted him to study medicine, but in August 1762, with the announcement of Russia's withdrawal from Königsberg, Herder started his studies with Kant. One of his first pieces of poetry was his ode to Peter III, who brought the occupation to an end (Ergang 1966: 60–3). In the treatise that Herder wrote in Riga for Catherine II in 1764, "Do we still have the public and Fatherland of Yore?" he glorified the German spirit but ended with an ode to the Russian Empress, who was also German after all:

> Yes, fatherland, you, mother, to whom the wise
> Will sacrifice the spirit's firstborn fruit . . .
> Yours is this house in Catherine's shadow . . .
> Here Russia's blessing, and there the sun's embrace. (Herder 1992: 64)

As Isaiah Berlin stated clearly, Herder's form of nationalism "remained unaltered" during his active life, which stretched from the Seven Years War to the Napoleonic wars (Berlin 2000: 180). However, Berlin, a great scholar of Russian thought and a native of Riga, did not focus on Herder's experience under Russian occupation, which was clearly important for his nationalism. It was there that Herder discovered the value of community and its autonomy from the state. For him, philosophy became a genre of public discourse, a way for people to understand themselves, like poetry or politics. There had to be as many philosophies as there were peoples. But when nations were at war or one people oppressed another, there could be no common understanding between them.

While distancing himself from Kant, Herder nevertheless shared with his teacher the great theme of self-determination. Though scholars derive this theme from Kant's and Herder's common spiritual tradition, Pietism, their experience under Russian rule was also important. For those who believed in self-reliance and an inner light, it was difficult to live under foreign rule. Hidden transcripts evolved into philosophy. The basis of the state – Russian and Prussian alike – is conquest; all wars are civil wars; the state robs men of themselves: in these inspired formulas Herder articulated a vision that was cultural, not political (Berlin 2000; Swift 2005). Though empires had "feet of clay," he worshiped the first and foremost Russian Emperor, Peter the Great, "the man and the marvel of our century," and Catherine the Great who finally stopped the war (Herder 1992: 62). Russian rule in Königsberg and Riga did not tolerate political opposition but negotiated cultural dissidence. This decoupling of culture and politics explains why it did not instill in Herder a hatred of Russians. Later in life, he wrote sublime words about the beautiful fate of the Slavs in the world to come (Gesemann 1965).[1] More importantly, he called for the exploration of Slavic folklore, "the archive of the people." Herder's ideal of the right life was about people living in communities that are united by culture and organizing their own affairs independently of the state. One could speculate that Herder based this idea on his observations of Slavic village life, in Prussia or in Livonia. He was very popular among the Romantic, early nineteenth-century Russian intellectuals, some of whom held surprisingly high positions in the imperial administration (Maiofis 2008). Focused on the Slavs, Herder's idea of anthropology competed with the Kantian, more scientific, and more orientalist ethnology that Schlözer and his colleagues developed at Göttingen (Knight 1998: 120). Later, these two projects collided with spectacular results. Herder's distant follower, Lucian Malinowski, a professor of Slavic who studied the folklore of northern Poland, was the father of Bronislaw Malinowski, a great anthropologist who went to the Pacific with the ideas of East European romanticism (Gellner 1998: 130).

The explosion of intellectual life, poetry, and philosophy is a common feature of postcolonial moments. The circle of Kant and Herder in Königsberg experienced it for the first time ever. Observing the dramatic, unaccountable events that were caused by human will but which changed their lives like earthquakes, local intellectuals came to a new and revolutionary understanding of rationality, autonomy, and history. Two figures of their circle add to my argument,

[1] Soviet propaganda missed its chance to refer to Herder as a prophet of the glorious Slavic future, but today Ukrainian history textbooks quote him at length (for examples, see Portnov 2010: 148).

Hamann and Abbt. Both were important for the young Herder while he was distancing himself from Kant (Zammito 2002: 164) and both were seriously involved in the Prussian-Russian conflict. Johann Georg Hamann, a philosopher from Königsberg, lived in Riga, under Russian rule, and worked for the major merchants of the area, the brothers Berens. Riga was the center of wartime efforts; the Russian headquarters were stationed there. Trading hemp and timber, the Berens had every reason to be concerned about the turn of European politics that put Russia and England at war. One of the brothers, Reinhold, left a memoir in which he mentions Hamann and Kant as friends of the family. After the Seven Years War ended, Reinhold Berens served in Russia as a military doctor, took part in the suppression of the Pugachev rebellion, and traveled as far as the Altai Mountains; he was so Russified that in his memoir he called his venerable schoolteacher Nestor (Berens 1812: 10).

In 1756, the Berens brothers sent Hamann to London with a "political as well as commercial" mission (Berlin 2000: 262; Betz 2008: 30). This secret mission started and finished with Hamann's visit to the Russian Ambassador in London, Aleksandr Golitsyn. Hamann handed over a proposal from the Berens brothers, which the Ambassador rejected outright. Later, during Catherine's coup, Golitsyn acted like a turnspit, so counting on his support was probably not wise. Isaiah Berlin suggested that the Berens brothers contemplated a secession of German Baltic lands from the Russian Empire; if so, it is difficult to explain why they would send their messenger to the Russian Ambassador in London. It is equally possible that they were struggling to preserve the Anglo-Russian alliance, which was profitable for their commerce. Whatever the message was, Hamann's failure to persuade the Ambassador changed his life. Somehow it led to his Christian reawakening, which triggered his new career as a bitter critic of the Enlightenment. From London, he returned to Königsberg, where he taught English to Herder and competed with Kant for influence over young minds.

The German public sphere was emerging during the Seven Years War; since Herder, a poem by Thomas Abbt, *On Death for the Fatherland* (1761), has been credited as a reflection on this process (La Vopa 1995; Redekop 1997). This poem responded to the Prussian defeat at the major battle of Kunersdorf, near Frankfurt (Oder), by calling the Germans to heroic resistance against the invaders. In 1760, Abbt became a professor of philosophy at Frankfurt during the Russian occupation of the city. After the war ended, in 1765, he left his professorship for a post at the court of Count Wilhelm von

Schaumburg-Lippe, one of the most successful Prussian commanders of the Seven Years War. Abbt contributed to the debate on theodicy, or the nature of evil:

> He formulated a grim parable for the human condition in terms of an army finding itself in hostile territory with no sense of what it has been sent to accomplish, so that each soldier had to make his separate peace with the situation. (Zammito 2002: 169)

Having recovered this wonderful tale from an old journal, Zammito failed to notice that for Abbt, the author of *On Death for the Fatherland*, this hapless army was the Russian army in Prussia and the pathetic soldier was someone like Bolotov.

Conjectural History

A century and half later, in August 1914, Russian troops were approaching Königsberg again. "The Cossacks are coming," was the cry in the city. Surrounded by a panicky crowd, the very young Hannah Arendt fled Königsberg with her mother. But in Berlin, Hannah suffered from homesickness, so they returned to the city 10 weeks later, after German troops had defeated Russian forces at the battle of Tannenberg. Hannah developed a recurrent ailment, a fever that occurred every time she had to leave Königsberg (Young-Bruehl 1982: 23). One can only speculate that this early experience of unsettledness had an effect on her later ideas; Ernest Gellner was right in seeing this situation as a philosophical parable (1987: 76). Kant aspired to worldly, universal knowledge without leaving his city, though this was the city that changed hands between the Prussians and the Russians. Arendt traversed the world haunted by statelessness, the banality of evil, and the German-Russian symmetry in totalitarianism. Though we do not know what would have happened to these philosophers in a different place, we can feel that their ideas, general as they are, were anchored in the history of Königsberg. But the meaning of the Königsberg parable went further than a dialectics of the particular and the universal. Built to colonize, but intermittently colonized, this failed imperial center proved to be a fertile ground for critical thinking about modernity.

After the Russian retreat from Königsberg, Kant recovered from his subaltern silence. Among his famous *Critiques*, he wrote a project of perpetual peace (1795), a utopian construction of the future federation of states, close and distant, which would be based on the prohibition against any state appropriating another state. This forward-looking idea had become popular in early-nineteenth-century Russia. In 1813, Sergei Uvarov, the future Minister of the Enlightenment, rewrote Kant's utopia as a project for the post-Napoleonic arrangement of Europe that would be led by the Russian Empire (Maiofis 2008: 74). Despite Uvarov's clout, his treatise did not gain much success in the Russian court or among international allies. Indeed, Kant stated clearly that the future federation would become possible only when every state became a republic. A European peace was realistic if it was based not on a utopian federation but on the balance of power, a British principle that Russian rulers mostly disliked.

With the advent of modernity, power became dependent not only on the size and resources of the state, but also on the knowledge and creativity of the people. In 1786, Kant published an essay, "Conjectural Beginnings of Human History," which provided a reading of *Genesis* but which actually outlined Kant's thinking about war and his polemics with Herder. Closer to the end of the essay, Kant broke the code and acknowledged that he was talking not only about Adam, but also about the events of today: "For the danger of war is also still today the sole thing that moderates despotism, because wealth is required for a state to be a might, but without *freedom*, no enterprise that could produce wealth will take place" (Kant 2007c: 172).

This is a strong form of liberalism that connects sovereignty to military power and this power to freedom. Despots need industriousness among their peoples and, because of that, have to restrict their despotism. This is where despots find their nemesis, from among the best smiths of their best weapons, who have enjoyed an exclusive freedom and wish to share it with others. This speculation would work particularly well during the twentieth century's Cold War. Arendt, who was passionate about Soviet dissidents and lived long enough to learn the news about Andrei Sakharov, would probably agree with this scheme of things. In earlier centuries, the Prussian Frederick and the Russian Catherine were such despots, who supported both gauntlets and sciences because they needed them for their survival. As usual, Kant tried to look at both sides from some kind of philosophical middle ground. In his biblical essay, the nomadic herdsmen, who were "sworn enemies of all landed property," attack peaceful farmers and urban dwellers. "There was continual war between them, or at least the continual threat of war, and both peoples were at least able to enjoy the priceless good of internal freedom." He continues the tale, twisting it unexpectedly: "With time the increasing luxury of the town dwellers, but chiefly the art of pleasing, in which the town women eclipsed the dingy maids of the deserts, must have been a mighty lure for those shepherds" (Kant 2007c: 172). Responding to this lure of the town women, the herdsmen enter into relations with them, which brings "the end of all danger of war" and with it, "the end of all freedom."

Whether Kant was thinking about Countess von Keyserlingk, his "ideal of a woman," and Baron von Korf, or whether the romance between the wild invader and the local beauty was taken solely from the Bible, the lesson is astonishingly modern. The greatest troubles come from wars and from war efforts. But if there were no threat of war, says Kant, people would not enjoy even the freedom that they have, because this threat is the only factor that forces rulers to respect freedom. In the current state of culture, he says, perpetual peace cannot be attained. At this stage, war, not peace, facilitates progress. Grass is needful for the ox and freedom is needful for man, and therefore war, the state, and even evil, should exist.

—10—

Sects and Revolution

On April 16, 1861, in provincial Kazan, Professor Afanasii Shchapov proffered a theory that would inspire several generations of Russian socialists. An expert in religious history, Shchapov spoke at a requiem service to commemorate the lives of the peasants who were shot by troops at a village meeting, after they questioned the announced Emancipation. Shchapov called these victims "Christs" and presented their genealogy: "In Russia, for the past century and a half . . . among you, peasants – your own Christs have appeared" (Shchapov 1923: 409; Field 1976: 98). Shchapov ended his eulogy by saying that the peasants lost their lives for the cause of "the Soviet of the people." Combining the Christs with the Soviets, this rhetoric was pregnant with meaning. In his academic works as well as in his eulogy, Shchapov proposed the twofold argument, that participants in Russian peasant revolts were usually non-Orthodox in religious matters, and that members of Schismatic groups usually opposed state power. As a historian, Shchapov knew that some of these groups called their leaders Christs. As a prophet, he predicted the Soviet terminology of the Russian future.

Peasant Christs

The Emancipation of serfs was announced in newspapers for those who were literate, and in churches for those who were not. One of many responses was the peasant unrest in Bezdna, in the Kazan province. Surrounded by thousands of peasants, Anton Petrov interpreted the tome containing the Emancipation legislation as if it were the Scriptures. He was literate, or so peasants believed, and he inter-

Figure 16: Afanasii Shchapov in 1872.
Source: Shchapov, Afanasii 1906. *Sochineniia*. St. Petersburg

preted the sign "%," which was scattered throughout the text, as the Holy Cross, and all the zeroes as symbols of liberation without redemption payments (Krylov 1892: 616). He so agitated the peasants that they refused to disperse even under fire from a military regiment, which killed or wounded several hundred people, including Petrov himself (Field 1976; Freeze 1988). The name of the place where it all happened added to its horror: Bezdna means "abyss."

Although historians are very familiar with these events, they have not elaborated on the explanation that was developed by Shchapov: that Anton Petrov and the peasant crowd were religious dissenters. In speaking about the periodic appearance of peasant "Christs," Shchapov identified Petrov as a leader of the Russian sect Khlysty. These sectarians believed in multiple reincarnations of Jesus Christ; in addition, they believed that Christ visited every worthy member of the community as he or she reached the apogee of religious ecstasy.

They called themselves "Khristy" (Christs), but hostile Orthodox observers distorted it into "Khlysty" (the Whips). The sect entered history with this negative designation, a fate that it shared with such groups as the Shakers and Quakers. The first observer to endow these sectarians with a romantic aura was the Prussian visitor August von Haxthausen. In the 1840s, he found among the Russian sects "the firm and stable organization of these rude masses . . . a remarkably powerful spirit of association, and unparalleled communal institutions" (Haxthausen 1856: 1/254). After describing sectarian manifestations of mystical orgies, self-mutilation, and, most importantly, collective property, Haxthausen introduced his story of the bloody ritual performed by the Khlysty. In this narrative, singing, whirling, and flagellating sectarians cut off the breast of a naked virgin. After her breast had been collectively eaten, the community of sectarians engaged in group intercourse. The young woman with one breast was called Mother of God and became a leader of the community. Her spiritual partner was called Christ. Haxthausen's rhetoric, an accomplishment of romantic orientalism, contained the potential for ambivalent, and even positive, readings. To eat a human breast is certainly barbaric. Still, the ritual empowered a woman to lead her community. As Haxthausen wrote, some French intellectuals "went to Egypt to discover the free woman; had they gone to Russia they would perhaps have returned better satisfied" (Haxthausen 1856: 1/44). The hidden truth of the Russian commune was not only economic and legal, but also spiritual and sexual.

Russian ethnographers trustfully retold the startling story of the eaten breast (Kelsiev 1867; Melnikov-Pechersky 1869). This racy ritual of the Khlysty became a common plotline for many stories whose ambition was to uncover the hidden life of the Russian provinces. Count Vladimir Sollogub, a rich socialite and writer, served in the Ministry of Internal Affairs and inspected the Tver province in 1836. One of his tasks was to investigate the crimes of the local sectarians. In his memoir, he retold the picturesque, Gothic story of the Khlysty ritual service that he himself allegedly saw through a peephole. A Kalmyk guardsman, whose tongue had been cut out by the sectarians, betrayed them and brought Sollogub into the underground temple. Surrounded by a mysterious crowd, an elder led into the dark room "an entirely naked beauty," 16 years of age and "astonishingly handsome." After some "Cabbalistic gestures," the elder and everyone else beat her with a whip until she was nearly dead; at this moment though, the gendarmes arrived and arrested everyone present. Sollogub, who had never had a legal education or practice, led the investigation (1998: 133). Written much later, this memoir was most probably inspired by Haxthausen or some of his Russian readers; there is no doubt that this was a story that men liked to share. One can find similarly pleasant scenes, also from the life of Russian sects, in the major texts of writers as different as Leopold Sacher-Masoch and Maksim Gorky (Etkind 1998). For the radical readers of Haxthausen, the sectarian ritual complemented his discovery of the Russian commune with the striking image of its collective body, identified with God in ecstatic unity.

Cannibalism, flagellation, and group sex among the Khlysty were never confirmed. In actual fact, they practiced a ritual whirling dance that resembled the dances of American Shakers. In ecstasy, they spoke in tongues, made prophecies, and healed the sick. Largely forgotten today, the Khlysty deserve a place among other phenomena of the Eurasian religious tradition (Siniavsky 1991; Etkind 1998; Clay 2001; Zhuk 2004). But as political agents, they were neutral, nonviolent, or just passive. There were only two cases of mass unrest attributed to the Khlysty and related sects. The first of these took place in 1861 when, according to Shchapov, "democratic, purported Christs" organized the rebellion in Bezdna. The second, in 1901, took place in the village of Pavlovki in Kharkov province, when a crowd vandalized the local church and some experts attributed the event to the Khlysty (Gamfield 1990). Though the statistics were notoriously unreliable, by the beginning of the twentieth century estimations of the number of Khlysty were still as high as 100,000 (Klibanov 1982). Many communities split from the Khlysty or simply resembled them; they preferred to call themselves by other, usually exotic names. Many of these movements shared broadly millennial beliefs, which were common to the natives of other colonized regions of the world (Curtin 2000). By identifying with the early Christians in their struggle against the Romans, they articulated their feelings toward modern empires. Most of these "sectarians," as they were officially called in Russia, were illiterate, but there were educated, including self-educated, people among them. To characterize their religious movements as "cargo cults" is entirely wrong. The nineteenth-century history of these communities feature permanent interactions between high and low cultures, which culminated in the synthesis that was achieved by Lev Tolstoy, an admirer and correspondent of several sectarian communities, and his fellow Tolstovians who claimed leadership in the world of sects.

The path-breaking historian of Russian radicalism, Franco Venturi, claimed that those activists who famously "went to the People" in the 1870s were guided, "above all," by the ethnographers (1982: 270). Being different from urbane society and unknown to it, the people (as Russian peasants were called) were intelligible only through the lens of the exoticizing "science" of ethnography. An amalgam of socialist activism and lay ethnography, the populist movement saw the peasantry as silent, dispossessed, obscure, exotic, virtuous – in short, different. Whatever the people did or thought was known to the intelligentsia through authors who were themselves part of that same intelligentsia (Frierson 1993; Offord 2010). The colonial past, argued Gayatri Spivak, is incommunicable. The subaltern does not speak; when he or she speaks to us, her speech is not authentic, and her language is already contaminated by western meanings. To put it in postcolonial terms, the people were the subaltern. The emerging Russian science of ethnography confronted the same paradox in the nineteenth century that the scholars of subalternity in India noted in the twentieth century (Prakash 1994; Spivak 1994). Dominant discourses presented the superstitious peasant as a figure beyond the realm of reason, outside the authorized categories of rationality and progress. However, these discourses claimed that this subaltern figure was knowable and actually known; he was believed to be reachable and transparent for the specialized methods of scholarship. This paradox proved to be fruitful for several fields of Russian scholarship, from ethnography to history to literary studies. Its internationally acclaimed achievements developed as offspring of the studies of sectarian and peasant folk life. Vladimir Propp's structuralist analysis of folk tales has become famous. It is less known that Viktor Shklovsky's formalist theory of estrangement started with his analysis of the songs of the Khlysty (Etkind 1998: 153).

The Politicization of the Schism

The requiem in Kazan was arguably the first public commemoration of victims of the Russian monarchy. Church authorities wanted to incarcerate Shchapov in a monastery, but Alexander II considered him a layperson and instead ordered his arrest. In February 1862, on the first anniversary of the emancipation of the serfs, the Tsar pardoned Shchapov. In a sensational turn of events, the disgraced professor was then appointed to the Ministry of Internal Affairs. His new position was in the "Committee for Schismatics, Skoptsy and other Especially Dangerous Sects," which was responsible for dealing with religious dissidents by the means of police. Shchapov held this position for a few months until, in another sensational development, the Minister of Internal Affairs dismissed him. The Minister of Enlightenment proposed sending him to eastern Siberia for ethnographic studies, but instead Alexander II sent him into exile there under police surveillance.

Shchapov's short governmental service radicalized his thought. In a series of essays published in populist journals, he reappraised the whole variety of Russian sectarian experience, providing it with a new combination of nationalistic and utopian meanings. Describing an exceptionally rich range of cases, Shchapov saw a common element in all of them: anti-governmental protest. He blurred the traditional distinction between "Old-Believers" and "sectarians," which favored Old-Believers as the lesser evil, though nobody could clearly explicate their difference. He disregarded those Schismatics, and there were many, who were solely concerned with eternal salvation and who turned their backs upon the political world. To be sure, there was a great variety of beliefs and modes of behavior among different creeds of non-Orthodox Russians.[1] Still, according to the formulations of Shchapov, all Russian sectarians and Old-Believers disguised social protest under religious masks, uniting themselves into the "democratic party of the Schismatics" (1906: 1/451–505). Shchapov's collection of Russian sects followed along with the better-known achievements of Russian ethnography, such as Vladimir Dal's dictionary of the Russian language, the surveys of peasant rites and mores organized by Nikolai Nadezhdin, the collection of historical legends by Pavel Rybnikov, and the collection of fairytales by Alexander Afanasiev. Ethnography, "the science of the people," became an instrument of national self-fashioning (Slezkine 1994; Gellner 1998). Alluding to the pure virtues and mystical practices of the people, ethnography demonstrated their spectacular difference from the life of cynical, commercialized, urban civilization.

External and internal factors cooperated in the nineteenth-century discovery of Russian sects. They were constructed as uniquely Russian, whereas the terms and genres of this discursive formation were predominantly European. Frequent dialogue with western travelers,

[1] Nineteenth-century literature on these sects was enormous and is partially summarized in Etkind 1998. The current literature is large and growing; see Crummey 1993; Robson 1995; Engelstein 1999; Clay 2001; Paert 2004; Zhuk 2004; Breyfogle 2005; Steinberg and Coleman 2007; Heretz 2008.

hungry for social wonders and oriental exotica, played a defining role in the burgeoning discourse about Russian sects. For many decades, European authors like August von Haxthausen, Alexander Dumas-père, William H. Dixon, Leopold Sacher-Masoch, and René Fülöp-Miller referred to Russian sects while projecting onto Russia their favorite ideas, such as deep spirituality, free eroticism, love of suffering, and collective property. Russian intellectuals knew too well that these curiosities were absent in their own circles. In order to give an affirmative response to the western projections, they produced imaginary constructions of their own. The sectarians were real but inaccessible to the profane gaze, which provided experts with an excellent chance to manipulate the political vision of their readers.

In the rich history of Russian ethnography of sectarian movements, we observe the three stages that Miroslav Hroch (1985) described in his classical study of East European nationalisms. First, scholars produce and disseminate knowledge about minority groups. Second, activists seek to access and employ these groups for the project of the future nation, which would be radically different from the existing one. Third, a mass movement is formed, which shapes itself into a different form from the one projected by early enthusiasts. At the crucial second stage, lay ethnographers used two strategies to radicalize their debate about Russian sects. They emphasized sectarian eccentricities by appropriating Orthodox missionaries' accusations against them, changing the tone of these narratives from the hostile to the romanticized and even the utopian. As an aspect of this modernizing effort, they used comparisons between Russian and American sects, such as Shakers, Mormons, and the Bible Communists (for details, see Etkind 2001b). Lay ethnographers also conflated different religious groups, thereby producing mammoth numbers that encompassed total statistics rather than specific numbers for individual sects. In 1861, a proclamation estimated the number of "Russian sectarians who do not honor the Tsar" at nine million (Shelgunov and Mikhailov 1958: 96). In 1867, a political émigré, Nikolai Ogarev, wrote that "almost half of our population" are Schismatics (1952: 773). In 1924, Vladimir Bonch-Bruevich wrote in the newspaper *Pravda* that 35 million, "no less than one-third of the population of the country," are "sectarians and Old-Believers." What was decisive was the combination of the inflated statistics, which included all of these variegated groups, and the vivid descriptions of radical communities that were purposefully taken for typical portraits of all of them.

The Militant Pilgrims

At the same time that the Ministry of Internal Affairs was employing Shchapov for police purposes, the political émigré Vasilii Kelsiev was employing Shchapov's essays for subversive politics. An orientalist by training and a revolutionary by profession, Kelsiev described his reading experience in a mixture of romantic, oriental, and sectarian symbols, including the most salient one – the New Man:

> I almost went berserk. My life literally split in two, and I became a new man. . . . It seemed to me while reading that I was entering a supernatural, secret world, the world of Hoffman, Edgar Allan Poe or *The Thousand and One Nights*. Suddenly, in one night, there was revealed to me the Skoptsy (Castrates) with their mystic rites . . . ; the Khlysty with their strange beliefs; . . . the intrigues of the leaders of Old-Believers. . . . Sect followed sect, images passed before me one after the other, as in a magic lantern. (Kelsiev 1941: 285)

In the light of this lantern, Kelsiev directed his revolutionary activities from London to the sectarian communities on the southern Russian frontier. Through them, he hoped to organize the smuggling of arms via Odessa and the distribution of propaganda literature in the Volga region. In 1862, he illegally re-entered Russia with a Turkish passport, presenting himself as an academic researcher on the Russian Schism. Thirty-two individuals were tried in court for having had contact with this self-proclaimed ethnographer. Shchapov, subpoenaed, denied meeting Kelsiev, but there was evidence of earlier correspondence, which resulted in Shchapov's exile to Siberia. In 1863, Kelsiev moved to Constantinople to make contact with the local Schismatics of Russian origin there, who served the Sultan and from time to time took part in military actions against Russia. The Turkish administration appointed Kelsiev "chief and protector of all Russians before the local authorities." Then, Kelsiev once more returned to Russia, surrendered to the police, wrote his "Confession" in prison, earned a pardon, and ended his days in quiet disgrace. The exciting saga of Kelsiev was fully covered in the literature of the time. Before his return to Russia, he served as a prototype of Rakhmetov in Chernyshevsky's novel *What is to be Done?* After his return, he served as a prototype of Shatov in Dostoevsky's *The Possessed* (Etkind 2001b: 83). In this novel, a conspiratorial group aims to spread among the people a subversive legend "that would surpass even that of the Skoptsy" (Castrates). The failure of his project leads its fictional participants to a murder and a suicide.

As for Shchapov, he never returned from Siberia, where he is credited for promoting Siberian separatism. Echoing him, the famous anarchist, Mikhail Bakunin, declared in 1862 that the Schism was a political protest against the Russian government and that the sects were a resource for the future revolution (Dragomanov 1896: 75). Looking to the Radical Reformation as a model for the Russian revolution, Bakunin said that socialism was the way peasants had led their lives from the beginning of time. He specifically referred to two ethnographic discoveries, the land commune and the Schism, to which he added "bandits." Following Shchapov, Bakunin chose the Beguny (Runners) sect as his favorite idiom of revolution. A splinter group of the Khlysty, the Beguny rejected not only the family, but also the home and any connections whatsoever to the state. They forbade money, printed books, and the use of their own names. The sect was discovered in 1849 on the northern Volga by an expedition of the Ministry of Internal Affairs with Ivan Aksakov as the leading expert. Relying on his evidence, Shchapov claimed that in the sectarian "capital" Sopelki, on the Volga river, the Beguny annually summoned "Federal Land Councils," which gathered "representatives" who came on foot from all over Russia, from the Carpathians to Siberia. The intrepid Beguny and their periodic Soviets were supposed to resolve the irresolvable question of populism: integration between the local communes (1906: 1/505–80).

Reading Shchapov in their adolescence, his best readers put his lessons into practice as adults. In the summer of 1874, the populists fanned out across the villages of Russia. The "Going to the People" movement had begun, "the most genuinely original social movement of modern Russian history" (Billington 1966: 204). In Kiev, Ivan Fesenko gathered around him 15 students, each of whom had to choose a sect according to his taste and then live among them. The sectarians would proselytize the radicals and the radicals would propagandize the sectarians. As a result, their ideas would draw closer to each other and the number of adherents would grow. Using Shchapov's essay of 1862 as a guidebook, most of Fesenko's followers went to the lower reaches of the Volga to locate the Beguny, but none succeeded in finding a single member of the sect. Another group went to the Molokane (the Milk-Drinkers), and several others chose to go to the Shtundisty (the Protestant-like sect influenced by German Mennonites). Fesenko himself went to a southern community of sectarians who whirled like the Khlysty. A participant in these events reported:

> As a former seminarian . . . Fesenko spouted quotes and freely interpreted texts. His listeners were amazed . . . his appearance strongly resembled that of a prophet. Towards the end of the session, Fesenko exalted these impressionable sectarians to such a degree that many of them were brought to a state of religious ecstasy. And then something totally improbable happened . . . the sectarians, having surrounded Fesenko in a tight circle, picked him up and started whirling about in ritual manner, joyously exclaiming, "He has come! He is here! He is with us!" (Deich 1923: 220)

Fesenko was ready to take on his new role, but the police would not allow him to be a village Christ for long. Vladimir Bonch-Bruevich, a future Bolshevik leader, claimed that he used the same method. According to his account, the ecstatic community of the Beguny thought that he was the Prophet Elijah, and the bespectacled Bonch-Bruevich, "as a representative of God, participated in their rituals which were accompanied by songs, hopping around, and what was almost an orgy" (Iordanskaia 1994: 208). Dmitrii Rogachev traveled along the Volga region, hiring himself out as a barge hauler. Reading the Psalms to illiterate sectarians, he was able to insert propaganda without their noticing it (Itenberg 1960: 48). In 1874, Katerina Breshko-Breshkovskaia, who was later nicknamed "the grandmother of the Russian Revolution," conducted propaganda work among the Shtundisty. Settling among the sectarians, she studied the Gospels for days, preparing herself for debates. After her first attempt, the leader of the community threatened her with the police, forcing her to flee (Breshkovskaia 1931: 51). More successful was Sofiia Subbotina, who resettled from Switzerland in 1873 to her estate in Kursk province to practice the healing arts and to politicize the local Skoptsy (Field 1987). The terrorist Mikhail Frolenko remembered that "in 1875, while we were spending time with the peaceful Shtundists, nobody even thought about taking up arms" (1932: 2/94). However, like other leaders of the movement, Frolenko became bitterly disillusioned with the sectarians and, as a result, turned to terror tactics. Ivan Kovalsky worked with a sectarian community in southern Russia, but all he succeeded in doing was, in his own words, "convince the elders not to fall down in ecstasy during prayer." Still, he presented his case as if the sects were a united movement and the author their leader:

> The Kherson and Kiev regions will surrender to the Shtundisty, and in the Poltava and Ekaterinoslav regions the Shaloputy are sprouting like mushrooms, and Novorossiia . . . was long ago made into a gathering

> place of the Molokane and Dukhobory. . . . The city of Nikolaev . . . has become a kind of massive laboratory in which various sects remake and perfect themselves. (Kovalsky 1878)

In August 1878, Kovalsky was executed for armed resistance against the police. In 1881, two student radicals made a pilgrimage to a sect of Sutaevtsy, in the Tver province. Founded in 1874 by Vasilii Sutaev, who argued that holding property was sinful, this small community was adopted by Lev Tolstoy and, later, by the Tolstovian movement, as their spiritual model. Inspired by their fieldwork with the Sutaevtsy, the students founded the "Christian Brotherhood," whose aim was to integrate student activism and peasant sectarianism under a common socialist ideal. When they were arrested, they reported to the police that they learned about this communist sect from a literary journal (Volk 1966: 377). According to one of these inspiring publications, a community of the southern Khlysty integrated a dozen villages in an efficient arrangement, a task that peasant communes usually failed to accomplish. Allegedly, the religious enthusiasm of sectarians helped them create a hierarchical, state-like structure while avoiding authoritarianism (Uimovich-Ponomarev and Ponomarev 1886; Saiapin 1915).

The Russian Luther

The idea of proselytizing among sects was specifically included in the first 1876 program of the revolutionary organization "Land and Liberty." The program recognized "a mass of great and small movements, sects of a religious-revolutionary character, and sometimes, gangs of bandits, who express the active protest of the Russian people." Therefore, the program called for revolutionaries "to merge with already existing People's organizations that have a revolutionary character" (Arkhiv 1932: 56–7). Aleksandr Mikhailov, the most powerful figure in this movement, traveled to the Volga Schismatics. He recalled: "I had to literally become an Old Believer. Those who know Old Believers know what this means. For an educated man, that means to carry out ten thousand Chinese ceremonies" (1906: 163–5). Mikhailov's task among the peaceful, hard-working Spasovtsy (the Savior's people) was to find the connection to the mythical sects of Beguny, but he failed in this project. The young Georgii Plekhanov, the future leader of Russian Marxism, accompanied Mikhailov during this trip. Plekhanov (1925) recalled a public debate in a church between Mikhailov, who was performing as a Schismatic preacher, and two Orthodox priests. Mikhailov stammered but still argued with great force; that, at least, was Plekhanov's view. The subject of debate was the Apocalypse, a relevant theme for Mikhailov, who disguised his revolutionary project under a religious mask, but in this double masquerade also shaped a way to realize his religious craving. Coming back to St. Petersburg in 1878 and joining terrorist activities, Mikhailov continued to prepare himself "for his future role as the Schism's Reformer," as Plekhanov put it. In practice, that meant that Mikhailov and his fellow guerrillas visited the public library to study the literature on the Schism, which mainly followed in Shchapov's footsteps. But they also prepared a sophisticated plan for a terrorist assassination of the tsar.[2]

In March 1881, Mikhailov's group murdered Alexander II, though Mikhailov was arrested several months before his triumph. The assassination created a new situation for the movement. Populists returned from the countryside to the capitals, changing their roles from propagandists to terrorists and their means from ethnographic tourism to armed guerilla warfare. Explosions of external aggression were accompanied by an epidemic of suicides (Paperno 1997). Marxist scholars have attributed this transition, from populism to terrorism, to the class-based disappointment of activists with the peasantry, thus paving the way to the later enchantment with the proletariat. Class analysis, however, has obscured more specific explications of the events (Hardy 1987). The populists' disillusionment with the sectarians provides a more precise explanation of the movement's crisis.

Neglected by historians, this explanation was known to the participants. Having fled from the Russian police to England, Sergei Stepniak-Kravchinskii explained that the "Going to the People" was a religious rather than political movement. He compared the populist propagandists to the early Christians, their collective journey to the Russian heartland to a "crusade," and their efforts to settle among

[2] Characteristically, Samuel Baron (1953, 1995), the prominent American expert on Plekhanov, mentions his work with the peasants on the Volga but ignores its crucial aspect: that Plekhanov and Mikhailov spread propaganda and acquired their formative experience not among the common peasants but among the peculiar Spasovtsy. In an illuminating essay, Baron (1995: 188–206) self-critically analyzes the pro-Soviet, "leftish" roots of his lifelong infatuation with Plekhanov. As it happened, this interest did not help the historian to appreciate the religious episodes in his subject's itinerary.

peasants to "the colonies." When these "colonies" failed, the crusaders became terrorists. Two Jewish activists, Osip Aptekman and Lev Deich, began their political careers as propagandists among the Molokane (Haberer 1995: 102–5). Aptekman later illuminated the intellectual roots of the populist drama:

> Many of us, without any impetus from the government, ran without a backward glance from the countryside: the countryside, obviously, was more offensive than the government itself. . . . Shchapov, and then Kelsiev and others, had carelessly let it be known beyond any doubt that the Schism was a hidden reserve force for the Revolution. . . . Many gatherings of young people came together and read verbose essays about Schismatics. (Aptekman 1924: 434–6)

Fascination with texts led to fascination with sects; disillusionment with sects led to violence. Among the most faithful, these acts repeated in cycles. In 1874, the peasants of Chernigov converted Nikolai Tchaikovsky, the organizer of an important group of student radicals in St. Petersburg, to the Khlysty (Lavrov 1974: 1/147). After his return to the capital, Tchaikovsky preached non-violence and tried to transform his group into a religious commune. His friends had already become terrorists, and so Tchaikovsky left for America to join the peaceful Shakers. After some years, he returned to Europe to take part in revolutionary activities. In 1907, he made another trip to the sectarian regions of the Volga and was arrested. In 1918, President Wilson consulted with Tchaikovsky during the Versailles negotiations; the Bolsheviks condemned Tchaikovsky to death in absentia. As his biography aptly demonstrates, Tchaikovsky did not really choose between revolutionary activism and sectarian mysticism, but rather synthesized these two options (Hecht 1947; Etkind 2001b). Though extraordinary, his itinerary was not unique. Viktor Danilov, a nobleman and terrorist from Ukraine, was exiled to Siberia from whence he fled to Europe, but he returned illegally to Russia to undertake numerous pilgrimages to the Khlysty, whom he described in a series of amateurish essays. He was again exiled to Yakutia, where he married a native and called himself an ethnographer. At the start of his fascinating career, Danilov was first arrested in the Caucasus among the Dukhobory (Spirit-Wrestlers) in 1874. At the end of his career, in 1911, the Russian Prime Minister Petr Stolypin consulted with Danilov on his expertise about the Khlysty (Etkind 1998: 641).

In 1898, in a provincial library near Tambov, Viktor Chernov read an old review of Shchapov's work (Subbotin 1867) and was so inspired that he revealed in the local community of Molokane a ready-made clandestine organization with a subversive program (Chernov 1922: 1/302). Having found his way to the people in the library, Chernov then established a new library among the Molokane. On its shelves, books by Shchapov stood next to those by western utopian writers such as Charles Fourier and Edward Bellamy. Working with the Molokane, Chernov found that these people, as well as many others, were ready for "the Russian Luther." He hoped to play this role himself. It was the Russian way of doing politics, Chernov believed, to converge the Revolution with "our native Reformation, which is far too belated" (Chernov 1922: 1/275). The young Chernov was a future celebrity, the founder of the Socialist–Revolutionary party and a leader of the February 1917 Revolution. In his tragic life, he presided over decades of the terrorist politics of the Socialist–Revolutionaries and led this party from victory to victory, until they lost to the even more radical Social Democrats, the future Communists.

Founded by Georgii Plekhanov after his return from a pilgrimage to the Spasovtsy on the Volga, the Social Democrats changed the perspective of the Russian revolutionary movement. The agnostic proletariat, rather than the religious peasantry, would be the bulwark of revolution. Two big issues were at stake, the people and the state. The early enthusiasts, Shchapov and Bakunin, believed in the secret wisdom of the common people, which would manifest itself if they were freed from interference from the state. The professional revolutionaries, Plekhanov and Lenin, found this unacceptable: it was precisely the state, understood as the apparatus of violence, which they singled out as their tool. For them, that traditional hope of Russian socialists, the commune, was a feature and creation of Russia's "oriental society", an outdated institution that had to be overcome (Baron 1958).

The populists exaggerated their cultural distance from the peasantry precisely in those instances when they wished to overcome that distance. Among the people, they imagined harems and cannibalism, compared their experience to Arabic tales, and spoke about Chinese ceremonies. Disappointed with popular sects or, rather, the historical account of these sects, they reverted to terrorism, which launched a vicious cycle of violence that led to the Revolution. Worshipping the heroic past of revolutionary terrorism, they repressed a part of its historical legacy that connected it to the Russian sects. Nevertheless, even the Social Democrats continued working with the sects. The young Leon Trotsky began his revolutionary career with propaganda among urban sectarians (Trotsky 1990: 1/130).

The Exemplary Farm

The emphasis on the religious underpinnings of the Russian revolution has become popular in more recent literature (Etkind 1998, 2003; Manchester 1998, 2008; Rowley 1999; Halfin 2000; Malia 2006; see also fictional accounts: Sharov 2003; Meek 2005). Indeed, religion and revolution were allied in the minds of the two pre-revolutionary generations, but the specific mechanisms of their interaction were complex and sometimes deceitful. Revolutionary leaders proclaimed their atheism, and there is no reason to distrust them. Most of them were, indeed, secular intellectuals. But the revolutions they produced, or planned to produce, were not necessarily secular. An heir and revisionist of the populist tradition, Lenin suggested a combination of the "progressive vanguard" and the "backward peasantry" as the route to Russian revolution. Leading peasantry to the civilization of the future was a radically new version of that internal colonization that Lenin perceptively found in Russian provinces (see Chapter 2). This project was dependent on the perception of the peasantry as a disguised, non-self-conscious world of religious dissent and political protest. The Orthodox clergy remained faithful to the monarchy, but the peasantry was religious in a different way. To capture the leadership over the selected groups of the dissenting peasantry and to exploit them for political purposes meant a chance for revolution in Russia. The deep hybridization between religion and politics manifested itself in varied, unstable versions.

Aware of the cultural gap that separated them from the peasants, radicals hoped to use religious symbols to communicate their political aims. Many of the populists were children of priests. Those who graduated from church schools and seminaries knew the Orthodox rhetoric, but were typically discontent with church practices. Others were noblemen with university degrees who pursued highly individualized versions of religious-political synthesis. Populists were fascinated with the social structures of sects, which they identified with the primordial socialism. They interpreted the sects' apocalyptic expectations as a promise of the coming revolution. Though the task of the young socialists was to turn themselves into the leaders of mystical communities and, then, to bring them to the goals that were entirely foreign for these communities, not all these propagandists were cynical manipulators, like Kurtz from Conrad's *Heart of Darkness*. The whole spectrum from the most pragmatic cynicism to the most naive enthusiasm was tested. In this spiritual domain, the enthusiasts were more successful than the manipulators.

Academic scholarship, political activism, and religious fervor were often indistinguishable for these intellectuals. While the academic aspects of their activism shaped public display, the religious ones remained in the private imagery, which left its traces mainly in personal diaries or memoirs. Within the Party of Socialist Revolutionaries that was led by Chernov, the leading expert on the Schism was Aleksandr Prugavin, an ethnographer who, like many of his Russian colleagues, acquired his profession in political exile; he believed in the approaching union of sectarianism and socialism until the day he died in a Bolshevik prison (Prugavin 1881, 1904, 1917). Within the Party of Social Democrats that was led by Lenin, Vladimir Bonch-Bruevich provided the ethnographic expertise (Etkind 1996, 1998; Engelstein 1999). Leading the double life of a terrorist networker and a sectarian aficionado, he visited many sectarian communities, but

Figure 17: Lenin and Bonch-Bruevich, October 16, 1918. Moscow, Kremlin.

found his ideal in the émigré Dukhobory (Spirit-Strugglers) villages in Canada. Bonch-Bruevich's book about them is the ode to mystical socialism, perhaps the most mesmerizing portrait of "the people" ever written in Russian. Ironically, this people had already moved to Canada, while the author moved to the Kremlin (Bonch-Bruevich 1918).

The commandant of the Smolny headquarters of the Bolsheviks in 1917 and the chief-of-staff in the first Lenin government, in 1921 Bonch-Bruevich organized the exemplary *sovkhoz* (Soviet farm) near Moscow, on an estate that earlier belonged to Savva Morozov. He resettled there a community of the Khlysty from St. Petersburg, who called themselves the Chemreki, with their leader Pavel Legkobytov. Relying on their efficiency in dairy farming and trusting their honesty in accounting, Bonch-Bruevich hoped to establish an example of practical communism that other Russian communes and communities would follow. In 1922, together with a number of agricultural officials, he signed the "Call to Sectarians and Old-Ritualists in Russia and Abroad." This document praised sectarians for their "millennial experience" with collective agriculture and invited them to emerge from their underground and to return from emigration. An analogue to Catherine's Manifesto of 1763 (see Chapter 7), this document promised the sectarian communities the land that was confiscated from the noble landowners, thereby presenting the sectarians as beneficiaries of the Revolution. Also like Catherine, the People's Comissariat of Agriculture established a governmental body to oversee the new resettlement, the "Committee for the Settlement of Sectarians and Old-Ritualists in State Farms, Free Lands, and the Former Estates." During the Civil War in 1919, the Lenin administration gave sectarians an exemption from military service, a sign of their favored but passive status. As much as the Bolsheviks admired the non-acquisitive character of sectarian economies, they detested the non-violence that was preached and practiced by them (Etkind 1998).

Never fulfilled, promises of popular support led Bonch-Bruevich to the summit of very real power. From 1917 to 1920, hundreds of the top governmental orders were signed with two names, Lenin's and Bonch-Bruevich's. The long-standing friendship between the two shows that the fascination with sectarians remained a respected preoccupation among revolutionary leaders. After Lenin's death, Bonch-Bruevich focused on creating the Lenin cult and, in this context, initiated a new discussion on the affinity between the sectarians and the Bolsheviks at the Thirteenth Party Congress in 1924. Outliving his academic subjects and political opponents, Bonch-Bruevich died in 1955, while serving as director of the academic Museum of the History of Religion and Atheism that was, meaningfully, located in a cathedral. In this museum, he himself was the most unique exhibit.

While the Russian revolutionaries were abandoning their belief in the political potential of sects, the Russian literati were developing their interest in the subject. The most important writers of the early twentieth century, such as Lev Tolstoy and Andrei Bely, depicted sectarians in their writings (Vroon 1994). Tolstoy favored the Dukhobory, but he was also interested in the Khlysty and he corresponded with the Skoptsy (Tolstoy 1908; Heier 1970; Fodor 1989). Sects and revolution were central subjects for Andrei Platonov in *Chevengur*, Boris Pil'niak in *The Naked Year*, Maksim Gorky in *Klim Samgin*, and Vsevolod Ivanov in his underappreciated *Kremlin*. Lev Trotsky had a point when he accused fellow-travelers of the Revolution of having a "half-Khlystovian perspective on events"; the true Bolsheviks shave themselves, added Trotsky (1991: 68). Mystical populism constituted an important part of the governing ideology of the years that preceded and followed the Revolution, and sectarianism was at the center of Russian public debate (Etkind 1998). But in the real politics of revolutionary Russia, there was nothing akin to the sectarian mobilization found in the English revolution of the seventeenth century, in antebellum America, or in nineteenth-century England (Nordhoff 1875; Hobsbawm 1959; Walzer 1965; Taves 1999).

The most important case of direct political action by members of Russian religious dissent in the early twentieth century was the financial contributions made by some Moscow Old-Believer merchants to extremist parties, including the Bolsheviks. The most important, Savva Morozov (1862–1905), was a descendant of the radical community of Old-Believers who taught about the imminent coming of the Anti-Christ. Reportedly because of his youthful fascination with fireworks, he studied chemistry at Cambridge. He later owned major textile enterprises and breweries near Moscow and in the Urals. A major philanthropist, he financed the Moscow Artistic Theater and was close to its actress, the wife of Maksim Gorky. Through Gorky, he also financed the underground Bolshevik newspaper and some terrorist activities. He told Gorky about the experiments of Ernest Rutherford at Cambridge; they also discussed Nietzsche, whose philosophy Morozov compared to pyrotechnics. After Morozov's suicide, Gorky's wife received a big sum of money and passed it to the Social–Democratic underground. Morozov was buried at an Old-Believers' cemetery; many were convinced that the Bolsheviks killed him (Felshtinsky 2009). Other Old-Believer merchants, however, contributed to moderate parties (Williams 1986; West 1991). Many of them were secularized to an extent that makes it difficult to speculate about the religious sources of their politics.

The only figure of national significance who could arguably be considered a sectarian was Grigorii Rasputin, a radical in his own way, but hardly a revolutionary. The controversial and well-publicized evidence of his sectarianism did nothing to hinder his success at the court of the Romanovs. On the contrary, his populist performance determined his success at court and with the Synod. After 50 years of glorification of Russian sects by the Left, the regime of Nicholas II boasted a live sectarian who symbolized popular support for the crown (Jonge 1982; Etkind 1998). This deal was not an easy one; resistance to Rasputin's ascendance to cultural power raged furiously.

As the dynasty went native, the imperial period was approaching its end. Lev Tolstoy told a British guest that he had a sectarian peasant as his "spiritual father" and that he, Count Tolstoy, was nothing but "the interpreter to the world at large of what the Russian peasants have always known" (Stead 1888: 440). This manner of self-presentation did not hamper Tostoy's popularity but instead boosted it to new heights. After the 1905 Revolution, the famous *Vekhi* anthology warned the intelligentsia of its future destruction by the people. But the leading authors of the *Vekhi*, such as Nikolai Berdiaev, remained infatuated with the Khlysty and other sects (Berdiaev 1916, 1989). As happened earlier in Europe, many Russian intellectuals felt that "modernity impoverishes" and that religious enthusiasm "compensate[s] for modernity's costs" (Klein and La Vopa 1998: 3). Feeling a keen interest in Russian sects, Max Weber was hesitant to extend his analysis of the Protestant ethics to their variety (Weber 1995: 64, 161; Radkau 2009: 246; also Gerschenkron 1970). In keeping with his famous thesis on the Protestant ethic, some sociologists have speculated that the success of religious reformation would have facilitated capitalist development in Russia. In fact, the very same populists and socialists who talked about the Russian Luther wished to prevent the development of capitalism in Russia. Partially due to their activities, the failure of the reformation led to an anticapitalist revolution. Even though one could argue that Weber's thesis was proven in the negative, the variety of the sectarian experience in Russia, the political aims of intellectual pilgrimages to the sectarian communities, and the massive disillusionment that the intellectuals found there are all very different from the universe of *The Protestant Ethic*. A different kind of sociology is needed in this case and I argue that this sociology is Emil Durkheim's. He helps to appreciate the deep affinity between the rituals of popular Russian sects, such as the Khlysty, and the theories of nineteenth-century socialists.

Whirling together in an ecstatic ritual and inviting God to inhabit their collective body, the Khlysty worshipped the Durkheimian "society writ large," an organic, cohesive community that was higher, stronger, and more real than the individuals who compose it. This image matched the aspirations that many Russian socialists projected onto their society of the future. The alleged indifference of the Khlysty to property, their abstinence from marital sex, and rumors about the ritual orgies in their communities all added to the charms that many populists, some socialists, and even a few Bolsheviks could not resist. They imagined themselves leading the enthusiastic masses of Russian sectarians, colonizing them from within and directing them towards the "scientific" goals that they believed to be not much different from the ideals of the sectarians. The religious nature of sectarian worship differed from the technocratic imagination of the faithful Marxists, but the overlap was in communitarian ideas that the activists hoped to expand and exploit. The notion of a Russian historical affinity with communism also satisfied nationalist sentiment, which the fantasy of world revolution never managed to suppress.

With the collectivization of 1928, the sectarian diversions of Russian socialists were forgotten in Russia and remained unknown abroad. However, some critics still used them to understand the nature of the new Bolshevik society. Having visited Moscow in the 1920s, the Austrian writer and Freud's editor, René Fülöp-Miller alleged that the Bolsheviks borrowed some of their ideas and rituals from the Khlysty (1927: 71). An author of books on Dostoevsky and Rasputin, Fülöp-Miller illustrated his point by yet another scene of sectarian sex, "the most wild and unbridled orgies, in which complete promiscuity is the rule" (1927: 82).

Having little to do with the historical reality of Bolshevik rule, this narrative matched the literary convention of anti-utopian writing. When Aldous Huxley wrote his *Brave New World* (1932) with its memorable Solidarity Service, he took inspiration from Fülöp-Miller's book, *The Mind and Face of Bolshevism*, which he reviewed while he was working on the novel (Huxley 1958: 191; Etkind 2004). As it happened, Huxley based his frightening scene of the compulsory group sex of the future on the mid-nineteenth-century fantasy of the mythical orgy of the Khlysty.

—11—

Re-Enchanting the Darkness

In the late nineteenth century, two writers composed a novella each that was set in oddly similar settings. In both novels, on the deck of a freshwater vessel, one of the passengers entertains the others by telling stories of his distant adventures. In the story by Joseph Conrad, a ship is anchored in the Thames. In the story by Nikolai Leskov, a passenger vessel sails on the lake of Ladoga. Although the passengers listen, question, and express doubts in similar ways, the storytellers are vastly different and so are their relations with their public. The English storyteller, Marlow, a commercial seaman who has traveled to the Indian Ocean and the Pacific, describes a freshwater trip into the heart of Africa that was even more exotic than his travels on the high seas. The Russian storyteller, Fliagin, a horse groom who pretends to be a monk, tells the passengers the tales of his travels, by foot and on horseback, across Eurasia. Russian literature has focused on ground transportation as much as English literature has on the sea. But the two novellas in question, Leskov's *The Enchanted Pilgrim* (1873) and Conrad's *Heart of Darkness* (1899), are both stories told on river vessels. These works have become highly popular in their respective traditions – national, imperial, and postcolonial. Read together, they provide an exciting perspective on their deep, unacknowledged peculiarities. In this chapter, I will re-read these novellas together with two lesser-known non-fiction texts by the same authors that present helpful self-commentaries to the better-known ones.

Darkness Was Here

Observing the Thames, Conrad's Marlow imagines a Roman colony on its banks:

> Darkness was here yesterday. . . . The very end of the world, a sea the color of lead, a sky the color of smoke. . . . Sandbanks, marshes, forests, savages. . . . Here and there a military camp lost in a wilderness like a needle in a bundle of hay – cold, fog, tempests, disease, exile, and death. (p. 9)[1]

Marlow is not an intellectual but an adventurer. However, he introduces his story of the modern colonizer, Kurtz, by outlining his ancient genealogy. Such a long-term historical perspective is surprising not only for Marlow the sailor, but even for Conrad the writer; he probably received it from a particular kind of romanticized Hegelian historicism that was popular in the Poland of his youth (Niland 2010). Looking at the Thames and thinking about the Congo, Marlow describes a Roman who came to England "in the train of some prefect, or tax-gatherer, or trader even, to mend his fortunes." Whatever he traded in England, though it was certainly not ivory, Marlow sees two differences between the ancient and the modern. "What saves us is efficiency," he says with irony. "What redeems it is the idea." Apart from these two ambiguous phrases, he describes the ancient colonizer in a way that is strikingly similar to his modern counterpart:

> Land in a swamp, march through the woods, and in some inland post feel the savagery. . . . There's no initiation either into such mysteries. He has to live in the midst of the incomprehensible, which is also detestable. And it has a fascination, too, that goes to work upon him. The fascination of the abomination – you know. (pp. 9–10)

Here on the Thames, the colonized have become the colonizers. At length, Marlow recounts his attempt to rescue the fabulously efficient Kurtz, an agent who "collected, bartered, swindled, or stole more ivory than all the other agents together," but who got sick or went mad at his Central Station. Though the story centers on ivory, there is no mention of elephants. Kurtz did not hunt; he delivered the "fossil" ivory that the "niggers" had hunted and stored beforehand. Kurtz's secret was to make the natives dig up the product and deliver it in an organized, ritual manner. The natives "adored him"; he approached them "with thunder and lightning. . . . He could be very terrible. . . . The chiefs came every day to see him. They would crawl"

[1] For quotes from *Heart of Darkness*, see Conrad 1988; page numbers are indicated in parentheses.

(pp. 56–8). Organizing these commercial miracles, Kurtz also raided one tribe with the help of another. Marlow observed heads drying on the stakes near Kurtz's dwelling.

For Marlow and also for Conrad, this hybridized kind of terror, which imitated wilderness by means of civilization, was worse than the wilderness itself. Kurtz made his business by digging into the belief system of the natives and making them adore him as their god. "The wilderness . . . loved him" and he loved the wilderness, with the result that this alliance manifested "the inconceivable ceremonies of some devilish initiation." He "presided at certain midnight dances ending with unspeakable rites" and these rites led to swindling the ivory from the natives. From Marlow's common-sense perspective, these "unspeakable rites" felt "more intolerable than those heads drying on the stakes under Mr. Kurtz's windows" (p. 58) As a result, he did not learn much about these improvised rituals. We know only that Kurtz developed "the power to charm or frighten rudimentary souls into an aggravated witch-dance in his honor" and that part of the same business was "aggravated murder on a great scale." The rites and raids worked together to create a profit.

The reader might be disappointed in Marlow's anthropological skills, but Kurtz's were officially recognized. A member of the International Society for the Suppression of Savage Customs, Kurtz argued in his report to this learned society that the whites must necessarily appear to the savages "in the nature of supernatural beings." At the end of this "beautiful piece of writing," Marlow found "a kind of note . . . scrawled evidently much later, in an unsteady hand . . . : 'Exterminate all the brutes!' " (p. 50). Marlow sees these two aspects of Kurtz's business plan as intimately connected. The re-enchantment of the world by the enlightened colonizers for the sake of "the idea" ignites violence and is impossible without it.

Erebus and Terror

In 1870, a Polish boy, Józef, became addicted to map-gazing (Conrad 1921: 19). He studied in a high school in Krakow and his favorite subject was geography. It was there that he fell in love with multicolored maps, a passion Marlow also feels in *The Heart of Darkness*. Józef's family consisted of Russian subjects who lived and worked in a complex colonial situation. His grandfather and father managed leaseholds on land estates in Western Ukraine, which became part of the Russian Empire after the second partition of Poland. Józef was born in these colonized lands, in the Ukrainian-Jewish town of Berdyczów. His father, Apollo Korzeniowski, received his education at the St. Petersburg Imperial University, in the Department of Oriental Studies, which was chaired by Osip Senkovsky, the Pole who established academic orientalism in Russia. Korzeniowski was also a poet and playwright whose work developed under the obvious influence of his Russian predecessors. After having lost his fortune on leaseholds, he turned to underground politics and became a hero of the anti-imperial struggle. He led an underground movement in the Ukrainian city of Żytomierz and later in Warsaw with the goal of emancipating Poland, along with its ancient domains in Ukraine, from the Russian rule. He was arrested in October 1861 when, in anticipation of the Polish rebellion, the Russians introduced martial law.

In the Austrian-Polish Krakov, Józef was an orphan and he was stateless. His parents died after being exiled by the Russian Empire to Vologda. Together with Józef, they had traveled thousands of miles by foot and by horse carriage. Not quite as far as the Arctic, Vologda was nevertheless cold and dangerous enough to justify Józef's obsession with Arctic maps and the lonely heroes who had died on their way through the ice. At school, Józef wrote an essay on the subject and, decades later, remembered it as "an erudite performance." But his professors were "persons with no romantic sense for the real" and were not interested in the Arctic (Conrad 1921: 17).

In his late memoirs, Conrad was still coming to terms with events from the distant past. He revisited, more than once, the scene of his sick mother's return from Vologda to Poland for a few months before she went back through the cold, despotic Russia to rejoin her husband. With some irony, Conrad later related the stories that he had heard in his youth from his Polish relatives. An uncle, an officer of the Napoleonic army that invaded Russia, was hiding from the Cossacks in a peasant hut when a dog betrayed him by barking. In response, the uncle cut off the dog's head and devoured the little body. "He had eaten him to appease his hunger, no doubt, but also for the sake of an unappeasable and patriotic desire," wrote Conrad (1919: 78).

John A. McClure was right to state that "Conrad lived both as a native of a colonized country and as a member of a colonizing community." His father was a colonial manager *and* a victim of foreign imperialism. As a Polish subject of the Russian Empire, he was a victim of external colonization; as a Polish manager of the Ukrainian peasants, he was a colonizer. This double experience was unique among British writers: "Conrad achieved what . . . some, like Kipling, tried: a view from the other side of the compound wall" (McClure 1981: 92; Fleishman 1967). The multilayered experience of Russian colonialism, in which the roles of the colonizer and the colonized repeatedly flipped, provided Conrad with this stereoscopic ability. In Conrad's Eastern Europe, the very idea of progress, with its double effects, was experienced as a colonial conquest: "Progress leaves its dead by the way, for progress is only a great adventure . . . a march into an undiscovered country; and in such an enterprise victims do not count" (Conrad 1921: 156).

The young Józef's hero was Sir John Franklin, the commander of an Arctic expedition undertaken by two British ships, the *Erebus* and the *Terror*. The expedition departed in 1845 to search for the Northwest Passage between Greenland and North America. When the ships disappeared, several attempts were made to find them. In 1859, Sir Leopold McClintock led another expedition that was organized by Franklin's widow, Lady Jane. On an island, McClintock discovered a note that was left by Franklin's expedition, which read: "All well." A second message, written a year later on the margins of the same sheet of paper, reported that the *Erebus* and the *Terror* were trapped in the ice and that the crew had abandoned the ships (Conrad 1926: 15–16). The Inuits later said that they saw the sailors eating their dead. These reports of cannibalism among the dying Brits have been confirmed by the later findings of their remains (Keenleyside et al. 1997).

McClintock's book describing the search for Franklin in the Arctic seas was the favorite reading of the young Józef. "I have read the work many times since," Conrad later wrote; "the realities of the story sent me off on the romantic explorations of the inner self; to the discovery of the taste for poring over maps." This essay, "Geography and Some Explorers," juxtaposed those voyages that were driven by "an acquisitive spirit, the idea of lucre" and those that were "free from any taint of that sort." Examples of the first type were travelers who went south; examples of the second type were polar explorers such as Franklin, "whose aims were as pure as the air of those high latitudes." Even though Conrad's maturation meant a shift of his interests from the north to the south and from purity to lucre, he claimed, "it must not be supposed that I gave up my interest in the polar regions" (1926: 14, 17, 21). In *Heart of Darkness* Marlow repeated after his creator: "Now when I was a little chap I had a passion for maps. . . . At that time there were many blank spaces on the earth. . . . The North Pole was one of these places, I remember. Well, I haven't been there yet, and shall not try now. The glamour's off" (p. 11).

Marlow's tropical narrative starts with a reference to John Franklin and his ships, the *Erebus* and the *Terror*, which had also departed from the Thames (p. 8). These two names foreshadow Marlow's story. The Greek god Erebus, the son of Chaos, is the personification of darkness. Terror culminates in the last words of Kurtz: "The Horror! The Horror!" Marlow's rescue expedition works in contrast to the extraordinary saga of McClintock's search for Franklin. Marlow lied to Kurtz's fiancée; McClintock did tell the truth to Franklin's wife, by then a widow. Marlow's suspicion of cannibalism amongst black Africans, which has infuriated some of Conrad's critics (Achebe 2001), was also inspired by Franklin's saga.

Heart of Darkness mentions the Thames where the story is told but not once does it name the Congo where the action takes place. Usually a precise geographer, Conrad situates Marlow's travel by using the most general terms – the river, darkness, earth:

> Going up that river was like traveling back to the earliest beginnings of the world. . . . There were moments when one's past came back to one. . . . And this stillness of life did not in the least resemble a peace. It was the stillness of an implacable force brooding over an inscrutable intention. It looked at you with a vengeful aspect. (p. 35)

With all the difference between the frost and the heat, there is nonetheless an uncanny resemblance between Conrad's depictions of the Congo under Leopold II and Russia under Nicolas II:

> The snow covered the endless forests, the frozen rivers, the plains of an immense country, obliterating the landmarks, the accidents of the ground, levelling everything under its uniform whiteness, like a monstrous blank page awaiting the record of an inconceivable history. (Conrad 2001: 25)

There is no doubt that the story about Kurtz was situated in the Congo. However, the fact is that Conrad did not locate the heart of darkness in any specific place but, rather, gave a summary image of the imperial conquest. There were such places on the map "in every sort of latitude" and every time in history; Conrad, like Marlow, had visited some of them. For Locke, "in the beginning all the world was America." For Conrad, at its roots, all the world was Poland.

The Thick Description of Kurtz

The central protagonist, Kurtz, is almost mute in Conrad's novel. The first, unnamed narrator learns about Kurtz from the second narrator, Marlow, who learned about Kurtz from the third narrator, who knew him well. This third source was a Russian. To meet a Russian in the heart of Africa was a surprise of course; Marlow is "lost in astonishment." The son of a priest of the provincial Russian town of Tambov, this self-employed ivory trader stayed, traveled, and traded with Kurtz. He nursed Kurtz during his illness like a civilized man, but adored him and supplied him with ivory like a native. We do not know the name of this Russian. He is a bizarre fellow but, strangely enough, Marlow takes his words at face value:

> There he was before me, in motley, as though he had absconded from a troupe of mimes, enthusiastic, fabulous. His very existence was improbable, inexplicable, and altogether bewildering. He was an insoluble problem. . . . His clothes had been made of some stuff that was brown holland probably, but it was covered with patches all over, with bright patches, blue, red, and yellow. (pp. 53–4)

Marlow likes the strange son of Tambov and solves at least one of his problems. His bizarre outfit "reminded me of something I had seen – something funny I had seen somewhere," he says. At the start of his story, he describes a map that he had seen in the office of the company that hired him. It was a "large shining map, marked with all the colors of a rainbow. There was a vast amount of red – good to see at any time, because one knows that some real work is done in there, a deuce of a lot of blue, a little green, smears of orange, and, on the East Coast, a purple patch" (p. 13). Conrad could base this colorful map on Cecil Rhodes's aphorism, "I contend that we are the first race in the world. . . . If there be God, I think that what he would like me to do is to paint as much of the map of Africa British red as possible" (quoted in Spivak 1999: 13). There was no color to represent Russia on the map of Africa; Russia did not have colonies there. Instead, the colonial colors were all "painted" on a Russian adventurist, who represented for Conrad a personal symbol of imperialism (GoGwilt 1995) and nothingness (Said 1966: 146).

Creating his harlequin to embody the colorful darkness of the colonial endeavor, Conrad smuggled into the tragedy of the European colonization of Africa the trauma of the Russian colonization of Poland. Tambov is even further from the Arctic Circle than Vologda, but the temper of this Russian matched those selfless souls of Arctic explorers whom Conrad adored in his youth:

> He surely wanted nothing from the wilderness but space to breathe in and to push on through. . . . If the absolutely pure, uncalculating, unpractical spirit of adventure had ever ruled a human being, it ruled this bepatched youth. I almost envied him the possession of this modest and clear flame. (p. 55)

These are almost the same words that Marlow had used at the start of his story, when he contrasted the greedy travelers to the south with the pure explorers of the north, "whose aims were as pure as the air of those high latitudes." This Russian's purity was connected to his glamor, a word that Marlow used with some insistence. "Well, I haven't been there [to the North Pole] yet, and shall not try now. The glamour's off," Marlow said at the start of his story. It is the same northern glamor that he found in his new Russian acquaintance. "Glamour urged him on, glamour kept him unscathed" (p. 55).

As Marlow approaches the Central Station, he makes "an extraordinary find" in an abandoned hut: a technical book, *An Inquiry Into Some Points of Seamanship*. The copy is 60 years old, published about the time of John Franklin's travels. In the margins, there are penciled notes that refer to the text. These notes are in a cipher that Marlow cannot read. He sees it as "an extravagant mystery," but when he meets the motley-dressed Russian he realizes that the notes were written in Cyrillic. The whole episode reads out of context, as a kind of textual cipher in itself. It is strange, of course, to meet a Russian adventurist in Central Congo; but, given that fact, there can be nothing mysterious about his annotating a book in his own language. In a text bursting with meaning, what is the meaning of these Cyrillic notes?

Post factum notes play significant roles in the *Heart of Darkness* and "Geography and Some Explorers," Conrad's self-commentary on *Heart of Darkness*. Kurtz's note, "Exterminate all the brutes!" changed the meaning of his anthropological report. Added to their previous message, "All is well," the dying sailors' note reported John Franklin's death. In both cases, Kurtz's and Franklin's, the texts were untrue but the later comments revealed the truth. Conrad's later essay, "Geography and Some Explorers," plays exactly this same role, partly explanatory and party deconstructive, in relation to *The Heart of Darkness*. The unread comments in the margins of the British book of seamanship play the same role.

Almost all that Marlow learned, and that we know, about Kurtz, came from the Russian (Brooks 1996: 70). This is particularly true of the most interesting part of Kurtz's story, his methods of treating the natives: "[T]his amazing tale that was not so much told as suggested to me in desolate exclamations . . . in interrupted phrases . . . in hints" of the Russian (p. 56). Marlow could not verify this interpretation of Kurtz's activities because, when he finally reaches Kurtz, he is about to die. But this interpretation made sense for Marlow; he did not question it, his interlocutors did not question it, and we the readers rarely do so, either. However, Marlow says that this Russian harlequin crawled before Kurtz "as much as the veriest savage of them all" (p. 58), which makes the Russian a little bit too involved for an observer.

Interpretation is important; it is terribly important if it is the only source of evidence, raw or processed. Told in Africa by the Tambovian to the Londoner, the story of Kurtz is very Russian indeed. Kurtz did not just go native (Rothberg 2009: 83). Like his Russian friend, he also became more savage than the savages, installing himself into the native system of beliefs with an amazing "efficiency." Combining charismatic leadership with violent coercion, Kurtz reformed the natives with the sole purpose of enriching himself in a way that was foreign to them. He did not act as a missionary, struggling to replace the belief system of the natives with his own. He worked, rather, as a virus, entrenching himself in the center of the native spiritual system and forcing this system to offer sacrifices to him. It was an internal colonization of a sort.

Imperialism was at its worst not when it acted by pure force but when it sought a project of hegemony on top of the usual domination, a religious or ideological faith in its activities that would be felt by the exploited population. Reading about the fictional colonizer, Kurtz, in the *Heart of Darkness*, we find a composite of various sources, from the inherited knowledge of Polish methods of leasehold management in Ukraine, to memories of Russian massacres in Poland, to British massacres in India, to Conrad's feelings about his own visit to the Congo, to his vague expectations for the Russian and colonial revolutions that would, he knew, create new kinds of darkness. Going to the people, inhabiting their religion and forcing them to work for his own "idea," Kurtz did what two generations of Russian radicals did before and after him. Though these Russian populists were driven not by the lure of profit but, rather, by their utopian ideals, Conrad saw their methods as similar. On top of the violent capability of his firearms, Kurtz's particular sort of "efficiency" needed social sciences and humanities. This is why Conrad made his brutal, greedy character a scholar who was respected by learned societies. In the late nineteenth century, sociology and anthropology opened new vistas for understanding the people and, also, for trying to change them. In the transformationist spirit of the time, some enthusiastic experts called this process "God-building."[2] Reading Durkheim and Marx together, these radical intellectuals asked themselves: If rituals instill values, why not create new rituals? If gods replace one another like tsars, why not enthrone new gods? Since Russia did not feature a rational proletariat but, rather, a mystical peasantry, would it be not the disenchanting enlightenment but, instead, the re-enchantment of the world that would launch the Russian revolution? This process of purposeful, pre-planned God-building would absorb the beliefs among the common folk and direct them toward revolution. Since only the experts – ethnographers, historians, and sociologists – could claim knowledge of these beliefs, these experts became essential for the social revolution (see Chapter 10). In fact, these sons of priests and connoisseurs of sectarian communities, some of them professional revolutionaries and convinced God-builders, looked and sounded like Conrad's harlequin, though they chose to go to the Volga rather than to the Congo. Working among the exotic sectarians with the aim of becoming their leaders and exploiting them for the revolution, these intellectuals would emulate Kurtz in his "unspeakable" inventions. I can imagine finding the note, "Exterminate all the brutes!" in the vast archive of Anatolii Lunacharsky, a prominent God-builder. It would be "an extraordinary finding" but it would not change history as we know it. After studying philosophy in Zurich, writing plays about Faust and Cromwell, and recanting his God-building teachings, the pan-European Lunacharsky became the first People's Commissar of the Enlightenment.

Product of Nature

Nikolai Leskov was the prolific author of novels and essays on many aspects of Russian imperial life. He wrote about peasant recruits,

[2] For the experimental God-building of the revolutionaries who lost in the competition with Lenin, see Williams 1986; Stites 1989; Scherr 2003; Rosenthal 2004. On the popularity of Durkheim in the early-twentieth-century Russia, see Gofman 2001.

forensic medicine, the alcoholism of the lower classes, and other social questions. On top of that, he was interested in religion, both high and popular. He started his career as a small official in the provincial courts in Kiev and later became a local representative for the military draft. But then, his British relative, Alexander Scott, who was married to his aunt, changed Leskov's life. Scott managed the enormous estate of the Minister of Internal Affairs, Lev Perovsky (see Chapter 8), and owned the commercial company *Scott and Wilkins*, which sold British agricultural equipment to Russian landlords. In 1857, the young Leskov left governmental service to work for Scott. An entrepreneurial Brit, Scott failed in his Russian business despite his high connections. He turned into a bitter old man who, looking at a collection of unused, top-end machinery, addressed to his nephew, the future writer, the classical complaint of an unsuccessful imperialist: "Machines do not work in Russia. . . . Nothing good works here because the people living here are wild and vicious." Leskov thought that his uncle was joking, but he was not. Much later, in 1893, Leskov remembered the amazing words of his British relative:

> You are Russian and you do not want to hear it, but I am foreign and I can judge: these people are vicious, but this is not the worst. What is the worst is that these people are deceived. They are led to believe that what is bad is good, and what is good, bad. Remember my words: the retribution will come when you least expect it! (p. 368)[3]

Under Scott's supervision, Perovsky's estate "exploited everything the land could provide," which first and foremost was the peasants. At the start of his new career, Leskov had to oversee the resettling of serfs, whom Perovsky bought from small owners in two central provinces, Orel and Kursk, and transferred to his estates in the southern steppes. The count had died a few months earlier and passed his estate to one of his brothers; the manager, Scott, used the opportunity to populate the land in anticipation of the coming Emancipation of 1861. There was nothing unusual in this operation. In previous transfers, Perovsky's peasants were moved thousands of miles by horse carts, so that about half of them fled or died on the way. This time, Scott hired barges to carry the serfs, whom he called "a product of nature," down the great rivers, the Oka and the Volga. He commis-

[3] For quotes from Leskov's "Product of Nature," see Leskov 1958, vol. 9; page numbers are indicated in parentheses.

Figure 18: Nikolai Leskov, by Ilia Repin, 1888.

sioned his nephew to oversee the action in an improvised regime of indirect rule. "Be a tsar, not a ruler," Scott instructed his nephew. The ruler was a strong man, Piotr, whom Scott called, in a colonial manner, 'Pizarro' after the sixteenth-century conqueror of Peru. Writing about the horror of this type of resettlement, which was formative for the Russian Empire, Leskov presented it in a way that suggested the transportation of the black Africans across the Atlantic. Reimagining Piotr-Pizarro many decades later, Leskov described everything in him – his eyes, hair, beard, and more – as black. All the white men in the story – the dead Perovsky, the British Scott, the feeble Leskov, and the self-proclaimed policeman – were absent, weak, or fake. The only strong man was this black-colored leader of the peasants' Middle-Passage.

When Leskov and Pizarro loaded the peasants on barges, they asked the police for help. Otherwise, they were left with three barges and several hundred peasant families, on the long trip down the great rivers. According to Leskov, the peasants did not look unusually desolated:

> They were sitting on the barges barefoot, half-dressed, as pathetic and unfortunate as they usually appear in the Russian village. Then I still believed that everywhere peasants had to be in the same condition as we were accustomed to seeing them in Russia. They were as humble as they usually were. (p. 345)

During the trip, everyone was busy with one kind of entertainment, called "searching." The peasants combed their bodies looking for lice; there was no way to get rid of them. They could not start a fire on the barge to treat the clothing and they did not swim in the river because they believed that the water was bad for people and good for lice. They suffered immensely and eagerly demonstrated their horrible scratches. Leskov tried to help, but in vain. When he expressed his concern to Pizarro, he received the response: "He who has pity for the people should not be in charge of them." Leskov felt it was true; however, he prevented Pizarro from flogging the peasants on board. Once, the peasants spotted a bathhouse on the bank and begged Leskov to let them go to it. They swore that they would return right away; how could they not return, leaving their wives and children on the barge? Leskov allowed 40 of the men to go. Reaching the bank of the river, they did not go to the bathhouse but ran home, which was hundreds of miles away. Leskov had to call the police; three Cossacks caught and flogged these 40 men. While the peasants were being punished, the head of the local police (later he turned out to be an impostor) invited Leskov to his home, and locked him in so that he would not be a nuisance. Trapped there, Leskov browsed the books from his library, which included texts by the illustrious Russian democrats Herzen and Granovsky. Then, everyone returned to the barge:

> It was nighttime but I saw how they led them. It rained before and the clay was slippery and it was funny and pitiful to see how they splashed through the mud and their feet shuffled and slid over the wet clay, and if the front pair slid and fell down all the rest did the same, as if it was a Cotillion. (p. 351)

As a salesman in his uncle's company, Leskov traveled across the Russian provinces. He published compassionate novels about the people and satirical essays about the intelligentsia, which made him a controversial figure. But always a practical man, he loved a quotation that he attributed to Heinrich Heine: "He who loves the people should take them to the bathhouse."

Horse Trading

Marlow talked to his colleagues on the deck of the yawl as a peer to peers. He was telling them about those who were unequal to them, the blacks in the ivory country, and about the European superman there, Kurtz. His story is unusual but his interlocutors and we, the readers, believe Marlow. With Fliagin, the narrator of Leskov's novella, *The Enchanted Wanderer* (1873), it is different. As he tells his long story, the random group of passengers becomes increasingly critical toward him and his message. However, they are uniformly curious, indeed more curious about him than he was about the natives among whom he lived. Scholars also perceive him in various ways, which range from "the Russian superman" (McLean 1977: 241) to "the Russian Everyman" (Franklin 2004: 108). On deck, Fliagin looks like a monk, though actually he is a groom; the enchanted passengers gradually recognize an impostor, similar to that fake monk whom Vladimir Dal recognized by his accent (see Chapter 8). Beginning as an exchange among peers, the situation turns into a cultural encounter between Europeans and a noble savage.

Fliagin tells his life story on board a ship that is carrying pilgrims and supplies to the island monasteries on the lake of Ladoga. They are about a day-trip's distance from St. Petersburg, north of the source of the Neva. The way to the heart of Russia goes through this ancient land. Like the Thames, the Neva has had its moments of darkness, light, and flickering. Like England, Russia was a colonized and a colonizing country. The Romans never reached these banks, but Finns, Russians, Swedes, and Germans came and left, some of them more than once. If Rurik did come from his Scandinavia, he would have sailed there, through the Neva and Ladoga to Novgorod. The medieval fur trade went in the opposite direction. Now, Fliagin narrates on this great lake the story of his nomadic life, which carried him across Eurasia, from the Russian heartlands to the Central Asian deserts and the Caucasus and, then, to the lakes and islands of the north. For Marlow, going from England to Europe and then to Africa meant crossing high seas and political borders. Fliagin's adventures all happened within Russia. Crossing steppes, deserts, and mountains, finding himself among strange and hostile peoples, Fliagin never left what he believed was his "land." Marlow is a critical, self-conscious imperialist, one of those who took part in the colonialist endeavors and also in decolonizing the world. Epically strong and competent, Fliagin is destitute of curiosity and critical ability.

Unavoidably, the reader finds himself closer to the passengers of the ship than to Fliagin, an eloquent but impenetrable narrator. His exotic dwellings, incredible survivals, hyper-masculine physicality, bizarre religiosity, immoral hubris, deep contact with animals, and lack of human touch and connection all make him an impossible target for identification. If he is a Superman, he is depicted with a healthy dose of irony.

Sadness

Born into the poor family of a priest in provincial Orel, Leskov finished two classes at the local school and learned everything else as an autodidact. He matured into a sophisticated ironist, British-style liberal, and soul-seeker who became a follower of one of the greatest dissidents of all times, Lev Tolstoy. Misunderstood by Walter Benjamin (1968) as an exemplary storyteller who was still close to the "immediate" oral tradition, Leskov was prone to narrative games and mocking experiments with his characters and readers.

Leskov started his novella with a brief visit by passengers to a small coastal town, Korela, on the lake of Ladoga. "This poor, though extremely ancient, Russian town was so sad that it was hard to imagine a place on earth that was more sad than this one." Founded by a Finnish tribe, Korela was colonized by Novgorod in 1310, taken by the Swedes in 1580, by the Muscovites in 1595, by the Swedes in 1617, by the Russians in 1710; it became a part of Finland in 1920, and was taken by the USSR in 1940. Having changed its name four times and now known as Priozersk, the town has survived as a hub of dacha-style resorts on the lake of Ladoga. Many times colonized and never liberated, the town had no reason to cheer, but its record-winning sadness is perhaps an overstatement. In Fliagin's narrative, sadness is projected onto the deserts, where natives enslaved and mutilated him; onto his native province of central Russia, where his life was all about whipping; and onto the imperial capital, where he played the devil on the stage of a theater. But for Leskov, the heart of sadness was Korela, a town like myriad others. Leskov did not specify what exactly was so sad in Korela, but in another story he described another Russian town, Penza, where he lived for a while and where Fliagin also spent some time:

> Penza was one of the darkest. . . . Everything there was instituted the other way around. . . . The streets were like swamps and the sidewalks were made of boards; nails slid away and a pedestrian fell down in the cesspit. . . . The police robbed people on the square; the marshal's dogs tore people apart . . . in front of the city officials; the governor whipped people on the street with his own hands; there were terrible but true rumors about violence toward the women, who were invited to parties in the homes of the nobility. (Leskov 1958: 9/369)

Fliagin emerges out of this environment very organically. Leskov gave him a narrative gift, merged it with a muscular, destructive character, and reserved the irony for himself. Born as a serf, Fliagin grew up in a stable and fled from his master after being whipped for cutting the tail of a cat. He wandered with the Gypsies before taking part in a Tartar competition, in which the rivals whipped each other, "as in a duel among nobles." Having mastered this "Asian practice," Fliagin whipped his rival Tartar to death. His prize was a beautiful horse, but he had to flee again. Far out in the desert, he was captured by an Asian tribe, which mutilated him by cutting his heels and putting bristles into the cuts. He lived among these "Tartars" for 11 years, learned their language, healed them with herbs and magic, married their women, and fathered many children. He combined his success among the natives with an entire lack of interest toward them. Nothing among the "Tartars" was of any value, with the only exception being horses. In the desert, he met Russian missionaries. "An Asian should be brought to God by fear, so that he would be trembling with awe," believes Fliagin; but the missionaries preached a humble Christ and were killed by the natives.

Then British spies came to the desert from India by way of Khiva. In this variant of Kipling's *Kim*, fantasized from the other side of the Himalayas, the Brits are preparing for a war with Russia and want to buy horses from the natives somewhere in Central Asia. When Fliagin destroys this trade, the Brits frighten the tribe with fireworks, steal the horses, and disappear. Fliagin used the remaining fireworks to baptize the tribe with lightening and thunder. After he turns himself into their god, they let him flee across the desert. The Russians return him to his old master, who diligently flogs him for running away.

Fliagin resumes his horse trade, with Asians as before. For a while, he trades on behalf of a prince who entrusts Fliagin with his money, horses, and women. But both of them then fall in love with a Gypsy beauty, Grusha. Selflessly, Fliagin buys Grusha for his patron and secures their romance. When the prince gets tired of the pregnant Grusha, she begs Fliagin to kill her. Because of his love for her, he throws her into the river, thereby creating another sacrificial plotline with a female offering (see Chapter 12). Fliagin then flees again to serve in the standing army in the Caucasus. After heroic service and other adventures, he finds his ultimate destination as a horse groom in a northern monastery. The ghosts of Grusha and the others whom he killed chase him, but he repels them by fasting and bowing to the ground.

After Fliagin tells the passengers about the murder of Grusha, something happens to his storytelling. His rich, creative narrative becomes an inarticulate sermon. There is no end to his story; it deteriorates into wordy, meaningless speculation. Grusha's ghost is still with him, despite his bows and chanting.

What Conrad calls darkness, Leskov calls sadness. Three stories unfold on boats that have made freshwater tours, with "pilgrims" on board. *The Heart of Darkness* and *The Enchanted Pilgrim* are both shaped as first-person narratives installed within a third-person frame. Both stories create a superhuman image only to demolish it. Having unusual gifts like Kurtz, Fliagin failed to realize them. A true hero of the empire, he knew animals, not humans. His life was punctuated by murders. He loved a woman and killed her: it is a sad story indeed. Fliagin "is magnificent and appalling," writes one historian (Franklin 2004: 109); it is instructive to note the similarity of this perception to Marlow's words with which he concluded his story of the Roman colonizer of England: "The fascination of the abomination – you know" (Conrad 1988: 9–10).

Sitting on the deck and telling the story of his wonders and wanderings in distant lands, Fliagin is both a witness to *and* an agent of colonialism, Marlow *and* Kurtz in one person, a narrative position that is less analytical but more enchanting than Marlow's. Fliagin is also a native informer, a third position that is conspicuously absent in *The Heart of Darkness*, where subalterns do not speak. In contrast to Fliagin, Marlow and Kurtz have never been whipped; in contrast to the black victims of Kurtz, Fliagin is able to tell his story. Marlow's is also not a nice story, but he feels compelled to tell it because he is doing so for others who cannot speak. In Russia, the natives were colonized and colonizing, and they did speak. And so does Fliagin.

—12—

Sacrificial Plotlines

In 1850, a rich nobleman, Aleksandr Sukhovo-Kobylin, who divided his time between translating Hegel and womanizing in high quarters, got rid of his French mistress. He brought her from Paris to Moscow, lived with her for a number of years and was reasonably attached to her, but at this point he had other liaisons. The French woman was found on the road, beaten by an iron bar and with her throat slashed. Although Sukhovo-Kobylin blamed his servants and bribed the police, the authorities suspected him. The investigation lasted for seven years, after which all suspects, including the master and his serfs, were acquitted. To this day, this story has attracted scholars, who have been invariably divided in their judgments as to who is to blame (Murav 1998; Seleznev and Selezneva 2002). Under police investigation Sukhovo-Kobylin began writing comedies; he worked on his trilogy, which made him famous, for 30 years. In the first comedy, a rich bride is seduced by a rogue and barely survives. In the second, her father sells his wealth in order to save her from the police, and dies. In the third, a police officer plays a werewolf, imitating death and resurrection. From the 1850s to the 1880s, the female character stepped back from the cycle, allowing the corrupted, entirely irrational men around her to annihilate themselves without any help from her. With a dark irony, the epigraph to the trilogy is taken from Hegel: "If you look rationally at this world it will look rationally at you."

In novelistic fiction as opposed to historical non-fiction, the relationship between the Empire and the people was intrinsically connected with the relationship between men and women. Two romantic and colonial themes, the Russian woman as tragic sacrifice and the Russian peasant as noble savage, became crucial elements for the national imagery. Great writers developed these themes, or rather these themes made great writers. Almost invariably, Russian literature depicted men and women, on the one hand, and those from high culture and those from the people, on another hand, as creatures of a fundamentally different nature.

The Contact Zone of the Novel

In her comparative study of travel writings, Mary Louise Pratt introduced a helpful concept of the contact zone, "the space in which peoples geographically and historically separated come into contact with each other and establish ongoing relations, usually involving conditions of coercion, radical inequality, and intractable conflict" (1992: 6). I argue that the classical Russian novel was such a contact zone, where historically and culturally separated men and women played out their conflictual relations. In his treatment of the historical poetics of the novel, Mikhail Bakhtin identified, among other "persistent" chronotopes, the chronotope of the road. In Bakhtin's classification there are two lines of development in the travel novel: in the first, the road takes the hero "through his own *native country*, and not some exotic *alien world*"; in the second, "an 'alien world,' separated from the native country by sea and distance . . . has an analogous function to that of the road" (Bakhtin 1975: 392–4). In both cases, Bakhtin argued, the hero is aware of the exotic nature of what is taking place, but in the first type of novel this is a "social exotic," whereas in the second it is a natural or ethnographic exotic associated with overseas travel.

The first, internal type of novel is represented by Goethe's *Wilhelm Meister*, the second, external by Defoe's *Robinson Crusoe*. All the Russian examples given by Bakhtin, from Radishchev to Nekrasov, belong to the internal type. The travel in social space, between classes, is as fruitful for the novel as the travel in geographical space, between continents. The road takes on the capacity of estrangement. It makes the everyday feel exotic and the boring, foreign and interesting. These ideas are connected to another of Bakhtin's typological innovations, the "idyllic chronotope." Utopia is located in distant islands; the idyll is located in local depths. Literature, Bakhtin wrote in 1937, has created idylls "from the time of Antiquity right up until recent times"; literary scholars, however, had failed to understand or evaluate this fact, "as a result of which all perspectives on the history of the novel are distorted." Bakhtin briefly surveyed the "sublimation of the idyll" in Rousseau, the "return of the idyll" in Tolstoy, and the "demise of the idyll" in Flaubert, arguing that "in Russian literature the chronological boundaries of this phenomenon are of course shifted to the second half of the nineteenth century." At this time, the novel was overwhelmed by "the idyllic complex" and Bakhtin concentrates on its chief character: "The 'man of the people' in the novel is often of idyllic provenance" (1975: 384).

Developing Bakhtin's argument somewhat further, I observe that in the Russian novel, the Man of the People is usually counterpoised to the Man of Culture. Each lives, by definition, in a different milieu, but they encounter one another in the idyllic chronotope – the contact zone of the novel. They are brought together by their occupation or by chance, but most often by "the road." In the plots of the novel, these two character-types, the Man of Culture and the Man of the People, engage in multiple relations, from mortal rivalry to redeeming brotherhood. One character-type is historical, another idyllic. Usually, the Man of Culture firmly belongs to his own time; in contrast, the Man of the People has transhistorical but national features. Endowed with the capacity and desire to move through cultural space, the Man of Culture penetrates the atemporal space of the Man of the People. And there, more often than not, he remains forever.

Love between man and woman is the eternal subject of the novel. However, the French-American literary theorist René Girard (1965), who was, like Bakhtin, initially inspired by Dostoevsky, argues that in the novel, erotic desire requires a mediator. To tell the story of love, the novel usually depicts three characters rather than two. The competition between two men for a woman gives rise to a paradoxical effect of mediation. They wish to get rid of one another, but instead they create mutual dependencies that sometimes make the reader suspect that the object of their passion, the woman, does not matter at all. This relationship between the rivals is interpreted in different texts as mystical, political, or even erotic. Girard explains this triangular structure in general terms, but I am mostly interested in its specific modification in the Russian nineteenth-century novel.

In René Girard's theory (1965, 1995), if a society is unable to achieve peace through law and the courts, it falls back on ancient mechanisms of sacrifice, as collective participation in an act of violence. Historical societies progressed by substituting human sacrifices with animal sacrifices and, then, actual sacrifices with symbolic ones. What happens in a secular society where religious rites are increasingly irrelevant but the court system is still underdeveloped? One can expect an uncontrollable growth of violence and development of various means of its symbolic substitution. Making another step, we can speculate about the novel itself as a mechanism of substitutional sacrifice. Here, it is not humans who die for the sake of the collective, but their representations. Along with drama and opera, which used similar mechanisms, the novel was the nineteenth-century method of choice for sacrificial matters. In the next century, the cinema would take this place. To be sure, not every novel ends with a corpse, but many do. And corpses had gender.

"The Man of the People appears in the novel as a bearer of a wise attitude towards life and death, which has been lost by the ruling classes," wrote Bakhtin (1975: 384). More often than not, this character is the enigmatic one who possesses a mystical and threatening, God-like power. In such narratives, Eve is a classless but national object of desire. Sometimes she is passive, but often she is endowed with the power of choice between the rivals for her affections. Gender structure intersects with class structure and both are contained within a national space, which is symbolized by the woman character-type, the Russian Beauty. Relations between these character-types are based on the story from Genesis. The Man of Culture, a descendant of the sinful Adam, argues with the Man of the People about the possession of the Russian Eve.

In its interactions with historical situations, this triangular plot produced the variety of Romantic literature, Russian style. This is a reductive reading, of course. There are many stories that have little to do with this plotline, and in those novels that generally comply with this scheme, there are many characters and many branches of the story that do not fit into the triangle. However, I will argue that in its multiple versions, this narrative structure replicates the intricacies of internal colonization in rich, diverging narratives. At the close of these stories we can often discern the ancient motif of sacrifice, which resolves what Girard describes as a "sacrificial crisis." Depending on which of them the novel sacrifices – the Man of the People, the Man of Culture, or the Russian Beauty – we can identify different types of this triangular narrative. Throughout the nineteenth century, male characters largely replaced female characters as objects of novelistic sacrifice.

Exchange and Mercy

In 1882, the French historian Ernest Renan grounded his definition of "nation" on the common experience of suffering and sacrifice.

"Suffering in common unifies more than joy does. . . . A nation is a large-scale solidarity, constituted by the feeling of the sacrifices" (1996: 53). Renan was referring to wars and revolutions, but the fictional life of culture plays out these constitutive, sacrificial narratives without actually spilling blood. Forty years earlier, a character of a Russian novel contemplated: "We are no longer capable of great sacrifices for the good of mankind nor even for our very own happiness, for we realize its impossibility." This was Pechorin from Mikhail Lermontov's novel *A Hero of Our Time* (1840). There are at least four violent deaths in this story, but most of them are women; for Pechorin's idea of a "great sacrifice," women do not count. In his poem "Demon," Lermontov portrayed a fallen angel in love with a woman from the Caucuses. Ruined by his sublime desire, she dies after a kiss. A demon flies away in sorrow. Nothing more occurred; just another colonial woman was killed. If it had been the other way round – that the male demon, contaminated by the filth of flesh, had died or decomposed – we could expect an overthrow of hell and heavens, a revolution of a sort. But this, in the course of Russian literature, was not to happen until somewhat later. A sacrificial death was clearly important for Romantic fiction. No less important was the choice of the sacrificial object: was it a man or a woman? The gender of sacrifice was a historically changing variable, and it was crucial for the function of the narrative.

Pushkin constructed a triangular structure in his novella *The Captain's Daughter* (1836), with a Cossack rebel Pugachev as Man of the People, the young officer of the imperial army, Grinev, as the Man of Culture, and Mashenka as the Russian Beauty. On the side of the people, there are horrifying depths, undeclared strength, and untold wisdom; behind the state there is poor discipline and alien rationality. Pugachev, a Cossack, Old-Believer, and romantic rebel, fascinates even the loyal member of the imperial hierarchy, Grinev. The story is played out between St. Petersburg and Orenburg – the center of the Empire, located on the periphery, and a distant province in its geographical center. Ethnically and culturally, the mixture of Cossacks, Bashkirs, and runaway serfs who rebelled in the Orenburg steppe was not much different from the irregular troops who represented the Empire. The struggle belongs to the history of colonial uprisings, but both sides fought against their own kind. Many characters in this historical novel – the rebels like Pugachev and the imperial officers – started their careers in the Russian–Prussian war that occurred two decades earlier (Kretinin 1996); Grinev is close to the historical Bolotov (see Chapter 9). Rebels have Russian beards and wear Eastern-style pantaloons, Pugachev in the Tartar style, his lieutenant in the Kyrgyz style. Pushkin depicted the rebels with a mixture of orientalist prejudice and human respect; those occidentals who personified imperial power in the steppe are described with much irony.

The Captain's Daughter should be read in the comparative context of such events as the Sepoy mutiny in British India in 1857, now remembered as the First War of Independence. In British narratives of the mutiny, common motifs include the executions and rapes of the English by the insurgents (Sharpe 1991). Pushkin's story is much the same, but there is one exception: the captain's daughter, who is captured by Pugachev, remains unharmed. Against the background of the oriental brutality that Pushkin describes in a straightforward manner, the absence of violence toward the object of all the characters' desire is a kind of negative device. The honor of the heroine is of critical importance not only for the characters of the story, but also for its entire colonial construction. By saving Mashenka, Pushkin allows her to recount her unlikely adventure to the Empress, appealing to her – and to the reader – for mercy toward those who rose up and perished. The narrative is full of migrations in the cultural space, but the most unlikely of these – going at first to the very depths of a rebellious people, then to the very heights of the imperial order – is accomplished by a woman. Her salvation halts the vicious circle of violence, symbolizes the renewal of the civil peace, and promises the viability of the colonial order. The reader who was aware of the reality of peasant uprisings would notice the unusualness of this plotline, and would therefore be able to apprehend its ideological significance.

Impervious to imperial power, the province obeys its own rules of exchange, in wealth and violence alike. Throughout *The Captain's Daughter*, the native rites of gift-giving interact with the rationalism and unforgiving justice of the imperial state. Pushkin's analysis reveals these two conflicting principles and tries to find a balance between them. It is in this middle ground that the hope of maintaining the colonial situation resides. The first gift in this novel is, appropriately, one of fur. Grinev gives Pugachev a hare fur coat: "The tramp was extraordinarily pleased with my gift." Just as in Marcel Mauss's anthropological studies of the Maoris, so too with Pushkin's literary studies of the Cossacks: the gift obliges the recipient to repay it, not because of some external law, but rather because the thing in itself – here, the fur coat – carries with it something of its former owner that must be returned. The two authors, Mauss and Pushkin, were equally ambivalent in their attitudes toward the customs described: which is better, justice and the settling of accounts, or mercy and giving? In native rites, each successive gift is greater than the previous one. In return for the fur coat, Pugachev gives Grinev a sheepskin, a horse, and life. Pugachev begins another chain of giving by preserving Mashenka's honor and gifting her to Grinev. In return, Grinev "passionately" wants to save Pugachev's neck, and he and Mashenka will pray for the salvation of his soul. In Mauss's formulation, the gift is thus a way of "buying the world," the very same world that in "civilized" conditions is protected by the state (Mauss 2002; Bethea 1998). When Grinev returns from the rebellious people to the civilized world and goes on trial, Mashenka circumvents the state and returns to the world of the gift, asking Catherine II for "mercy, and not justice." She receives not only mercy, but also, according to the rules of ritual giving, her dowry. Pushkin's compromise has worked. Many generations of readers will be captivated not only by the black-bearded and inscrutable Pugachev, but also by that extra-legal mercy of the Empress. The novel ends, however, with Pugachev's execution on the scaffold. *The Captain's Daughter* was the first work to embody the horror of Russian rebellion, and the first to reify the equally familiar "charm" of the Russian people that even in the twentieth century many felt to be irresistible (Tsvetaeva 2006).

The Gender of Sacrifice

Fyodor Dostoevsky's writings fit neatly between two major sacrificial events, his own mock execution along with other members of an early revolutionary circle in 1849 and the assassination of the Tsar in 1881. In his works, Dostoevsky shows one murder after another, and most of them had women as their victims. In *Crime and Punishment*, a male student murders two females, a pawnbroker and her sister. One can speculate that a premeditated murder evokes more guilt when directed against a woman, and the doubling-up of killed females reinforces this guilt. In this narrative, however, a theme of female suffering is illustrated by another female character, the prostitute. The prostitute, a victim of social abuse, is the opposite of the victim of murder, the pawnbroker. One suffers, another is killed, but both are females. The story of *Idiot* (1868) elevates these themes by merging them. The novel culminates in the murder of Nastasia Filippovna, who carries two features of Russian heroines, beauty and suffering, to the possible limits.

There are three main characters: prince Myshkin, the Man of Culture, merchant Rogozhin, the Man of the People, and Nastasia, the Russian Beauty. The action takes place in St. Petersburg, to where the prince comes from Switzerland and the merchant, from the depths of Russian mysticism, with a family connection to the sect of Skoptsy (Castrates). The strange dynamics of the relationship between Myshkin and Rogozhin reflect, as in a laboratory experiment, the structure of internal colonization. At the same time, the friendship and rivalry between these two men, united by their desire toward Nastasia, is a definitive example of the mediation of desire in Girard's sense. The plotline displays the characteristic drive towards the reduction of cultural distance and foreshadows the catastrophic consequences of such 'fraternization'.

Many men loved Nastasia; she kept running from one to another, and finally she preferred Rogozhin. Why did he kill Nastasia instead of marrying her? Trying to understand it in terms of common sense leads nowhere. However, prince Myshkin, with his ability to understand people, did understand Rogozhin. Why did he not prevent the murder or seek revenge for it? Why did he collaborate in concealing the murder? Why did he spend that night together with the corpse of his loved one and with her murderer? Of course, this experience was hugely important for him; afterwards, he went insane. Because we feel that Myshkin understood Rogozhin's reasons, why do we not know these reasons, either from Rogozhin himself or from Myshkin? Why do Rogozhin and Myshkin not talk about it? Actually, we are deprived of any possibility of understanding these events from the inside. In this particular situation, neither the characters nor the narrator perform a dialogue. In many preceding scenes, we heard their voices. They performed that very exchange between the internal positions of the actors, different but communicable, in which Bakhtin found the key to Dostoevsky. Rather than being a part and an outcome of human dialogue, the murder of Nastasia is presented as something that just happened. It permits only external observation. This is how sacrifice works, and this is where Girard complements Bakhtin.

Sharing the object of their passions, these two men who loved Nastasia became increasingly close. They were endowed with every possible difference: they came from two different estates, the old nobility and the rising capitalists; they belonged to different religious backgrounds, one to high Orthodoxy, another to a mysterious cult; they had opposite temperaments. But, united by their love for Nastasia and by their interest in each other, they become as close as twins.

They exchange crosses, performing a ritual of acquired brotherhood, and they read together "all of Pushkin." As a result of their friendship, competition, and mutual influence, they outgrow their personal limits. Relations between them are dialogical and ideological, and reading Bakhtin helps a lot to understand their substance. However, these relations cannot be explained without reference to the third person, whom both of them love. This process is explicable by an important concept of Girard, the concept of mimetic, or triangular, desire. As Girard insists, mimetic desire merges two components, a longing for the object and a competition with the rival, in such a way that one cannot tell what is primary and what is secondary. While passions develop, both parts become progressively dependent upon each other as mediators of their desires. As Girard says, mimetic desire is contagious, and an epidemic of it can be resolved only by a sacrifice. Mimetic brothers Rogozhin and Myshkin, who compete and collaborate in their desire for Nastasia, have their female counterparts in the mimetic sisters, Nastasia and Aglaia, whose passions are addressed to Myshkin. Nastasia, who is at the center of this mimetic network, logically becomes the sacrificial victim. Importantly, there is no word in *The Idiot* to suggest that Nastasia deserved her fate, from anyone's point of view. Sacrifice is neither punishment nor revenge; actually, the least guilty are the better victims for a true sacrifice.

The irrationality of this relationship is created in equal measure by all three protagonists. We never understand why Myshkin attempts to marry Nastasia, why she runs out from underneath the wedding wreath, why Rogozhin murders her, or why Myshkin forgives him. Scholars have suggested many partial explanations: the homoerotic attraction between the male heroes; class struggle between old nobility and the new bourgeoisie; a confessional debate that ends in Nastasia's initiation as a member of the Skoptsy sect. Without wishing to suggest one more such explanation, I will attempt to re-read Myshkin's speeches.

There is a wonderful episode in the novel, which involves Myshkin, St. Petersburg society, and a Chinese vase. Rogozhin is absent, although Myshkin constantly speaks about him. A society gathering is composed of a German-born general, an anglophile noble, a Russian poet, etc. The anglophile recounts with displeasure "certain outbreaks of disorder on the landed estates" and refers with sympathy to a relative who has converted to Catholicism. Myshkin replies that Catholicism is an unchristian faith and gives rise to socialism. He argues that "our Christ must shine forth in rejection of the West" and also that "he who has no roots beneath his feet has no God." In this speech, Russia is a country of the authentic east and God is, by definition, "our God." Just as in totemic cults, what is not our God is not God at all. Religion is thus inseparable from politics; both relate to geography, and all three are locked together in the national idea. Myshkin also says that "the most educated of our people have stooped so low as to become the Khlysty," a popular sect. Referring to Rogozhin, Myshkin sends his audience the message of internal orientalism: "Reveal to the yearning and feverish companions of Columbus the 'New World', reveal to the Russian the 'world' of Russia, let him find the gold, the treasure hidden from him on earth!" (Dostoevsky 1996: 511). The main colonial event – the discovery of America – is turned inwards on Russia: the interior provinces where Myshkin has recently traveled are, for him, the New World. The depths of these regions must be discovered in order to resurrect Russia and the world. But St. Petersburg society prevents genuinely Russian people from accomplishing their transfiguration. As Myshkin says:

> I'm afraid for you, for all of you, for all of us together. I am a prince myself, of ancient family, and I am sitting with princes. I speak to save us all, that our class [the gentry estate] may not vanish in vain, in darkness, without realizing anything, abusing everything, and losing everything. (Dostoevsky 1996: 518)

The class of internal colonization, Myshkin warns, has lost the game. This class can only be saved, he thinks, by pilgrimage to the country of the east, to the interior regions of Russia. And soon, in 1874, many would indeed take this journey, "going to the people," which, more precisely, meant the Khlysty and other sects (see Chapter 10).

The positive orientalism of the imperial elite is characteristic of the later stages of colonization and coincides with the advent of nationalist movements in the colonies. From Rousseau to Lévi-Strauss, the romanticization of the distant and noble savage has been an important element of the western tradition. Russia has also made its contribution to this, a contribution that is, as always, centripetal. Myshkin wishes to be the Russian Columbus, while Rogozhin guards his treasure like Montezuma, in that he is ready to give it up to whoever asks properly for it, and with similar consequences. Meanwhile, the society of the capital, blind to the genuine idyll of the interior, worships false idols like the "enormous, beautiful Chinese vase, standing on its pedestal." External orientalism can be smashed with a single gesture, thus revealing the treasures within; this is exactly what

Myshkin does at the peak of his ecstasy. The east is doubled; one version is embodied in the Chinese vase, the other in Myshkin's speech.

The Idiot, as has long been realized, is an ideological novel. One of the aspects of the bizarre union between Myshkin and Rogozhin is their ideological exchange. The prince has read "all" of Pushkin to the merchant, while the merchant has told the prince of the unity of God and soil. None of this explains, however, why it was necessary to kill Nastasia Fillipovna. This act resolves the triangular structure in the gravest of ways. The sacrifice of an innocent woman is the most malignant of all possible outcomes of the ritual action. As we see in the story, Myshkin and Rogozhin, who constitute the sacrificial community, are destroyed along with their victim. The novel's terrible conclusion is proof that its author did not believe in the resurrection of mankind through "the Russian idea, the Russian God," a belief he puts in the words of caricatured murderers. Such belief leads to terrible evil, and is entirely exposed in the process. Myshkin was not the Christ – and Dostoevsky not the idiot – they are made to look like in some interpretations.

The Real Day

If the social sciences rely on statistical criteria to demonstrate the significance of observed differences, the humanities rely on the reader's memory and the age-long work of selection that it does. When readers think about the Russian novel or drama of the 1860–70s, they remember the deaths of female characters: Ostrovsky's *Thunderstorm*, suicide; Dostoevsky's *Idiot,* murder; Tolstoy's *Anna Karenina*, suicide . . . too many Ophelias, too few Hamlets. Before and sometimes after the murder of Nastasia, violent deaths in Russian literature were predominantly those of women. A scholar of European opera observes a similar plotline of "undoing women" in the major masterpieces that were widely influential throughout the nineteenth century (Clément 1988).

Contemporaneous criticism was well aware of the special role that Russian stories, and Russian history, attributed to women. Reviewing Ostrovsky's play, *Thunderstorm*, which ended with the suicide of the central heroine, the radical critic Nikolai Dobroliubov speculated that two human conditions, males' "sovereign stupidity" and females' "wholesome decisiveness," interact in such a way that the only outcome is the death of the woman. Foreshadowing Joseph Conrad's metaphor of the heart of darkness, Dobroliubov wrote that provincial Russia was the tsardom of darkness. A suicidal woman was the only beam of light: the public was "glad to watch the escape of Katerina, even though through death" (1962: 6/362). Rather than giving a "realistic analysis of social issues," which was believed to be the task of literature, Ostrovsky's play, Dobroliubov's essay, and Dostoevsky's novel all produced simple, memorable symbols of human suffering. On the threshold of the 1861 Emancipation of the serfs, the public was in need of gestures of self-accusation, as strong as possible. Seeing female suffering and death, the public felt guilty. They hoped that men in power would change their ways. When they did not, the public, including men in power, read about even more female deaths in books, or watched them at the theatre. Collective participation in sacrificial rites, which were performed by high culture, enacted these men's guilt.

But the most radical men had further thoughts. In his famous review, "When Will the Real Day Come?," Dobroliubov attacked Turgenev's novel *On the Eve* (1860) for showing another beautiful and suffering Russian woman. She was in love with a revolutionary, but he was foreign. This Bulgarian nationalist brought Elena to his country and she died on the road. The Russian critic envies the Bulgarian character who lives and fights in an alliance with all groups of his society, because they all have a common enemy, the Turks. "Russian life has no such monotony; every estate, every little group lives its own life, has its particular goals," which confront each other. The real day will come, prophesized the critic, when a Russian revolutionary will come to struggle with "with our internal enemies." But his task will be challenging. In a memorable metaphor, Dobroliubov compares society to an empty box, which is easy to flip from the outside but impossible to overthrow for someone who sits inside of it. It is easier to be a nationalist who fights with a foreign oppressor than to fight one's own oppressors inside the same space:

> A Russian hero . . . is connected by blood with all those that he rebels against. He is in a position of, say, a son of a Turkish sultan who would decide to emancipate Bulgaria from the Turks. . . . This is horribly difficult; such a decision demands a very different development from the one that the son of a Turkish sultan usually gets. (Dobroliubov 1962: 6/163)

For this critic of the 1860s, internal colonization was already connected with gender. The oppression of Russian women correlated with the internal colonization of Russian men. Women in Russia were like Bulgaria under the Turks: external colonization made things clear and heroism possible. "The real day" would come when Russian men would, like this son of the Turkish sultan, rebel against themselves.

Catechism of a Revolutionary, a programmatic document of Russian political terrorism that was composed by Sergei Nechaev in 1869, called for new sacrifices: "The revolutionary is a doomed man. He has no pity for the state . . . and expects no pity for himself. . . . Every day he must be prepared for death. . . . Day and night he must have one single purpose: merciless destruction" (Nechaev 1997: 244). There was no gender ambivalence in this text. Both parts of the sacrificial act, executors and victims, were imagined to be men.

The sacrifice of the Man of the People restored the political balance and, therefore, promised the preservation of the colonial order. From the point of view of the characters, the author, and many readers, Pushkin's Pugachev was a criminal and was executed by a legal court. The sacrifice of an innocent woman raised the narrative to the level of a final, apocalyptic catastrophe. The sacrifice of the Man of Culture represents the victory of the colonized people, which the metropolitan elite cannot, indeed does not want to, resist. Possessed by a sense of historical guilt, the elite oversees its own destruction, organizes its own sacrifice. A good example is Andrei Bely's *Silver Dove* (1909), in which we observe, once again, a familiar triangular structure. Darialsky is a poet-symbolist and typical intellectual of late populism. The idyll that attracts him is as irrepressible as it is nonsensical; as usual for idylls, it combines three vectors – the mystical, the political, and the erotic. The Wise Man of the People, Kudeiarov is described in more expressive terms than either Pugachev or Rogozhin. But Matrena, a subject of fatal attraction for Darialsky, is faceless. Her only secret is the nature of her relationship to Kudeiarov: is she a mistress? a daughter? a spiritual sister?

The new resolution of the triangular narrative – the sacrifice of the Man of Culture – sends a different message. Like Myshkin before him, Darialsky descends "into the depths" of the mystical sectarians. His sectarian guru, Kudeiarov, is close to the Khlysty and the author describes their rituals with many ethnographical details. Along with his Russian contemporaries, the erudite Andrei Bely was aware of Durkheim's writings on religion and many volumes by the nineteenth-century classicists who depicted the redeeming effects of pagan sacrifices. But the collective murder of Darialsky is entirely senseless; the purposelessness of this sacrifice is emphasized throughout the entire plot. Neither the victim, who did not expect to be killed, nor the murderers, who experience no redemption afterwards, invest any meaning in the sacrifice. In attempting to grasp and accept the faith of the people, Darialsky ends up being ritually murdered because of his desperate search for a popular tradition. Constructing this story, Bely used the living memory of the populists' journeys to the countryside and the rich ethnography of the Russian sects (see Chapter 10). In performing for revolution, the intelligentsia – a group whose existence is justified by its civilizing mission in relation to the people – attempts to find some religious or political meaning in its own self-sacrifice. Aware of the consequences, Bely has deconstructed the idea of sacrifice itself. The murder of Darialsky is presented as an evil deed, behind which there is the contact of two systems of belief that have nothing in common with one another, those of the people and those of the populists.

Darialsky and his murderer, Kudeiarov, are distinct from one another in every possible way, except in race and gender. Once again, we see the paradoxical situation of internal colonization, which makes it so suitable for literary development. In this contact zone, the colonies were as close to the metropolitan center as suburbs, and utterly different people had the same skin color. The meaning of *The Silver Dove* could be clarified by comparing it with Conrad's *The Heart of Darkness*, which Bely probably read (Lavrov 2004). Like Darialsky, Kurtz had his own local woman, but all the natives in Conrad's text are nameless, and we do not see a single witch-doctor here, let alone any rival to Kurtz. By way of contrast, Bely showed Darialsky in the detailed context of the rituals of the Khlysty sect; their leader Kudeiarov's spiritual hegemony over the intellectual Darialsky is clear from the story. In contrast to Darialsky's, Kurtz's religious innovations were "efficient": his rituals allowed him to extract more ivory than his colleagues. Colonial power does not require the eradication of local customs, but rather their reconstruction from within and their exploitation by Men of Culture. In pursuing their colonial projects, Darialsky failed where Kurtz succeeded. But as both stories teach us, these projects were equally doomed.

The Double

Carried to its extreme, the situation of internal colonization brings us back to Girard's concepts of the "crisis of difference" and "the monstrous double." In mythology and literature, doubles and monsters are often the same, writes Girard. Nobody understood their dynamics better than Dostoevsky, he states, though he does not explain how Dostoevsky managed to reach an understanding that others, from Sophocles on, have not (1995: 160–1). A re-reading of Dostoevsky's crucial text, *The Double* (1846), helps to grasp the historical sources of his inspiration.

As in Gogol's "The Nose," a low-level St. Petersburgclerk, Goliadkin, has met his double. This clone carries his name, works in the same position, and is one day a friend, another day a foe. Worst of all, the double is always quicker, smarter, and more beloved than the original. Goliadkin is insane, of course, but he does not know it. He feels the apparition of the double as a personal and a cultural catastrophe, an overthrow in the heart of the social order; he is amazed that others do not share his sentiment. The story develops within a narrow social space, which is defined by an inverted pyramid of power, from the undifferentiated crowd of Goliadkin's superiors to his servant, Petrusha. The only horizontal relationship that Goliadkin seems to have ever had is the one with his clone. He is unhappy with himself and his place in the world. He always pretends to be someone else, to take someone's role, to be "an impostor." He rents a carriage that is appropriate to a higher rank and drives around the city with no purpose; he bargains for expensive purchases that he does not need, promises to come and pay, and never does. Pretending to be someone else, he is punished by someone else who pretends to be him, his double.

A St. Petersburgdweller, Goliadkin was born "elsewhere" and this birthplace made him alien to his fellow officials. Still, he is a gentleman who owns his apartment, hires a servant, and has savings. His ninth rank in the Table of Ranks was the first that, according to the law of 1845, guaranteed him rights that belonged to the gentry, such as the ability to own serfs and freedom from corporal punishment. By law and status, he is a master; but his mind and speech are destroyed to such an extent that he looks and sounds like he does not belong to himself. Though he speaks often, nobody – neither his doctor, nor his superiors, nor his servant – understands him. He is listened to as if he is a subaltern, i.e. he is not listened to at all. Only his unreliable double understands him; but the double is always ready to betray him in order to take his place. Now that he is in two places at once, the gaze of power cannot control him. He pays for it dearly.

We do not know in which Ministry Goliadkin served. From what we do know, his knowledge and interests are all connected to what Russians then considered to be their orient. In his conversations with his double, Goliadkin mentions Turkey, Algeria, and India. The only writer that he ever refers to is the prolific Osip Senkovsky, the orientalist scholar and also author, editor, and censor. Goliadkin and his double "smiled a lot about the simple-mindedness of the Turks" and talked about the Turks' "fanaticism which is aroused by opium." There is no further word in the story about Goliadkin's national sentiments or political views; his only allegiance seems to be his self-affirmation at the cost of those whom he considers inferior because they are more oriental than the Russians. There is not a word in the story about serfs either, though the servant Petrusha is a pertinent object of rivalry between Goliadkin and his double. As Goliadkin's delirium unfolds, Petrusha works as his reality check; when Petrusha leaves Goliadkin for his double, Goliadkin collapses. Superiors sack Goliadkin-the-original, hire Goliadkin-the-copy, and send the original Goliadkin to the asylum. There is a gloomy anti-utopian message in this early fantasy of Dostoevsky's. In order to be listened to and understood, the subaltern needs his equals; if he does not have them, he creates them; but these equals, inescapably, subject our subject to a new kind of oppression. His doctor, the embodiment of his horror, carries the name Rutenshpits, an inverted double of the Russian word *shpitsruten*, the gauntlet.

In Bhabha's words, which were evoked by his readings of Fanon rather than Dostoevsky, in the colonial situation, "in place of the symbolic unconsciousness that gives the sign of identity its integrity and unity, its *depth*, we are faced with the dimension of doubling" (1994: 71). But Dostoevsky's fantasy goes further than Bhabha's theories. Goliadkin's multiplication does not terminate with his doubling; as his delirium develops, he sees more and more copies of himself: St. Petersburgis full of them; flocking together like geese, they chase Goliadkin; a policeman brings them all in to jail, but in vain. "A horrible abyss of perfect simulacra," wrote Dostoevsky about Goliadkin's experience (1993: 1/242).

The intensity of the competition between Goliadkin and his double always surprised Dostoevsky's readers. As Mikhail Bakhtin (2000: 118) put it in his brilliant reading of *The Double*, "the foreign word settled in Goliadkin's consciousness and took power there." The "foreign word" is one of Bakhtin's most frequent and favorite concepts, but here it acquires a political, colonial connotation, that of a foreign settler who is also an invader, an occupant. According to Bakhtin, three voices interact in Goliadkin's internal conversations: the voice which affirms Goliadkin's independence from the foreign word of those in power; the voice which simulates Goliadkin's indifference to this foreign word; and the voice which imitates the foreign word as if it is his – Goliadkin's – own. These three voices model the dynamics of internal colonization, which results not in dialogue and integrity but in doubling and madness. The story of Goliadkin is told by someone else, a conventional observer who, as happens in novels, holds narratorial and also disciplinary power over the character, someone like a doctor or a detective who reconstructs the internal life of another person. But Bakhtin shows that this framing, objectifying narrative of *The Double* is often mixed with words that could be attributed only to Goliadkin. The circle closes here: the voice of power is also infected with the madness of the subject. Simultaneously with Bakhtin's discovery of dialogism in Dostoevsky, Walter Benjamin (1999: 13) wrote about the Russian peasants' incapability of "following two simultaneous narrative strands" as a problem that was recognized by the early Soviet filmmakers. Essentially, Bakhtin's "dialogism" is the subject's ability to follow and develop "two simultaneous narrative strands" without collapsing into doubling. If Goliadkin's obsessive dialogue with his double illustrates the problem which was noticed by Benjamin, Bakhtin's focus on the open, creative dialogue – a process that always resists the monologic interference that comes from power – may be understood as his solution.

Dostoevsky's reader feels that there is no exit from Goliadkin's suffering precisely because he is possessed by a double, his exact and strangely modern clone, rather than an old-fashioned monster of the kind that Gogol and other Gothic predecessors of Dostoevsky loved to portray. Monsters are playful and picturesque; they are humans hybridized with animals and spirits; they come from afar and they might return there, like Transylvanian vampires or Haitian zombies. Monsters can be explored and tamed; doubles cannot be colonized because they are failed products of colonization. As the experience of horror movies teaches us, "To transform the double back into a monster is to retain a residual sense of oneself as *one* self" (Coates 1991: 87; see also Webber 1996). This is exactly what Goliadkin fails to accomplish. While external colonization finds its symbolic representation in hybrids, internal colonization finds it in doubles. The circular character of this imaginary matches the reflective character of self-colonization, which is striving to define its Other and ends up with doubles of the Self. Jean-Paul Sartre (1963: 22) wrote that "the European has only been able to become a man through creating slaves and monsters." His undoing has been through creating serfs and doubles.

Internal colonization led to the unlimited sophistication of cultural differentiations which had as its limit the replication of subjects' vicious doubles. In the mid-nineteenth century, this process targeted the middle men of the imperial system who found themselves split by the unstable but razor-sharp colonial frontier that cut through their selves, leaving them alone with their doubles. Goliadkin's despair produces a community of his own simulacra: a parody of the socialism of Fourier and his Russian followers with whom Dostoevsky, at the moment of writing, was increasingly disenchanted. When the self collapses, its split produces a double and then a multitude, a society of equals. Readers of Bakhtin and Dostoevsky use the notion of the dialogical as a paradigm for the postcolonial utopia, a proof of the human ability to relate to the other as other. *The Double* is also a blueprint for the post-totalitarian anti-utopia, a document of human collapse when the other is purged.

The geography and history of internal colonization compressed nineteenth-century Russian culture into folds, which connected different levels that in other western cultures were separated either by oceans or by millennia. On the level of high professional culture – among Russian authors and their cultured heroes such as Grinev, Myshkin, and Darialsky – there developed rationality, individualism, writing, and discipline. On the level of folk culture – among millions of Russian peasants – life was "eastern," "native," "communal," "oral," and "mystical." This is the level of Pugachev, Rogozhin, and Kudeiarov. There was also the middle-ground level of the imperial officials, managers, and executors of colonization, people like Maksim Maksimovich, Kovalev, or Goliadkin. The heart of darkness was there; their terrible conflicts developed in an imperial solitude, in the conspicuous absence of women and worldliness that triggers the dynamics of a novel. Representing the short circuits of sacrifice and doubling that punctured the folds of history, the Russian novel portended the modern condition, in which internal colonization gradually takes over from external colonization. As Iurii Tynianov put it in 1924: "Russian literature was subjected to many demands, but all were futile. It was ordered to discover India, but instead it discovered America" (Tynianov 2001: 458).

Conclusion

Things move fast in the postcolonial world. Just a few decades ago, the idea that Ukraine or even Central Asia were colonies of the Soviet Empire evoked furious resistance on both sides of the Iron Curtain. In the 1990s, postcolonial experts still debated the reasons for not applying their concepts to the emerging countries of the post-Soviet space. The current literature resolves these problems but reveals new ones. Focusing on ethnicity, nationalism, and sovereignty in this part of the world, many scholars have turned their backs on the peculiar institutions of the Russian Empire that defined the life of northern Eurasia for several centuries and brought it to its twentieth-century turmoil. Russian serfdom provides a good example. A central subject for nineteenth-Russian politics and historiography, it is reduced to a footnote in the twenty-first-century textbooks of Russian history. Abolished at the same time as American slavery and involving much greater numbers, serfdom must have had at least as deep and lasting an impact. However, nothing similar to the North American attention to the legacy of slavery has emerged. This reveals a double standard, in academia and elsewhere.

The constructivist paradigm downplays the notions of legacy and historical continuity that inspired several generations of Sovietologists. During the Cold War, many scholars justified their interests by deriving the Soviet institutions from the history of the Russian Empire. Ignoring the changing agency of the rulers and the populus, these straightforward explanations do not seem convincing now. There is no more reason to believe that the Soviet regime was a reincarnation of the Russian Empire than to deduce the peculiarities of post-Soviet Russia from the Soviet regime. Every generation makes its own choice within the window of opportunities that it receives from the past.

However, some of these opportunities and constraints have proven to be surprisingly stable in this part of the world. There are continuities in Russia's geography and ecology that one cannot deny. Russia acquired most of its territory before the institution of the Empire, and the main reason for amassing this territory was fur. With the exhaustion of this natural resource, the state underwent a catastrophic and productive transformation that laid the foundation for the Empire. This was a period of multiple experiments with discovering, appropriating, populating, cultivating, and domesticating – in a word, colonizing – lands within and beyond the moving boundaries of the Empire. For centuries, the Russian state combined its territorial expansion with a strong immigration policy. It imported people, settled and resettled them, and launched experimental forms of population management. Illicit or organized, these movements spanned the elastic continuums of internal versus external, native versus foreign, assimilated versus alien. These spatial oppositions were subordinated to intuitive ideas of temporal order. Old areas of colonization were felt as domestic, recently occupied areas as foreign. Political categories of space emerged from the perception of historical time. The external and the internal swapped ceaselessly. Königsberg was outside Russian borders for the larger part of its millennial history; but when Russian troops took it, the dwellers of Königsberg more than once became subjects of the Russian state, as had the people of Ingria where St. Petersburg stands, and as, much earlier, had those who lived where Moscow stands. While military and political borders were expanding outside, the heartland remained underdeveloped. It had to be colonized again, and again. In the mid-nineteenth century, Russian mainstream historians started to use this colonial terminology, and gradually the bureaucratic circles of St. Petersburg accepted it. In 1907–17, *Problems of Colonization* (*Voprosy kolonizatsii*) was the title of the official journal of the Resettlement Administration, an agency that had been founded in 1896 within the Ministry of Internal Affairs and later moved into the Ministry of Agriculture. Led by their "etatist and technocratic ethos," officials of this administration oversaw the colonial efforts of the state that were directed both onto the reorganization of the Russian heartlands (Stolypin reforms) and the migration of the peasantry to Siberia, Central Asia, and Transcaucasia (Holquist 2010a). This terminology survived the Bolshevik Revolution but did not outlive Stalinism. In 1922, the Bolshevik government opened the State Scientific Research Institute of Colonization, which functioned until 1930 (Rybakovsky 1998; Hirsch 2005).

In the nineteenth century, Russia was a colonial empire alongside those of Britain or Austria, *and* a colonized territory like Congo or the West Indies. In its different aspects and periods, Russian culture was both the subject *and* the object of orientalism. The main paths of colonization led not only outwards, but also into the Russian heartland. These paths led to Eastern Europe, Central Asia, the Middle East, and the Pacific, but also to the lands around Novgorod, Tula, Orenburg, and Odessa. It was there in the heartland that the Empire settled foreign "colonists" and established military "colonies." There in the heartland, Russian nobles owned millions of "souls" and punished millions of bodies. There in the heartland, imperial experts discovered the most unusual communes and collected the most exotic folklore. And it was to these heartlands that Russian pilgrims went in search of their chosen groups of people. The characteristic phenomena of colonialism, such as missionary work, exotic journeys, and ethnographic scholarship, were directed inwards toward the Russian villages as well as outwards and overseas. Expanding into huge spaces, Russia colonized its own people. This was the process of internal colonization, the secondary colonization of one's own territory.

Having "discovered" an alien tribe, the Empire never left it as it was. Mixed, separated, destroyed, or instituted, ethnicities were more like cooked imperial cuisine than the raw products of nature. The imperial situation superimposed multiple dualities. Imperial and colonial elites defined themselves against their lower-class compatriots and also against one another. These correlated processes of self-definition and othering featured different mechanisms from those typical for overseas empires. Like a structuralist, the Empire imposed these binary categories onto the chaotic mosaic of religious differences, property rights, and, finally, geography itself; but the flow of history, a deconstruction in action, inescapably mixed and overruled these dichotomies.

The internal colonization of Russia was more akin to the British colonization of America than that of India: non-Europeans were either assimilated or annihilated, leaving the Empire to embark on colonization of its own people, who gradually formed new identities for themselves. Many spoke the same language and almost all had the same color of skin. Dialectal variation, which had played a critical role in many European cultures, was less characteristic of Russia. In agrarian societies, the cultural distance between the upper and lower strata secured their stability (Gellner 1983, 1998). The main distinctions in such societies, those between the rulers and the commoners, were made visible through all means available to the culture. Because of the contingencies of geography, ecology, and even zoology, in Russia agrarian society became an imperial one, with social distances of the former compounded by political distances of the latter. Instead of naturalizing social and linguistic differences in a racist way, the state codified them in a legal way, creating a system of estates that regulated the access of subjects to education, career, and prosperity.

The reflexivity of internal colonization has lent Russian cultural history a characteristic inconsistency, confusion, and incompleteness, which western observers have sought to explain in a typically orientalist style. The two modes of colonial expansion, the British and the Russian, were so different that Bismarck famously compared them to a whale and a bear. For empires, their different ways of expanding around the globe determined their different methods of colonial administration and military methods, but also their different forms of culture and scholarship. The Russian Empire defined its others by estate and religion; western empires defined them by geography and race. A stable imperial order created a ceaseless, manageable exchange between culture, nature, and the law, with cultural difference naturalized smoothly and legalized effectively. But this exchange turned into an explosive mix every time things went wrong, or in anticipation of such crises. In revolutionary situations, differences were de-naturalized and de-legitimized. The very same intellectuals who were entrusted by the Empire with managing cultural distances realized their cultural, constructed character.

Unusually for European powers, the Russian Empire demonstrated a reversed imperial gradient: people on the periphery lived better than those in the central provinces. The Empire settled foreigners on its lands, giving them privileges over Russians and other locals. Among all ethnicities in the Empire, only Russians and some other eastern Slavs were subject to serfdom. Emancipation began with reforms on the periphery of the Empire and from there moved to the heartland. After Emancipation, Russians were still subjected to heavier economic exploitation than non-Russians.

No cultural distance, no empire. In Russia, the metropolitan elite often perceived cultural distances in paradoxical ways, with subjugated peoples – Russians and non-Russians – imagined as endowed with higher culture or morals than the elite attributed to itself. Though the concept of orientalism is sometimes interpreted in an exclusively negative way, the colonial subject was frequently idealized as superior to the metropolitan observer. For many in the nineteenth century, "the Orient was a place of pilgrimage, an exotic yet especially attractive reality" (Said 1978: 168). Once embedded in the public imagination, the idea of difference became a double-edged mechanism, an ideological swing. When the ruling and writing elites attributed to "noble savages" and "simple peasants" the most improbable virtues, such as primordial equality, unselfish proficiency, and a love of suffering, such idealizations did not prevent native populations from being oppressed. In fact, these creative constructs supported exploitation in subtle and paradoxical ways. For those who enjoyed living off the income from their estates, it was comfortable to believe that peasants did not need private property because of their sublime beliefs. Some intellectuals are always able to convince themselves that peasants, or women, or Slavs, or students just love to suffer.

From the triumph of Peter I to the collapse of Nicholas II, the Empire was ceaselessly concerned with constructing, demonstrating, affirming, and re-affirming its cultural hegemony. It heavily invested in showing the world an inspired and inspiring face that would evoke loyalty among subjects, respect among friends, and fear among enemies. But the challenges of domination for this Empire proved to be easier than the challenges of hegemony. Building St. Petersburg was the most ambitious project of the imperial hegemony, but the cultural mythology of the city overflows with visions of flood, guilt, and apocalypse. Despite the large-scale programs of cultural import and ambitious technologies such as fireworks, the Empire constantly reverted to force in its dealings with the nationalism of non-Russians and the discontent of Russians. Against this backdrop, the truly successful institution of cultural hegemony in the Empire was Russian literature. While performing its crucial function of providing the dispersed subjects of the Empire with a common pool of cultural symbols, Russian literature became increasingly critical toward other imperial institutions. The prevalence of imaginative literature as a major institution of transformation, culture and anti-imperial protest expanded throughout the nineteenth century and then into the Soviet period. Playing this role, Russian literature attracted myriad fans both inside and outside Russia. However, its cultural power within the Empire demonstrated an uneasy dialectics. The more productive a literary text was in the machinery of hegemony, the more destructive it became to the hierarchy of domination.

Over three centuries, Russian literature created a saga of political dissidence and proof of the autonomy of culture. Populating the unexplored space between retreating imperialism, emerging nationalism, and ambitious utopianism, it created a paradigm for post-imperial humanity. Its central texts were applauded by colonial readers around the world.

Postcolonial theory, with its explicitly political way of reading, is important for the understanding of canonical Russian texts. In those cases where the canon is produced by the dominant culture, contemporary critics look to marginal texts in order to hear the suppressed parts of historical experience. In Russian literature, however, the canonical texts were created by those who suffered political persecution in its purest form, not necessarily accompanied by economic hardships. Sometimes deceiving imperial censorship and sometimes going into exile, many Russian writers were victims of their own country. These white, educated, and sometimes rich men belonged to an oppressed minority within their society. From their marginalized feelings emerged canonical texts. British admirers compared Gandhi to Tolstoy just as often as Franz Fanon or the writers of the Harlem Renaissance cited Dostoevsky. One group of writers belonged to an imperial elite, the other to the colonized peoples, but the similarities between them turned out to be more important than the differences. These were the similarities between external and internal colonization.

In France and Germany, the nationalization of agrarian culture was also similar to self-colonization: the "people," who were divided into classes, provinces, dialects, and sects, were transformed into a "nation" (Weber 1976). In Russia, this process took the tragic form of a series of catastrophes that the future historian will probably describe, with reference to Trotsky, as the permanent revolution. While the British sought oriental knowledge and pleasures overseas, the Russians sought them in the depths of their own country. In promoting state-sponsored nationalism and organizing ethnographic studies, the mid-nineteenth-century monarchy inadvertently sponsored the discovery of the Russian commune and its increasingly radical interpretations by Slavophiles, populists, and socialists. With the discovery of sects, German romantic clichés, French utopian ideas, and American dissident experience became applicable to the trivia of Russian life. Locked between the Empire that it failed to overthrow and the commune that it failed to preserve, Russian thought offered a brilliant, tragic, and deeply human lesson. As a result of this literature, serfs, sectarians, and other subaltern groups spoke and are still speaking to us. Written by the authors from higher classes, whose fate was sometimes different from and sometimes similar to that of their underprivileged characters, this literature became postcolonial not only *avant la lettre* but before its Empire collapsed.

Writing about "an intellectual historian of the year 2010, if such a person is imaginable," the anthropologist James Clifford (1988: 93–4) predicted that this historian would transcend the twentieth-century problematic of language and create a paradigm of "ethnographic subjectivity." In fact, even more has happened. After a period of fascination with ethnicity, scholars are developing non-ethnic concepts to apply to Eurasia (Hagen 2004; Kappeler 2009; Burbank and Cooper 2010). If the new paradigm transcends language, as Clifford correctly believed would happen, it also transcends ethnicity. But it is still mired in the conundrum of subjectivity. In the imperial context, the word "subject" has at least two meanings, subject as opposed to sovereign and subject as opposed to object. The English concept of the subject, with its derivatives of subjectivity and subjectness, retains this ambiguity; some other European languages, Russian included, have developed two different words for these two aspects of subject."[1] Subjectivity develops in relation to sovereignty, but surpasses it by far; it is this surplus of subjectivity over subjectness – hidden transcripts and much else – that makes imperial cultures so rich and so unstable. Michel Foucault (1997: 44) said "a sort of farewell" to the concept of sovereignty, as being insufficient for the analysis of power relations. The concept of subjectivity is equally one-sided, but the very oscillation of "subject" from its juridical to its epistemological meanings helps to address the problems of imperial power. Pressed between the sovereign, who is the super-subject of the domain, and the domain's usable and taxable objects (resources, products, etc.), the subjects develop their unique ways of life, love, and service. Upwards, this imperial *subjectness* ranges from identification with the sovereign to resistance and rebellion. Downwards, this imperial *subjectivity* confronts the variety of objects, from animals to landscapes, in circuitous attempts to conquer and explore, build and destroy, capture and exchange, forget and remember. Horizontally, this *subjectification* involves other subjects, those who are singular and those who are counted in the millions, with all their souls, bodies, and communities.

Bears and whales differ dramatically, but scholars know that deep under their skins they are alike. In colonizing India and Russia, the

[1] An important debate on "Soviet subjectivity" helped me to articulate this idea (Halfin 2000; Hellbeck 2000; Krylova 2000; Etkind 2005; Chatterjee and Petrone 2008).

British and the Russians enslaved, exploited, enlightened, and emancipated those "half devils, half children" (Kipling) who populated them. It was an impossible task implied by the "white man's burden," a task that I have named the "shaved man's burden" of the Russian imperial elite. Among many Russian stories revealing this burden is "A Product of Nature" by Nikolai Leskov. In this memoir, Leskov, a young gentleman, strives to save some peasants from being flogged by a local policeman. But the policeman locks him up in his own house, where Leskov browses through the policeman's books, a collection of forbidden literature that calls for justice and emancipation. In the meantime, the policeman flogs the serfs, and Leskov's only success is his discovery that the policeman is an impostor and not a policeman at all.

References

Abrams, M. H. 1953. *The Mirror and the Lamp: Romantic Theory and the Critical Tradition*. New York: Oxford University Press.

Achebe, Chinua 2001. "An Image of Africa: Racism in Conrad's Heart of Darkness," in Vincent B. Leitch (ed.), *The Norton Anthology of Theory and Criticism*. New York: Norton.

Agamben, Giorgio 1998. *Homo Sacer. Sovereign Power and Bare Life*. Stanford: Stanford University Press.

Aksakov, Ivan 1994. *Pis'ma k rodnym, 1849–1856*. Moscow: Nauka.

Anderson, Benedict 1991. *Imagined Communities*. London, New York: Verso.

Anderson, F. 2000. *Crucible of War: The Seven Years War and the Fate of Empire in British North America*. New York: Vintage.

Anisimov, Evgenii 1999. *Elizaveta Petrovna*. Moscow: Molodaia gvardiia.

Annenkov, Pavel 1989. *Literatirnye vospominaniia*. Moscow: Pravda.

[Anonymous] 1847. "Baron Haxthausen i ego puteshestvie po Rossii," *Finsky vestnik*, 22/10: 1–16.

Aptekman, O. B. 1924. *Obshchestvo "Zemlia i volia" 70-x godov po lichnym vospominaniiam*. Petrograd: Kolos.

Arendt, Hannah 1966. *Origins of Totalitarianism*. New York: Harcourt.

Arendt, Hannah 1968. *Men in Dark Times*. Orlando, FL: Harcourt.

Arendt, Hannah 1970. *On Violence*. Orlando, FL: Harcourt.

Arkhiv 1932. *Arkhiv "Zemli i Voli" i "Narodnoi Voli."* Moscow: Obshchestvo politkatorzhan.

Arneil, Barbara 1996. *John Locke and America: The Defense of English Colonialism*. Oxford: Oxford University Press.

Ashcroft, Bill, and Paul Ahluwalia 1999. *Edward Said. The Paradox of Identity*. London: Routledge.

Atkinson, D. 1990. "Egalitarianism and the Commune," in R. P. Bartlett (ed.), *Land Commune and Peasant Community in Russia*. Basingstoke: Macmillan.

Bakhtin, Mikhail 1975. "Formy vremeni i khronotopa v romane. Ocherki po istoricheskoi poetike," in *Voprosy literatury i estetiki. Issledovaniia raznykh let*. Moscow: Khudozhestvennaia literatura, 234–407.

Bakhtin, Mikhail 2000. *Problemy tvorchestva Dostoevskogo*. Moscow: Russkie slovari.

Balibar, E. 1999. "Is There a 'Neo-Racism'?," in E. Balibar and I. Wallerstein, *Race, Nation, Class: Ambiguous Identities*, trans. Chris Turner. London: Verso, 17–28.
Baranowski, Shelley 2011. *Nazi Empire. German Colonialism and Imperialism from Bismarck to Hitler*. Cambridge: Cambridge University Press.
Barnes, Hugh 2005. *Gannibal: The Moor of Petersburg*. New York: Profile Books.
Baron, Samuel H. 1953. *Plekhanov: The Father of Russian Marxism*. Stanford: Stanford University Press.
Baron, Samuel H. 1958. "Plekhanov's Russia: The Impact of the West upon an 'Oriental' Society," *Journal of the History of Ideas*, 19/3: 388–404.
Baron, Samuel H. 1995. *Plekhanov in Russian History and Soviet Historiography*. Pittsburgh: University of Pittsburgh Press.
Barrett, Thomas 1999. *At the Edge of Empire: The Terek Cossacks and the North Caucasus Frontier*. Boulder, CO: Westview.
Bartlett, Robert 1993. *The Making of Europe. Conquest, Colonization, and Cultural Change*. London: Penguin.
Bartlett, Roger 1979. *Human Capital. The Settlement of Foreigners in Russia, 1762–1804*. Cambridge: Cambridge University Press.
Bassin, Mark 1993. "Turner, Solov'ev, and the 'Frontier Hypothesis': The Nationalist Signification of Open Spaces," *Journal of Modern History*, 65: 473–511.
Bassin, Mark 1999. *Imperial Visions: Nationalist Imagination and Geographic Expansion in the Russian Far East, 1840–1865*. Cambridge: Cambridge University Press.
Bates, Robert H. 2001. *Prosperity and Violence: The Political Economy of Development*. New York: Norton.
Bauman, Whitney 2009. *Theology, Creation, and Environmental Ethics: From Creatio Ex Nihilo to Terra Nullius*. London: Routledge.
Beissinger, Mark 2006. "Soviet Empire as 'Family Resemblance'," *Slavic Review*, 65/2: 294–303.
Belinsky, Vissarion 1954. *Polnoe sobranie sochinenii*. Moscow: AN SSSR.
Benes, Tuska 2004. "Comparative Linguistics as Ethnology. In Search of Indo-Germans in Central Asia," *Comparative Studies of South Asia, Africa, and the Middle East*, 24/2: 117–32.
Benjamin, Walter 1968. "The Storyteller. Reflections on the Works of Nikolai Leskov," in his *Essays and Reflections*, ed. Hannah Arendt. New York: Schocken, 83–110.
Benjamin, Walter 1999. "On the Present Situation in Russian Film," in his *Selected Writings*, vol. 2, pt. 1 (1927–1930). Cambridge, MA: Belknap, 12–15.
Bentham, Jeremy 1995. *The Panopticon Writings*, ed. Miran Bozovic. London: Verso.
Beratz, Gottlieb 1991. *The German Colonies on the Lower Volga*. Lincoln, NE: American Historical Society of Germans from Russia.
Berdiaev, Nikolai 1916. "Tipy religioznoi mysli v Rossii," *Russkaia mysl'*, 6.
Berdiaev, Nikolai 1989. "Dukhovnoe khristianstvo i sektantstvo v Rossii," in his *Sobraniie sochinenii*, vol. 3. Paris: YMCA-Press.
Berens, Reinhold 1812. *Geschichte der seit hundert und funzig Jahren in Riga einheimischen Familie Berens aus Rostock*. Riga: Julius Müller Verlag.

Berezin, Ilia 1858. "Metropoliia i koloniia," *Otechestvennye zapiski*, 118/5: 74–115.

Berlin, Isaiah 1978. "A Remarkable Decade," in his *Russian Thinkers*. New York: Penguin.

Berlin, Isaiah 1996. "Kant as an Unfamiliar Source of Nationalism," in his *Sense of Reality*. London: Chatto.

Berlin, Isaiah 2000. *Three Critics of the Enlightenment*. London: Pimlico.

Berman, Russell A. 1998. *Enlightenment or Empire: Colonial Discourse in German Culture*. Lincoln: University of Nebraska Press.

Bethea, David 1998. "Slavic Gift Giving: The Poet in History and Pushkin's 'The Captain's Daughter'," in Monika Greenleaf and Stephen Moeller-Sally (eds.), *Russian Subjects: Empire, Nation, and the Culture of the Golden Age*. Evanston, IL: Northwestern University Press, 259–76.

Betz, John 2008. *After Enlightenment: The Post-Secular Vision of J. G. Hamann*. Oxford: Wiley-Blackwell.

Bhabha, Homi 1994. *The Location of Culture*. London: Routledge.

Bideleux, Robert, and Ian Jeffries 2007. *A History of Eastern Europe: Crisis and Change*. London: Routledge.

Billington, James H. 1966. *The Icon and the Axe*. New York: Vintage.

Black, J. L. 1986. *G.-F. Müller and the Imperial Russian Academy*. Kingston: McGill University Press.

Blackbourn, David 2007. *The Conquest of Nature. Water, Landscape, and the Making of Modern Germany*. London: Pimlico.

Blackbourn, David 2009. "The Conquest of Nature and the Mystique of the Eastern Frontier in Nazi Germany," in Robert L. Nelson (ed.), *Germans, Poland, and Colonial Expansion to the East*. London: Palgrave, 141–70.

Blauner, Robert 1969. "Internal Colonialism and Ghetto Revolt," *Social Problems*, 16/4: 393–408.

Bockstoce, John R. 2009. *Furs and Frontiers in the Far North*. New Haven, CT: Yale University Press.

Boeck, Brian J. 2007. "Containment vs. Colonization. Muscovite Approaches to Settling the Steppe," in Nicholas B. Breyfogle, Abby Schrader, and William Sunderland (eds.), *Peopling the Russian Periphery. Borderland Colonization in Eurasian History*. London: Routledge, 41–60.

Bogucharsky, V. 1912. *Aktivnoe narodnichestvo semidesiatykh godov*. Moscow: Sabashnikovy.

Bojanowska, Edyta M. 2007. *Nikolai Gogol. Between Ukrainian and Russian Nationalism*. Cambridge, MA: Harvard University Press.

Bolotov, Andrei 1931. *Zhizn' i prikliucheniia Andreia Bolotova, opisannye samim im dlia svoikh potomkov*, vols. 1–3. Moscow: Academia.

Bolotov, Andrei 1986. *Zhizn' i prikliucheniia Andreia Bolotova, opisannye samim im dlia svoikh potomkov*, ed. Arsenii Gulyga. Moscow: Sovremennik.

Bonch-Bruevich, Vladimir 1918. *Dukhobortsy v kanadskikh preriiakh*. Petrograd.

Bonch-Bruevich, Vladimir 1924. "Vozmozhnoe uchastie sektantov v khoziastvennoi zhizni SSSR," *Pravda*, May 15.

Boucher, David 2010. "The Law of Nations and the Doctrine of Terra Nulius," in Olaf Asbach and Peter Schroder (eds.), *War, the State and International Law in Seventeenth-Century Europe*. London: Ashgate, 63–82.

Boym, Svetlana 2010. *Another Freedom. The Alternative History of an Idea*. Chicago: University of Chicago Press.

Braudel, Fernand 1967. *Capitalism and Material Life, 1400–1800*, trans. Miriam Kochan. London: Weidenfeld.
Breshkovskaia, E. K. 1931. *Hidden Springs of the Russian Revolution*. Stanford: Stanford University Press.
Breyfogle, Nicolas B. 2005. *Heretics and Colonizers. Forging Russia's Empire in the South Caucasus*. Ithaca: Cornell University Press.
Brooks, Peter. 1996. "'An Unreadable Report.' Conrad's *Heart of Darkness*," in Elaine Jordan (ed.), *Joseph Conrad*. London: Macmillan, 67–86.
Brower, Daniel R., and Edward J. Lazzerini (eds.) 1997. *Russia's Orient. Imperial Borderlands and Peoples*. Bloomington: Indiana University Press.
Brubaker, Rogers 1992. *Citizenship and Nationhood in France and Germany*. Cambridge, MA: Harvard University Press.
Buchowski, Michał 2006. "The Specter of Orientalism in Europe: From Exotic Other to Stigmatized Brother," *Anthropological Quarterly*, 79/3: 463–82.
Bulgarin, Faddei 1830. "Poezdka v Pargolovo," in his *Sochineniia*. St. Petersburg: Smirdin, vol. 11, 150–61.
Bulgarin, Faddei 1836. "Russkii teatr. Revizor N. Gogolia," *Severnaia pchela*, 98.
Burbank, Jane, and Frederick Cooper 2010. *Empires in World History*. Princeton: Princeton University Press.
Burbank, Jane, and David Ransel (eds.) 1998. *Imperial Russia. New Histories for the Empire*. Bloomington: Indiana University Press.
Bushkovitch, Paul 1980. *The Merchants of Moscow. 1580–1650*. Cambridge: Cambridge University Press.
Butterfield, Herbert 1955. *Man on His Past: The Study of the History of Historical Scholarship*. Cambridge: Cambridge University Press.
Calvert, Peter 2001. "Internal Colonisation, Development and Environment," *Third World Quarterly*, 22/1: 51–63.
Cannadine, David 2001. *Ornamentalism. How the British See Their Empire*. Oxford: Oxford University Press.
Césaire, Aimé 1955. Discours sur le colonialism. Paris: Editions Presence Africaine.
Chaadaev, Petr 1914. *Sochineniia i pis'ma*, ed. Mikhail Gershenzon. Moscow.
Chari, Sharad, and Catherine Verdery 2009. "Thinking between the Posts: Postcolonialism, Postsocialism, and Ethnography after the Cold War," *Comparative Studies in Society and History*, 51/1: 1–29.
Chatterjee, Choi, and Karen Petrone 2008. "Models of Selfhood and Subjectivity: The Soviet Case in Historical Perspective," *Slavic Review*, 67/4: 967–86.
Chatterjee, Partha 1993. *The Nation and its Fragments. Colonial and Post-Colonial Histories*. Princeton: Princeton University Press.
Chernov, Viktor 1922. *Zapiski sotsialista-revoliutsionera*, vol. 1. Berlin: Grzhebin.
Chicherin, Boris 1856. "Obzor istoricheskogo razvitiia sel'skoi obshchiny v Rossii," *Russkii vestnik*, 4.
Christie, Ian R. 1993. *The Benthams in Russia*. Oxford: Berg.
Clay, J. Eugene 2001. "Orthodox Missionaries and 'Orthodox Heretics' in Russia, 1886–1917," in Robert Geraci and Michael Khodarkovsky (eds.), *Of Religion and Empire: Missions, Conversions, and Tolerance in Tsarist Russia*. Ithaca: Cornell University Press.

Clément, Catherine 1988. *Opera. The Undoing of Women*, trans. Betsy Wing. Minneapolis: University of Minnesota Press.
Clifford, James 1988. *The Predicament of Culture. Twentieth-Century Ethnography, Literature, and Art*. Cambridge, MA: Harvard University Press.
Coates, Paul 1991. *The Gorgon's Gaze. German Cinema, Expressionism, and the Image of Horror*. Cambridge: Cambridge University Press.
Collier, Stephen, Alex Cooley, Alexander Etkind, Bruce Grant, Jon Kyst, Harriet Murav, Marc Nichanian, and Gayatri Chakravorty Spivak 2003. "Empire, Union, Center, Satellite: Post-Colonial Theory and Slavic Studies," *Ulbandus. The Slavic Review of Columbia University*, 7.
Condee, Nancy 1995. "The Relentless Cult of Novelty," in Daniel Orlovsky (ed.), *Beyond Soviet Studies*. Washington, DC: Woodrow Wilson Center Press, 289–304.
Condee, Nancy 2006. "Drowning or Waving? Some Remarks on Russian Cultural Studies," *The Slavic and East European Journal*, 50/1: 197–203.
Condee, Nancy 2008. "From Emigration to E-Migration: Contemporaneity and the Former Second World," in Terry Smith, Okwui Enwezor, and Nancy Condee (eds.), *Antinomies of Art and Culture. Modernity, Postmodernity, and Contemporaneity*. Durham, NC: Duke University Press, 235–49.
Condee, Nancy 2009. *The Imperial Trace: Recent Russian Cinema*. Oxford: Oxford University Press.
Confino, Michael 1963. *Domaines et seigneurs en Russie vers la fin du XVIIIe siècle*. Paris: Institut d'Études slaves de l'Université de Paris.
Confino, Michael 2008. "The *soslovie* (estate) paradigm," *Cahiers du monde russe*, 49/4: 681–704.
Conrad, Joseph 1919. *A Personal Record*. London: Dent.
Conrad, Joseph 1921. "Crime of Partition," in his *Notes on Life and Letters*. London: Dent.
Conrad, Joseph 1926. "Geography and Some Explorers," in his *Last Essays*. London: Dent.
Conrad, Joseph 1988. *Heart of Darkness*. New York: Norton.
Conrad, Joseph 2001. *Under Western Eyes*. New York: Random House.
Cook, Malcolm 1994. "Robinson Crusoe in Siberia: The Writing of a Novel in the Late Eighteen Century," *Studies on Voltaire and the Eighteenth Century*, 317: 1–43.
Cook, Malcolm 2006. *Bernardin de Saint-Pierre. A Life of Culture*. London: Legenda.
Cooper, Frederick, and Ann Laura Stoler 1997. "Between Metropole and Colony: Rethinking a Research Agenda," in Cooper and Stoler (eds.), *Tensions of Empire. Colonial Cultures in a Bourgeois World*. Berkeley: University of California Press, 1–58.
Coulanges, Fustel de 1908. *Rimskii kolonat*, trans. I. M. Grevs. St. Petersburg: Stasiulevich.
Cracraft, James 1997. *The Petrine Revolution in Russian Imagery*. Chicago: University of Chicago Press.
Cracraft, James 2004. *The Petrine Revolution in Russian Culture*. Cambridge, MA: Harvard University Press.
Crummey, Robert 1993. "Old Belief as Popular Religion: New Approaches," *Slavic Review*, 52: 700–12.

Curtin, Philipp 1984. *Cross-Cultural Trade in World History*. Cambridge: Cambridge University Press.
Curtin, Philipp 2000. *The World and the West*. Cambridge: Cambridge University Press.
Curzon, George N. 1889. *Russia in Central Asia in 1889, and the Anglo-Russian Question*. London: Longmans.
Dabag, Mihran, Horst Gründer, and Uwe-K. Ketelsen (eds). 2004. *Kolonialismus, Kolonialdiskurs und Genozid*. Munich: Wilhelm Fink.
Dal, Vladimir 2002a. "Poltora slova o nyneshnem russkom iazyke," in his *Neizvestnyi Vladimir Dal*. Orenburg: Knizhnoe izdatel'stvo.
Dal, Vladimir 2002b. "Avtobiographicheskie zapiski," in his *Kartiny iz russkogo byta*. Moscow: Novyi kliuch.
Dameshek, L. M., and Remnev A. V. (eds). 2007. *Sibir' v sostave Rossiiskoi imperii*. Moscow: Novoe literaturnoe obozrenie.
Defoe, Daniel 1925. *The Farther Adventures of Robinson Crusoe, Being the Second and Last Part of his Life, Written by Himself*. London: Constable.
Deich, L. G. 1923. *Za polveka*. Berlin: Grani.
Dekhnewallah, A. 1879. "The Great Russian Invasion of India," in *A Sequel to the Afghanistan Campaign of 1878–9*. London: Harrison.
Dennison, T. K., and A. W. Carus 2003. "The Invention of the Russian Rural Commune: Haxthausen and the Evidence," *The Historical Journal*, 46/3: 561–82.
Derrida, Jacques 2009. *The Beast and the Sovereign*. Chicago: University of Chicago Press.
Dettelbach, Michael 1996. "Forster as Linnean," in *Johann Reinhold Forster. Observations Made During A Voyage Round The World*. Honolulu: University of Hawaii Press.
Diderot, Denis 1992. "Observations sur le Nakaz," in his *Political Writings*. Cambridge: Cambridge University Press.
Dimou, Augusta 2009. *Entangled Paths Towards Modernity: Contextualizing Socialism and Nationalism in the Balkans*. Budapest: CEU Press.
Dirks, Nicholas B. 2001. *Castes of Mind. Colonialism and the Making of Modern India*. Princeton: Princeton University Press.
Dixon, William H. 1870. *Free Russia*. New York.
Dobroliubov, Nikolai 1962. *Sobranie sochinenii v deviati tomakh*. Moscow: GIKhL.
Dolbilov, Mikhail 2010. *Russkii krai, chuzhaia vera*. Moscow: Novoe literaturnoe obizrenie.
Domar, Evsey 1970. "The Causes of Slavery or Serfdom," *Journal of Economic History*, 30/1, 18–32.
Dostoevsky, Fyodor 1993. "Riad statei o russkoi literature," in his *Sobranie sochinenii v 15 tomakh*, vol. 11. St. Petersburg: Nauka, 12–13.
Dostoevsky, Fyodor 1996. *The Idiot*. London: Wordsworth.
Dragomanov, M. P. 1896. "Introduction," in Bakunin, *Pis'ma k A.I. Gertsenu i N.P. Ogarevu*. Geneva.
Druzhinin, N. M. 1968. "Krest'ianskaia obshchina v otsenke A. Gakstgauzena i ego russkikh sovremennikov," in *Ezhegodnik germanskoi istorii*. Moscow: Nauka, 28–50.
Dubie, Alan 1989. *Frank A. Golder, An Adventure of a Historian in Quest of Russian History*. Boulder: East European Monographs.

Dubnow, Simon, and Israel Friedlaender 1920. *History of the Jews in Russia and Poland*. New York.
Dunning, Chester, 1989. "James I, the Russia Company, and the Plan to Establish a Protectorate over North Russia," *Albion*, 21/2: 206–26.
Dunning, Chester S. L. 2001. *Russia's First Civil War: The Time of Troubles and the Founding of the Romanov Dynasty*. University Park: Penn State University Press.
Durylin, S. N. 1932. "Russkie pisateli u Gete v Veimare". *Literaturnoe nasledstvo*, 4/6: 83–496. Moscow: Zhurnal'no-gazetnoe ob'edininenie.
Eaton, Henry 1980. "Marx and the Russians," *Journal of the History of Ideas*, 41/1: 89–112.
Eidelman, Nathan 1965. "Pavel Ivanovich Bakhmet'ev," in Militsa Nechkina (ed.), *Revoliutsionnaia situatsiia v Rossii v 1859–1861*. Moscow: Nauka, vol. 4, 387–98.
Eidelman, Nathan 1993. "Gde i chto Liprandi?," in N. Ia. Eidelman, *Iz potaennoi istorii Rossii 18–19 vekov*. Moscow: Vysshaia shkola, 429–64.
Ekaterina II 1869. "Antidot," in *Osmnadcatyi vek*, vol. 4. Moscow.
Ekaterina II 1990. *Sochineniia*, ed. O. N. Mikhailov. Moscow: Sovetskaia Rossiia.
Ekaterina II 2008. *Rossiiskaia istoriia*. Moscow: EKSMO.
Emmons, Terence 1999. "On the Problem of Russia's 'Separate Path' in Late Imperial Historiography," in Thomas Sanders (ed.), *Historiography of Imperial Russia*. Armonk, NY: Sharpe, 163–85.
Emmons, Terence, and Bertrand M. Patenaude 1992. *War, Revolution, and Peace in Russia: The Passages of Frank Golder*. Stanford, CA: Hoover Press.
Engels, Frederick 1940. *The Origin of the Family, Private Property, and the State*. London: Lawrence.
Engelstein, Laura 1999. *Castration and the Heavenly Kingdom. A Russian Folktale*. Ithaca: Cornell University Press.
Engelstein, Laura 2009. *Slavophile Empire. Imperial Russia's Illiberal Path*. Ithaca: Cornell University Press.
Ergang, Robert Reinhold 1966. *Herder and the Foundation of German Nationalism*. New York: Octagon.
Ermichev, A. A., and A. A. Zlatopol'skaia (eds.) 1989. *Chaadaev. Pro et Contra*. St. Petersburg: RKhGI.
Eshevsky, Stepan 1870. *Sochineniia*, vol. 1. Moscow: Soldatenkov.
Etkind, Alexander 1996. "Russkie sekty i sovetskii kommunism: proekt Vladimira Bonch-Bruevicha," *Minuvshee*, 19: 275–319.
Etkind, Alexander 1997. *Eros of the Impossible. The History of Psychoanalysis in Russia*, trans. Noah and Maria Rubins. Boulder, CO: Westview.
Etkind, Alexander 1998. *Khlyst. Sekty, literatura i revolutsia*. Moscow: Novoe literaturnoe obozrenie.
Etkind, Alexander 2001a. "Foucault i imperskaia Rossiia: Distsiplinarnye praktiki v usloviiakh vnutrennei kolonizatsii," in Oleg Kharkhordin (ed.), *Foucault i Rossiia*. St. Petersburg: Evropeiiskii universitet, 166–91.
Etkind, Alexander 2001b. *Tolkovaniie puteshestvii. Rossiia i Amerika v travelogakh i intertextakh*. Moscow: Novoe literaturnoe obozrenie.
Etkind, Alexander 2002. "Bremia britogo cheloveka, ili Vnutrenniaia kolonizatsiia Rossii," *Ab Imperio* (Kazan'), 1: 265–99.

Etkind, Alexander 2003. "Whirling with the Other: Russian Populism and Religious Sects," *Russian Review*, 62/4: 565–88.
Etkind, Alexander 2004. "Sex, Sects, and Texts: Russian Sectarians in Russian and Other Literatures," *Wiener Slawistischer Almanach*, 54: 45–56.
Etkind, Alexander 2005. "Soviet Subjectivity: Torture for the Sake of Salvation?" *Kritika: Explorations in Russian and Eurasian History*, 6/1: 171–86.
Etkind, Alexander 2007. "Internalizing Colonialism: Intellectual Endeavors and Internal Affairs in mid-19th-century Russia," in Peter J. S. Duncan (ed.), *Convergence and Divergence. Russia and Eastern Europe into the Twenty-First Century*. London: SSEES, 103–20.
Etkind, Alexander 2009. "The Kremlin's Double Monopoly" in *Russia Lost or Found?* Helsinki: Ministry of Foreign Affairs, 186–213.
Etkind, Alexander 2010. "The Shaved Man's Burden: The Russian Novel as a Romance of Internal Colonization," in Alastair Renfrew and Galin Tihanov (eds.), *Critical Theory in Russia and the West*. London: Routledge, 124–51.
Fanon, Frantz 1967. *The Wretched of the Earth*. New York: Weidenfeld.
Felshtinsky, Iurii 2009. *Vozhdi v zakone*. Moscow: Terra.
Fernández-Armesto, Felipe and James Muldoon (eds.) 2008. *Internal Colonization in Medieval Europe*. London: Ashgate.
Ferro, Marc 1997. *Colonization: A Global History*. London: Routledge.
Field, Daniel, 1976. *Rebels in the Name of the Tsar*. Boston: Houghton Mifflin.
Field, Daniel 1987. "Peasants and Propagandists in the Russian Movement to the People of 1874," *Journal of Modern History*, 59: 415–38.
Fisher, Henry Raymond 1943. *The Russian Fur Trade, 1550–1700*. Berkeley: University of California Press.
Fitzpatrick, Sheila 1993. "Ascribing Class: The Construction of Social Identity in Soviet Russia," *The Journal of Modern History*, 65/4: 745–70.
Fleishman, Avrom 1967. *Conrad's Politics. Community and Anarchy in the Fiction of Joseph Conrad*. Baltimore, MD: Johns Hopkins Press.
Fodor, Alexander 1989. *A Quest for Non-Violent Russia: The Partnership of Leo Tolstoy and Vladimir Chertkov*. Lanham, Md.: University Press of America.
Forster, John Reinhold 1768. "A Letter from Mr. J. R. Forster Containing Some Account of a New Map of the River Volga," *Philosophical Transactions*, 58: 214–16.
Foucault, Michel 1979. *Discipline and Punish. The Birth of the Prison*, trans. Alan Sheridan. New York: Vintage.
Foucault, Michel 1998. *The History of Sexuality*. Vol. 1: *The Will to Knowledge*. London: Penguin.
Foucault, Michel 2003. *Society Must Be Defended*, trans. David Macey. New York: Picador.
Foust, Clifford M. 1969. *Muscovite and Mandarin: Russia's Trade with China and Its Setting, 1727–1805*. Chapel Hill: University of North Carolina Press.
Frank, Stephen P. 1999. *Crime, Cultural Conflict, and Justice in Rural Russia*. Berkeley: University of California Press.
Franklin, Simon 2004. "Identity and Religion," in Simon Franklin and Emma Widdis (eds.), *National Identity in Russian Culture*. Cambridge: Cambridge University Press, 95–115.
Franklin, Simon, and Jonathan Shepard 1996. *The Emergence of Rus, 750–1200*. London: Longman.

Free, Melissa 2006. "Un-Erasing Crusoe: Farther Adventures in the Nineteenth Century," *Book History*, 9, 89–130.
Freeze, Gregory 1986. "The Estate (Soslovie) Paradigm and Russian Social History," *American Historical Review*, 91/1: 11–36.
Freeze, Gregory 1988. "A Social Mission for Russian Orthodoxy: The Kazan Requiem of 1861 for the Peasants in Bezdna," in M. Shatz and E. Mendelsohn (eds.), *Imperial Russia, 1700–1917: State, Society, Opposition*. DeKalb, IL: Northern Illinois University Press, 115–35.
Friedman, Thomas 2006. "First Law of Petropolitics," *Foreign Policy*, 154: 28–39.
Frierson, Cathy A. 1993. Peasant Icons. *Representations of Rural People in Late Nineteenth-Century Russia*. Oxford: Oxford University Press.
Friesen, P. M. 1978. *The Mennonite Brotherhood in Russia (1789–1910)*, trans. and ed. J. B. Toews. Fresno: Mennonite Brethren.
Frolenko, M. F. 1932. *Sobranie sochinenii*, vol. 2. Moscow, 94.
Frost, Robert I. 2000. *The Northern Wars: War, State and Society in Northeastern Europe, 1558–1721*. Harlow: Longman.
Fülop-Miller, René 1927. *The Mind and Face of Bolshevism: An Examination of Cultural Life in Soviet Russia*, trans. F. S. Flint and D. F. Tait. London: Putnam.
Gamfield, G. P. 1990. "The Pavlovtsy of Khar'kov Province, 1886–1905: Harmless Sectarians or Dangerous Rebels?," *Slavic and East European Review*, 68/4: 692–717.
Gates, Henry Louis 1985. "Writing 'Race' and the Difference it Makes," in Gates (ed.), *Race, Writing, and Difference*. Chicago: University of Chicago Press, 1–20.
Gellner, Ernest 1983. *Nations and Nationalism*. Ithaca, NY: Cornell university press.
Gellner, Ernest 1987. *Culture, Identity, and Politics*. Cambridge: Cambridge University Press.
Gellner, Ernest 1998. *Language and Solitude. Wittgenstein, Malinowski and the Habsburg Dilemma*. Cambridge: Cambridge University Press.
Geraci, Robert P. 2001. *Window on the East: National and Imperial Identities in late Tsarist Russia*. Ithaca: Cornell University Press.
Gerasimov, Ilia et al. 2004. *Novaia imperskaia istoriia postsovetskogo prostranstva*. Kazan: Ab Imperio.
Gerasimov, Ilia, Jan Kusber, and Alexander Semyonov, 2009. *Empire Speaks Out. Languages of Rationalization and Self-Description in the Russian Empire*. Leiden: Brill.
Gerould, Katharine Fullerton 1919. "The Remarkable Rightness of Rudyard Kipling," *Atlantic Magazine*, January.
Gerschenkron, Alexander 1970. *Europe in the Russian Mirror*. Cambridge: Cambridge University Press.
Gershtein, Emma 1964. *Sud'ba Lermontova*. Moscow: Sovetskii pisatel'.
Gesemann, Wolfgang 1965. "Herder's Russia," *Journal of the History of Ideas*, 26/3: 424–34.
Gilmour, David 1994. *Curzon*. London: John Murray.
Girard, René 1965. *Deceit, Desire, and The Novel: Self and Other in Literary Structure*. Baltimore: Johns Hopkins Press.
Girard, René 1995. *Violence and the Sacred*. New York: Continuum.
Gleason, Abbot 1980. *Young Russia. The Genesis of Russian Radicalism in the 1860s*. New York: Viking.

Glebov, Sergey 2009. "Siberian Middle Ground: Languages of Rule and Accommodation of the Siberian Frontier," in Ilia Gerasimov et al. (eds.), *Empire Speaks Out*. Leiden: Brill, 121–54.

Gofman, A. B. 2001. *Emil Durkheim v Rossii*. Moscow: GUVShE.

Gogol, Nikolai 1984. *Sobranie sochinenii*, 7 vols. Moscow: Khudozhestvennaia literatura.

GoGwilt, Christopher 1995. *The Invention of the West: Joseph Conrad and the Double-Mapping of Europe and Empire*. Stanford: Stanford University Press.

Golder, Frank 1914. *Russian Expansion on the Pacific, 1641–1850*. New York: The Arthur H. Clark Co.

Goldman, Marshall 2008. *Petrostate: Putin, Power and the New Russia*. Oxford: Oxford University Press.

Golovnin, Aleksandr 2004. *Zapiski dlia nemnogikh*, ed. B. D. Gal'perin. St. Petersburg: Nestor.

Gorski, Philip 2003. *The Disciplinary Revolution: Calvinism and the Growth of State Power in Early Modern Europe*. Chicago: University of Chicago Press.

Gosden, Chris 2004. *Archaeology and Colonialism: Cultural Contact from 5000 BC to the Present*. Cambridge: Cambridge University Press.

Gouldner, Alvin W. 1977. "Stalinism: A Study of Internal Colonialism," *Telos*, 34: 5–48.

Gradovsky, G. K. 1882. "K istorii russkoi pechati," *Russkaia starina*, 2: 494–509.

Gramsci, Antonio 1957. "The Southern Question," in his *The Modern Prince and Other Writings*. London: Lawrence, 28–54.

Griboedov, Aleksandr 1999a. "Proekt uchrezhdeniia Rossiiskoi zakavkazskoi kampanii," in his *Sochineniia v trekh tomakh*, vol. 1. Moscow: Notabene, 614–41.

Griboedov, Aleksandr 1999b. "Zagorodnaia poezdka (Otryvok iz pis'ma iuzhnogo zhitelia)," in his *Sochineniia v trekh tomakh*, vol. 2. Moscow: Notabene, 275–8.

Grigoriev, V. V. 1846. "Evreiskie religioznye sekty v Rossii," *Zhurnal Ministerstva vnutrennikh del*, 15/3–49: 282–309.

Grinev, Andrei n.d. "Tuzemcy-amanaty v Russkoi Amerike," http://america-xix.org.ru/library/grinev-indeans/.

Grossman, Leonid 1929. "Istoricheskii fon Vystrela," *Novii Mir*, 5: 203–23.

Groys, Boris 1993. "Imena goroda," in his *Utopia i obmen*. Moscow: Znak, 358.

Guha, Ranajit 1997. *Dominance without Hegemony. History and Power in Colonial India*. Cambridge, MA: Harvard University Press.

Guha, Ranajit 1998. "A Conquest Foretold," *Social Text*, 54: 85–99.

Gulyga, Arsenij 1987. *Immanuel Kant. His Life and Thought*, trans. Marijan Despalatovic. Boston: Birk.

Gutiérrez, Ramón A. 2004. "Internal Colonialism: An American Theory of Race," *Du Bois Review: Social Science Research on Race*, 1: 281–95.

Haberer, Erich 1995. *Jews and Revolution in Nineteenth-Century Russia*. Cambridge: Cambridge University Press.

Habermas, Jürgen 1987. *The Theory of Communicative Action*, trans. Thomas McCarthy. Cambridge: Polity.

Hagen, Mark von 2004. "Empires, Borderlands, and Diasporas: Eurasia as Anti-Paradigm for the Post-Soviet Era," *American Historical Review*, 109/42: 445–69.
Halfin, Igal 2000. *From Darkness to Light: Class, Consciousness, and Salvation in Revolutionary Russia*. Pittsburgh: University of Pittsburgh Press.
Hardy, Deborah 1987. *Land and Freedom. The Origins of Russian Terrorism, 1876–1879*. Westport, CT: Greenwood Press.
Haxthausen, August von 1856. *The Russian Empire, Its People, Institutions, and Resources*. London: Chapman & Hall.
Hecht, David 1947. *Russian Radicals Look to America, 1825–1894*. Cambridge, MA: Harvard University Press.
Hechter, Michael 2001. *Containing Nationalism*. Oxford: Oxford University Press.
Hechter, Michael 1975. *Internal Colonialism. The Celtic Fringe in British National Development*. London: Routledge.
Heier, Edmund 1970. *Religious Schism in the Russian Aristocracy 1860–1900*. The Hague: Nijhoff.
Hellbeck, Jochen 2000. "Speaking Out: Languages of Affirmation and Dissent in Stalinist Russia," *Kritika* I/1: 71–96.
Hellie, Richard 1971. *Enserfment and Military Change in Muscovy*. Chicago: University of Chicago Press.
Herder, J. G. 1992. *Selected Early Works*, trans. Ernest A. Menze and Michael Palma. University Park: Penn State University Press.
Heretz, Leonid 2008. *Russia on the Eve of Modernity: Popular Religion and Traditional Culture under the Last Tsars*. Cambridge: Cambridge University Press.
Herzen, Alexander 1956. "Le peuple Russe et le socialisme," in his *Sobranie sochinenii*, vol. 7. Moscow: AN SSSR, 271–306.
Herzen, Alexander 1957. "Russian Serfdom", in his *Sobranie sochinenii*, vol. 12. Moscow: AN SSSR, 7–33.
Hess, Jonathan M. 2000. "Johann David Michaelis and the Colonial Imaginary," *Jewish Social Studies*, 6/2: 56–101.
Hill, Fiona, and Clifford Gaddy 2003. *The Siberian Curse. How Communist Planners Left Russia Out in the Cold*. New York: Brookings Press.
Hind, Robert J. 1984. "The Internal Colonial Concept," *Comparative Studies in Society and History*, 26/3: 543–68.
Hirsch, Francine 2005. *Empire of Nations: Ethnographic Knowledge and the Making of the Soviet Union*. Ithaca: Cornell University Press.
Hitler, Adolph 1969. *Mein Kampf*, trans. Ralph Manheim. London: Hutchinson.
Hobsbawm, E. J. 1959. *Primitive Rebels*. Manchester: Manchester University Press, 126–49.
Hobson, John Atkinson 1902. *Imperialism: A Study*. London: Nisbet
Hoch, Stephen 1989. *Serfdom and Social Control in Russia: Petrovskoe, a Village in Tambov*. Chicago: University of Chicago Press.
Hokanson, Katya 1994. "Literary Imperialism, Narodnost' and Pushkin's Invention of the Caucasus." *Russian Review*, 53/3: 336–52.
Hokanson, Katya 2010. *Writing at Russia's Border*. Toronto: University of Toronto Press.

Holquist, Peter 2010a. "'In Accord with State Interests and the People's Wishes': The Technocratic Ideology of Imperial Russia's Resettlement Administration," *Slavic Review*, 69/1: 151–79.

Holquist, Peter 2010b. Review of Brian J. Boeck, *Imperial Boundaries. Journal of Interdisciplinary History*, 41/3: 461–3.

Hopkirk, Peter 1996. *Quest for Kim: In Search of Kipling's Great Game*. Ann Arbor: University of Michigan Press.

Horvath, Robert J. 1972. "A Definition of Colonialism," *Current Anthropology*, 13/1: 45–57.

Hosking, Geoffrey 1997. *Russia. People and Empire*. London: Fontana Press.

Hroch, Miroslav 1985. *Social Preconditions of National Revival in Europe*. Cambridge: Cambridge University Press.

Hughes, Lindsey 1998. *Russia in the Age of Peter the Great*. New Haven, CT: Yale University Press.

Hughes, Lindsey 2004. "A Beard is an Unnecessary Burden: Peter I's Laws on Shaving and Their Roots in Early Russia, in Russian Society and Culture and the Long 18th century," in Hughes (ed.), *Essays in Honour of Anthony Cross*. Munich: Lit Verlag, 21–34.

Hunter, Ian 2001. *Rival Enlightenments. Civil and Metaphysical Philosophy in Early Modern Germany*. Cambridge: Cambridge University Press.

Huxley, Aldous 1958. *Music at Night and Other Essays*. New York: Harper.

Iadrintsev, Nikolai 2003. *Sibir kak koloniia*. Novosibirsk: Sibirskii khronograf.

Iastrebtsov, Ivan 1833. *O sisteme nauk, prilichnykh v nashe vremia detiam*. Moscow.

Iordanskaia, M. K. 1994. "Novyi table-talk," *Novoe literaturnoe obozrenie*, 9.

Istoriia Russkoi Ameriki 1997. ed. N. N. Bolkhovitinov. Moscow: Mezhdunarodnye otnosheniia.

Itenberg, B. 1960. *Dmitrii Rogachev, revoliutsioner-narodnik*. Moscow: Sotsialno-ekonomicheskoe izdatel'stvo.

Jabotinsky, Vladimir (Zeev) 1989. *Povest'moikh dnei*. Jerusalem: Alia.

Jones, Robert E. 2001. "Why St. Petersburg?," in *Peter the Great and the West. New Perspectives*. New York: Palgrave, 189–205.

Jonge, Alex de 1982. *The Lives and Times of Grigorii Rasputin*. New York: Coward, McCann and Geoghegan.

Juel, Just 1899. *Zapiski datskogo poslannika pri Petre Velikom*. Moscow.

Kagarlitsky, Boris 2003. *Periferiinaia imperia*. Moscow: Ultra-Kultura.

Kant, Immanuel 1992. *Theoretical Philosophy*, ed. David Walford. Cambridge: Cambridge University Press.

Kant, Immanuel 2007a. *Critique of Judgment*, trans. G. H. Bernard. New York: Cosimo.

Kant, Immanuel 2007b. "On the Different Races of Human Beings," in his *Anthropology, History, and Education*, ed. Günter Zöller and Robert B. Louden. Cambridge: Cambridge University Press.

Kant, Immanuel 2007c. "Conjectural Beginnings of Human History," in his *Anthropology, History, and Education*, ed. Günter Zöller and Robert B. Louden. Cambridge: Cambridge University Press.

Kaplan, Herbert H. 1968. *Russia and the Outbreak of the Seven Years War*. Berkeley: University of California Press.

Kappeler, Andreas 2001. *The Russian Empire: A Multiethnic History*, trans. Alfred Clayton. Harlow: Longman.
Kappeler, Andreas 2009. "From an Ethnonational to a Multiethnic to a Transnational Ukrainian History," in Georgiy Kasianov and Philipp Ther (eds.), *A Laboratory of Transnational History: Ukraine and Recent Ukrainian Historiography*. Budapest: Central European University Press, 51–80.
Karamzin, Nikolai 1989. *Istoriia gosudarstva Rossiiskogo*. Moscow: Nauka.
Karamzin, Nikolai 1991. *Zapiska o drevnei i novoi Rossii*. Moscow: Nauka.
Kartsev, P. P. 1890. "O voennykh poseleniiakh pri grafe Arakcheeve," *Russkii vestnik*, 3.
Kaufman, A. A. 1908. *Russkaia obshchina v processe ee zarozhdeniia i rosta*. Moscow: Sytin.
Kavelin, Konstantin 1989. "Mysli i zametki o russkoi istorii," in his *Nash umstvennyi stroi*. Moscow: Pravda.
Kavelin, Konstantin, and Boris Chicherin 1974. "Pis'mo k izdateliu," in *Golosa iz Rossii. Sbroniki Gerzena i Ogareva*, vol. 1. Moscow: Nauka.
Keenleyside, Anne, Margaret Bertulli, and Henry Fricke 1997. "The Final Days of the Franklin Expedition: New Skeletal Evidence," *Arctic*, 50/1: 36–46.
Kellogg, Michael 2005. *The Russian Roots of Nazism: White Émigrés and the Making of National Socialism, 1917–1945*. New York: Cambridge University Press.
Kelsiev, Vasilii 1867. "Sviatorusskie dvoevery," *Otechestvennye zapiski*, October.
Kelsiev, Vasilii 1941. "Ispoved'" in *Literaturnoe nasledstvo*, vols. 41–42, pt. II. Moscow.
Kempe, Michael 2007. "The Anthropology of Natural Law: Debates about Pufendorf in the Age of Enlightenment," in Larry Wolff and Marco Cipolloni (eds.), *The Anthropology of the Enlightenment*. Stanford: Stanford University Press.
Kennan, George 1870. *Tent-life in Siberia and Adventures among the Koraks and Other Tribes in Kamtchatka and Northern Asia*. New York: Putnam.
Kennan, George 1946. "Long Telegram," http://www.gwu.edu/~nsarchiv/coldwar/documents/episode-1/kennan.htm.
Khalfin, N. A. 1990. *Vozmezdie ozhidaet v Dzhagdalake*. Moscow: Nauka.
Khalid, Adeeb, Nathaniel Knight, and Maria Todorova 2000. "Ex Tempore: Orientalism and Russia," *Kritika*, 1/4: 691–728.
Kharkhordin, Oleg 1999. *The Collective and the Individual in Russia: A Study of Practices*. Berkeley: University of California Press.
Khodarkovsky, Michael 1992. *Where Two Worlds Met: The Russian State and the Kalmyk Nomads*. Ithaca: Cornell University Press.
Khodarkovsky, Michael 2002. *Russia's Steppe Frontier: The Making of a Colonial Empire, 1500–1800*. Bloomington, IN: Indiana University Press.
Khomiakov, Aleksei 1832. *Ermak*. Moscow: Selivanovsky.
Khomiakov, Aleksei 1871. *Zapiski o vsemirnoi istorii*. Moscow.
Khomiakov, Aleksei 1988. *O starom i novom. Stat'i i ocherki*. Moscow: Sovremennik.
King, Robert J. 2008. "The Mulovsky Expedition and Catherine II's North Pacific Empire," *Australian Slavonic and East European Studies*, 21/1: 97–122.
Kipling, Rudyard 1925. *Verse*. Inclusive Edition. London: Hodder.
Kipling, Rudyard 1952. *A Choice of Kipling's Prose*. Selected by W. Somerset Maugham. London: Macmillan.

Kireeva, R. A. 1996. "Vasilii Osipovich Kliuchevskii," in A. N. Sakharov (ed.), *Istoriki Rossii*. Moscow: Institut rossijskoj istorii, 398–445.
Klaus, A. 1869. *Nashi kolonii*. St. Petersburg: Nusval't.
Klein, Lawrence E., and Anthony J. La Vopa (eds.) 1998. *Enthusiasm and Enlightenment in Europe, 1650–1850*. San Marino, CA: Huntington.
Klein, Lev 2009. *Spor o variagakh*. St. Petersburg: Evraziia.
Klibanov, Aleksandr 1982. *History of Religious Sectarianism in Russia, 1860s–1917*, trans. Ethel Dunn. New York: Pergamon
Klier, John Doyle 1986. *Russia Gathers Her Jews*. DeKalb: Northern Illinois University Press.
Kliuchevsky, Vasilii 1913. *Istoriia soslovii v Rossii*. Moscow.
Kliuchevsky, Vasilii 1956. *Kurs russkoi istorii*, Moscow.
Kliuchevsky, Vasilii 1959. "Russkii rubl' 16–18 vekov v ego otnoshenii k nyneshnemu," *Sochineniia*, vol. 7. Moscow.
Kliuchevsky, Vasilii 1983. "Nabroski po 'variazhskomu voprosu,'" in his *Neopublikovannye proizvedeniia*. Moscow: Nauka.
Kliuchevsky, Vasilii 1990. "Evgenii Onegin i ego predki," *Sochineniia*, vol. 9. Moscow.
Kliuchevsky, Vasilii 2001. *Tetrad' s aforizmami*. Moscow: EKSMO.
Kloberdanz, Timothy J. 1975. "The Volga Germans in Old Russia and in Western North America," *Anthropological Quarterly*, 48/4: 209–22.
Knei-Paz, Baruch 1978. *The Social and Political Thought of Leon Trotsky*. Oxford: Clarendon.
Knight, Nathaniel 1998. "Science, Empire, and Nationality: Ethnography in the Russian Geographical Society, 1845–1855," in Jane Burbank and David Ransel (eds.), *Imperial Russia. New Histories for the Empire*. Bloomington: Indiana University Press, 108–48.
Knight, Nathaniel 2000. "Grigor'ev in Orenburg, 1851–1862: Russian Orientalism in the Service of Empire?" *Slavic Review*, 59/1: 74–100.
Koehl, Robert Lewis 1953. "Colonialism inside Germany, 1886–1918," *Journal of Modern History*, 25/3: 255–72.
Kolchin, Peter 1987. *Unfree Labor. American Slavery and Russian Serfdom*. Cambridge: Cambridge University Press.
Kopp, Kristin 2011. "Gray Zones: On the Inclusion of 'Poland' in the Study of German Colonialism," in Michael Perraudin and Jürgen Zimmerer (eds.), *German Colonialism and National Identity*. London: Routledge, 33–44.
Kordonsky, Simon 2008. *Soslovnaia struktura postsovetskoi Rossii*. Moscow: FOM.
Korf, Modest 2003. *Zapiski*. Moscow: Zakharov.
Koselleck, Reinhart 2004. *Futures Past*, trans. Keith Tribe. New York: Columbia University Press.
Kostiushev, Iu. V., and G. V. Kretinin 1999. *Petrovskoe nachalo: Kenigsbergskii universitet i rossiiskoe prosveshchenie v XVIII veke*. Kaliningrad: Iantarnyi skaz.
Kovalsky, I. 1878. "Ratsionalizsm na iuge Rossii," *Otechestvennye zapiski*, March, 204–24; May, 199–230.
Kozlov, Sergei 2003. *Russkii puteshestvennik epokhi Prosveshcheniia*. St. Petersburg: Istoricheskaia illiustratsiia.
Kretinin, G. V. 1996. *Pod Rossiskoi koronoi ili, Russkie v Kenigsberge*. Kaliningrad: Kaliningradskoe knizhnoe izd-vo.

Kristeva, Julia 1991. *Strangers to Ourselves*. New York: Columbia University Press.

Krylov, N. A. 1892. "Vospominaniia mirovogo posrednika pervogo prizyva," *Russkaia starina*, 7.

Krylova, Anna 2000. "The Tenacious Liberal Subject in Soviet Studies," *Kritika: Explorations in Russian and Eurasian History*, 1/1: 119–46.

Kuehn, Manfred 2001. *Kant: A Biography*. Cambridge: Cambridge University Press.

Kuehn, Manfred, and Heiner Klemme n.d. "Daniel Heinrich Arnoldt," http://www.manchester.edu/kant/bio/FullBio/ArnoldtDH.html.

Lantzeff, George V. 1972. *Siberia in the Seventeenth Century. A Study of the Colonial Administration*. New York: Octagon.

Lantzeff, George V., and Richard A. Pierce 1973. *Eastward to Empire. Exploration and Conquest on the Russian Open Frontier, to 1750*. Montreal: McGill-Queen's University Press.

Laurentian Text 1953. *The Russian Primary Chronicle*, trans. Samuel Hazzard Cross and Olgerd P. Sherbowitz-Wetzor. Cambridge, MA: Mediaeval Academy of America.

La Vopa, Anthony J. 1995. "Herder's Publikum: Language, Print, and Sociability in Eighteenth-Century Germany," *Eighteenth-Century Studies*, 29/1: 5–24.

La Vopa, Anthony J. 2005. "Thinking about Marriage: Kant's Liberalism and the Peculiar Morality of Conjugal Union," *The Journal of Modern History*, 77 (March): 1–34.

Lavrov, Alexander 2004. "Andrei Belyi mezhdu Conradom i Chestertonom," *Lotmanovskii sbornik*, 3. Moscow: OGI, 443–57.

Lavrov, Petr 1974. *Gody emigratsii*, compiled by Boris Sapir. Dordrecht: Reidel, vol. 1.

Layton, Susan 1994. *Russian Literature and Empire: Conquest of the Caucasus from Pushkin to Tolstoy*. Cambridge: Cambridge University Press.

Lebedev, Kastor 1888. "Iz zapisok senatora". *Russkii arkhiv*, vol. 7.

Leetz, G. 1980. *Abram Petrovich Gannibal*. Tallinn: Eestii Raamat.

Lenin, Vladimir 1967. "Razvitie kapitalizma v Rossii," in his *Polnoe sobranie sochinenii*, vol. 3. Moscow: Politizdat.

Lermontov, Mikhail 1958. *Sobranie sochinenii*. Moscow: GIKhL.

Leskov, Nikolai 1958. *Sobranie sochinenii*. Moscow: GIKhL.

Leskov, Nikolai 1988. "O russkom rasselenii i Politiko-Ekomomicheskom komitete," in his *Chestnoe slovo*. Moscow: Sovetskaia Rossiia, 57–73.

Levshin, A. I. 1994. "Dostopamiatnye minuty v moei zhizni," in V. A. Fedorov (ed.), *Konets krepostnichestva v Rossii*. Moscew: Izd–vc Moskovskogo universiteta.

Liapunova, R. G. 1987. *Aleuty. Ocherki etnicheskoi istorii*. Leningrad: Nauka.

Lieven, Dominic 2003. *Empire: The Russian Empire and Its Rivals*. London: Random House.

Lincoln, Bruce W. 1982. *In the Vanguard of Reform. Russia's Enlightened Bureaucrats*. DeKalb: Northern Illinois University Press.

Liprandi, Ivan 1870a. "O prirodnykh granitsakh i stremlenii nemtsev na Vostok ('Drang nach Osten'). *Chteniia v Imperatorskom obshchestve istorii i drevnostei Rossiiskikh*, vol. 1.

Liprandi, Ivan 1870b. «Kratkoe obozrenie russkikh raskolov, eresei i sekt». *Chteniia v Imperatorskom obshchestve istorii i drevnostei Rossiiskikh*, vol. 2.

Liu, John 2000. "Towards an Understanding of the Internal Colonial Model," in Diana Braun (ed.), *Postcolonialism. Critical Concepts in Literary and Cultural Studies*, vol. 4. London: Routledge, 1347–65.

Liubavsky, Matvej 1996. *Obzor istorii russkoi kolonizatsii*. Moscow: MGU.

Love, Joseph L. 1989. "Modeling Internal Colonialism: History and Prospect," *World Development*, 17/6: 905–22.

Lowe, Heinz-Dietrich 2000. "Poles, Jews, and Tartars: Religion, Ethnicity, and Social Structure in Tsarist Nationality Policies," *Jewish Social Studies*, 6/3: 52–96.

Luxemburg, Rosa 2003. *The Accumulation of Capital*. London: Routledge.

Macaulay, Thomas B. 1862. *Minutes on Education in India*, collected by H. Woodrow. Calcutta: Lewis.

Maiofis, Maria 2008. *Vozzvanie k Evrope. Literaturnoe obshchestvo Arzamas i rossiiskii modernizatsionnyi proekt 1815–1818 godov*. Moscow.

Maiorova, Olga 2010. *From the Shadow of Empire. Defining the Russian Nation through Cultural Mythology, 1855–1870*. Madison: University of Wisconsin Press.

Malia, Martin 2006. *History's Locomotives. Revolutions and the Making of the Modern World*. New Haven: Yale University Press.

Malik, Charles 1953. "The Relations Between East and West," *Proceedings of the American Philosophical Society*, 97/1: 1–7.

Malkin, Irad 2004. "Postcolonial Concepts and Ancient Greek Colonization," *Modern Language Quarterly*, 65/3: 341–64.

Manchester, Laurie 1998. "The Secularization of the Search for Salvation: The Self-Fashioning of Orthodox Clergymen's Sons in Late Imperial Russia," *Slavic Review*, 57/1: 50–76.

Manchester, Laurie 2008. *Holy Fathers, Secular Sons. Clergy, Intelligentsia, and the Modern Self in Revolutionary Russia*. DeKalb: Northern Illinois University Press.

Mann, Michael 1996. *The Sources of Social Power*. Cambridge: Cambridge University Press.

Mann, Michael 2005. *The Dark Side of Democracy. Explaining Ethnic Cleansing*. Cambridge: Cambridge University Press.

Mantena, Karuna 2010. "Genealogies of Catastrophe: Arendt on the Logic and Legacy of Imperialism," in Seyla Benhabib (ed.), *Politics in Dark Times. Encounters with Hannah Arendt*. Cambridge: Cambridge University Press, 83–112.

Martin, Janet 2004. *Treasure of the Land of Darkness: The Fur Trade and Its Significance for Medieval Russia*. Cambridge: Cambridge University Press.

Martin, Virginia 2001. *Law and Custom in the Steppe: The Kazakhs of the Middle Horde and Russian Colonialism in the Nineteenth Century*. Richmond, UK: Curzon Press.

Marx, Karl 1990. *Capital. Manifesto of the Communist Party*, ed. F. Engels. Chicago: University of Chicago Press.

Mauss, Marcel 2002. *The Gift: The Form and Reason for Exchange in Archaic Societies*. London: Routledge.

McClure, John A. 1981. *Kipling and Conrad. The Colonial Fiction*. Cambridge, MA: Harvard University Press.

McLean, Hugh 1977. *Nikolai Leskov: The Man and His Art*. Cambridge, MA: Harvard University Press.

Meek, James 2005. *The People's Act of Love*. London: Canongate.
Meek, Ronald, 1976. *Social Science and Ignoble Savage*. Cambridge: Cambridge University Press.
Melnikov-Pechersky, Pavel 1869. "Belye golubi," *Russkii vestnik*, vol. 3.
Melnikov-Pechersky, Pavel 1873. "Vospominaniia o Vladimire Ivanoviche Dale," *Russkii vestnik*, vol. 3.
Meyer, Priscilla 2009. *How the Russians Read the French: Lermontov, Dostoevsky and Tolstoy*. Madison: University of Wisconsin Press.
Mikhailov, A. D. 1906. "Avtobiograficheskie zametki," *Byloe*, 2: 163–5.
Miliukov, Pavel 1895. *Kolonizatsiia Rossii, Enciklopedicheskii slovar'*, vol. 30. St. Petersburg: Brokgauz, 740–6.
Miliukov, Pavel 1990. *Vospominaniia*. Moscow: Sovremennik.
Miliukov, Pavel 2006. *Glavnye techeniia russkoi istoriheskoi mysli*, Moscow: GPIBR.
Millward, Robert 1982. "An Economic Analysis of the Organization of Serfdom in Eastern Europe," *Journal of Economic History*, 42: 513–48.
Mironov, Boris 1985. "The Russian Peasant Commune After the Reforms of the 1860s," *Slavic Review*, 44/3: 438–67.
Mironov, Boris 1999. *Sotsialnaia istoriia Rossii*. St. Petersburg: Bulanin.
Mogilner, Marina 2008. *Homo imperii. Istoriia fizicheskoi antropologii v Rossii*. Moscow: Novoe literaturnoe obozrenie.
Moon, David 1999. *The Russian Peasantry. The World the Peasants Made*. London: Longman.
Moon, David 2010. "The Russian Academy of Sciences Expeditions to the Steppes in the Late Eighteenth Century," *Slavonic and East European Review*, 88/1: 204–36.
Moore, David Chioni 2001. "Is the Post- in Postcolonial the Post- in Post-Soviet?" *PMLA*, 116/1: 111–28.
Morozov, P. O. 1891. "Baron August Haxthausen i ego sochinenie o Rossii (1842–1854)," *Istoricheskie materialy iz arkhiva Ministerstva gosudarstvennykh imushchestv*, vol. 1. St. Petersburg, 189–207.
Morris, Henry C. 1900. *The History of Colonization*. New York: Macmillan.
Morrison, Alexander S. 2008. *Russian Rule in Samarkand, 1868–1910: A Comparison with British India*. Oxford: Oxford University Press.
Müller, Gerhard Friedrich 1996. *Akademik G. F. Müller – pervyi issledovatel' Moskvy i Moskovskoi provintsii*. Moscow: Ianus.
Murav, Harriette 1998. *Russia's Legal Fictions*. Ann Arbor: University of Michigan Press.
Nadezhdin, Nikolai 1998. "Dva otveta Chaadaevu," in A. A. Zlatopolsky and A. A. Ermichev (eds.), *Chaadaev. Pro et Contra*. Moscow: RKhGI.
Nadezhdin, Nikolai 2000. "Sovremennoe napravlenie prosveshcheniia", in his *Sochineniia*. St. Petersburg: RKhGI.
Nash, Gary B. 2000. *Red, White, and Black: The Peoples of Early North America*. New York: Prentice Hall.
Nathans, Benjamen 2002. *Beyond the Pale: The Jewish Encounter with Late Imperial Russia*. Berkeley: University of California Press.
Nechaev, Sergei 1997. "Katekhizis revoliutsionera," in E. L. Rudnitskaia (ed.), *Revoliutsionnyi radicalism v Rossii*. Moscow: Arkheotsentr.
Nechkina, Militsa 1974. *V. O. Kliuschevsky. Istoriia zhizni i tvorchestva*. Moscow: Nauka.

Nelson, Robert L. 2009. "The Archive for Inner Colonization, the German East, and World War I," in Robert L. Nelson (ed.), *Germans, Poland, and Colonial Expansion to the East*. London: Palgrave, 65–94.
Nelson, Robert L. 2010. "From Manitoba to the Memel: Max Sering, Inner Colonization, and the German East", *Social History*, 35/4: 439–57.
Netzloff, Mark 2003. *England's Internal Colonies: Class, Capital, and the Literature of Early Modern English Colonialism*. London: Palgrave.
Newlin, Thomas 2001. *The Voice in the Garden: Andrei Bolotov and the Anxieties of Russian Pastoral, 1738–1833*. Evanston, IL: Northwestern University Press.
Niland, Richard 2010. *Conrad and History*. Oxford: Oxford University Press.
Nolde, Boris 1952. *La formation de l'Empire russe*, vol. 2. Paris: Institut des Études Slaves.
Nordhoff, Charles 1875. *The Communistic Societies of the United States*. New York: Harper & Brothers.
North, Douglass C., John Joseph Wallis, and Barry R. Weingast 2009. *Violence and Social Orders: A Conceptual Framework for Interpreting Recorded Human History*. Cambridge: Cambridge University Press.
N.R. 1895. "Kolonizatsia", *in Entsikopedicheskii slovar'*. St. Petersburg: Brokgauz, 736–40.
Obolensky, Dimitri 1982. "The Varangian-Russian Controversy: the First Round," in his *The Byzantine Inheritance of Eastern Europe*. London: Variorum.
Ocherki po istorii kolonizatsii Severa, 1922. vol. 1. St. Petersburg: Gosudarstvennoe izdatel'stvo.
Offord, Dereck 2010. "The People," in William Leatherbarrow and Derek Offord (eds.), *History of Russian Thought*. Cambridge: Cambridge University Press.
Ogarev, N. P. 1952. *Izbrannye sotsial'no-politicheskie i filosofskie proizvedeniia*. Moscow: MGU.
Orlovsky, Daniel T. 1981. *The Limits of Reform: The Ministry of Internal Affairs in Imperial Russia, 1802–1881*. Cambridge, MA: Harvard University Press.
Ovsianiko-Kulikovskii, D. N. 1880. "Sekta liudei bozhiikh," *Slovo*, 9: 55–74.
Paddock, Troy R. E. 2010. *Creating the Russian Peril: Education, the Public Sphere, and National Identity in Imperial Germany*. New York: Camden House.
Paert, Irina 2004. *Old Believers: Religious Dissent and Gender in Russia*. Manchester: Manchester University Press.
Palmer, Alan 2005. *Northern Shores: A History of the Baltic Sea and its Peoples*. London: John Murray.
Paperno, Irina 1997. *Suicide as a Cultural Institution in Dostoevsky's Russia*. Ithaca: Cornell University Press.
Patterson, Orlando 1982. *Slavery and Social Death. A Comparative Study*. Cambridge, MA: Harvard University Press.
Pavlov, V. N. 1972. *Pushnoi promysel v Sibiri 17-go veka*. Krasnoiarsk: Krasnoiarskii rabochii.
Peterkin, Allan 2001. *One Thousand Beards. A Cultural History of Facial Hair*. Vancouver, BC: Arsenal Pulp Press.
Petrov, A. N. 1871. *Ustroistvo i upravlenie voennykh poselenii v Rossii*. St. Petersburg: Russkaia starina.

Pettengill, John S. 1979. "The Impact of Military Technology on European Income Distribution," *Journal of Interdisciplinary History*, 10/2: 201–25.
Pietz, William 1988. "The 'Post-Colonialism' of Cold War Discourse," *Social Text*, 19/20: 55–75.
Pintner, Walter 1967. *Russian Economic Policy under Nicolas I.* Ithaca: Cornell University Press.
Pipes, Richard 1950. "The Russian Military Colonies 1810–1831," *Journal of Modern History*, 22: 205–19.
Pirozhkova, T. V. 1997. *Slavianofil'skaia zhurnalistika.* Moscow: MGU.
Plekhanov, G. V. 1925. "Vospominaniia ob A.D. Mikhailove," in A. P. Pribyleva-Korba and V. N. Figner (eds.), *A. D. Mikhailov.* Leningrad.
Pletsch, Carl E. 1981. "The Three Worlds, or the Division of Social Scientific Labor," *Comparative Studies in Society and History*, 23/4: 565–90.
Pogodin, Mikhail 1846. *Issledovaniia, zamechaniia i lektsii o russkoi istorii.* Moscow.
Pogodin, Mikhail 1859. *Normanskii period russkoi istorii.* Moscow.
Pogosian, Elena 2001. *Petr I. Arkhitektor Rossiiskoi istorii.* St. Petersburg: Iskusstvo.
Pokrovsky, Mikhail 1920. *Russkaia istoriia v samom szhatom ocherke.* Moscow.
Pokrovsky, Mikhail 1922. "Svoeobrazie istoricheskogo processa i pervaia bukva marxizma," *Krasnaia nov'* (republished in *Vostok,* 12(24), December 2004).
Pokrovsky, Mikhail 2001. *Rossiia v kontse XVIII veka, in Istoriia Rossii v XIX veke. Doreformennaia Rossiia.* Moscow: Tsentrpoligraph
Pokshishevskii, V. V., and V. A. Krotov 1951. *Zaselenie Sibiri.* Irkutsk: Irkutskoe oblastnoe izd-vo.
Polanyi, Karl 1944. *The Great Transformation: Economic and Political Origins of Our Time.* New York: Rinehart.
Polian, Pavel (ed.) 2001. *Gorod i derevnia v sovremennoi Rossii. Sto let peremen.* Moscow: OGI.
Portnov, Andrei 2010. *Uprazhneniia s istoriei po-ukrainski.* Moscow: OGI.
Prakash, Gyan 1994. "Subaltern Studies as Postcolonial Criticism," *American Historical Review,* 99/5: 1475–90.
Prakash, Gyan 1996. "Who is Afraid of Postcoloniality?" *Social Text*, 49: 187–203.
Pratt, Mary Louise 1992. *Imperial Eyes. Travel Writing and Acculturation.* London: Routledge.
Pravilova, Ekaterina 2006. *Finansy imperii. Den'gi i vlast' v politike Rossii na natsional'nykh okrainakh.* Moscow: Novoe izdatel'stvo.
Priamursky, G. G. 1997. "Peterburgskii panoptikon," in *Peterburgskie chteniia - 97.* St. Petersburg: Russko-Baltiskii tsentr, 165–8.
Proskurina, Vera 2006. *Mify imperii.* Moscow: Novoe literaturnoe obozrenie.
Prugavin, Aleksandr 1881. "Znachenie sektantstva v russkoi narodnoi zhizni," *Russkaia mysl'*, 1.
Prugavin, Aleksandr 1904. *Staroobriadchestvo vo vtoroi polovine 1 veka. Ocherki po noveishei teorii raskola.* Moscow.
Prugavin, Aleksandr 1917. *Bunt protiv prirody (o khlystakh i khlystovschine).* Moscow.
Pufendorf, Samuel, 1764. *An Introduction to the History of the Principal States of Europe.* London.

Pufendorf, Samuel 2002. "On the Law of Nature and Nations" [1670], in Thomas Hobbes, *Leviathan*, Broadway.
Pushkin, Aleksandr 1950. *Polnoe sobranie sochinenii.* Moscow: GIKhL.
Pushkin, Aleksandr 1995. "Biografiia A. P. Gannibala," in his *Dnevniki. Zapiski.* St. Petersburg: Nauka.
Pypin, Aleksandr 1869. "Russkie otnosheniia Bentama," *Vestnik Evropy*, 2.
Pypin, Aleksandr 1890. *Istoriia russkoi etnographii.* St. Petersburg.
Radishchev, Nikolai 1941. *Polnoe sobranie sochinenii.* Moscow: ANSSSR.
Radishchev, Nikolai 1992. *Puteshestvie iz Peterburga v Moskvu.* St. Petersburg: Nauka.
Radkau, Joachim 2009. *Max Weber. A Biography.* Cambridge: Polity.
Raeff, Marc 1983. *The Well-Ordered Police State: Social and Institutional Change Through Law in the Germanies and Russia, 1600–1800.* New Haven: Yale University Press.
Ram, Harsha 2003. *The Imperial Sublime. A Russian Poetics of Empire.* Madison: University of Wisconsin Press.
Raynal, Abbé, 1777. *A Philosophical and Political History of the Settlements and Trade of the Europeans in the East and West Indies*, trans. J. Justamond. London: Cadell.
Redekop, Benjamin W. 1997. "Thomas Abbt and the Formation of an Enlightened German 'Public'," *Journal of the History of Ideas*, 58/1: 81–103.
Reitblatt, A. I. (ed.) 1998. *Vidok Figliarin: Pis'ma i zapiski Bulgarina v III otdelenie.* Moscow: Novoe Literaturnoe Obozrenie.
Renan, Ernest 1996. "What is a Nation?" in Geoff Eley and Ronald Grigor Suny (eds.), *Becoming National.* Oxford: Oxford University Press, 42–56.
Reynolds, Reginald 1949. *Beards: Their Social Standing, Religious Involvements, Decorative Possibilities, and Value in Offence and Defence Through the Ages.* New York: Doubleday.
Riasanovsky, Nicholas V. 1959. *Nicholas I and Official Nationality in Russia.* Berkeley: University of California Press.
Riasanovsky, Nicholas V. 1985. *The Image of Peter the Great in Russian History and Thought.* Oxford: Oxford University Press.
Robson, Roy R. 1995. *Old-Believers in Modern Russia.* DeKalb, IL: Northern Illinois University Press.
Rogger, Hans 1960. *National Consciousness in Eighteenth-century Russia.* Cambridge, MA: Harvard University Press.
Rogger, Hans 1993. "Reforming Jews – Reforming Russians," in Herbert A. Strauss (ed.), *Hostages of Modernization. Studies on Modern Anti-Semitism*, vol. 2. Berlin: de Gruyter.
Rosenthal, Bernice Glatzer 2004. *New Myth, New World: From Nietzsche To Stalinism.* Philadelphia: Penn State University Press.
Ross, Kristin 1996. *Fast Cars, Clean Bodies. Decolonization and the Reordering of French Culture.* Cambridge, MA: MIT Press.
Ross, Michael L. 2001. "Does Oil Hinder Democracy?" *World Politics*, 53: 325–61.
Rothberg, Michael 2009. *Multidirectional Memory.* Stanford: Stanford University Press.
Rowley, David G. 1999. "'Redeemer Empire': Russian Millenarianism," *American Historical Review*, 104/5: 1582–602.

Rybakovsky, L. L. 1998. "Issledovaniia migratsii naseleniia v Rossii," in *Sotsiologiia v Rossii*. Moscow: Instutut sotsiologii, 436–51.

Sacher-Masoch, Leopold 1883. *Die Gottesmutter*. Leipzig.

Sachs, Ignacy 1976. *The Discovery of the Third World*. Cambridge, MA: MIT Press.

Sahadeo, Jeff 2007. *Russian Colonial Society in Tashkent*. Bloomington: Indiana University Press.

Sahni, Kalpana 1997. *Crucifying the Orient: Russian Orientalism and the Colonization of Caucasus and Central Asia*. Bangkok; Oslo: White Orchid Press.

Saiapin, M. 1915. "Obshchie. Russkaia kommunisticheskaia sekta," *Ezhemesiachnyi Zhurnal*, 1: 65–77; 2: 60–9.

Said, Edward W. 1966. *Joseph Conrad and the Fiction of Autobiography*. Cambridge, MA: Harvard University Press.

Said, Edward W. 1978. *Orientalism*: New York: Vintage.

Said, Edward W. 1985. *Beginnings. Intention and Method*. New York: Basic Books.

Said, Edward W. 1993. *Culture and Imperialism*. New York: Knopf.

Said, Edward W. 1999. *Out of Place*. London: Granta.

Said, Edward W. 2003. *Freud and the Non-European*. London: Verso.

Saltykov-Shchedrin, Nikolai 1936. *Polnoe sobranie sochinenii*. Moscow.

Sarieva, E. A. 2000. "Feierverki v Rossii XVIII veka," in *Razvlekatel'naia kul'tura Rossii XVIII-XIXvv*. St. Petersburg: Bulanin, 88–98.

Sartre, Jean-Paul, 1963. "Preface" to Frantz Fanon's *The Wretched of the Earth*. New York: Grove Press.

Scherr, Barry 2003. "Gorky and God-Building," in Joan Delaney Grossman and Ruth Rischin (eds.), *William James in Russian Culture*. Lanham, MD: Lexington, 189–210.

Schimmelpenninck van der Oye, David 2010. *Russian Orientalism. Asia in the Russian Mind from Peter the Great to the Emigration*. New Haven: Yale University Press.

Schlözer, Avgust 1809. *Nestor*. St. Petersburg.

Schmitt, Carl 1976. *The Concept of the Political*, trans. George Schwab. New Brunswick, NJ: Rutgers University Press.

Schmoller, Gustav 1886. "Dic preußische Kolonisation des 17. und 18. Jahrhundert," in *Verein fur Socialpolitik, Zur Inneren Kolonisation in Deutschland: Erfahrungen und Vorschlage*. Leipzig: Duncker & Humblot, 1–43.

Schumann, Matt, and Karl W. Schweizer 2008. *The Seven Years War: A Transatlantic History*. London: Routledge.

Schweizer, Karl 1989. *England, Prussia, and the Seven Years War*. Lewiston, NY: Edwin Mellen Press.

Scott, H. M. 2001. *The Emergence of the Eastern Powers*. Cambridge: Cambridge University Press.

Scott, James C. 1990. *Hidden Transcripts. Domination and the Arts of Resistance*. New Haven: Yale University Press.

Scott, James C. 1998. *Seeing Like a State*. New Haven: Yale University Press.

Seddon, J. H. 1985. *The Petrashevtsy. A Study of the Russian Revolutionaries of 1848*. Manchester: Manchester University Press.

Seleznev V. M., and E. O. Selezneva (eds.) 2002. *Delo Sukhovo-Kobylina*. Moscow: Novoe literaturnoe obozrenie.
Semenov-Tian-Shansky, Veniamin 1915. *O mogushchestvennom territorial'nom vladenii primenitel'no k Rossii. Oherki po politiheskoi geografii*. Petrograd.
Shanin, Teodor 1983. *Late Marx and the Russian Road*. London: Monthly Review Press.
Shannon, John 1990. "Regional Variations in the Commune: The Case of Siberia," in R. P. Bartlett (ed.), *Land Commune and Peasant Community in Russia*. Basingstoke: Macmillan.
Sharov, Vladimir 2003. *Voskreshenie Lazaria*. Moscow: Vagrius.
Sharpe, Jenny 1991. "The Unspeakable Limits of Rape: Colonial Violence and Counter-Insurgency," *Genders*, 10: 25–46.
Shchapov, Afanasii 1862. *Zemstvo i raskol*. St. Petersburg.
Shchapov, Afanasii 1906. *Sochineniia*. St. Petersburg.
Shchapov, Afanasii 1923. "Rech' posle panikhidy po ubitym v Bezdne krest'ianam," *Krasnyi arkhiv*, 4.
Shelgunov Nikolai, and M. Mikhailov 1958. "K molodomu pokoleniiu" [1861], in N. Karataev (ed.), *Narodnicheskaia ekonomicheskaia literature*. Moscow, 96.
Shkandrij, Miroslav 2001. *Russia and Ukraine. Literature and the Discourse of Empire from Napoleonic to Postcolonial Times*. Montreal: McGill University Press.
Shumakher, A. D. 1899. "Pozdnie vospominaniia o o davno minuvshikh vremenakh," *Vestnik Evropy*, 3: 89–128.
Sieyès, Emmanuel Joseph 2003. *Political Writings*. Indianapolis: Hackett.
Siniavsky, Andrey 1991. *Ivan-Durak. Ocherk russkoi narodnoi very*. Paris: Syntaxes.
Slezkine, Yuri 1994. *Arctic Mirrors. Russia and the Small Peoples of the North*. Ithaca: Cornell University Press
Slezkine, Yuri 2004. *The Jewish Century*. Princeton: Princeton University Press.
Slovtsov, Piotr 1886. *Istoricheskoe obozrenie Sibiri*. Moscow: Skorokhodov.
Snyder, Timothy 2010. *Bloodlands. Europe between Hitler and Stalin*. London: The Bodley Head.
Sollogub, Vladimir 1998. *Vospominaniia*. Moscow: Slovo.
Soloviev, Sergei 1856. "Schlözer i anti-istoricheskoe napravlenie," *Russkii vestnik*, 8/4: 489–533.
Soloviev, Sergei 1983. *Izbrannye trudy. Zapiski*. Moscow: MGU.
Soloviev, Sergei 1988. *Istoriia Rossii s drevneishikh vremen*. Moscow: Mysl'.
Sopelnikov, S. V. 2000. *Doroga v Arzrum: Russkaia obshchestvennaia mysl' o Vostoke*. Moscow: Vostochnaia literatura.
Spivak, Gayatri Chakravorty 1994. "Can the Subaltern Speak?," in Patrick Williams and Laura Chrisman (eds.), *Colonial Discourse and Post-Colonial Theory*. Harlow: Pearson, 66–112.
Spivak, Gayatri Chakravorty 1999. *A Critique of Postcolonial Reason: Toward a History of the Vanishing Present*. Cambridge, MA: Harvard University Press.
Spurr, David 1993. *The Rhetoric of Empire. Colonial Discourse in Journalism, Travel Writing, and Imperial Administration*. Durham, NC: Duke University Press.

Stagl, Justin 1995. *A History of Curiosity. The Theory of Travel.* Chur: Harwood.

Stanislawski, Michael 1983. *Tsar Nicholas I and the Jews.* Philadelphia: Jewish Publication Society of America.

Stanziani, Alessandro 2008. "Free Labor–Forced Labor: An Uncertain Boundary?," *Kritika: Explorations in Russian and Eurasian History* 9/1: 27–52.

Starr, S. Frederick 1968. "August von Haxthausen and Russia," *The Slavonic and East European Review*, 46/107: 462–78.

Stead, W. T. 1888, *Truth about Russia.* London: Cassell & Company.

Stebnitsky, M. (Nikolai Leskov) 1863. "S lud'mi drevlego blagochestiia," *Biblioteka dlia chteniia*, 9.

Steinberg, Mark, and Heather J. Coleman 2007. *Sacred Stories: Religion and Spirituality in Modern Russia.* Bloomington: Indiana University Press.

Stites, Richard 1989. *Revolutionary Dreams.* Oxford: Oxford University Press.

Stoler, Ann Laura 1995. *Race and Education of Sexuality.* Durham: Duke University Press.

Stoler, Ann Laura 2009. "Considerations on Imperial Comparisons," in Ilia Gerasimov et al. (eds.), *Empire Speaks Out.* Leiden: Brill, 33–58.

Struve, Piotr 1894. *Kritisheskie zametki k voprosu ob ekonomicheskom razvitii Rossii.* St. Petersburg.

Subbotin, Nikolai 1867. "Raskol kak orudie vrazhdebnykh Rossii partii," *Russkii vestnik*, 5: 316–48.

Sukhomlinov, M. L. 1888. "I. S. Aksakov v sorokovykh godakh," *Istoricheskii vestnik*, February.

Sunderland, Willard 1993. "Peasants on the Move: State Peasant Resettlement in Imperial Russia, 1805–1830," *Russian Review*, 52/4: 472–85.

Sunderland, Willard 1996. "Russians into Iakuts? 'Going Native' and Problems of Russian National Identity in the Siberian North," *Slavic Review*, 55/4: 806–25.

Sunderland, Willard 2004. *Taming the Wild Field: Colonization and Empire on the Russian Steppe.* Ithaca: Cornell University Press.

Sunderland, Willard 2010. "The Ministry of Asiatic Russia: The Colonial Office That Never Was But Might Have Been," *Slavic Review*, 69: 120–50.

Suny, Ronald Grigor 2001. "The Empire Strikes Out: Imperial Russia, 'National' Identity, and Theories of Empire," in his *Empire and Nation-Making in the Soviet Union, 1917–1953.* Oxford: Oxford University Press.

Svin'in, Pavel 2000. "Poezdka v Gruzino," in E. E. Davydova et al. (eds.), *Arakcheev. Svidetel'stva sovremennikov.* Moscow: Novoe literaturnoe obozrenie.

Svod 1818. *Sistematicheskii svod sushchestvuiushchikh zakonov Rossiiskoi imperii.* St. Petersburg: Komissia sostavleniia zakonov.

Swift, Simon 2005. "Kant, Herder, and the Question of Philosophical Anthropology," *Textual Practice*, 19/2: 219–38.

Taagepera, Rein 1988. "An Overview of the Growth of the Russian Empire," in Michael Rywkin (ed.), *Russian Colonial Expansion to 1917.* London: Mansell, 1–8.

Tatishchev, Vasilii 1994. *Istoriia Rossiiskaia.* Moscow: Ladomir.

Taves, Ann 1999. *Fits, Trances and Visions.* Princeton: Princeton University Press.

Teletova, N. K. 1989. "Gerb Gannibalov," in *Vremennik pushkinskoi komissii.* vol. 23. Leningrad: AN SSSR, 140–51.

Teller, Edward, and Charles Malik 1960. "To Meet the Communist Challenge." Address delivered at St Louis University.

Thompson, Ewa 2000. *Imperial Knowledge: Russian Literature and Colonialism.* Westport, CT: Greenwood.

Tilly, Charles 1990. *Coercion, Capital, and European States.* Malden, MA: Blackwell.

Tolochko, Aleksei 2005. *"Istoriia Rossijskaia" Vasiliia Tatishcheva: Istochniki i izvestiia.* Moscow-Kiev: Novoe literaturnoe obozrenie.

Tolstoy, Lev 1908. "Pis'ma o skopchestve," in V. Bonch-Bruevich (ed.), *Materialy k istorii russkogo sektantsva i staroobriadchestva*, vol. 1. St. Petersburg.

Tolz, Vera 2005. "Orientalism, Nationalism, and Ethnic Diversity in late Imperial Russia," *The Historical Journal*, 48: 127–50.

Trotsky, Leon 1959. *The Russian Revolution*, trans. Max Eastman. New York: Doubleday.

Trotsky, Lev 1922. "Ob osobennostiakh istoricheskogo razvitiia Rossii," *Pravda*, 1–2 July.

Trotsky, Lev 1990. *Moia zhizn'*, vol. 1. Moscow: Kniga.

Trotsky, Lev 1991. *Literatura i revoliutsia.* Moscow: Politizdat.

Tsimbaev, N. I. 1986. *Slavianofil'stvo.* Moscow: MGU.

Tsvetaeva, Marina 2006. *Moi Pushkin.* Moscow: Azbuka.

Turgenev, Nikolai 1963. *Sobranie sochinenii.* Moscow.

Turner, Frederick Jackson 1920. *The Frontier in American History.* New York: Holt.

Tynianov, Iu. 2001. "Literaturnoe segodnia," in his *Istoriia literatury. Kritika.* St. Petersburg: Azbuka.

Uimovich-Ponomarev, P., and S. Ponomarev 1886. "Zemledelcheskoe bratstvo kak obychno-pravovoi institut sektantov," *Severny vestnik*, 9: 1–31; 10: 1–36.

Uvarov, Sergei 1810. *Projet d'une Academie Asiatique.* St. Petersburg.

Uvarov, Sergei 1817. *Essay on Eleusinian Mysteries*, trans. J. D. Price. London.

Uvarov, Sergei 1864. "Doklad k desiatiletiiu Ministerstva narodnogo prosvescheniia," in *Desiatiletie Ministerstva narodnogo prosvesccheniia.* St. Petersburg.

Valentinov, Nikolai 1953. *Vstrechi s Leninym.* New York: izdatelstvo imeni Chekhova.

Vasil'ev, Aleksandr 1946. *The Russian Attack on Constantinople in 860.* Cambridge, MA: Medieval Academy of America.

Veale, Elspeth M. 1966. *The English Fur Trade in the Later Middle Ages.* Oxford: Oxford University Press.

Vengerov, S. 1902. *"Turgenev," in Entsikopedicheskii slovar'.* St. Petersburg: Brokgauz, 96–106.

Veniaminov, I. 1840. *Zapiski ob ostrovakh Unalashkinskogo otdela.* St. Petersburg.

Venturi, Franco 1982. *Studies in Free Russia.* Chicago: University of Chicago Press.

Vermeulen, Han F. 2006. "The German Invention of Volkerkunde. Ethnological Discourse in Europe and Asia, 1740–1798," in Sara Eigen and Mark Lattimore (eds.), *The German Invention of Race.* New York: State University of New York Press, 123–47.

Vermeulen, Han F. 2008. "Early History of Ethnography and Ethnology in the German Enlightenment: Anthropological Discourse in Europe and Asia, 1710–1808." PhD thesis, University of Leiden.

Veselovsky, N. I. 1887. *Vasilii Vasil´evich Grigor´ev po ego pis´mam i trudam*. St. Petersburg: Imperatorskoe arkheologicheskoe obshchestvo.

Vigel, Philip 1998. Pis'mo (1836), in *Chaadaev. Pro et Contra,* ed. A. A. Ermichev, A. A. Zlatopol'skaia. St. Petersburg: RKhGI.

Vilkov, Oleg 1999. "Pushnoi promysel v Sibiri," *Nauka v Sibiri*, 45.

Viola, Lynne 2009. "Die Selbstkolonisierung der Sowjetunion und der Gulag der 1930er Jahre," in *United Europe-Divided Memory*, trans. Karl-Heinz Siber; special issue of *Transit. Europaeische Revue*, ed. Klaus Nelen, no. 38 (winter): 34–56.

Volk, S. S. 1966. *Narodnaia volia, 1879–1882*. Moscow-Leningrad: AN SSSR.

Volodarsky, Mikhail 1984. "The Russians in Afghanistan in the 1830s," *Central Asian Survey*, 3/1: 63–86.

Vrangel, Ferdinand 1841. *Puteshestvie po severnym beregam Sibiri i po Ledovitomu moriu*. St. Petersburg.

Vroon, Ronald 1994. "The Old Belief and Sectarianism as Cultural Models in the Silver Age," in Robert P. Hughes and Irina Paperno (eds.), *Christianity and the Eastern Slavs*. Berkeley, CA: University of California Press.

Wachtel, Andrew Baruch 1994. *An Obsession with History: Russian Writers Confront the Past*. Stanford: Stanford University Press.

Wakefield, Andre 2009. *The Disordered Police State. German Cameralism in Science and Practice*. Chicago: The University of Chicago Press.

Wakefield, Edward Gibbon 1849. *A View of the Art of Colonization*. London.

Walicki, A. 1969. *The Controversy Over Capitalism: Studies in the Social Philosophy of the Russian Populists*. Oxford: Clarendon.

Walzer, Michael 1965. *The Revolution of the Saints: A Study in the Origins of Radical Politics*. Cambridge: Cambridge University Press.

Walzer, Michael 2004. *Politics and Passion. Toward a More Egalitarian Liberalism*. New Haven: Yale University Press.

Washington, Booker T., W. E. B. DuBois, and James Weldon Johnson 1965. "The Souls of Black Folk," in *Three Negro Classics*. New York: Avon Books.

Watts, Edward 1998. *Writing and Postcolonialism in the Early Republic*. Charlottesville: University Press of Virginia.

Wcislo, Francis W. 1990. *Reforming Rural Russia: State, Local Society, and National Politics, 1855–1914*. Princeton: Princeton University Press.

Webber, Andrew 1996. *The Doppelgänger: Double Visions in German Literature*. Oxford: Clarendon Press.

Weber, Eugen 1976. *Peasants into Frenchmen: The Modernization of Rural France*. Stanford: Stanford University Press.

Weber, Max 1979. *Economy and Society*. Berkeley: University of California Press.

Weber, Max 1995. *The Russian Revolutions*, trans. Gordon C. Wells and Peter Baehr. Oxford: Oxford University Press.

Weizmann, Chaim 1949. *Trial and Error. An Autobiography*. London: Hamish.

Werrett, Simon 2010. *Fireworks: Pyrotechnic Arts and Sciences in European History*. Chicago: University of Chicago Press.

West, James L. 1991. "The Riabushinsky Circle: Burzhuaziia and Obshecestvennost in Late Imperial Russia," in his *Educated Society and the Quest for Public Identity in Late Imperial Russia*. Princeton: Princeton University Press, 41–56.

Whittaker, Cynthia H. 1984. *The Origins of Modern Russian Education: An Intellectual Biography of Count Sergei Uvarov*. DeKalb: Northern Illinois University Press.

Widdis, Emma 2004. "Russia as Space," in Simon Franklin and Emma Widdis (eds.), *National Identity in Russian Culture*. Cambridge: Cambridge University Press, 30–50.

Williams, Robert Chadwell 1986. *The Other Bolsheviks: Lenin and His Critics, 1904–1914*. Bloomington: Indiana University Press.

Wirtschafter, Elise Kimerling 1997. *Social Identity in Imperial Russia*. DeKalb: Northern Illinois University Press.

Wolff, Larry 1994. *Inventing Eastern Europe. The Map of Civilization on the Mind of the Enlightenment*. Stanford: Stanford University Press.

Wood, Michael 2003. "On Edward Said," *London Review of Books*, October 23.

Wortman, Richard 1995. *Scenarios of Power, Myth and Ceremony in Russian Monarchy*, vol. 1. Princeton: Princeton University Press.

Yampolsky, Vladimir 1994. "Iz istorii germanskoi geopolitiki," *Rossiia – 21*, 6/7: 158–68.

Yapp, Malcolm 1987. "British Perceptions of the Russian Threat to India," *Modern Asian Studies*, 21: 647–65.

Young, Robert 1772. *Political Essays Concerning the Present State of the British Empire*. London: Strahan and Cadell.

Young-Bruehl, Elisabeth 1982. *Hannah Arendt. For Love of the World*. New Haven: Yale University Press.

Zammito, John H. 2002. *Kant, Herder, and the Birth of Anthropology*. Chicago: University of Chicago Press.

Zhuk, Sergei 2004. *Russia's Lost Reformation: Peasants, Millennialism, and Radical Sects in Southern Russia and Ukraine*. Washington, DC: Woodrow Wilson Center Press.

Zimmerman, Andrew 2006. "Decolonizing Weber," *Postcolonial Studies*, 9/1: 53–79.

Znamenski, Andrei A. 2007. "The Ethic of Empire on the Siberian Borderland," in Nicholas B. Breyfogle, Abby Schrader, and William Sunderland (eds.), *Peopling the Russian Periphery. Borderland Colonization in Eurasian History*. London: Routledge, 106–28.

Zorin, Andrei. 1997. "Ideologiia 'Pravoslavie-Samoderzhavie-Narodnost': opyt rekonstruktsii," *Novoe literaturnoe obozrenie*, 26.

Zorin, Andrei 2001. *Kormia dvuglavogo oral. Literatura i gosudarstvennaia ideologiia v Rossii*. Moscow: Novoe literaturnoe obozrenie.

INDEX

Abbt, Thomas 190–1
Afghanistan 33–5
African Americans 7, 21, 123, 125, 225
Agamben, Giorgio 77
Aksakov, Ivan 159, 202
Alaska 5, 66, 76, 82–3, 87–8
Aleuts 76, 86
Amanat 76.
Amazons 48–51, 114, 135
America 5, 17, 21–2, 64, 83–4, 104, 110, 113, 123, 133, 200, 240, 248–9, 251
Arakcheev, Aleksei 136
Archangel 5, 20, 29, 82, 101, 124–5
Arendt, Hannah 7, 20, 23–4, 27, 47, 89, 191–2
Argonauts 85, 87
Arnoldt, Daniel Heinrich 182–3

Bakhmetev, Pavel 132
Bakhtin, Mikhail 10, 16, 232–4, 238–9, 246–8
Bakunin, Mikhail 202
Balfour, Arthur James 37–9
Bashkiria 6, 69
Bassin, Mark 63
beards 95, 101–4, 140, 235
Belinsky, Vissarion 15–16, 45, 94–5, 97, 105
Bely, Andrei 211, 243–4
Benjamin, Walter 1–2, 228, 247
Bentham, Jeremy 134–5
Bentham, Samuel 134–5
Beratz, Gottlieb 131
Berlin, Isaiah 160, 181, 188–90
Berman, Russell 28
Bernal, Martin 56
Bhabha, Homi 13–15, 28, 61, 246
Bismarck, Otto 21–2, 26, 252
Blauner, Robert 7
Blok, Aleksandr 119
Bojanowska Edyta 119
Bolotov, Andrei 121, 175–93, 235
Bonch-Bruevich, Vladimir 200, 203, 209–11
boomerang effect 7, 22–5, 37, 53, 148, 154–5, 168
Boulainvilliers, Henri 47
Boym, Svetlana 23
Bulgarin, Faddei 14, 109, 152
Burbank, Jane 2, 255
Burke, Edmund 17
Byron, George Gordon 107

Calvinism 18, 98, 128
camera obscura 186–8
cameralism 151, 187
Cannadine, David 28

Catherine II the Great 48, 76, 83, 88, 101, 115, 128–31, 141, 176, 188, 192, 210, 237
Caucasus 4, 13, 70, 90, 110, 115–17, 144
Central Asia 90, 121, 144, 152, 161, 229, 249
Césaire, Aimé 7
Chaadaev, Piotr 17, 58
Chernov, Viktor 207, 209
Chernyshevsky, Nikolai 132–3, 140
Chicherin, Boris 141, 167
colonization, definition 2, 7, 248, 251
  colonization *vs.* colonialism 7–8, 86
  colonizers and colonized 215, 217–8, 230, 251
  external *vs.* internal 2, 7, 20–4, 64, 69–70, 115, 127, 154–5, 162–4, 178–80, 217, 240, 243, 247–8, 250, 254
  and inter-imperial mimesis 38, 71, 110, 134, 136.
  profitability 74, 80–1, 83, 89, 99, 124, 126, 216
  recent *vs.* ancient 142–3, 250
  and re-enchantment 216, 222
  and rivalry between empires 3–4, 6, 21, 33–5, 55, 65, 82–3, 98, 174–7, 189–92, 220, 229, 254
  terrestrial *vs.* overseas 5, 21, 62, 143, 174, 232, 252–4
Cold War 4, 9, 27, 33, 40–2, 249
commune (*obshchina*) 138–43, 145–8, 155, 207
  and colonization 142–3, 145–7
  destruction of 144, 148–9
  discovery of 138–43, 155, 254
  and *Kahal* 147–8
  and socialism 133, 140–1, 202, 208, 248
Condee, Nancy 3, 8, 17, 26
Conrad, Joseph 10, 14, 27, 29, 39, 79, 119, 169, 208, 214–23, 230, 241, 244
Constantinople 48, 71
contact zone 109, 111, 232
Cook, James 14, 83, 129
Cossacks 35, 76, 82, 152, 175, 236
Coulanges, Fustel 127
Crimean War 5, 16, 34–6, 65
Curzon, George Nathaniel 36–9

Dal, Vladimir 150–3, 156–164, 199, 227
Defoe, Daniel 29, 232
Dekhnewallah, A. 35
Derrida, Jacques 77
Derzhavin Gavriil 114, 146
Deutcher, Isaac 42
Diderot, Denis 51, 83, 101, 177
Dobroliubov, Nikolai 241–3
Dostoevsky, Fyodor 10, 19, 31, 119, 133, 156–7, 167–9, 201, 213, 233, 237–48
DuBois, W. E. B. 21, 61
Dukhobory (Spirit-Strugglers) 210
Durkheim, Emil 213, 223, 243
Durylin, Sergei 54

Egypt 39–42, 53–7, 196
Elizabeth I 152, 174–8, 182
emancipation of serfs (1861) 106–7, 132, 141, 144, 148, 194, 224
Engels, Friedrich 138
England 3, 8, 15–18, 28–9, 34–9, 55, 62, 77, 82, 112, 128, 133, 211, 215, 217–18, 220, 224, 229, 251–4
Enlightenment 9, 14, 17, 25, 51–2, 58–9, 90, 95, 98, 105, 115, 162, 179, 182, 187, 190–2, 223
Ermak 18, 79–80
Eshevsky, Stepan 112–14

estate (*soslovie*) 101, 103–7, 252
ethnography 52, 160, 189, 198–200, 244, 254–5

Fanon, Frantz 28, 93, 246, 254
Finns 4, 47–8, 97, 109, 114
firearms 75–6, 80, 120–1, 124
fireworks 120–2, 186–8, 211, 229, 253.
Forster, George, 83, 129
Forster, Johann Reinhold 129
Foucault, Michel 3, 8, 24, 26, 45, 47, 51, 54, 111–14, 133–5, 138, 255
Franklin, John 218, 221
Franklin, Simon 48, 227, 230
Frederick II the Great 21, 129, 173–9, 192
Freud, Sigmund 42, 156
Fülöp-Miller, René 200, 213
fur trade 4, 9, 31, 66, 72–90, 117–19, 227

Gandhi, Mahatma 19, 254
gauntlet (*shpitsruteny*) 138, 141–2, 175, 246
Gellner, Ernest 145, 189, 191, 199, 251
German colonies in the Russian Empire 128–33, 146–8, 154
Girard, René 10, 233–4, 238–9, 244
Gobineau, Arthur 113
God-builders 223
Goethe, Johann Wolfgang 55, 132, 232
Gogol, Nikolai 13–15, 17, 27, 34, 52, 119, 127, 158–9, 164, 245–7
Going-to-the-People movement 117, 198, 202–7
Golder, Frank A. 87
Golovnin, Aleksandr 129–30
Gorky, Maksim 197, 211
Göttingen 47, 53, 56, 138, 189
Gouldner, Alvin W. 8
Gramsci, Antonio 22, 41
Great Game 32–4, 62
Greece 53–7
Griboedov, Aleksandr 108–11, 115, 168
Grigoriev, Vasilii 51, 164–8
Guha, Ranajit 49
Gulyga, Arsenii 181–2

Habermas, Jürgen 7, 26
Hamann, George 190
Hansa 78–9, 81
Haxthausen, August 62, 138–40, 155, 165, 196–7
Hechter, Michael 8
hegemony *vs.* domination 6, 23, 59, 119–20, 178, 186, 222, 253
Heidegger, Martin 39
Herder, Johann Gottfried 52, 55, 105, 185, 188–92
Herodotus 50
Herrnhuters 129–30
Herzen, Alexander 105, 138
High Imperial Period (1814–1856) 16, 19, 61, 100, 120–1, 148, 168
historiography 6–9, 45, 53, 59, 62–71, 112, 123, 142, 249
Hitler 21, 26, 133
Hobbes, Thomas 49–51, 55–7, 60, 112
Hoch, Stephen 123
Holy Alliance 4, 55, 160
Huber, Eduard 132
hybridization 19, 28, 64, 113, 118, 208, 216, 247

Ignatiev, Nikolai 121
imperial gradient 16, 143–4, 252
imperialism 5, 7, 20–1, 24, 28, 41, 55, 70, 94, 124, 217, 220–2, 253

India 5–6, 16, 19, 23, 33–6, 77, 104, 236, 248, 251
Ingria 97, 99, 101, 250
internal colonization
  and collectivization 132, 137–8, 142–9, 154, 196–7, 210, 213
  definition 5–7, 9, 20–2, 24, 62, 65–6, 70, 129, 136, 222, 248
  and doubling 13, 18, 241
  and frontier 63–5, 144, 248
  and gender 231–44
  history of the concept 7–9, 24, 26, 62–6
  and indirect rule 145–9
  institutions 82, 89–90, 124–7, 141–3, 148, 196, 249
  legal acts 102, 128
  and reflexivity 6, 63, 67–70, 252
  as self-colonization 6, 63, 67–71
  and sovereignty *vs.* subjectivity 51, 58, 77, 98, 115, 255
  and transformationist culture 3, 6, 19, 64, 93, 97, 101, 132, 148, 168–9, 185, 235, 242, 251–3

Jews 22, 37, 42, 56, 59, 144, 146–8, 162, 165–8

Kalmyks 47, 132, 174–5, 179, 196
Kankrin, Egor (George) 126, 147
Karamzin, Nikolai 45, 48, 57
Kavelin, Konstantin 19
Kazakhs 115
Kazan 65, 79, 112–14, 118, 194, 198
Kelsiev, Vasilii 201–2
Kennan, George 4
Keyserlingk, Caroline 180, 193
Khomiakov, Aleksei 17, 62, 120, 138
Klaus Alexander, 132–3
Klaproth, Julius 54, 56
Königsberg 99, 121, 173–93, 250
Konstantin Romanov, Grand Duke 108, 160
Korf, Nikolai 180, 185, 193
Krichev 133–5
Kronstadt 131
Krusenstern, Johann 83
Kyrgyzes 47, 115, 165, 168
Kipling, Rudyard 27, 32–9, 229, 256
Kliuchevsky, Vasilii 2, 59, 61, 65–71, 82, 86, 106, 113, 125–7, 147
Kamchatka 13, 52, 82
Kant, Immanuel 9, 23, 52, 55, 173–93

Ladoga Lake 131, 214, 227–8
La Vopa, Anthony 180, 190, 212
Lenin, Vladimir 20, 26, 107, 133, 136, 159, 207–8, 210
Lermontov Mikhail 115–17, 152, 235
Leskov, Nikolai 10, 62, 158, 214, 223–30, 256
Liprandi, Ivan 155–8
Liubavsky, Matvei 69
Lobachevsky, Nikolai 113
Lomonosov, Mikhail
longue durée 9, 89
Luxemburg, Rosa 20, 41

Macaulay, Thomas Babington 15–19
Malik, Charles 39–42
Mann, Michael 25, 104
Martin, Janet 80
Marx, Karl 20, 85, 112, 138, 223
Melnikov-Pechersky, Pavel 157–8
Mennonites 131
Michaelis, Johann David 56
Mikhailov, Aleksandr 204–5
military colonies in the Russian Empire 135–7
Miliukov, Pavel 47, 69–70, 81, 106

Ministry of Internal Affairs 9, 65, 150–69, 198, 201
Ministry of State Properties 137–8, 155
monsters 244, 247
Moore, David Chioni 26
Moravian Brothers 130–2, 154
Morozov, Savva 210–11
Moscow 1, 5, 62, 66, 75, 77, 79–82, 88, 101, 107, 114, 123–5, 151, 210–11, 250
Müller, Gerhard Friedrich 5, 52, 107
Mulovsky, Grigory 83

Nadezhdin, Nikolai 106, 151, 160, 199
Napoleonic Wars 16–7, 25, 45, 55, 135, 156, 188, 217
Nasser, Gamal Abdel 39, 42
nationalism 25–6, 46, 140, 145, 156, 164–5, 213, 254
negative hegemony 114–20
Nestor 45, 52–3, 60, 190
Netzloff, Mark 8
Neva River 78, 97, 101, 121, 131, 187, 227
New Zealand 93, 126, 132
Norman Conquest 48, 51, 58, 112, 140
novel 6, 10, 16, 46, 85, 95, 115–16, 127, 129, 132, 152–3, 157–8, 168, 185–6, 201, 214–30, 231–48
Novgorod 46, 65, 74, 79, 88, 131, 135, 227

Odessa 87, 108, 131, 160, 201, 251
Old-Believers 47, 125, 157, 159, 169, 199–201, 204, 211–12, 235
Olenin, Aleksei 56–7
Oprichnina 82
Orenburg 115, 152, 161, 165, 235
orientalism 9, 27–42, 95, 115, 159, 165–8, 196, 207, 217, 240, 251–2
  positive 168, 196, 240, 252–3
  reversed 17, 95, 119
Orlov, Grigorii 128–9, 180–1
Orlov, Mikhail 45
orthodoxy 18, 75, 104, 125, 208

pan-Slavic movement 23
Panopticon 23, 133–6
Patterson, Orlando 125–6
Peace of Westphalia 49–52, 128
Perovsky, Lev 150–69, 224
Perovsky, Vasilii 152–4, 165
Persia 35, 110
Peter I the Great 15, 19, 47, 50, 59, 61, 85, 102, 120, 174
Pietists 131, 179, 188
Plekhanov, Grigorii 204–5, 207
Pogodin, Mikhail 58
Pokrovsky, Mikhail 86–7, 127
Poland 4, 22, 70, 189, 216–19
populism (*narodnichestvo*) 55, 103, 127, 141, 148, 169, 198–9, 202, 204–8, 211–13, 215, 233, 222, 243–4, 254
post-Soviet Russia 4, 26, 72, 88, 104, 249
postcolonial theory 8, 26–8, 254
Potemkin, Grogorii 134
Prakash, Gyan 28
Primary Chronicle 45–53, 58–60, 73–4
Prokopovich, Feofan 50
Prussia 7, 21–2, 131, 138, 141, 173–93
Pufendorf, Samuel 49–52, 60, 84
Pugachev, Emelian 132, 178, 235–7
Pushkin, Aleksandr 10, 16, 61, 95, 107–8, 115–20, 132, 137, 153, 156–63, 169, 235–43

Quakers 130, 136

race 9, 23–4, 35, 51, 56, 66, 93, 101–7, 110–14, 125, 138, 140, 166, 174, 252
Radical Reformation 129, 133, 202
Radishchev, Nikolai 84, 105, 232
Rasputin, Grigorii 103, 212
Raynal, Guillaume Thomas 105, 107, 129
Razumovsky, Aleksei 150–3
Reed, John 41
resettlements 25, 109, 123, 126, 177, 224–7
resource-bound state 72–3, 77, 89
revolution in Russia 2–3, 16, 23–4, 37–8, 41, 69, 95–8, 104, 129, 133, 139, 144, 148–9, 157, 194–213, 223, 237, 242–4, 250–4
Riga 13, 101, 165, 174, 188–90
Romanovs 45, 47, 59, 112, 149, 174, 212
Roosevelt, Eleanor 39–40
Rosenberg, Alfred 133
Ross, Kristin 8
Rousseau, Jean-Jacques 55, 232
Rurik 45–60, 66, 94–5, 112, 131, 140, 227
Rurikides 45, 47, 51, 125, 159
Russian Geographical Society 62, 108, 160
Russian sects 9, 132, 155–7, 194–213, 240, 244, 254
  Beguny (Runners) 159, 202
  Dukhobory (Spirit-Strugglers) 210
  Khlysty (Christs or Whips) 194–8, 201–6, 210–13, 240, 243–4
  Molokane (Milk-Drinkers) 202, 206
  Skoptsy (Castrates) 157, 162, 201–3, 211, 238–9

sables 78, 84–5
Sacher-Masoch, Leopold 85, 200
Said, Edward 5, 9, 27–42, 45, 55, 95, 168, 220, 253
Saint-Pierre, Bernardin 128
Saltykov-Shchedrin, Nikolai 24–5, 152, 159, 169
Sarepta 132–3
Sartre, Jean-Paul 41, 247
Schism 140, 155–9, 198–206, 209
Schlözer, August 47–8, 51–4, 56, 62, 151, 189
Schmidt, Isaak Jacob 132
Schmitt, Carl 72
Schmoller, Gustav 21
Scott, James C. 8, 182–4
Second World 25–7, 39–42, 55
Semenov-Tian-Shansky, Veniamin 71
serfdom 82, 106–7, 123–8, 249
Sering, Max 21
Seven Years War 52, 128, 174–7, 181, 188–91, 235
Shakers 196–7, 200
Shchapov, Afanasii 7, 65–7, 70, 82, 86, 112, 118, 158, 194–9, 201, 207
Siberia 5, 19–20, 30–1, 65–6, 75, 79, 84, 88, 118, 142, 144, 146, 156, 173, 201–2, 250
Slavophiles 17–18, 62, 102, 140, 157
Slezkine, Yuri 74, 76, 83, 145, 148, 199
Slovtsov, Piotr 84
Soloviev, Sergei 19, 59, 61–70, 113, 127
Soviet Union 3–4, 23–4, 27, 40–1, 71, 72, 88, 104, 143, 249
Spivak, Gayatri Chakravorty 173, 198
St. Petersburg 4, 13, 17, 59, 65, 69, 83, 111, 121, 131, 135, 227, 238, 250, 253
Steller, Georg Wilhelm 51

Stoler, Ann Laura 8, 23, 29, 71, 112, 136, 155
Stroganov family 84–6
Struve, Petr 20
subaltern 181, 191, 198, 230, 245–6
Sunderland, Willard 64, 67, 119, 127, 150

Tambov 114, 123, 220
Tartars 115, 229
Tashkent 24–5
Tatishchev, Vasilii 47–51, 60
Tchaikovsky, Nikolai 206
terra nullius 94–7
Time of Troubles (1598–1613) 82, 124
Tocqueville, Alexis 17, 58
Tolstoy, Lev 6, 16, 19, 103, 131, 137, 152, 168–9, 197, 204, 211–12, 228, 232, 241, 254
totalitarianism 23–4
Trotsky Lev 16, 86–7, 89, 133, 207, 211, 254
Tunguses 30, 86, 109
Turgenev, Ivan 102, 158, 169
Turner, Frederick J. 63

Ukraine 14, 22–3, 131, 133–4, 161, 167–8, 189, 217, 222, 249
Urals 4, 47
Uvarov, Sergei 18–19, 53–8, 153, 192

Varangians 45–53, 57–60, 111
Veniaminov, Innokentii 76
Veniukov, Mikhail 62
Vikings 47–8, 60–2, 114, 140
violence 25, 75, 104, 112, 123–4, 149, 195, 216, 222, 233, 236
Vitkevitch Ivan (Yan) 36
Volga River 20, 22, 47, 131–3, 159, 202, 224
Vrangel, Ferdinand 117–18

Weber, Eugen 8, 254
Weber, Max 21, 26, 73, 151, 212–13
Weizmann, Chaim 38–9
Weymann, Daniel 179
Wolff, Christian 50
World War I 4, 47, 71
World War II 133

Yadrintsev Nikolai 70, 78
Yakuts 117–19, 173
Yasak 76
Young, Arthur 110

Zammito, John 178–81, 190–1
Zinzendorf, Nicolaus Ludwig 129